PENGUIN (🐧) CLASSICS

THE NEW NEGRO AESTHETIC

ALAIN LEROY LOCKE (1885–1954) was a philosopher, writer, and educator. He graduated with honors from Harvard University in 1907 and became the first African American to be selected as a Rhodes Scholar at Oxford University. Locke returned to the United States and began teaching English, philosophy, and education at Howard University in 1912, where he helped launch *The Stylus*, a literary society and magazine, and the Howard Players, which produced Eugene O'Neill's *Emperor Jones*. After receiving his PhD in philosophy from Harvard in 1918, Locke continued teaching philosophy but began to publish occasional articles on Black literature, music, and drama and advise an emerging group of writers that included Georgia Douglas Johnson, Jean Toomer, Countee Cullen, Zora Neale Hurston, and Langston Hughes. Locke is best known as the creator of the philosophical concept of the New Negro that anchored the Harlem Renaissance (1925–1945), a period of significant contributions of African American artists, writers, poets, and musicians. In 1925, he edited *The New Negro: An Interpretation*, a landmark anthology of African American fiction, poetry, and social commentary, and charted the road forward in numerous critical essays and articles on African American art and culture afterward.

JEFFREY C. STEWART is the MacArthur Foundation Professor of Black Studies at the University of California, Santa Barbara. His biography *The New Negro: The Life of Alain Locke* was the winner of the 2019 Pulitzer Prize for Biography, the 2019 Mark Lynton History Prize, the 2019 James A. Rawley Prize, and the 2018 National Book Award in Nonfiction. He has been a Fulbright Professor of American Studies at the University of Rome III; a W. E. B. Du Bois and a Charles Warren fellow at Harvard University; and a lecturer at the Terra Foundation for American Art in Giverny, France. He has also been a guest curator of *To Color America: Portraits by Winold Reiss* (1989) at the Smithsonian's National Portrait Gallery and *Paul Robeson: Artist and Citizen* (1998) at the Zimmerli Art Museum at Rutgers University. His Wyeth Symposium volume, *Beauty Born of*

Struggle, The Art of Black Washington, will be published by the National Gallery of Art in 2022.

HENRY LOUIS GATES, JR., is the Alphonse Fletcher University Professor and founding director of the Hutchins Center for African and African American Research at Harvard University. He is editor in chief of the Oxford African American Studies Center and TheRoot.com, and creator of the highly praised PBS documentary *The African Americans: Many Rivers to Cross*. He is general editor for a Penguin Classics series of African American works.

ALAIN LOCKE

The New Negro Aesthetic

SELECTED WRITINGS

Edited with an Introduction by
JEFFREY C. STEWART

General Editor:
HENRY LOUIS GATES, JR.

PENGUIN BOOKS

PENGUIN BOOKS

An imprint of Penguin Random House LLC
penguinrandomhouse.com

Introduction, compilation, and suggestions for further reading
copyright © 2022 by Jeffrey C. Stewart
General introduction copyright © 2008 by Henry Louis Gates, Jr.
Penguin supports copyright. Copyright fuels creativity, encourages diverse voices,
promotes free speech, and creates a vibrant culture. Thank you for buying an authorized edition
of this book and for complying with copyright laws by not reproducing, scanning, or distributing
any part of it in any form without permission. You are supporting writers and allowing
Penguin to continue to publish books for every reader.

Frontispiece courtesy of the Moorland-Spingarn Research Center,
Howard University Archives, Howard University, Washington, D.C.

"Paul Laurence Dunbar" by Alain Locke is reprinted with permission of the
Manuscript Division of the Moorland-Spingarn Research Center at Howard University.

The author wishes to thank the Crisis Publishing Co., Inc., the publisher of The Crisis,
the magazine of the National Association for the Advancement of Colored People, for the use of
"Freedom Through Art" by Alain Locke from the July 1938 edition of The Crisis.

The volume editor wishes to thank Lela J. Sewell-Williams, curator of the Manuscript Division,
Moorland-Spingarn Research Center at Howard University, for her outstanding efforts to obtain
the frontispiece photo of Alain Locke for this volume.

LIBRARY OF CONGRESS CATALOGING-IN-PUBLICATION DATA
Names: Locke, Alain, 1885–1954 author. | Stewart, Jeffrey C., 1950– editor. |
Gates, Henry Louis, Jr. editor.
Title: The new Negro aesthetic : selected writings / Alain Locke ; edited with an
introduction by Jeffrey C. Stewart ; general editor: Henry Louis Gates, Jr.
Description: [New York] : Penguin Books, [2022] |
Includes bibliographical references. |
Identifiers: LCCN 2021038793 | ISBN 9780143135210 (paperback) |
ISBN 9780525506881 (ebook)
Subjects: LCSH: African Americans—Intellectual life—20th century. |
African-American arts. | American literature—African American authors—History
and criticism. | African Americans—Race identity. | LCGFT: Essays.
Classification: LCC E185.97.L79 A5 2022 |
DDC 305.896/073—dc23/eng/20211018
LC record available at https://lccn.loc.gov/2021038793

Printed in the United States of America
1st Printing

Set in Sabon LT Pro

For Curmie

Contents

What Is an African American Classic?

I have long nurtured a deep and abiding affection for the Penguin Classics, at least since I was an undergraduate at Yale. I used to imagine that my attraction for these books—grouped together, as a set, in some independent bookstores when I was a student, and perhaps even in some today—stemmed from the fact that my first-grade classmates, for some reason that I can't recall, were required to dress as penguins in our annual all-school pageant, and perform a collective side-to-side motion that our misguided teacher thought she could choreograph into something meant to pass for a "dance." Piedmont, West Virginia, in 1956, was a very long way from Penguin Nation, wherever that was supposed to be! But penguins we were determined to be, and we did our level best to avoid wounding each other with our orange-colored cardboard beaks while stomping out of rhythm in our matching orange, veined webbed feet. The whole scene was madness, one never to be repeated at the Davis Free School. But I never stopped loving penguins. And I have never stopped loving the very audacity of the idea of the Penguin Classics, an affordable, accessible library of the most important and compelling texts in the history of civilization, their black-and-white spines and covers and uniform type giving each text a comfortable, familiar feel, as if we have encountered it, or its cousins, before. I think of the Penguin Classics as the very best and most compelling in human thought, an Alexandrian library in paperback, enclosed in black and white.

I still gravitate to the Penguin Classics when killing time in an airport bookstore, deferring the slow torture of the security

lines. Sometimes I even purchase two or three, fantasizing that
I can speed-read one of the shorter titles, then make a dent in
the longer one, vainly attempting to fill the holes in the liberal
arts education that our degrees suggest we have, over the course
of a plane ride! Mark Twain once quipped that a classic is
"something that everybody wants to have read and nobody
wants to read," and perhaps that applies to my airport pur-
chasing habits. For my generation, these titles in the Penguin
Classics form the canon—the canon of the texts that a truly
well-educated person should have read, and read carefully and
closely, at least once. For years I rued the absence of texts by
Black authors in this series, and longed to be able to make even
a small contribution to the diversification of this astonishingly
universal list. I watched with great pleasure as titles by African
American and African authors began to appear, some two
dozen over the past several years. So when Elda Rotor approached me about editing a series of African American classics and collections for Penguin's Portable Series, I eagerly
accepted.

Thinking about the titles appropriate for inclusion in these
series led me, inevitably, to think about what, for me, constitutes a "classic." And thinking about this led me, in turn, to
the wealth of reflections on what defines a work of literature
or philosophy somehow speaking to the human condition beyond time and place, a work somehow endlessly compelling,
generation upon generation, a work whose author we don't
have to look like to identify with, to feel at one with, as we
find ourselves transported through the magic of a textual time
machine; a work that refracts the image of ourselves that we
project onto it, regardless of our ethnicity, our gender, our
time, our place. This is what centuries of scholars and writers
have meant when they use the word *classic*, and—despite all
that we know about the complex intersubjectivity of the production of meaning in the wondrous exchange between a
reader and a text—it remains true that classic texts, even in
the most conventional, conservative sense of the word *classic*,
do exist, and these books will continue to be read long after
the generation the text reflects and defines, the generation of

readers contemporary with the text's author, is dead and gone. Classic texts speak from their authors' graves, in their names, in their voices. As Italo Calvino once remarked, "A classic is a book that has never finished saying what it has to say."

Faulkner put this idea in an interesting way: "The aim of every artist is to arrest motion, which is life, by artificial means, and hold it fixed so that a hundred years later, when a stranger looks at it, it moves again since it is life." That, I am certain, must be the desire of every writer. But what about the reader? What makes a book a classic to a reader? Here, perhaps, Hemingway said it best: "All good books are alike in that they are truer than if they had really happened and after you are finished reading one you will feel that all that happened to you, and afterward it belongs to you, the good and the bad, the ecstasy, the remorse and sorrow, the people and the places and how the weather was."

I have been reading Black literature since I was fifteen, yanked into the dark discursive universe by an Episcopal priest at a church camp near my home in West Virginia in August 1965, during the terrifying days of the Watts Riots in Los Angeles. Eventually, by fits and starts, studying the literature written by Black authors became my avocation; ultimately, it has become my vocation. And, in my own way, I have tried to be an evangelist for it, to a readership larger than my own people, people who, as it were, look like these texts. Here, I am reminded of something W. S. Merwin said about the books he most loved: "Perhaps a classic is a work that one imagines should be common knowledge, but more and more often isn't." I would say, of African and African American literature, that perhaps classic works by Black writers are works that one imagines should be common knowledge among the broadest possible readership but that less and less are, as the teaching of reading to understand how words can create the worlds into which books can transport us yields to classroom instruction geared toward passing a state-authorized standardized exam. All literary texts suffer from this wrongheaded approach to teaching, mind you; but it especially affects texts by people of color, and texts by women—texts still struggling, despite enormous gains over the last twenty years, to gain a solid foothold in anthologies and syllabi. For every anthology, every syllabus, every publishing series such as the Penguin Classics constitutes a distinct "canon," an implicit definition of all that is essential for a truly educated person to read.

James Baldwin, who has pride of place in my personal canon of African American authors since it was one of his books that that Episcopal priest gave me to read in that dreadful summer of 1965, argued that "the responsibility of a writer is to excavate the experience of the people who produced him." But surely Baldwin would have agreed with E. M. Forster that the books that we remember, the books that have truly influenced us, are those that "have gone a little further down our particular path than we have yet ourselves." Excavating the known is a worthy goal of the writer as cultural archeologist; yet, at the same time, so is unveiling the unknown, the unarticulated yet shared experience of the colorless things that make us human: "something we have always known (or thought we knew)," as Calvino puts it, "but without knowing that this author said it first." We might think of the difference between Forster and Baldwin, on the one hand, and Calvino, on the other, as the difference between an author representing what has happened (Forster, Baldwin) in the history of a people whose stories, whose very history itself, has long been suppressed, and what could have happened (Calvino) in the atemporal realm of art. This is an important distinction when thinking about the nature of an African American classic—rather, when thinking about the nature of the texts that constitute the African American literary tradition or, for that matter, the texts in any under-read tradition.

One of James Baldwin's most memorable essays, a subtle meditation on sexual preference, race, and gender, is entitled "Here Be Dragons." So much of traditional African American literature, even fiction and poetry—ostensibly at least once removed from direct statement—was meant to deal a fatal blow to the dragon of racism. For Black writers since the eighteenth-century beginnings of the tradition, literature has been one more weapon—a very important weapon, mind you, but still one weapon among many—in the arsenal Black people have drawn upon to fight against anti-Black racism and for their equal rights before the law. Ted Joans, the Black surrealist poet, called this sort of literature from the sixties' Black Arts Movement "hand grenade poems." Of what possible use are the niceties of figuration when one must slay a dragon? I can hear you say, give me the blunt weapon anytime! Problem is, it is more difficult than some writers seem to think to slay a dragon with a poem or a novel. Social problems persist; literature too tied to addressing those social problems tends to enter the historical archives, leaving the realm of the literary. Let me state bluntly what should be obvious: Writers are read for how they write, not what they write about.

Frederick Douglass—for this generation of readers one of the most widely read writers—reflected on this matter even in the midst of one of his most fiery speeches addressing the ironies of the sons and daughters of slaves celebrating the Fourth of July while slavery continued unabated. In his now-classic essay "What to the Slave Is the Fourth of July?" (1852), Douglass argued that an immediate, almost transparent form of discourse was demanded of Black writers by the heated temper of the times, a discourse with an immediate end in mind: "At a time like this, scorching irony, not convincing argument, is needed . . . a fiery stream of biting ridicule, blasting reproach, withering sarcasm, and stern rebuke. For it is not light that is needed, but fire; it is not the gentle shower, but thunder. We need the storm, the whirlwind, and the earthquake." Above all else, Douglass concludes, the rhetoric of the literature created by African Americans must, of necessity, be a purposeful rhetoric, its ends targeted at attacking the evils that afflict Black people: "The feeling of the nation must be quickened; the conscience of the nation must be roused; the propriety of the nation must be startled; the hypocrisy of the nation must be exposed; and its crimes against God and man must be proclaimed and denounced." And perhaps this was so; nevertheless, we read Douglass's writings today in literature classes not so much for their content but to understand, and marvel at, his sublime mastery of words, words—to paraphrase Calvino—that never finish saying what it is they have to say, not because of their "message" but because of the language in which that message is inextricably enfolded.

There are as many ways to define a classic in the African American tradition as there are in any other tradition, and these ways are legion. So many essays have been published entitled "What Is a Classic?" that they could fill several large anthologies. And while no one can say explicitly why generations of readers return to read certain texts, just about everyone can agree that making a best-seller list in one's lifetime is most certainly not an index of fame or influence over time; the longevity of one's readership—of books about which one says, "I am rereading," as Calvino puts it—on the other hand, most certainly is. So, the size of one's readership (through library use, Internet access, and sales) cumulatively is an interesting factor to consider; and because of series such as the Penguin Classics, we can gain a sense, for our purposes, of those texts written by authors in previous generations that have sustained sales—mostly for classroom use—long after their authors were dead.

There can be little doubt that *Narrative of the Life of Frederick Douglass* (1845), *The Souls of Black Folk* (1903), by W. E. B. Du Bois, and *Their Eyes Were Watching God* (1937), by Zora Neale Hurston, are the three most classic of the Black classics—again, as measured by consumption—while Langston Hughes's poetry, though not purchased as books in these large numbers, is accessed through the internet as frequently as that of any other American poet, and indeed profoundly more so than most. Within Penguin's Portable Series list, the most popular individual titles, excluding Douglass's first slave narrative and Du Bois's *Souls*, are:

Up from Slavery (1901), Booker T. Washington
The Autobiography of an Ex-Colored Man (1912), James
    Weldon Johnson
God's Trombones (1927), James Weldon Johnson
Passing (1929), Nella Larsen

The Marrow of Tradition (1901), Charles W. Chesnutt
Incidents in the Life of a Slave Girl (1861), Harriet Jacobs
The Interesting Narrative (1789), Olaudah Equiano
The House Behind the Cedars (1900), Charles W. Chesnutt
My Bondage and My Freedom (1855), Frederick Douglass
Quicksand (1928), Nella Larsen

These titles form a canon of classic African American literature, judged by classroom readership. If we add Jean Toomer's
novel *Cane* (1923), arguably the first work of African American modernism, along with Douglass's first narrative, Du
Bois's *The Souls*, and Hurston's *Their Eyes*, we would most
certainly have included many of the touchstones of Black literature published before 1940, when Richard Wright published *Native Son*.

Every teacher's syllabus constitutes a canon of sorts, and I
teach these texts and a few others as the classics of the Black
canon. Why these particular texts? I can think of two reasons:
First, these texts signify or riff upon each other, repeating,
borrowing, and extending metaphors book to book, generation to generation. To take just a few examples, Equiano's
eighteenth-century use of the trope of the talking book (an
image found, remarkably, in five slave narratives published between 1770 and 1811) becomes, with Frederick Douglass, the
representation of the quest for freedom as, necessarily, the quest
for literacy, for a freedom larger than physical manumission;
we might think of this as the representation of metaphysical
manumission, of freedom and literacy—the literacy of great
literature—inextricably intertwined. Douglass transformed the
metaphor of the talking book into the trope of chiasmus, a
repetition with a stinging reversal: "You have seen how a man
becomes a slave, you will see how a slave becomes a man." Du
Bois, with Douglass very much on his mind, transmuted chiasmus a half century later into the metaphor of duality or double
consciousness, a necessary condition of living one's life, as he
memorably put it, behind a "veil."

Du Bois's metaphor has a powerful legacy in twentieth-
century Black fiction: James Weldon Johnson, in *Ex-Colored*

Man, literalizes the trope of double consciousness by depicting as his protagonist a man who, at will, can occupy two distinct racial spaces, one Black, one white, and who moves seamlessly, if ruefully, between them; Toomer's *Cane* takes Du Bois's metaphor of duality for the inevitably split consciousness that every Negro must feel living in a country in which her or his status as a citizen is liminal at best, or has been erased at worst, and makes of this the metaphor for the human condition itself under modernity, a tellingly bold rhetorical gesture—one designed to make the Negro the metaphor of the human condition. And Hurston, in *Their Eyes*, extends Toomer's revision even further, depicting a character who can gain her voice only once she can name this condition of duality or double consciousness and then glide gracefully and lyrically between her two selves, an "inside" self and an "outside" one.

More recently, Alice Walker, in *The Color Purple*, signifies upon two aspects of the narrative strategy of *Their Eyes*: First, she revisits the theme of a young Black woman finding her voice, depicting a protagonist who writes herself into being through letters addressed to God and to her sister, Nettie—letters that grow ever more sophisticated in their syntax and grammar and imagery as she comes to consciousness before our very eyes, letter to letter; and second, Walker riffs on Hurston's use of a vernacular-inflected free indirect discourse to show that Black English has the capacity to serve as the medium for narrating a novel through the Black dialect that forms a most pliable and expansive language in Celie's letters. Ralph Ellison makes Du Bois's metaphor of the veil a trope of blindness and life underground for his protagonist in *Invisible Man*, a protagonist who, as he types the story of his life from a hole underground, writes himself into being in the first person (in contradistinction to Richard Wright's protagonist, Bigger Thomas, whose reactive tale of fear and flight is told in the third person). Walker's novel also riffs on Ellison's claim for the revolutionary possibilities of writing the self into being, whereas Hurston's protagonist, Janie, speaks herself into being. Ellison himself signified multiply upon Richard Wright's *Native Son*, from the title to the use of the first-person bildungsroman to chart the coming to consciousness of a sensitive protagonist moving from blindness and an inability to do little more than react to his environment, to the insight gained by wresting control of his identity from social forces and strong individuals that would circumscribe and confine his life choices. Toni Morrison, master supernaturalist and perhaps the greatest Black novelist of all, trumps Ellison's trope of blindness by returning over and over to the possibilities and limits of insight within worlds confined or circumscribed not by supraforces (à la Wright) but by the confines of the imagination and the ironies of individual and family history, signifying upon Faulkner, Woolf, and García Márquez in the process. And Ishmael Reed, the father of Black postmodernism and what we might think of as the hip-hop novel, the tradition's master parodist, signifies upon everybody and everything in the Black literary tradition, from the slave narratives to the Harlem Renaissance to Black nationalism and feminism.

This sort of literary signifying is what makes a literary tradition, well, a "tradition," rather than a simple list of books whose authors happen to have been born in the same country, share the same gender, or would be identified by their peers as belonging to this ethnic group or that. What makes these books special—"classic"—however, is something else. Each text has the uncanny capacity to take the seemingly mundane details of the day-to-day African American experience of its time and transmute those details and the characters' actions into something that transcends its ostensible subject's time and place, its specificity. These texts reveal the human universal through the African American particular: All true art, all classics, do this; this is what "art" is, a revelation of that which makes each of us sublimely human, rendered in the minute details of the actions and thoughts and feelings of a compelling character embedded in a time and place. But as soon as we find ourselves turning to a text for its anthropological or sociological data, we have left the realm of art; we have reduced the complexity of fiction or poetry to an essay, and this is not what imaginative literature is for. Richard Wright, at his best, did this, as did his signifying disciple Ralph Ellison; Louis

Armstrong and Duke Ellington, Bessie Smith and Billie Holi-
day achieved this effect in music; Jacob Lawrence and Romare
Bearden achieved it in the visual arts. And this is what Wole
Soyinka does in his tragedies, what Toni Morrison does in her
novels, what Derek Walcott did in his poetry. And while it is
risky to name one's contemporaries in a list such as this, I
think that Rita Dove and Jamaica Kincaid achieve this effect
as well, as do Colson Whitehead and Edwidge Danticat, in a
younger generation. (There are other writers whom I would
include in this group had I the space.) By delving ever so deeply
into the particularity of the African and African American experience, these authors manage, somehow, to come out the
other side, making the race or the gender of their characters
almost translucent, less important than the fact that they stand
as aspects of ourselves beyond race or gender or time or place,
precisely in the same magical way that Hamlet never remains
for long stuck as a prince in a court in Denmark.

Each classic Black text reveals to us, uncannily, subtly, how
the Black Experience is inscribed, inextricably and indelibly,
in the human experience, and how the human experience
takes one of its myriad forms in blackface, as it were. Together,
such texts also demonstrate, implicitly, that African American
culture is one of the world's truly great and eternal cultures, as
noble and as resplendent as any. And it is to publish such texts,
written by African and African American authors, that Penguin has created this new series, which I have the pleasure of
editing.

HENRY LOUIS GATES, JR.

Introduction

Imagine the scene: A middle-aged, still youthful African American sits at an outdoor café on the Italian Riviera, in the town of San Remo, sometime in August 1924. Barely taller than the little children playing in the street before him, the man is dressed in all-white clothes to shield him, barely, from the pounding rays of the summer sun. Tourists saunter by him, taking no notice, while the Italian organ grinder leans in for a tip, which the notoriously parsimonious Alain Locke obliges by giving him a dime. As he soaks up the sun and the scene, however, his mind is somewhere else—in the cafes of Harlem, that inner suburb of New York City, whose speakeasies, nightclubs, and basement dives he also habituates (only at night and often incognito), where Black people are dancing, drinking, and writhing the night away. For months in the United States, he struggled to find his footing in an assignment to edit a special issue of a magazine, *Survey Graphic*, on the meaning of Harlem and the new movement of Black creatives who claim it as their spiritual home. Lying in front of him on his outdoor table in San Remo are not tourist guides or restaurant menus but poems, short stories, and essays by these writers who are Black, youthful, sexually ambiguous, and unafraid to identify themselves in print as Negro—the respectful term for African Americans in the 1920s.[1] For Locke, a Philadelphia aesthete, it is difficult to marry his own sense of the aesthetic, the love of beautiful form in all creation, with the particular self-assertion and pride bubbling up in places far removed from the summer splendor of Italy, like Harlem.

Something in Locke's trip abroad dislodged his Victorian

resistance to seeing Black people en masse as inherently creative, as quintessentially beautiful. What changed his perception? Was it getting away from the segregation of America to suffuse himself in the world of art without fear of being denied entrance to cultural events because of the color of his skin? Was it his encounter with Langston Hughes, one of the young poets featured in the forthcoming magazine, whom he had met in Paris and wined and dined throughout Europe only to be dragged into the slums of places like Venice by this young radical in search of the poor people whom Hughes believed were the true artists of any culture? Perhaps Locke did not know. But something in his summer opened his eyes to seeing Black people aesthetically and not as the victims of social forces that sociologists and political scientists decreed they were. Instead, Locke began to unearth a connection between the young Black creatives he wanted to introduce to America and the Black masses whose agency in leaving the South and pouring into the urban North had transformed Harlem into a "crucible" of diversity that would welcome even queer Black expatriates like himself.

Sitting thousands of miles away from Black America, in transatlantic privilege, Locke began to see the papers in front of him with enlightened eyes. He realized that the boldness he found in the writings of these largely middle-class Black writers was connected to the agency of young Black working-class people who had not only left the South but left behind an old identity. These two distinct classes had found one another in Harlem and together were changing what it meant to be a Negro in America. Searching for a metaphor of that changed consciousness, Locke seized on the term "the New Negro," habitually if inconsistently used by young Blacks since the end of Reconstruction to describe a manly Black identity, as a metaphor for the new synthesis of agency he saw evidenced in the 1920s in places like Harlem. In drafts titled "The New Setting" and "The New Negro," Locke would finally be able to say what he could see—that a fundamental swerve in the consciousness of Black Americans had occurred, and the Negroes' future would never be the same as the Old Negro past. The

New Negro aesthetic was a dance Alain Locke had to learn, ironically, abroad. Only away from the racism and homophobia of America could he fuse his thinking about aesthetics—why art, literature, music, and performance mattered—with his thinking about the Negro experience in the 1920s to offer something new, a conception of Black modernity as a New Negro creativity that would transform America as well as Black people. As he wrote Paul Kellogg, the editor of *Survey Graphic*, before leaving Italy, Locke was returning to America with a "full kit" of essays. Getting outside of America, Locke had gotten outside of the usual ways of portraying Black people in America and finally been able to see the Negro *aesthetically*.[2]

The essays and articles collected in this volume are the result of that new attitude and the struggle to inculcate that New Negro aesthetic, as I am calling it here, into the minds of the twentieth century. Locke spent the rest of his life trying to redefine what it meant to be Black in America and to suggest that there were rich cultural rewards that came from realizing that being African American was not a problem at all. Because we tend to associate the word "aesthetics" with a search for the universal principles of art, bereft of the dirty business of race, it is important to recognize that in putting race and aesthetics in conversation with one another, Locke forever changed our understanding of both. For Locke refused to turn the discussion of the New Negro aesthetic into simply an exercise in "art for art's sake" or deploy aesthetics simply for the purpose of better propaganda for the race. Locke's critique of the American scene was simultaneously a critique of the Negro scene—the way that reacting against racism had contorted Black thinking into asserting one of two untenable monotheisms: either race had nothing to do with one's creative expressions as a human being or race completely determined all one needed to know about the humanity of Black people, especially their efforts at self-expression. Art was thus crucially important when discussing the attempt to escape this double bind—epitomized in the notion of a New Negro, a rebel against all old configurations of the Negro streaming out of the nineteenth century—because art was one of the very few spaces in which Negroes, according to Locke, could be completely and utterly themselves. To be a New Negro poet, novelist, actor, musician, dancer, or filmmaker was to commit oneself to an arc of self-discovery, an exploration of what and who the Negro was—and was "gonna be"—without fear that one would disappoint the White or Black bystander. In committing to that path, Locke asserted, Negro artists would access something inaccessible through the natural attitudes of American racial politics—one would uncover a reality, a domain, a being-in-the-world that was rich and bountiful in its creative possibilities. They could turn off the noise of racism and see people of African descent for who we really are—an abundantly creative people who have transformed, powerfully and perpetually, the culture of wherever history or social forces have landed us. The New Negro, in other words, need think of herself not as America's vexing problem but as a crucible of creativity for the whole world.

But why Europe? Why did Locke have to go to San Remo, Italy, to see Harlem and Black aesthetics in their proper light? Six months after Locke's special Harlem issue of *Survey Graphic* appeared on March 1, 1925, Josephine Baker would open in La Revue Nègre, at the Théâtre des Champs-Élysées in Paris, and become an international celebrity, headlining a series of sold-out shows throughout Europe that would propel her into European society. Nothing like it existed in America. The next year, Paul Robeson would head to London on the start of a European tour performing African American spirituals and, in 1928, he would become an international celebrity for his performance in the London production of *Show Boat*. By the 1930s, Robeson, now living in London, would be the most famous American abroad. Europe seemed to recognize the Negro as the quintessential artist she in fact was but could not become in America, as Locke suggested in his tribute "Roland Hayes: An Appreciation," about that Negro singer's success among highly critical European audiences. It was the modernist European dramatist Max Reinhardt who showed Locke and his ally Charles S. Johnson—the editor of *Oppor-*

tunity, the journal of the National Urban League, and the publisher of many of Locke's articles—that Black musical comedy was one of the purest forms of modernist theater he had ever seen. His enthusiasm, as Locke recorded in his article "The Negro and the American Stage," went beyond that of Locke and Johnson, who saw Black musical comedy through the lens of their bourgeois upbringing in Black Victorian culture. Europe provided the doorway into a new consciousness that form, rather than sociopolitical content, was in fact the terrain of genius for Black expression. As Locke wrote in "A Note on African Art," European modernist artists had been the first to view African sculpture as art and not grist for theories of race and anthropology. But Europeans' prescient appreciation was not limited to visual and performing arts; African diasporic writers like Claude McKay, René Maran, and Langston Hughes found recognition, awards, and appreciation as artists in Europe that eluded them in America.[3]

African Americans were able to reinvent themselves as artists in Europe, and thus fulfill one of the core values of the New Negro—reinvention through aesthetic form, which had been Black people's contribution to American culture for over a hundred years. In fact, Locke's conception of the New Negro, which he began to explore in "Enter the New Negro" but developed over decades of thinking and writing about it, was the most radical conceptual frame for aesthetics that Locke developed in his lifetime. Indeed, the articles "Harlem" and "Enter the New Negro" begin this collection precisely because the Great Migration, on the one hand, and Harlem, on the other, made visible to the public for the first time, according to Locke, that African Americans were fundamentally a people of reinvention. This was not simply some wild theory of a Black academic. As the literary critic and historian Eleanor Traylor noted, the folk tradition of Black Americans was fundamentally a tradition of creating agency out of the depths of depravity and social death.[4] Locke articulated this first as a social movement when he wrote, in "Harlem," that the Great Migration had filled Northern cities and states with hundreds of thousands of Negroes beginning in World War I not because they were pushed out of the South but because they chose to leave. Rather than social forces, Locke believed that the Great Migration occurred because of an act of consciousness, a willingness on the part of Black Americans to seize, as he put it, an opportunity for a different future than the present had saddled them with. To leave the South, to leave the land where one's ancestors were buried, was an act of reinvention, a fostering of a new self out of a vision of a new future, that redefined what it meant to be Negro. While Europeans like Reinhardt saw Black improvisational genius as not simply a fact of superlative individuals but an aesthetic, a set of principles of performance that revolutionized Western culture, Locke's innovation was to apply this aesthetic approach to identity and see Harlemites as improvising new identities and in the process becoming a new people.

It was not, of course, necessary to go to Europe to see the Negro in this new perspective, and simply going to Europe did not automatically result in this transforming vision for Locke. Ideally, as he asserted in his discussion of the possible impact of African art on African American artists in America, his goal was that once American-born Black artists had their eyes opened to the beautiful in African forms, they would render that beauty anew in their own ways. But to achieve that kind of seeing in America was difficult, and the vision once seen was hard to hold on to and build upon, given the constant brainwashing effects of discursive racism. Locke had first glimpsed the workings of the New Negro aesthetic as a literacy seventeen years earlier, as an undergraduate at Harvard College in Cambridge, Massachusetts. That such a change occurred in Locke at all was something of a miracle. Bred in the Black Victorian tradition of Philadelphia's upper middle class around the turn of the century, Locke had entered Harvard trained to socialize only with upper-middle-class Whites from his days as a brilliant student at Central High and the School of Pedagogy in Philadelphia. His voluminous letters to his mother during those years were filled with vitriolic condemnation of the other Black students in Cambridge as "uncultured" and lacking in the intellectual qualities of civilized people. He took most of his classes from professors like Irving Babbitt and Barrett Wendell, who asserted the absolute superiority of European literature over all of the rest of world literature.[5]

But a funny thing happened on the way to Locke's graduation. The death of Paul Laurence Dunbar, in 1906, led Locke to pen a eulogy to this poet that showed an opening in Locke's Europhilic thinking—or, more precisely, a consciousness to ignore the usual dismissal of African American literature at places like Harvard in favor of a remarkable first assessment of what it meant to be a New Negro writer. Partly inspired by his Irish student friend Charles Dickerman's love of the Irish Renaissance, Locke delivered a 1907 speech in a Black church in Roxbury, Massachusetts, that asserted that Dunbar, while not the greatest poet of the English language, and not even the best poet of African descent in the English language, was nevertheless the first poet to express the Negro mind unapologetically in the English language. Particularly important, Dunbar had captured the speech of the "peasant Negro," and thereby made a unique contribution to the English language. In effect, Dunbar had done what Locke wanted poets in the 1920s to do—mine working-class creative literacy and translate it into fine-art poetry that transformed the body of literature written in English. Because Locke was speaking to a Black audience, the resulting text was different from those he wrote in his Harvard classes. While speaking as a critic, Locke epitomized what Russian critic and philosopher Mikhail Bakhtin theorized about the novel: the writer, the thinker, the New Negro intellectual is always dialoguing with an Other, an audience (literally, in this case). Out of that dialogue came Locke's first statement of the New Negro aesthetic, a statement he would refine and update over and over again in relation to other audiences, seen and unseen, throughout his lifetime. Standing before that Roxbury audience, Locke executed a swerve in literary criticism in the West: he broke with the Eurocentric tradition of literary White supremacy.

But it did not last. Locke left for England four months after delivering that speech, having become the first African American Rhodes Scholar to Oxford. Here was the tension in Locke: he found it hard to follow the swerve toward a fuller, more complete statement of the New Negro aesthetic without first trying to abandon the study of Black culture—indeed, of Black people in general—as a permanent expatriate abroad.[6]

What makes the New Negro aesthetic interesting today is that it makes visible this tension in the career of many Black artists, writers, and intellectuals, a tension between the constant drumbeat of Eurocentrism in the fine arts, whether in the United States or abroad, and the reaction against that mentality that continues to erupt among people of color who study the arts and wish them to reflect another aesthetic consciousness. In that respect, what's remarkable about the formation of the New Negro aesthetic is that it occurred at all. Why did it erupt? How does one explain this recurring breakout of a different consciousness in a thoroughly Europeanized intellectual like Locke? Black places curate Black thinkers, but as San Remo reminds us, place is not sufficient to explain the awakening of a New Negro aesthetic consciousness in Locke. What happened?

Locke experienced what another philosopher, Edmund Husserl, called an epoché—a break in the natural attitude of daily life—here, the daily life of racist thinking about what Black people had accomplished in America—a suspension, really, of the taken-for-granted reasoning by which Americans, in this case, routinely went about their daily lives with people of every race, sexuality, and gender pigeonholed in neat hierarchical boxes.[7] The prompt for this break in the natural attitude toward Black people probably came from Charles Dickerman, his Harvard classmate, who was infatuated not only with Locke but also with the Irish Renaissance and its taking of the folk songs and stories of the Irish peasants and translating them into some of the most powerful English-language poetry and theater of the early twentieth century. Dickerman broke the spell of Locke's natural way of thinking of Negroes as without culture and allowed Locke to take a transcendental view of Black folk culture as the source of a unique revision of the English language that expressed an independent Negro subject in America. As in Irish literature, the aesthetics subjectivized the people, showed their efficacy and agency in creating something new in the world that transcended the social and economic conditions of their lives. It was potentially a platform even for political emancipation because, once aroused and confirmed as a new identity, out of the revelation of a distinct cultural efficacy found in Black literature, the Black subject could foster a new political agenda.

Locke had difficulty holding on to and building on that thought in 1907. The natural attitude of Black Victorian culture came roaring back to him, in part because that same year Locke began his own European grand tour. Mastery of European forms snapped him back into older beliefs that Black people's culture was inferior and reinforced his desire to escape the whole question of race, if he could, by becoming a permanent African American expatriate abroad. But England corrected this illusion. Locke received a rude awakening when he arrived at Oxford in 1907, as Southern Rhodes Scholars from the United States made his life a living hell by convincing the Rhodes authorities to exclude him from celebrations for Americans at Oxford. Academically, he faltered as well, failing to keep up in his Greek and Latin studies at Oxford in Literae Humaniores or to secure a degree for his philosophy thesis in value theory, which he completed once he moved to Berlin. The New Negro aesthetic is formed out of this dialectic of culture that is almost unavoidable, or at least often encountered, by almost every Black creative who seeks to create art or an art space inside even the contemporary literary and art worlds of the West in the twenty-first century, given the trajectory made visible by this one Black aesthetician of the twentieth century.

Another part of that dialectic was in operation at Oxford, where Locke encountered a community of young intellectuals from the colonies of the British Empire—Egypt, India, South Africa, and Sri Lanka—who were developing an antithesis to the cultural supremacy of English colonialism that was rooted in celebration of their indigenous aesthetic traditions and resistance to complete assimilation and worship of English aesthetic norms. Dialogue with these non-European intellectuals, struggling themselves to turn their predicament as the Other in English imperialist narcissism into something fresh, offered Locke a model of how to be a New Negro aesthetic intellectual. Bonding with and learning from them also gave him his first real opportunity of praxis as a creative midwife, when he helped his Oxford friend Lionel de Fonseka write *On the Truth of Decorative Art*, a dialogue between "Oriental and Occidental" that led almost inexorably to the radical conclusion that English cultural arrogance was unearned; Eastern aesthetics, De Fonseka had his dialogue conclude, were superior to those of the English. In De Fonseka, Locke found his model—to assert the beauty and even superiority of marginalized and racialized aesthetic traditions as a key not only to creating great African American art but also to fostering a great African American people as a powerful subject on the world-historical stage. By the time he secured a job at Howard University in 1912 and finished his PhD in philosophy in value theory at Harvard in 1918, Locke had come full circle. He had developed a synthetic view of Negro aesthetics as that which the Negro community *values* and now was ready to lead a Black renaissance of beauty in the 1920s.[8]

Locke began to institutionalize Negro aesthetics at Howard University in the late 1910s as he started *The Stylus*, a campus literary club and magazine, and helped Thomas Montgomery Gregory start the Howard Players, a student-run theater at Howard. Locke chronicled the modest success and outsized promise of the university theater to advance Negro self-expression in the article "Steps Toward a Negro Theater" and outlined the self-affirming agency of culture as an end of education in "The Ethics of Culture." But when Charles S. Johnson asked Locke to play the role of master of ceremonies at a Civic Club dinner in 1924, which would introduce emerging Black writers to liberal White publishers in New York, Locke jumped at the chance to institutionalize Negro aesthetics in the White publishing world. His remarks at this dinner made such an impression on *Survey Graphic* editor Paul Kellogg that he asked Locke and Johnson to edit the special issue devoted to the new consciousness bubbling up in Harlem and making itself visible in the younger writers he had met at the dinner. Locke seized on that opportunity to push himself forward as the prime interpreter and later defender of that movement, by arguing that Negro creative writing could be an American cultural revolution, not just for the artists but for Black people generally.[9]

That's because, from his temporary perch in San Remo, Locke was able to see that Harlem was an epoché—a transcendental space in the United States where the soul-numbing natural attitude of cultural racism and homophobia were suspended, if only for a few years, and Southern and Northern Negroes, recently arrived West Indians, Africans, young students, old criminals, and queer artists congregated in a safe space made possible by Harlem. The New Negro aesthetic had a particular relation to space and a relationship to sexuality, representing the emergence of a Black Queer Aesthetic from the Harlem drag queen balls to the intimate spaces in public places that Black gays and lesbians curated in clubs like Smalls Paradise in Harlem. Even though gay men like Countee Cullen, Langston Hughes, and even Locke himself remained closeted open secrets during the 1920s, because of the homophobia of Black progressive circles, the New Negro aesthetic embraced Richard Bruce Nugent not only as person but as writer of same sex stream-of-consciousness interracial love poems like "Smoke, Lilies and Jade." While not officially a member of the New Negro movement, James Baldwin and his work, especially *Go Tell It on the Mountain and Giovanni's Room*, built on the New Negro aesthetic's urging to find a new language to explore identity and sexuality without hypersensitivity over race "representativeness" and "propaganda." African principles of design, however changed from their originals in Africa, had a place-making effect, such that spaces like cabarets, speakeasies, even tight tenement apartments, became performance venues that exuded a distinctive form of community taking shape in America. Rather than ghettos, urban enclaves like Harlem, the South Side of Chicago, and others, were crucibles of new aesthetics that made room for new racial and sexual identities to flourish, and in the process redefine what it meant to be Black in America.

What can be frustrating about Locke's writings, however, is that he is not a system builder, like Husserl, or the author of a large number of single-authored books, like John Dewey, that establish the architecture of his aesthetic theory. Rather, Locke developed the New Negro aesthetic as a running conversation with reviewed books, exhibitions, collections, and performances that he witnessed, and recorded a slew of speeches, essays, and articles that constitute intellectual milestones in the path his thinking on aesthetics took. At a time of intense Jim Crow segregation of intellectual life in America (during his forty-year teaching career, with a PhD from Harvard, he never received an offer for a permanent job at a predominantly White institution of higher education), Locke wrote primarily for Black magazines and liberal journals that, except for the extremely popular Harlem issue of *Survey Graphic*, had limited readership. Nonetheless, the benefits of his chosen form of self-expression are many. Short-form writing—essays, articles, drafts of speeches—combined with an intimate, often Black or liberal White audience, shaped his writing creatively, giving it a clarity and pugnacity sometimes missing from his larger works aimed at a more diffuse and national audience. Those qualities make his short critical writings, scattered though they have been, the best of Locke's writings on what the implications are of the New Negro aesthetic for what we face as a nation and a people in the twenty-first century.

These essays exist in such abundance because of an irony in Locke's professional career. For reasons that remain unclear, Locke was fired from his job as a professor of philosophy at Howard University two months after the publication of the Harlem *Survey Graphic*. Immediately after learning, in June 1925, that his services would no longer be needed at Howard, Locke threw himself into turning the Harlem issue of *Survey Graphic* into a full-length anthology, with new and supplemental material, that would appear as *The New Negro: An Interpretation*, in December 1925. The success of that publication made it possible for Locke to launch himself into a schedule of almost constant travel and writing, delivering modestly paid lectures and writing dozens of articles each year to sustain himself economically until he got his job back in 1927 and returned to teaching at Howard in 1928. Being unemployed not only released Locke to write and speak publicly more than he otherwise would have, it also taught him that the New Negro aesthetic was an economy. It was a new way of making a living for Locke—his circulation throughout the country mirrored the experience of itinerant Black blues singers and Black jazz performers migrating from New Orleans to Chicago to New York, stitching together an income from a professional lifestyle that, while stress inducing, also freed them from the cotton field, the domestic service job, and, in Locke's case, the drudgery of the teaching profession. It uncovered what might be called an early post-Fordist economy of Black performers in the music industry who, like Josephine Baker, Florence Mills, and Paul Robeson, all escaped from the "natural attitude" of segregated Jim Crow jobs available for smart Negroes in early-twentieth-century America. Having observed from San Remo that the genius of Black people was to adopt circulation around the country as the mechanism of emancipation during the Great Migration, Locke applied that insight to himself and recognized that was what the New Negro aesthetic meant for the Negro of the future—one could create one's own opportunity as a Black person by being a creative, and White people and Black people would pay you for it. While advocating Negro aesthetics as an emancipatory platform, Locke was forced to emancipate himself through intellectual labor, shooting out a rapid-fire succession of articles, making the period from 1925 to 1928 one of the most productive periods of critical writing in African American intellectual history.

What saved Locke and, perhaps more accurately, drove him was that he was a polemicist, who reacted quickly and deftly to challenges to his position with literary missiles sent out to bring down his detractors, or at least parry their critical thrusts. When some Harlemites objected to the portraits of darker-skinned Negroes that the German artist Winold Reiss had done for *Survey Graphic*, Locke fired off a sharply worded critique, "To Certain of Our Philistines," not long after the forum in which the objections were raised. The New Negro aesthetic was not simply a Black artistic movement but a movement to find a new aesthetic to project Negro identity and culture. "Of all the arts," Locke wrote, "painting is most bound by social ideas," with the result that even such good American artists as Winslow Homer or Robert Henri had approached Negro portraiture as an "artistic curiosity" rather than a serious opportunity to develop a new strain of American art. "Negro artists, themselves victims of the academy-tradition, have had the same attitude and have shared the blindness of the Caucasian eye." Reiss, by contrast, had taken "a new approach," since a new subject requires a new style.

Reiss's art was revolutionary because he had "achieved what amounts to a revealing discovery of the significance, human and artistic, of one of the great dialects of human physiognomy, of some of the little but powerful idioms of nature's speech," as Locke put it in "Harlem Types," his article on Reiss in *Survey Graphic*. On canvas and paper, his Negro subjects were unapologetically Negro, and his abstract designs embodied "the pattern of the culture" from which they came. Reiss had done for New Negro visual aesthetics what Dunbar had done for Negro literature—translated the pattern of the people into a new visual literacy. That a European had made this breakthrough should not be derided, Locke argued, but celebrated and followed. As if to emphasize the point, Locke included full-color reproductions of Reiss's portraits in *The New Negro: An Interpretation* when it was published in December that year.

Perhaps motivated by criticism of the decision to continue to feature art by a European artist in a narrative of a Negro renaissance, Locke followed up his defense of Winold Reiss with a series of articles on European art that took the Negro as its subject. At first, his articles, such as "The Art of Auguste Mambour," built on the argument that European artists brought to the artistic depiction of the Negro a fresh modernism that rendered Africans and people of African descent as beautiful. As in drama, Locke wanted to create a space within the New Negro aesthetic for White, Latin American (the drawings of

Miguel Covarrubias, for example, were also included in *The New Negro*), and other artists to respond favorably to his call to invest their talent in depiction of the Negro, whether in art or drama, as a revolutionary act.

But just as Locke argued that the European tradition in art and theater could not be ignored by Negro art and Negro artists, so too he emphasized that African art could not be ignored by Negro American artists either. After writing "A Note on Negro Art," which was based on African art in the collection of the Barnes Foundation, Locke became a curator himself, using the money of Edith J. R. Isaacs, editor in chief of *Theatre Arts Monthly*, to purchase the Blondiau Collection of Congo art. In a series of articles based on that collection, Locke reiterated his belief that viewing African art should liberate African American artists from "lily-whitism" and internalized racism that, he believed, hampered the development of a robust Negro visual art. Then, in 1931, Locke discovered while helping to put together an exhibition on Negro art for the Harmon Foundation that Negro visual artists were doing outstanding work, some of it, like the sculpture of Sargent Johnson, inspired by African art. He discussed this coming of age for Negro visual artists in "The American Negro as Artist," suggesting that the flourishing of this new visual art was taking place because Black visual artists had stopped trying to escape the depiction of the Negro image in their work. Perhaps drawing on his own struggles with identification with the masses of Black people, Locke gave his aesthetics a praxis based on his update of the Freudian thesis—that racism formed a kind of disabling unconscious in most Negro American artists, who could only get over its handicapping effect in their creative lives by identifying with themselves through art. Acquaintance with African art was part of the healing process needed to allow Negro American artists to emerge as world-historical artists on their own terms, without deference to European models. Unlike some aesthetes involved in promoting African American artists of the time, Locke had no use for "art for art's sake": true art, he asserted, advanced a philosophy of beauty that was both an end in itself and also a tool of self-empowerment and revival of Negroes' ancient primacy as artists in Africa. Art, therefore, revealed a deeper truth about who and what was Negro, not only for the artist but for the community such art ultimately should serve and enhance.

Locke's essays on art had perhaps greater effect on contemporary visual artists than his literary criticism had on the writers of his time. For while Locke's recommendations to model African art or choose a Negro theme alienated some young artists, like Romare Bearden and Norman Lewis, others such as William H. Johnson, Richmond Barthé, Lois Mailou Jones, and Jacob Lawrence heeded Locke's call to "do something on your own people," as he put it to Jones. Johnson, for example, excelled in using African forms of abstraction to produce uniquely modernist studies of African American performance culture. Lawrence, perhaps the most talented of all the artists of his generation, did "something on your own people" by chronicling their history in multipanel art series that culminated in *Migration Series* (1941), which won a Rosenwald Fellowship and became part of the permanent collections of the Museum of Modern Art and the Phillips Collection.[10] A child of the Great Migration, Lawrence seemed to have no problem utilizing African principles of design and European abstraction to create works that excelled both as modern art and as interpretations of Negro history and struggle. Similarly, in 1941, William H. Johnson created a spectacular series of prints called *Jitterbugs* (one of which appears on the cover of this anthology) that fused African principles of design with European abstraction to render Black nightclub dancing as the aesthetic language of the Black modern. Locke's demand that visual artists make the Negro experience the focal point of Negro art anticipated the position of the Black Arts Movement of the 1960s. Of course, a key philosophical difference between Locke and AfriCOBRA and other Black aesthetic collectives of the 1960s and 1970s was that Locke refused to jettison the European, either as tradition or artists, as collaborator in the creation of the New Negro Renaissance, whereas the later Black Arts movements did so emphatically.

The New Negro aesthetic was a more complex and capa-

cious transnational cultural formation than America had seen
in the 1930s—or since. Locke chose as his calling to delineate
the transnational truths of the Negro and resist simplistic formulas that claimed that Black art was simply another part of
American or Western aesthetics, on the one hand, or something
completely separate and autonomous from Western aesthetics,
on the other. Locke was a dialogical thinker who believed that
African American aesthetics was a dialectical formation, in
which both European and African elements were taken up and
transformed into something new, but something which nevertheless echoed, reverberated with, and spoke to the aesthetics
of both continents.

One drawback of Locke's emphasis on the European and
African transnationalism implicit in African American—indeed,
in American—art was that he sometimes failed to evaluate
American cultural innovations purely on their own terms, at a
time when artists and critics were turning away from seeing
American art, music, and literature through a European or
even African frame. In the visual arts, the American Scene
painting replaced Cubism, for example, as the driving conceptual frame for many American artists who sought to depict the
unique struggles of Americans, especially workers, in the face
of the Great Depression. Even in African American art circles,
Southern Black folk art displaced African-inspired painting as
the African American works most desired by collectors in the
1930s. Locke's Europhilia also blinded him, at times, to the genius of African American art forms. For example, Locke was
famous for his distaste for ragtime and jazz, with only a passing tolerance for the blues, which Langston Hughes helped him
learn to appreciate. Locke could recognize the astounding originality of the blues but was unable to come to terms with it
emotionally because his taste was formed by European classical
music. When he critiqued contemporary Black musicians and
composers in the 1930s in his article "Toward a Critique of
Negro Music," he revealed that his model for development of
the music into "fine art" was the European classical model.
Controversial in 1934 and since, that article has anchored a
view that Locke was unable to understand Black popular music

forms such as jazz on their own terms. Rather than continue that debate, I have chosen to include instead a little referenced excerpt from *The Negro and His Music*, written in 1936, which shows how much Locke grew as a student of Black music and, in particular, recognized that working-class Black people were the drivers of innovation in jazz. While he still retained his hope for classical elevation of the form, the passage from the Bronze Booklet shows Locke was already one of the most astute interpreters of contemporary Negro music by 1936.

The tendency to engage in critical commentary across so many diverse fields of Negro expression also cost Locke in his work on African art. Having sustained the backlash from his effrontery in trying to tell Negro artists how they should create Negro art, Locke began to deepen his study of African art in the 1930s, especially as he realized that younger, more singularly focused students of African art in America were about to eclipse him. His article "African Art: Classic Style," written in response to James Johnson Sweeney's 1935 exhibition of African art at the Museum of Modern Art, was hampered by an already out-of-date terminology of the "classical" when discussing Black art. While still in play among collectors of African art in the 1930s, it smacked, yet again, of too close a reliance on European categories to discuss art that had developed autonomously, even after European contact. Nonetheless, his discussion of African art in another Bronze Booklet he authored in 1936, entitled *Negro Art: Past and Present*, provides a remarkably sophisticated analysis of African art, albeit hampered still, in comparison to today's scholarship, by some outworn terminology. By the mid-1930s, with less writing by young Black authors being published and his access to Europe curtailed by the rise of Nazism, Locke slowed down and devoted the time and attention to refine his earlier theses with fresh insights that until now were buried in out-of-print pamphlets. Stepping back from being such an active critic of the contemporary scene, as had been the case in the late 1920s and early 1930s, allowed Locke to develop the architecture for more powerful interpretations of the cultural foundations for the New Negro aesthetic during the mid- to late 1930s.

Being a different kind of Black visionary meant that Locke's call for the Negro to embrace aesthetics and beauty as tools for self-empowerment and Black renewal led him into conflict with other advocates of liberation on the American scene. How exactly was African American art to transform America? The idea that beauty was important to the Black freedom struggle in the United States was not in itself controversial. What was controversial after the publication of *The New Negro: An Interpretation*, the book version of the Harlem issue of *Survey Graphic*, was precisely what kind of art and beauty Black people in America should advance. W. E. B. Du Bois, then the dominant theorist of African American cultural and political life, was also interested in beauty, but he was alarmed by the emphasis on beauty on its own terms in Locke's anthology, and mentioned it in his review of the book. If beauty alone was to be the focus of Negro art, Du Bois declared, it would lead to decadence. In one sense, Du Bois's reaction was a fig leaf for homophobia, since Du Bois knew from his study of English literature that aesthetes like Walter Pater and Oscar Wilde were connected with the cult of beauty for its own sake and not for the sake of responsible society, as had been the cultural philosophy of Matthew Arnold. For Du Bois, art served the interests of the larger society as a place of enlightenment and civilization, even though he deeply appreciated the Platonic triad of Truth, Justice, and Beauty as the cornerstone of civilization.

But just as important, Du Bois worried that White America would concede beauty to the Negro in exchange for not granting what Negroes really needed—justice. He also observed something Locke would later confirm: the rapid appropriation and commodification of Negro literature by White publishers eager to profit from what David Levering Lewis calls the "vogue of the Negro." Thus, six months after Locke's anthology appeared, Du Bois penned a serious attack on the whole notion of the New Negro aesthetic in his article "Criteria of Negro Art," which began as a speech he delivered to the convention of the NAACP in 1926. Du Bois rejected the notion that an expansive Negro literature, one that explored Black working-class and queer cultures as sites of beauty, was an emancipatory platform of change. Negro art needed to be a robust apologetics that produced stories that countered the misrepresentations of Black character in White popular and intellectual culture; beauty, for Du Bois, was a weapon. Du Bois declared that "all Art is propaganda and ever must be, despite the wailing of the purists. I stand in utter shamelessness and say whatever art I have for writing has been used always for propaganda for gaining the right of black folk to love and enjoy. I do not care a damn for any art that is not used for propaganda."[11] Embedded in this argument was the sense of injury suffered by most African Americans because of how they were presented in the media. In the 1920s, the Negro in print media appeared either as Aunt Jemima or Uncle Tom, or as something worse—stereotypes and grotesque caricatures that conveyed Blacks as either destined to serve or horrible criminals.[12] One seldom saw an art portrait of a Negro. So, Du Bois thought that the art needed was one that would counter these misrepresentations with formal portraits—what professor Evelyn Brooks Higginbotham calls "respectable images"—which would prove to Whites that Negroes were human and middle class.

Locke knew that Du Bois's position violated the fundamental principle of aesthetics in Western philosophy, perhaps best articulated by Immanuel Kant in his *Critique of Judgment*, that to view an object aesthetically was to apprehend it with disinterest, without any preconceived concept or agenda.[13] But Locke knew too that Western philosophers did not view beauty disinterestedly; Kant also wrote that the European possessed a "more beautiful body, works harder, is more jocular, more controlled in his passions, more intelligent than any other race of people in the world. . . . Humanity is at its greatest perfection in the race of whites."[14] Thomas Jefferson made plain his view that Black people were excluded from the realm of beauty as a species of persons, regardless of individual attributes. Is, Jefferson asked, the "black of the negro . . . not the foundation of a greater or less share of beauty in the two races? Are not the fine suffusions of colour in the one, preferable to the eternal monotony . . . that immoveable veil of black which covers all the emotions of the other race?"[15] For thinkers like Kant and Jefferson, Blacks couldn't even appreciate beauty because the Black body "veiled" their emotions. As a queer Black man in love with the Black body, Locke knew how devastating it was that the anti-Black, anti-beauty discourse of Western and especially American culture alienated the Black person from himself.

But, Locke argued, Du Bois's war of representation was too narrow and confining. The *work* to be done by the New Negro aesthetic went beyond simply producing counternarratives to White racism. In a series of articles, "Beauty Instead of Ashes," "Art or Propaganda?" and "Beauty and the Provinces," Locke outlined a Black program of beauty to overcome the alienation from the Black body and the Black experience that was internalized in Black people themselves. Immersion in African art, for example, taught the "lesson" of seeing one's body outside of Western standards of representation handed down to Negroes from the nineteenth century—standards that were themselves being revolutionized by an African-art-inspired modernism overtaking the world. Answering White racism was a conceptual trap that undermined Black subjectivity, because it distracted the artist into believing that eighteenth- and nineteenth-century racist art and philosophies were relevant to the twentieth-century Negro artist. Protest art reduced Negro ontology to being merely an answer to racist narratives and confirmed what those like Kant and Jefferson implied—that Black people lacked the capacity to conceive of themselves as beautiful away from Whites. The real work of a New Negro aesthetic was not answering racism but exploring a diverse modern Black subjectivity and imagining a new world of beauty in which race was but one defining characteristic, along with class, gender, and sexual orientation (although the famously closeted Alain Locke never mentioned sexuality in his answers to Du Bois and other critics).

But the deeper question remained: What was the relation of aesthetics to the larger predicament of being an oppressed and racialized class at the bottom of the economic and social structure called America? Locke's own brilliant article "The Modern Literary Tradition and the Negro"—a challenge to another Du Bois article, "The Social Uses of Art"—came to confirm the basic Marxist theoretical position underlying Du Bois's and later critics' charges, such as that launched by Richard Wright in the 1930s, that art, literature, and culture were connected to, even dependent on, the changing dynamics of economic bases of modern capitalist society. If the image of the Negro changed in relation to the changes in the economics of America, then how could a self-conscious art do anything more than reflect the larger conditions of Black life in America? During the 1930s, Marxist literary aesthetics in Black America answered that question by arguing that the only meaningful art was "proletarian art," as Locke called it in one of his finest articles in this collection, "Deep River, Deeper Sea: Retrospective Review of the Literature of the Negro for 1935." What separated Locke from Du Bois's Black propaganda progressivism or Wright's Marxist proletarianism was his demand that the Negro not lose sight of the sea, of spiritual emancipation, as not a luxury but a necessity for oppressed African Americans, whether working- or middle-class. The "work" that the New Negro aesthetic was sent to do was nothing less than to activate a catharsis of the spirit, a reinvention of the soul in changing times, and a reconceptualization of what it meant to be human even while being trapped in a system of oppression that denied one's humanity.

The potential for an emancipatory art went beyond simply escape from the conditions of oppression without challenge to those conditions, as was generally the limitation imposed on art by a radical critique of aesthetics. For Locke, the art of the spirituals, for example, was not simply an escape from the daily drudgery and dehumanization of slavery but a realm of the imagination that could create the conditions for a better sense of humanity than that existing among those who were White and nominally "free" of enslavement in antebellum America. There was something more possible in humanity than had even been realized so far among those who did not carry the burdens of being Black in White-obsessed America.

In articles like "The Negro's Contribution to American Art and Literature," Locke acknowledged not only that an African "spirit" existed in antebellum Negro aesthetics but also that it carried with it a vision of a better America than that imagined by the enslavers whom Black people served.

Fifty years later, the Marxist scholar Herbert Marcuse expressed what Locke was getting at: rather than merely serve as an answer to the social determination or discursive discrimination of day-to-day life, true revolutionary art transcends its social grounding—the base in Marxist sociology—and subverts reality by creating a realm of the possible. At its most revolutionary, art elevates subjectivity, the possibility of the human to go beyond what is and imagine what could be. As Locke wrote in an undergraduate essay at Harvard, art at its highest level produces a catharsis in us as humans that turns us from objectifications of our social determination into *subjects*, who find in literature, art, music, a new world. Marcuse put it this way: "The catharsis itself is grounded in the power of aesthetic form to call fate by its name, to demystify force, to give the word to the victims—the power of recognition which gives the individual a modicum of freedom and fulfillment in the realm of unfreedom."[16] Or, as Locke suggested in his talk at the Library of Congress, the spirituals translate the particular experience of suffering under slavery into a universal message of freedom through aesthetic form. Through art, experience is transmuted into a symbol that allows all who suffer to feel spiritual freedom. That symbol was not so much an answer to racism or class conflict as a transcendence of them that stimulates the hearer to make a place—whether in a physical space, like Harlem, or in the imagination—for that freedom to take root. It was not so much a tension between reality and the imagination as a way for the singer, the poet, the dancer, the actor to access a deeper reality than that perceived through the senses or impressions. The most powerful art by Black people, as Locke suggested in "Deep River, Deeper Sea," was a kind of alchemy by which the particularity of the Black experience was translated into a call for a universal freedom that did not yet exist.

As persuasive as this theory was from a spiritual standpoint, it was not easy to explain how suspending one's consciousness of racism and class oppression could be a sustainable program for Black subjectivity in a world increasingly characterized according to race and class. Locke's assertion of the emancipatory potential of the New Negro aesthetic was also challenged by Black conservatives like George S. Schuyler at *The Messenger*, who critiqued the notion that anything like a Negro culture existed or that it had any revolutionary aspirations at all, being in Schuyler's mind nothing more than "hokum," a smoke-and-mirrors attempt to secure White support.[17] This argument would surface again in the 1930s, when Black Marxists like Richard Wright and John Wright would critique the New Negro aesthetic as little more than a reflection of the capitalist system of exploitation of all workers, but especially Black workers, who needed an explicitly working-class propaganda art to deliver Black folk from loyalty to the economic structure of racialized capitalism that enslaved them. Also during the 1930s, the Negro movement itself changed its focus, moving from a mainly race-based analysis of the causes of Black oppression to a more class-based analysis. Finally in this period, Black writers themselves embraced protest more aggressively and thoroughly as the through line of their artistic subjectivity in creative writing, drama, visual art, and dance. The strength of the New Negro concept was its recognition that African diasporic peoples reinvented themselves continuously throughout their history, especially in the West. Locke, as the steward of that concept, realized by 1936 that he had to update his concept, drop its rejection of protest art as somehow foreign to the New Negro aesthetic, and create a new synthesis and a stronger statement of exactly what the emancipation program of the New Negro was. The update of Locke's concept of the New Negro aesthetic took place largely in his retrospective reviews, especially one published not in *Opportunity* magazine, but in *The Crisis*. "Freedom Through Art" stands as a signpost of Locke and the aesthetics he codified in his essays, making explicit that the New Negro (or "Newest Negro," as he called the idea elsewhere) had evolved, taken on new signification, and

incorporated protest as the most legitimate and powerful itera-
tion of Black aesthetics in the 1930s and 1940s.

In these later retrospective reviews, Locke toned down the
note of optimism that had crept into his 1920s assessments
of the work of young Negro writers and fused a stronger criti-
cality of social conditions with a still-insistent demand that
Negro art be *art* as much as a critique of the conditions of life
experienced by most Negroes. Tempered in his later writings
was his characteristic belief in progressive change, matched
now with a deeper awareness of the resilience of American
racism in the face of progressive forces. In the late 1930s and
1940s, Locke had less of the John Dewey–like faith that intelligence alone would prevail, both in the Negro and in America, in delivering success in race relations. Now, in the late
1930s, influenced principally by Richard Wright and Ralph
Bunche, Locke focused more attention on the issue of power,
positing that the New Negro aesthetic was a quest toward the
power of cultural literacy to change the whole person and the
whole community that was Negro throughout the Black diaspora.

For us, in the third decade of the twenty-first century, the
real question is: What does the New Negro aesthetic explain
about today? If one thinks about the cultural landscape of
present-day America, Locke was very prescient; the entertainment world dominates the American economy of the twenty-
first century, and Black artists are dominant within it. Locke
uncovered that Black art was an economy that would create
outsized careers for African Americans of talent, who would
also have the opportunity to shape the entire culture at large.
People such as Beyoncé, for example, are not just providing an
image for other Black people, they're actually shaping all of
American culture. I think that is the larger vision implicit in
Locke—not only should African Americans reposition and re-
state our beauty to ourselves but to emancipate beauty for all
Americans. It is worth noting that in 2018 the rapper Kend-
rick Lamar, then thirty years old, won the Pulitzer Prize for
Music, becoming the first winner who was not a jazz or classi-
cal European performer or composer. Locke's vision did not

see that coming! But he laid the intellectual groundwork for it to happen, when he suggested that if Black people developed their art in relation to the Black experience, it would convey a universal message and be great art.

The signs are not just in music. The late Toni Morrison, who won the Nobel Prize in Literature in 1993, knew of Alain Locke as a teacher while she was at Howard University. Locke, of course, was infamous for his misogyny and probably never anticipated that it would be a Black woman who would secure the highest award one can receive in literature—the European stage, mind you, of culture. But she did, and she did so by writing novels of enormous complexity that were not simply race propaganda books that presented "respectable," middle-class images of Black people. Hers were complex characters who often outlined, as in *Song of Solomon*, the treacherous emotional path of catharsis that African Americans charted for themselves in segregated communities. In the contemporary world of visual arts, a number of Black artists have become quite prominent, including Mark Bradford, Arthur Jafa, Kara Walker, Jean-Michel Basquiat, Betye Saar, and others who have plumbed the American psyche in ways that move far beyond propaganda to carry forth a visual arts of catharsis for the entire nation.

But Locke would argue the New Negro aesthetic should result in more than simply the emergence of Black artists as the most spectacular artists in America. Certainly, the minds of Black people have been embodied in contemporary productions like Beyoncé's *Lemonade* and Childish Gambino's "This Is America." But the deeper significance of these and other works is not the elevation of Black artists but the start of a transformation in the contemporary American mind, the development of a deeper consciousness and reflection on who we are as a people. Here, Locke would applaud Colson Whitehead's Pulitzer Prize– and National Book Award–winning novel, *The Underground Railroad*, and the emotionally transfixing Amazon Prime Video series based on the novel, for exposing the realities of slavery for a contemporary American audience in an unflinching manner. In that sense, the epoché

Locke proposed in the New Negro was not so much an escape from racism but a willingness to see it in new ways that allow for agency and paths of liberation. Conversely, Locke's epiphany, late in life, that protest was an important part of the New Negro aesthetic means we should not ignore the way that Black Lives Matter is an aesthetic, one that manifests a distinctively African American creativity in the use of social media, street protest, and journalism, but also dance, music, and visual art to make visible the invisible—the epidemic of violence toward Black citizens—such that the killings of unarmed citizens like George Floyd, Breonna Taylor, Trayvon Martin, Ahmaud Arbery, and so many others become legible to a national and global community. The street performance and media spectacle created by BLM are worthy of admiration by Katherine Dunham (whose work Locke loved), who drew upon African and Haitian performance traditions to innovate in American dance and theater. Black activists are creating a new kind of global literacy out of rebellion.

If Locke were here today, he would challenge us to go deeper. What if we practiced a contemporary epoché, stepped out of the natural attitude of African American daily life and viewed our experience aesthetically—that is, as a wealth of unrealized opportunities for a better, more meaningful life for the Black community, a new consciousness that goes beyond protest against how others treat us? The deepest work of the New Negro aesthetic today, he would argue, is to change how we are treated but also how we treat ourselves. Is there an aesthetic that decolonizes the Black mind about the worth of the Black body and the ability of Black people to be agents of change on the world stage in every arena of knowledge, not simply the racial? The original weltanschauung of the New Negro was unfulfilled in Locke's lifetime and remains so in ours. For it to be realized, we as a people need to go deeper, act with a deeper sense of self-consciousness, in order to exercise the universal principles of justice and truth in our treatment of one another. The New Negro aesthetic is thus a program to love oneself as the first step toward liberation. That's why it relates to BLM—to say that Black lives matter means to love ourselves unapologetically and, because of that love, to demand equality and justice.

Locke's essays and articles created a swerve, a sweeping move away from a focus mainly on politics or economics and toward a path of spiritual deliverance charted through art. Once that path had been mapped out, despite the flaws in his approach to cultural politics—his class consciousness, his misogyny, his Europhilia—Locke set African American thinking, and really all of American thinking, in a completely new direction by viewing the Black experience as an aesthetic rather than a sociological revelation. His signature concept, that of the New Negro, was something that he embodied: the capacity to reinvent oneself over and over again in response to changing circumstances. That is what African American culture teaches us is possible, even under the worst of American racist regimes. That capacity for continual self-reinvention through the finding of something new in aesthetic form has also had the effect, Locke argued, of creating new forms of subjectivity for us as well. For if we continue to reinvent our aesthetic tradition with new forms, we reinvent ourselves and the world coming after us that others will inhabit and transform.

JEFFREY C. STEWART

NOTES

1. Over time, people of African descent within the United States have changed the nomenclature by which they wished to be referred to, sometimes as a reaction against racist or demeaning nomenclature used by whites. For example, in the 1700s and earlier, "sons and daughters of Africa" was a common appellation. By the 1830s, another designation became common: "Colored Americans" and "People of Color." For example, people of African descent in New York chose the title *The Colored American* for the name of their newspaper published between 1837 and 1842. Yet, during the same period, the term "Afro-American" was popular. By the end of the nineteenth century, "Colored"

was the preferred term of self-identification for progressive-minded African Americans. In the early 1900s, "Negro" became preferred among younger people as a term of self-identification, if not self-description. Some, like W. E. B. Du Bois, lobbied newspapers and magazines to capitalize this appellation; during the 1940s, the *New York Times* changed its practice to one of using the capitalized word "Negro." Similarly, in the 1960s, a young generation of activists chose the descriptor "Black" or "Black American," in part in reaction to the relentless criticism of the term "Negro" by Malcolm X in his speeches. During the 1970s, many chose "African American" to refer to themselves, in part in resistance to the insistence on the part of certain newspapers, such as the *New York Times*, on printing "black" in lowercase letters, since "white," when referring to European Americans, was usually printed with lowercase letters. After the murder of George Floyd, and the protests that followed, the *New York Times* as well as other newspapers have begun to print "Black" with an uppercase first letter. In this document, I have sought to retain the nomenclature of the times while at the same time following the practice of the *New York Times* and capitalizing "Black" when referring to peoples of African descent.

2. Jeffrey C. Stewart, *The New Negro: The Life of Alain Locke* (New York: Oxford University Press, 2018), 444–52.

3. See Cheryl A. Wall, *The Harlem Renaissance: A Very Short Introduction*, Very Short Introductions (New York: Oxford University Press, 2016) for the best recent survey of the movement. David Levering Lewis, *When Harlem Was in Vogue* (New York: Penguin, 1997) provides essential in-depth information on New York during the 1920s. Anne Anlin Cheng, *Second Skin: Josephine Baker and the Modern Surface* (New York: Oxford University Press, 2013) provides a provocative analysis of Baker's attractiveness to European modernists. I'm partial still to my own *Paul Robeson: Artist and Citizen* (New Brunswick, NJ: Rutgers University Press, 1998), for its collection of articles documenting Robeson's spectacular appeal in Europe.

4. See Eleanor W. Traylor, "A Blues View of Life (Literature and the Blues Vision)" in *The Blues Aesthetic: Black Culture and*

Modernism by Richard Powell (Washington, DC: Washington Project for the Arts, 1989), 43–44.

5. Stewart, *The New Negro*, 47–82.

6. Stewart, *The New Negro*, 83–93.

7. See Maurice Natanson, *Edmund Husserl: Philosopher of Infinite Tasks* (Evanston, IL: Northwestern University Press, 1971), 55 n, 77–78, 180–81, 186; Natanson, *The Erotic Bird: Phenomenology in Literature*, with a foreword by Judith Butler (Princeton, NJ: Princeton University Press, 1998), x–xi, 17–18. I am aware that I am taking a certain license in applying "epoché" in this manner, blending Husserl's "epoché" and Alfred Schutz's notion of the "epoché of the natural attitude." But Natanson suggests that "natural attitude" is an analogue of George Santayana's "animal faith"; Locke, of course, was a student of Santayana at Harvard College. I elaborated a bit more on my indebtedness to Maurice Natanson and this conceptualization here in my comments to the Before Columbus Foundation's 2019 American Book Awards ceremony in San Francisco; see "2019 American Book Awards," November 1, 2019, C-SPAN, video, 2:23:51, https://www.c-span.org/video/?465307-1/2019 -american-book-awards (beginning at 1:46:18).

8. Stewart, *The New Negro*, 161–225.

9. Stewart, *The New Negro*, 434–36.

10. Stewart, *The New Negro*, 629–44, 753. See Elizabeth Hutton Turner, ed., *Jacob Lawrence: Migration Series* (Washington, VA: Rappahannock Press, 1993).

11. W. E. B. Du Bois, "Criteria of Negro Art," *The Crisis*, October 1926, accessed June 13, 2020, http://www.webdubois.org/db CriteriaNArt.html.

12. See Michael D. Harris, *Colored Pictures: Race and Visual Representation* (Chapel Hill: University of North Carolina Press, 2003), 83–148. Also instructive is Elise Johnson McDougald's little-cited article "The Double Task: The Struggle of Negro Womanhood for Sex and Race Emancipation," *Survey Graphic* 51 (March 1, 1925): 689–91.

13. The most straightforward articulation of this position is in Mortimer J. Adler, *Six Great Ideas* (New York: Collier Books, 1981), 103–22. For a more detailed discussion, see Justin P.

Amoroso, *Kant on the Beautiful* (master's thesis, University of Maine, 2017), Electronic Theses and Dissertations, 2677, http:// digitalcommons.library.umaine.edu/etd/2677. The best source text is Immanuel Kant, *Kant's Critique of Judgement*, translated with introduction and notes by J. H. Bernard (2nd ed., revised) (London: Macmillan, 1914), accessed June 24, 2020, https://oll.libertyfund.org/titles/1217.

14. As quoted in Ibram X. Kendi, *Stamped from the Beginning: The Definitive History of Racist Ideas in America* (New York: Nation Books, 2016), 102.

15. Thomas Jefferson, *Notes on the State of Virginia*, Query 14, "Laws," 265.

16. Herbert Marcuse, *The Aesthetic Dimension: Toward a Critique of Marxist Aesthetics* (Boston: Beacon Press, 1978), 10.

17. George S. Schuyler, "The Negro-Art Hokum," in David Levering Lewis, ed., *The Portable Harlem Renaissance Reader,* Portable Library (New York: Penguin Books, 1994).

Suggestions for Further Reading

Baker Jr., Houston A. *Modernism and the Harlem Renaissance.* Chicago: University of Chicago Press, 1989.

Bambara, Toni Cade, ed. *The Black Woman: An Anthology.* With an introduction by Eleanor Traylor. New York: Washington Square Press, 2005.

Buck, Christopher. *Alain Locke: Faith and Philosophy.* Los Angeles: Kalimat Press, 2005.

Cruse, Harold. *The Crisis of the Negro Intellectual.* New York: William Morrow, 1969.

Dewey, John. *Art as Experience.* New York: Penguin, 1934.

Diagne, Souleymane Bachir. *African Art as Philosophy: Senghor, Bergson and the Idea of Negritude.* Translated by Chike Jeffers. Calcutta: Seagull Books, 2011.

Edwards, Brent Hayes. *The Practice of Diaspora: Literature, Translation, and the Rise of Black Internationalism.* Cambridge, MA: Harvard, 2003.

Gates Jr., Henry Louis, ed. *The Norton Anthology of African American Literature.* New York: Norton, 2014.

Gayle Jr., Addison, ed. *The Black Aesthetic.* New York: Anchor Books, 1971.

Godfrey, Mark, and Zoe Whitly, eds. *Soul of a Nation: Art in the Age of Black Power.* London: Tate, 2017.

Hutchinson, George, ed. *The Cambridge Companion to the Harlem Renaissance.* Cambridge: Cambridge University Press, 2007.

Jones, LeRoi. *Blues People: The Negro Experience in White America and the Music that Developed from It.* New York: William Morrow, 1963.

Lewis, David Levering. *When Harlem Was in Vogue*. New York: Penguin, 1997.

Locke, Alain. *The Negro in Art*. Washington, DC: Associates in Negro Folk Education, 1940.

Natanson, Maurice. *The Erotic Bird: Phenomenology in Literature*. Princeton, NJ: Princeton University Press, 1998.

Neal, Larry. *Visions of A Liberated Future: Black Arts Movement Writings*. New York: Basic Books, 1989.

O'Meally, Robert, ed. *The Jazz Cadence of American Culture*. New York: Columbia University Press, 1998.

Powell, Richard J., et al. *Rhapsodies in Black: Art of the Harlem Renaissance*. London: South Bank Centre, 1997.

———. *The Blues Aesthetic: Black Culture and Modernism*. Washington, DC: Washington Project for the Arts, 1989.

Reed, Ishmael, ed. *19 Necromancers from Now*. New York. Doubleday, 1970.

Scarry, Elaine. *On Beauty and Being Just*. Princeton, NJ: Princeton University Press, 1999.

Schwarz, A. B. Christa. *Gay Voices of the Harlem Renaissance*. Bloomington: Indiana University Press, 2003.

Stewart, Earl. *African American Music: An Introduction*. New York: Schirmer Books, 1998.

Stewart, Jeffrey C. *The New Negro: The Life of Alain Locke*. New York: Oxford University Press, 2018.

———, ed. *Paul Robeson: Artist and Citizen*. Rutgers, NJ: Rutgers University Press, 1998.

———. *Race Contacts and Interracial Relations: Lectures by Alain Locke*. Washington, DC: Howard University Press, 1992.

Thompson, Robert Ferris. *African Art in Motion: Icon and Act in the Collection of Katherine Coryton White*. Los Angeles: University of California Press, 1979.

Wall, Cheryl A. *Women of the Harlem Renaissance*. Bloomington: Indiana University Press, 1995.

A Note on the Text

These selected writings by Alain Locke have been Americanized, and spelling has been conformed to *Merriam-Webster's Collegiate Dictionary*, Eleventh Edition. Locke's overall punctuation style has been maintained and reflect the conventions of the time in which the pieces were written, however, the occasional comma or hyphen has been added or deleted to prevent misreading, and modern standards for representing titles of works have been employed to avoid confusion. Spellings of verifiable names and works, as well as other negligible spelling and typographical errors have been corrected, and a small number of obviously missing words have been provided for the sake of clarity.

Some of the pieces in this book are excerpted chapters from two Bronze Booklets that Locke authored in 1936 and privately printed and distributed: chapter 19, "Excerpt from *The Negro and His Music*," and chapter 27, "Excerpt from *Negro Art: Past and Present*."

The New Negro Aesthetic

A SPACE FOR
BEAUTY

I

HARLEM

If we were to offer a symbol of what Harlem has come to mean in the short span of twenty years it would be another statue of liberty on the landward side of New York. It stands for a folk-movement which in human significance can be compared only with the pushing back of the western frontier in the first half of the last century, or the waves of immigration which have swept in from overseas in the last half. Numerically far smaller than either of these movements, the volume of migration is such nonetheless that Harlem has become the greatest Negro community the world has known—without counterpart in the South or in Africa. But beyond this, Harlem represents the Negro's latest thrust toward Democracy.

The special significance that today stamps it as the sign and center of the renaissance of a people lies, however, layers deep under the Harlem that many know but few have begun to understand. Physically Harlem is little more than a note of sharper color in the kaleidoscope of New York. The metropolis pays little heed to the shifting crystallizations of its own heterogeneous millions. Never having experienced permanence, it has watched, without emotion or even curiosity, Irish, Jew, Italian, Negro, a score of other races drift in and out of the same colorless tenements.

So Harlem has come into being and grasped its destiny with little heed from New York. And to the herded thousands who shoot beneath it twice a day on the subway, or the comparatively few whose daily travel takes them within sight of its fringes or down its main arteries, it is a black belt and nothing more. The pattern of delicatessen store and cigar shop and restaurant and undertaker's shop which repeats itself a thousand times on each of New York's long avenues is unbroken through Harlem. Its apartments, churches, and storefronts antedated the Negroes and, for all New York knows, may outlast them there. For most of New York, Harlem is merely a rough rectangle of commonplace city blocks, lying between and to east and west of Lenox and Seventh Avenues, stretching nearly a mile north and south—and unaccountably full of Negroes.

Another Harlem is savored by the few—a Harlem of racy music and racier dancing, of cabarets famous or notorious according to their kind, of amusement in which abandon and sophistication are cheek by jowl—a Harlem which draws the connoisseur in diversion as well as the undiscriminating sightseer. This Harlem is the fertile source of the "shufflin'" and "rollin'" and "runnin' wild" revues that establish themselves season after season in "downtown" theaters. It is part of the exotic fringe of the metropolis.

Beneath this lies again the Harlem of the newspapers—a Harlem of monster parades and political flummery, a Harlem swept by revolutionary oratory or draped about the mysterious figures of Negro "millionaires," a Harlem preoccupied with naïve adjustments to a white world—a Harlem, in short, grotesque with the distortions of journalism.

Yet in final analysis, Harlem is neither slum, ghetto, resort, or colony, though it is in part all of them. It is—or promises at least to be—a race capital. Europe seething in a dozen centers with emergent nationalities, Palestine full of a renascent Judaism—these are no more alive with the spirit of a racial awakening than Harlem; culturally and spiritually it focuses a people. Negro life is not only founding new centers, but finding a new soul. The tide of Negro migration, northward and cityward, is not to be fully explained as a blind flood started by the demands of war industry coupled with the shutting off of foreign migration, or by the pressure of poor crops coupled with increased social terrorism in certain sections of the South and Southwest. Neither labor demand, the boll weevil, nor the Ku Klux Klan is a basic factor, however contributory any or all of them may have been. The wash and rush of this human tide on the beach line of the northern city centers is to be explained primarily in terms of a new vision of opportunity, of social and economic freedom, of a spirit to seize, even in the face of an extortionate and heavy toll, a chance for the improvement of conditions. With each successive wave of it, the movement of the Negro migrant becomes more and more like that of the European waves at their crests, a mass movement toward the larger and the more democratic chance—in the Negro's case a deliberate flight not only from countryside to city, but from medieval America to modern.

The secret lies close to what distinguishes Harlem from the ghettos with which it is sometimes compared. The ghetto picture is that of a slowly dissolving mass, bound by ties of custom and culture and association, in the midst of a freer and more varied society. From the racial standpoint, our Harlems are themselves crucibles. Here in Manhattan is not merely the largest Negro community in the world, but the first concentration in history of so many diverse elements of Negro life. It has attracted the African, the West Indian, the Negro American; has brought together the Negro of the North and the Negro of the South; the man from the city and the man from the town and village; the peasant, the student, the business man, the professional man, artist, poet, musician, adventurer and worker, preacher and criminal, exploiter and social outcast. Each group has come with its own separate motives and for its own special ends, but their greatest experience has been the finding of one another. Proscription and prejudice have thrown these dissimilar elements into a common area of contact and interaction. Within this area, race sympathy and unity have determined a further fusing of sentiment and experience. So what began in terms of segregation becomes more and more, as its elements mix and react, the laboratory of a great race-welding. Hitherto, it must be admitted that American Negroes have been a race more in name than in fact, or to be exact, more in sentiment than in experience. The chief bond between them has been that of a common condition rather than a common consciousness; a problem in common rather than a life in common. In Harlem, Negro life is seizing upon its first chances for group expression and self-determination. That is why our comparison is taken with those nascent centers of folk-expression and self-determination which are playing a creative part in the world today. Without pretense to their political significance, Harlem has the same role to play for the New Negro as Dublin has had for the New Ireland or Prague for the New Czechoslovakia.

It is true the formidable centers of our race life, educational, industrial, financial, are not in Harlem, yet here, nevertheless, are the forces that make a group known and felt in the world. The reformers, the fighting advocates, the inner spokesmen, the poets, artists, and social prophets are here, and pouring in toward them are the fluid ambitious youth and pressing in upon them the migrant masses. The professional observers, and the enveloping communities as well, are conscious of the physics of this stir and movement, of the cruder and more obvious facts of a ferment and a migration. But they are as yet largely unaware of the psychology of it, of the galvanizing shocks and reactions, which mark the social awakening and internal reorganization which are making a race out of its own disunited elements.

A railroad ticket and a suitcase, like a Baghdad carpet, transport the Negro peasant from the cotton-field and farm to the heart of the most complex urban civilization. Here, in the mass, he must and does survive a jump of two generations in social economy and of a century and more in civilization. Meanwhile the Negro poet, student, artist, thinker, by the very move that normally would take him off at a tangent from the masses, finds himself in their midst, in a situation concentrating the racial side of his experience and heightening his race-consciousness. These moving, half-awakened newcomers provide an exceptional seedbed for the germinating contacts of the enlightened minority. And that is why statistics are out of joint with fact in Harlem, and will be for a generation or so.

Harlem, I grant you, isn't typical—but it is significant, it is prophetic. No sane observer, however sympathetic to the new trend, would contend that the great masses are articulate as yet, but they stir, they move, they are more than physically restless. The challenge of the new intellectuals among them is clear enough—the "race radicals" and realists who have broken with the old epoch of philanthropic guidance, sentimental appeal, and protest. But are we after all only reading into the stirrings of a sleeping giant the dreams of an agitator? The answer is in the migrating peasant. It is the "man farthest down" who is most active in getting up. One of the most characteristic symptoms of this is the professional man himself migrating to recapture his constituency after a vain effort to maintain in some Southern corner what for years back seemed an established living and clientele. The clergyman following his errant flock, the physician or lawyer trailing his clients, supply the true clues. In a real sense it is the rank and file who are leading, and the leaders who are following. A transformed and transforming psychology permeates the masses.

When the racial leaders of twenty years ago spoke of developing race-pride and stimulating race-consciousness, and of the desirability of race solidarity, they could not in any accurate degree have anticipated the abrupt feeling that has surged up and now pervades the awakened centers. Some of the recognized Negro leaders and a powerful section of white opinion identified with "race work" of the older order have indeed attempted to discount this feeling as a "passing phase," an attack of "race nerves," so to speak, and "aftermath of the war," and the like. It has not abated, however, if we are to gauge by the present tone and temper of the Negro press, or by the shift in popular support from the officially recognized and orthodox spokesmen to those of the independent, popular, and often radical type who are unmistakable symptoms of a new order. It is a social disservice to blunt the fact that the Negro of the Northern centers has reached a stage where tutelage, even of the most interested and well-intentioned sort, must give place to new relationships, where positive self-direction must be reckoned with in ever increasing measure.

As a service to this new understanding, the contributors to this Harlem number have been asked, not merely to describe

Harlem as a city of migrants and as a race center, but to voice these new aspirations of a people, to read the clear message of the new conditions, and to discuss some of the new relationships and contacts they involve. First, we shall look at Harlem, with its kindred centers in the Northern and Mid-Western cities, as the way mark of a momentous folk-movement; then as the center of a gripping struggle for an industrial and urban foothold. But more significant than either of these, we shall also view it as the stage of the pageant of contemporary Negro life. In the drama of its new and progressive aspects, we may be witnessing the resurgence of a race; with our eyes focused on the Harlem scene we may dramatically glimpse the New Negro.

2

ENTER THE NEW NEGRO

In the last decade something beyond the watch and guard of statistics has happened in the life of the American Negro and the three norms who have traditionally presided over the Negro problem have a changeling in their laps. The Sociologist, the Philanthropist, the Race-leader are not unaware of the New Negro, but they are at a loss to account for him. He simply cannot be swathed in their formulae. For the younger generation is vibrant with a new psychology; the new spirit is awake in the masses, and under the very eyes of the professional observers is transforming what has been a perennial problem into the progressive phases of contemporary Negro life.

Could such a metamorphosis have taken place as suddenly as it has appeared to? The answer is no; not because the New Negro is not here, but because the Old Negro had long become more of a myth than a man. The Old Negro, we must remember, was a creature of moral debate and historical controversy. His has been a stock figure perpetuated as a historical fiction partly in innocent sentimentalism, partly in deliberate reactionism. The Negro himself has contributed his share to this through a sort of protective social mimicry forced upon him by the adverse circumstances of dependence. So for generations in the mind of America, the Negro has been more of a formula than a human being—a something to be argued about, condemned or defended, to be "kept down," or "in his place," or "helped up," to be worried with or worried over, harassed or patronized, a social bogey or a social burden. The thinking Negro even has been induced to share this same general attitude, to focus his attention on controversial issues, to see himself in the distorted perspective of a social problem. His shadow, so to speak, has been more real to him than his personality. Through having had to appeal from the unjust stereotypes of his oppressors and traducers to those of his liberators, friends, and benefactors he has subscribed to the traditional positions from which his case has been viewed. Little true social or self-understanding has or could come from such a situation.

But while the minds of most of us, black and white, have thus burrowed in the trenches of the Civil War and Reconstruction, the actual march of development has simply flanked these positions, necessitating a sudden reorientation of view. We have not been watching in the right direction; set North and South on a sectional axis, we have not noticed the East till the sun has us blinking.

Recall how suddenly the Negro spirituals revealed themselves; suppressed for generations under the stereotypes of Wesleyan hymn harmony, secretive, half-ashamed, until the courage of being natural brought them out—and behold, there was folk-music. Similarly the mind of the Negro seems suddenly to have slipped from under the tyranny of social intimidation and to be shaking off the psychology of imitation and implied inferiority. By shedding the old chrysalis of the Negro problem we are achieving something like a spiritual emancipation. Until recently, lacking self-understanding, we have been almost as much of a problem to ourselves as we still are to others. But the decade that found us with a problem has left us with only a task. The multitude perhaps feels as yet only a strange relief and a new vague urge, but the thinking few know that in the reaction the vital inner grip of prejudice has been broken.

With this renewed self-respect and self-dependence, the life of the Negro community is bound to enter a new dynamic phase, the buoyancy from within compensating for whatever pressure there may be of conditions from without. The migrant masses, shifting from countryside to city, hurdle several generations of experience at a leap, but more important, the same thing happens spiritually in the life-attitudes and self-expression of the Young Negro, in his poetry, his art, his education, and his new outlook, with the additional advantage, of course, of the poise and greater certainty of knowing what it is all about. From this comes the promise and warrant of a new leadership. As one of them has discerningly put it:

> We have tomorrow
> Bright before us
> Like a flame.
> Yesterday, a night-gone thing
> A sun-down name.
> And dawn today
> Broad arch above the road we came.
> We march!

This is what, even more than any "most creditable record of fifty years of freedom," requires that the Negro of today be seen through other than the dusty spectacles of past controversy. The day of "aunties," "uncles," and "mammies" is equally gone. Uncle Tom and Sambo have passed on, and even the "Colonel" and "George" play barnstorm roles from which they escape with relief when the public spotlight is off. The popular melodrama has about played itself out, and it is time to scrap the fictions, garret the bogeys, and settle down to a realistic facing of facts.

First we must observe some of the changes which since the traditional lines of opinion were drawn have rendered these quite obsolete. A main change has been, of course, that shifting of the Negro population which has made the Negro problem no longer exclusively or even predominantly Southern. Why should our minds remain sectionalized, when the problem itself no longer is? Then the trend of migration has not only been toward the North and the Central Midwest, but cityward and to the great centers of industry—the problems of adjustment are new, practical, local, and not peculiarly racial.

Rather they are an integral part of the large industrial and social problems of our present-day democracy. And finally, with the Negro rapidly in process of class differentiation, if it ever was warrantable to regard and treat the Negro en masse, it is becoming with every day less possible, more unjust, and more ridiculous.

The Negro, too, for his part, has idols of the tribe to smash. If on the one hand the white man has erred in making the Negro appear to be that which would excuse or extenuate his treatment of him, the Negro, in turn, has too often unnecessarily excused himself because of the way he has been treated. The intelligent Negro of today is resolved not to make discrimination an extenuation for his shortcomings in performance, individual or collective; he is trying to hold himself at par, neither inflated by sentimental allowances nor depreciated by current social discounts. For this he must know himself and be known for precisely what he is, and for that reason he welcomes the new scientific rather than the old sentimental interest. Sentimental interest in the Negro has ebbed. We used to lament this as the falling off of our friends; now we rejoice and pray to be delivered both from self-pity and condescension. The mind of each racial group has had a bitter weaning, apathy or hatred on one side matching disillusionment or resentment on the other; but they face each other today with the possibility at least of entirely new mutual attitudes.

It does not follow that if the Negro were better known, he would be better liked or better treated. But mutual understanding is basic for any subsequent cooperation and adjustment. The effort toward this will at least have the effect of remedying in large part what has been the most unsatisfactory feature of our present state of race relationships in America, namely the fact that the more intelligent and representative elements of the two race groups have at so many points got quite out of vital touch with one another.

The fiction is that the life of the races is separate, and increasingly so. The fact is that they have touched too closely at the unfavorable and too lightly at the favorable levels.

While interracial councils have sprung up in the South,

drawing on forward elements of both races, in the Northern cities manual laborers may brush elbows in their everyday work, but the community and business leaders have experienced no such interplay or far too little of it. These segments must achieve contact or the race situation in America becomes desperate. Fortunately this is happening. There is a growing realization that in social effort the cooperative basis must supplant long-distance philanthropy, and that the only safeguard for mass relations in the future must be provided in the carefully maintained contacts of the enlightened minorities of both race groups. In the intellectual realm a renewed and keen curiosity is replacing the recent apathy; the Negro is being carefully studied, not just talked about and discussed. In art and letters, instead of being wholly caricatured, he is being seriously portrayed and painted.

To all of this the New Negro is keenly responsive as an augury of a new democracy in American culture. He is contributing his share to the new social understanding. But the desire to be understood would never in itself have been sufficient to have opened so completely the protectively closed portals of the thinking Negro's mind. There is still too much possibility of being snubbed or patronized for that. It was rather the necessity for fuller, truer, self-expression, the realization of the unwisdom of allowing social discrimination to segregate him mentally, and a counter-attitude to cramp and fetter his own living—and so the "spite-wall" that the intellectuals built over the "color-line" has happily been taken down. Much of this reopening of intellectual contacts has centered in New York and has been richly fruitful not merely in the enlarging of personal experience, but in the definite enrichment of American art and letters and in the clarifying of our common vision of the social tasks ahead.

The particular significance in the reestablishment of contact between the more advanced and representative classes is that it promises to offset some of the unfavorable reactions of the past, or at least to resurface race contacts somewhat for the future. Subtly the conditions that are molding a New Negro are molding a new American attitude.

However, this new phase of things is delicate; it will call for less charity but more justice; less help, but infinitely closer understanding. This is indeed a critical stage of race relationships because of the likelihood, if the new temper is not understood, of engendering sharp group antagonism and a second crop of more calculated prejudice. In some quarters, it has already done so. Having weaned the Negro, public opinion cannot continue to paternalize. The Negro today is inevitably moving forward under the control largely of his own objectives. What are these objectives? Those of his outer life are happily already well and finally formulated, for they are none other than the ideals of American institutions and democracy. Those of his inner life are yet in process of formation, for the new psychology at present is more of a consensus of feeling than of opinion, of attitude rather than of program. Still some points seem to have crystallized.

Up to the present one may adequately describe the Negro's "inner objectives" as an attempt to repair a damaged group psychology and reshape a warped social perspective. Their realization has required a new mentality for the American Negro. And as it matures we begin to see its effects; at first, negative, iconoclastic, and then positive and constructive. In this new group psychology we note the lapse of sentimental appeal, then the development of a more positive self-respect and self-reliance; the repudiation of social dependence, and then the gradual recovery from hypersensitiveness and "touchy" nerves; the repudiation of the double standard of judgment with its special philanthropic allowances, and then the sturdier desire for objective and scientific appraisal; and finally the rise from social disillusionment to race pride, from the sense of social debt to the responsibilities of social contribution, and offsetting the necessary working and commonsense acceptance of restricted conditions, the belief in ultimate esteem and recognition. Therefore, the Negro today wishes to be known for what he is, even in his faults and shortcomings, and scorns a craven and precarious survival at the price of seeming

to be what he is not. He resents being spoken for as a social
ward or minor, even by his own, and being regarded a chronic
patient for the sociological clinic, the sick man of American
Democracy. For the same reasons, he himself is through with
those social nostrums and panaceas, the so-called "solutions"
of his "problem," with which he and the country have been so
liberally dosed in the past. Religion, freedom, education,
money—in turn, he has ardently hoped for and peculiarly
trusted these things; he still believes in them, but not in blind
trust that they alone will solve his life-problem.

Each generation, however, will have its creed and that of the
present is the belief in the efficacy of collective efforts in race
cooperation. This deep feeling of race is at present the mainspring of Negro life. It seems to be the outcome of the reaction
to proscription and prejudice; an attempt, fairly successful on
the whole, to convert a defensive into an offensive position, a
handicap into an incentive. It is radical in tone, but not in purpose and only the most stupid forms of opposition, misunderstanding, or persecution could make it otherwise. Of course,
the thinking Negro has shifted a little toward the left with the
world trend, and there is an increasing group who affiliate with
radical and liberal movements. But fundamentally for the present the Negro is radical on race matters, conservative on others,
in other words, a "forced radical," a social protestant rather
than a genuine radical. Yet under further pressure and injustice
iconoclastic thought and motives will inevitably increase. Harlem's quixotic radicalisms call for their ounce of democracy
today lest tomorrow they be beyond cure.

The Negro mind reaches out as yet to nothing but American
wants, American ideas. But this forced attempt to build his
Americanism on race values is a unique social experiment, and
its ultimate success is impossible except through the fullest
sharing of American culture and institutions. There should be
no delusion about this. American nerves in sections unstrung
with race hysteria are often fed the opiate that the trend of
Negro advance is wholly separatist, and that the effect of its
operation will be to encyst the Negro as a benign foreign body

in the body politic. This cannot be—even if it were desirable.
The racialism of the Negro is no limitation or reservation with
respect to American life; it is only a constructive effort to build
the obstructions in the stream of his progress into an efficient
dam of social energy and power. Democracy itself is obstructed and stagnated to the extent that any of its channels
are closed. Indeed they cannot be selectively closed. So the
choice is not between one way for the Negro and another way
for the rest, but between American institutions frustrated on
the one hand and American ideals progressively fulfilled and
realized on the other.

There is, of course, a warrantably comfortable feeling in
being on the right side of the country's professed ideals. We realize that we cannot be undone without America's undoing. It is
within the gamut of this attitude that the thinking Negro faces
America, but the variations of mood in connection with it are if
anything more significant than the attitude itself. Sometimes we
have it taken with the defiant ironic challenge of McKay:

> Mine is the future grinding down today
> Like a great landslip moving to the sea,
> Bearing its freight of debris far away
> Where the green hungry waters restlessly
> Heave mammoth pyramids and break and roar
> Their eerie challenge to the crumbling shore.

Sometimes, perhaps more frequently as yet, in the fervent
and almost filial appeal and counsel of Weldon Johnson's:

> O Southland, dear Southland!
> Then why do you still cling
> To an idle age and a musty page,
> To a dead and useless thing.

But between defiance and appeal, midway almost between
cynicism and hope, the prevailing mind stands in the mood of
the same author's "To America," an attitude of sober query
and stoical challenge:

How would you have us, as we are?
Or sinking 'neath the load we bear,
Our eyes fixed forward on a star,
Or gazing empty at despair?

Rising or falling? Men or things?
With dragging pace or footsteps fleet?
Strong, willing sinews in your wings,
Or tightening chains about your feet?

More and more, however, an intelligent realization of the
great discrepancy between the American social creed and the
American social practice forces upon the Negro the taking of
the moral advantage that is his. Only the steadying and sobering effect of a truly characteristic gentleness of spirit prevents
the rapid rise of a definite cynicism and counter-hate and a defiant superiority feeling. Human as this reaction would be, the
majority still deprecate its advent, and would gladly see it fore-
stalled by the speedy amelioration of its causes. We wish our
race pride to be a healthier, more positive achievement than a
feeling based upon a realization of the shortcomings of others.
But all paths toward the attainment of a sound social attitude
have been difficult; only a relatively few enlightened minds
have been able as the phrase puts it "to rise above" prejudice.
The ordinary man has had until recently only a hard choice
between the alternatives of supine and humiliating submission
and stimulating but hurtful counter-prejudice. Fortunately
from some inner, desperate resourcefulness has recently sprung
up the simple expedient of fighting prejudice by mental passive
resistance, in other words by trying to ignore it. For the few,
this manna may perhaps be effective, but the masses cannot
thrive on it.

Fortunately there are constructive channels opening out into
which the balked social feelings of the American Negro can
flow freely.

Without them there would be much more pressure and danger than there is. These compensating interests are racial but

in a new and enlarged way. One is the consciousness of acting as the advance guard of the African peoples in their contact with Twentieth Century civilization; the other, the sense of a mission of rehabilitating the race in world esteem from that loss of prestige for which the fate and conditions of slavery have so largely been responsible. Harlem, as we shall see, is the center of both these movements; she is the home of the Negro's "Zionism." The pulse of the Negro world has begun to beat in Harlem. A Negro newspaper carrying news material in English, French, and Spanish, gathered from all quarters of America, the West Indies, and Africa, has maintained itself in Harlem for over five years. Two important magazines, both edited from New York, maintain their news and circulation consistently on a cosmopolitan scale. Under American auspices and backing, three Pan-African congresses have been held abroad for the discussion of common interests, colonial questions, and the future cooperative development of Africa. In terms of the race question as a world problem, the Negro mind has leapt, so to speak, upon the parapets of prejudice and extended its cramped horizons. In so doing it has linked up with the growing group consciousness of the dark-peoples and is gradually learning their common interests. As one of our writers has recently put it: "It is imperative that we understand the white world in its relations to the nonwhite world." As with the Jew, persecution is making the Negro international.

As a world phenomenon this wider race consciousness is a different thing from the much asserted rising tide of color. Its inevitable causes are not of our making. The consequences are not necessarily damaging to the best interests of civilization. Whether it actually brings into being new Armadas of conflict or argosies of cultural exchange and enlightenment can only be decided by the attitude of the dominant races in an era of critical change. With the American Negro his new internationalism is primarily an effort to recapture contact with the scattered peoples of African derivation. Garveyism may be a transient, if spectacular, phenomenon, but the possible role of the American Negro in the future development of Africa is one of the most constructive and universally helpful missions that any modern people can lay claim to.

Constructive participation in such causes cannot help giving the Negro valuable group incentives, as well as increased prestige at home and abroad. Our greatest rehabilitation may possibly come through such channels, but for the present, more immediate hope rests in the revaluation by white and black alike of the Negro in terms of his artistic endowments and cultural contributions, past and prospective. It must be increasingly recognized that the Negro has already made very substantial contributions, not only in his folk art, music especially, which has always found appreciation, but in larger, though humbler and less acknowledged, ways. For generations the Negro has been the peasant matrix of that section of America which has most undervalued him, and here he has contributed not only materially in labor and in social patience, but spiritually as well. The South has unconsciously absorbed the gift of his folk-temperament. In less than half a generation it will be easier to recognize this, but the fact remains that a leaven of humor, sentiment, imagination, and tropic nonchalance has gone into the making of the South from a humble, unacknowledged source. A second crop of the Negro's gifts promises still more largely. He now becomes a conscious contributor and lays aside the status of a beneficiary and ward for that of a collaborator and participant in American civilization. The great social gain in this is the releasing of our talented group from the arid fields of controversy and debate to the productive fields of creative expression. The especially cultural recognition they win should in turn prove the key to that revaluation of the Negro which must precede or accompany any considerable further betterment of race relationships. But whatever the general effect, the present generation will have added the motives of self-expression and spiritual development to the old and still unfinished task of making material headway and progress. No one who understandingly faces the situation with its substantial accomplishment or views the new scene with its still more abundant promise can be entirely without hope. And certainly, if in our lifetime the Negro should not be able to celebrate his full initiation into American democracy, he can at least, on the warrant of these things, celebrate the attainment of a significant and satisfying new phase of group development, and with it a spiritual Coming of Age.

3

YOUTH SPEAKS

We might know the future but for our chronic tendency to turn to age rather than to youth for the forecast. And when youth speaks, the future listens, however the present may shut its ears. Here we have Negro youth, foretelling in the mirror of art what we must see and recognize in the streets of reality tomorrow.

Primarily, of course, it is youth that speaks in the voice of Negro youth, but the overtones are distinctive; Negro youth speaks out of a unique experience and with a particular representativeness. All classes of a people under social pressure are permeated with a common experience; they are emotionally welded as others cannot be. With them, even ordinary living has epic depth and lyric intensity, and this, their material handicap, is their spiritual advantage. So, in a day when art has run to classes, cliques, and coteries, and life lacks more and more a vital common background, the Negro artist, out of the depths of his group and personal experience, has to his hand almost the conditions of a classical art.

Negro genius today relies upon the race-gift as a vast spiritual endowment from which our best developments have come and must come. Racial expression as a conscious motive, it is true, is fading out of our latest art, but just as surely the age of truer, finer group expression is coming in—for race expression does not need to be deliberate to be vital. Indeed at its best it never is. This was the case with our instinctive and quite matchless folk art, and begins to be the same again as we approach cultural maturity in a phase of art that promises now to be fully representative. The interval between has been an awkward age, where from the anxious desire and attempt to be representative much that was really unrepresentative has come; we have lately had an art that was stiltedly self-conscious, and racially rhetorical rather than racially expressive. Our poets have now stopped speaking for the Negro—they speak as Negroes. Where formerly they spoke to others and tried to interpret, they now speak to their own and try to express. They have stopped posing, being nearer to the attainment of poise.

The younger generation has thus achieved an objective attitude toward life. Race for them is but an idiom of experience, a sort of added enriching adventure and discipline, giving subtler overtones to life, making it more beautiful and interesting, even if more poignantly so. So experienced, it affords a deepening rather than a narrowing of social vision. The artistic problem of the Young Negro has not been so much that of acquiring the outer mastery of form and technique as that of achieving an inner mastery of mood and spirit. That accomplished, there has come the happy release from self-consciousness, rhetoric, bombast, and the hampering habit of setting artistic values with primary regard for moral effect— all those pathetic overcompensations of a group inferiority complex which our social dilemmas inflicted upon several unhappy generations. Our poets no longer have the hard choice between an over-assertive and appealing attitude. By the same effort, they have shaken themselves free from the minstrel tradition and the fowling-nets of dialect, and through acquiring ease and simplicity in serious expression have carried the folk-gift to the altitudes of art. There they seek and find art's intrinsic values and satisfactions—and if America were deaf, they would still sing.

But America listens—perhaps in curiosity at first; later, we may be sure, in understanding. But—a moment of patience. The generation now in the artistic vanguard inherits the fine and dearly bought achievement of another generation of creative workmen who have been pioneers and pathbreakers in the cultural development and recognition of the Negro in the arts. Though still in their prime, as veterans of a hard struggle, they must have the praise and gratitude that is due them. We have had, in fiction, Chesnutt and Burghardt Du Bois; in drama, Du Bois again and Angelina Grimké; in poetry, Dunbar, James Weldon Johnson, Fenton and Charles Bertram Johnson, Everette Hawkins, Lucian Watkins, Cotter, Jameson; and in another file of poets, Miss Grimké, Anne Spencer, and Georgia Douglas Johnson; in criticism and belles lettres, Braithwaite and Dr. Du Bois; in painting, Tanner and Scott; in sculpture, Meta Warrick and May Jackson; in acting, Gilpin and Robeson; in music, Burleigh. Nor must the fine collaboration of white American artists be omitted; the work of Ridgley Torrence and Eugene O'Neill in drama, of Stribling and Shands and Clement Wood in fiction, all of which has helped in the bringing of the materials of Negro life out of the shambles of conventional polemics, cheap romance, and journalism into the domain of pure and unbiased art. Then, rich in this legacy, but richer still, I think, in their own endowment of talent, comes the youngest generation of our Afro-American culture: in music, Diton, Dett, Grant Still, and Roland Hayes; in fiction, Jessie Fauset, Walter White, Claude McKay (a forthcoming book); in drama, Willis Richardson; in the field of the short story, Jean Toomer, Eric Walrond, Rudolph Fisher; and finally a vivid galaxy of young Negro poets, McKay, Jean Toomer, Langston Hughes, and Countee Cullen.

These constitute a new generation not because of years only, but because of a new aesthetic and a new philosophy of life. They have all swung above the horizon in the last three years, and we can say without disparagement of the past that in that short space of time they have gained collectively from publishers, editors, critics, and the general public more recognition than has ever before come to Negro creative artists in an entire working lifetime. First novels of unquestioned distinction, first acceptances by premier journals whose pages are the ambition of veteran craftsmen, international acclaim, the conquest for us of new provinces of art, the development for the first time among us of literary coteries and channels for the contact of creative minds, and most important of all, a spiritual quickening and racial leavening such as no generation has yet felt and known. It has been their achievement also to bring the artistic advance of the Negro sharply into stepping alignment with contemporary artistic thought, mood, and style. They are thoroughly modern, some of them ultramodern, and Negro thoughts now wear the uniform of the age.

But for all that, the heart beats a little differently. Toomer gives a folk-lilt and ecstasy to the prose of the American modernists. McKay adds Aesop and irony to the social novel and a peasant clarity and naïveté to lyric thought, Fisher adds Uncle Remus to the art of Maupassant and O. Henry. Hughes puts Biblical fervor into free verse, Hayes carries the gush and depth of folk song to the old masters, Cullen blends the simple with the sophisticated and puts the vineyards themselves into his crystal goblets. There is in all the marriage of a fresh emotional endowment with the finest niceties of art. Here for the enrichment of American and modern art, among our contemporaries, in a people who still have the ancient key, are some of the things we thought culture had forever lost. Art cannot disdain the gift of a natural irony, of a transfiguring imagination, of rhapsodic Biblical speech, of dynamic musical swing, of cosmic emotion such as only the gifted pagans knew, of a return to nature, not by way of the forced and worn formula of Romanticism, but through the closeness of an imagination that has never broken kinship with nature. Art must accept such gifts, and revaluate the giver.

Not all the new art is in the field of pure art values. There is poetry of sturdy social protest, and fiction of calm, dispassionate social analysis. But reason and realism have cured us of sentimentality: instead of the wail and appeal, there is challenge and indictment. Satire is just beneath the surface of our latest prose, and tonic irony has come into our poetic wells. These are good medicines for the common mind, for us they are necessary antidotes against social poison. Their influence means that at least for us the worst symptoms of the social distemper are passing. And so the social promise of our recent art is as great as the artistic. It has brought with it, first of all, that wholesome, welcome virtue of finding beauty in oneself; the younger generation can no longer be twitted as "cultural nondescripts" or accused of "being out of love with their own nativity." They have instinctive love and pride of race, and, spiritually compensating for the present lacks of America, ardent respect and love for Africa, the motherland. Gradually too under some spiritualizing reaction, the brands and wounds of social persecution are becoming the proud stigmata of spiritual immunity and moral victory. Already enough progress has been made in this direction so that it is no longer true that the Negro mind is too engulfed in its own social dilemmas for control of the necessary perspective of art, or too depressed to attain the full horizons of self and social criticism. Indeed, by the evidence and promise of the cultured few, we are at last spiritually free, and offer through art an emancipating vision to America. But it is a presumption to speak further for those who have spoken and can speak so adequately for themselves.

4

BEAUTY INSTEAD OF ASHES

Like a fresh boring through the rock and sand of racial misunderstanding and controversy, modern American art has tapped a living wellspring of beauty, and the gush of it opens up an immediate question as to the possible contribution of the soil and substance of Negro life and experience to American culture and the native materials of art. Are we ever to have more than the simple first products and ground flow of this wellspring, and the fitful spurt of its released natural energies, or is the wellhead to be drummed over and its resources conserved and refined to give us a sustained output of more mature products and by-products?

To produce these second-process products is the particular raison d'être of a school of Negro poets and artists, and what most of our younger school really mean by an "acceptance of race in art" is the consciousness of this as an artistic task and program. Its group momentum behind the individual talent is largely responsible, I think, for the sudden and brilliant results of our contemporary artistic revival. The art movement in this case happens to coincide with a social one—a period of new stirrings in the Negro mind and the dawning of new social objectives. Yet most Negro artists would repudiate their own art program if it were presented as a reformer's duty or a prophet's mission, and to the extent that they were true artists be quite justified. But there is an ethics of beauty itself; an urgency of the right creative moment. Race materials come to the Negro artist today as much through his being the child of his age as through his being the child of his race; it is primarily because Negro life is creatively flowing in American art at present that it is the business of the Negro artist to capitalize it in his work. The proof of this is the marked and unusually successful interest of the white writer and artist in Negro themes and materials, not to mention the vogue of Negro music and the conquest of the popular mind through the dance and the vaudeville stage. Indeed in work like that of Eugene O'Neill, Ridgely Torrence, and Paul Green in drama, that of Vachel Lindsay and a whole school of "jazz poets," and that of Du-Bose Heyward, Julia Peterkin, Carl Van Vechten, and others in fiction, the turbulent warm substance of Negro life seems to be broadening out in the main course of American literature like some distinctive literary Gulf Stream. From the Negro himself naturally we expect, however, the most complete and sustained effort and activity. But just as we are not to restrict the Negro artist to Negro themes except by his own artistic choice and preference, so we are glad that Negro life is an artistic province free to everyone.

The opening up and artistic development of Negro life has come about not only through collaboration but through a noteworthy, though unconscious, division of labor. White artists have taken, as might be expected, the descriptive approach and have opened up first the channels of drama and fiction. Negro artists, not merely because of their more intimate emotional touch but also because of temporary incapacity for the objective approach so requisite for successful drama and fiction, have been more effective in expressing Negro life in the more subjective terms of poetry and music. In both cases it has been the distinctive and novel appeal of the folk life and folk temperament that has first gained general acceptance and attention; so that we may warrantably say that there was a third factor in the equation most important of all—this folk tradition and temperament. Wherever Negro life colors art distinctively with its folk values we ought, I think, to credit it as a cultural influence, and as in the case of Uncle Remus, without discrediting the interpreter, emphasize nevertheless the racial contribution. Only as we do this can we see how constant and important a literary and artistic influence Negro life has exerted, and see that the recent developments are only the

sudden deepening of an interest which has long been superficial. After generations of comic, sentimental, and genre interest in Negro life, American letters have at last dug down to
richer treasure in social-document studies like *Birthright* and
Nigger, to problem analysis like *All God's Chillun Got Wings*,
to a studied but brilliant novel of manners like *Nigger Heaven*,
and finally to pure tragedy like *Porgy* and *Abraham's Bosom*.
Negro intellectuals and reformers generally have complained
of this artistically important development—some on the score
of the defeatist trend of most of the themes, others because of
a "peasant, low-life portrayal that misrepresents by omission
the better elements of Negro life." They mistake for color prejudice the contemporary love for strong local color, and for
condescension the current interest in folk life. The younger
Negro artists as modernists have the same slant and interest,
as is unmistakably shown by Jean Toomer's *Cane*, Eric Walrond's *Tropic Death*, Rudolph Fisher's and Claude McKay's
pungent stories of Harlem, and the group trend of *Fire!!*, a
quarterly recently brought out to be "devoted to younger
Negro artists."

These critics further forget how protectively closed the
upper levels of Negro society have been, and how stiffly posed
they still are before the sociologist's camera. Any artist would
turn his back. But in the present fiction of the easily accessible
life of the many, the few will eventually find that power of objective approach and self-criticism without which a future
school of urbane fiction of Negro life cannot arise. Under
these circumstances the life of our middle and upper classes is
reserved for later self-expression, toward which Jessie Fauset's
There Is Confusion, Walter White's *Flight*, and James Weldon
Johnson's *Autobiography of an Ex-Colored Man* are tentative
thrusts. Meantime, to develop the technique of objective control, the younger Negro school has almost consciously emphasized three things: realistic fiction, the folk play, and type
analysis, and their maturing power in the folk play, the short
story, and the genre novel promises much for the future.

Though Negro genius does not yet move with full power
and freedom in the domain of the novel and the drama, in the

emotional mediums of poetry and music it has already attained self-mastery and distinguished expression. It is the popular opinion that Negro expression has always flowed freely in these channels. On the contrary, only recently have our serious artists accepted the folk music and poetry as an artistic heritage to be used for further development, and it is not quite a decade since James Weldon Johnson's "Creation" closed the feud between the "dialect" and the "academic" poets with the brilliant formula of emancipation from dialect plus the cultivation of racial idiom in imagery and symbolism. Since then a marvelous succession of poets, in a poetry of ever deepening lyric swing and power, have carried our expression in this form far beyond the mid ranks of minor poetry. In less than half a generation we have passed from poetized propaganda and didactic sentiment to truly spontaneous and relaxed lyricism. Fifteen years ago a Negro poet wrote:

> The golden lyre's delights bring little grace,
> To bless the singer of a lowly race,
> But I shall dig me deeper to the gold—
> So men shall know me, and remember long
> Nor my dark face dishonor any song.

It was a day of apostrophes and rhetorical assertions; Africa and the race were lauded in collective singulars of "thee"s and "thou"s. Contrast the emotional self-assurance of contemporary Negro moods in Cullen's

> Her walk is like the replica
> Of some barbaric dance,
> Wherewith the soul of Africa
> Is winged with arrogance

and the quiet espousal of race in these lines of Hughes

> Dream singers,
> Story tellers,
> Dancers,

> Loud laughers in the hands of Fate,
> My people.

It is a curious thing—it is also a fortunate thing—that the movement of Negro art toward racialism has been so similar to that of American art at large in search of its national soul. Padraic Colum's brilliant description of the national situation runs thus: "Her nationality has been a political one, it is now becoming an intellectual one." We might paraphrase this for the Negro and say: His racialism used to be rhetorical, now it is emotional; formerly he sang about his race, now we hear race in his singing.

Happily out of this parallelism much intuitive understanding has come, for the cultural rapprochement of the races in and through art has not been founded on sentiment but upon common interests. The modern recoil from the machine has deepened the appreciation of hitherto despised qualities in the Negro temperament, its hedonism, its nonchalance, its spontaneity; the reaction against over-sophistication has opened our eyes to the values of the primitive and the importance of the man of emotions and untarnished instincts; and finally the revolt against conventionality, against puritanism, has fought a strong ally in the half-submerged paganism of the Negro. With this established reciprocity, there is every reason for the Negro artist to be more of a modernist than, on the average, he yet is, but with each younger artistic generation the alignment with modernism becomes closer. The Negro schools have as yet no formulated aesthetic, but they will more and more profess the new realism, the new paganism, and the new vitalism of contemporary art. Especially in the rediscovery of the senses and the instincts, and in the equally important movement for re-rooting art in the soil of everyday life and emotion, Negro elements, culturally transplanted, have, I think, an important contribution to make to the working out of our national culture.

For the present, Negro art advance has one foot on its own original soil and one foot on borrowed ground. If it is allowed to make its national contribution, as it should, there is no anomaly in the situation but instead an advantage. It holds for the movement its racialism in solution, ready to pour it into the mainstream if the cultural forces gravitate that way. Eventually, either as a stream or as a separate body, it must find free outlet for its increasing creative energy. By virtue of the concentration of its elements, it seems to me to have greater potentialities than almost any other single contemporary group expression. Negro artists have made a creditable showing, but after all it is the artistic resources of Negro life and experience that give this statement force.

It was once thought that the Negro was a fine minstrel and could be a fair troubadour, but certainly no poet or finished artist. Now that he is, another reservation is supposed to be made. Can he be the commentator, the analyst, the critic? The answer is in process, as we may have shown. The younger Negro expects to attain that mastery of all the estates of art, especially the provinces of social description and criticism, that admittedly mark seasoned cultural maturity rather than flashy adolescence. Self-criticism will put the Negro artist in a position to make a unique contribution in the portrayal of American life, for his own life situations penetrate to the deepest complications possible in our society. Comedy, tragedy, satire of the first order are wrapped up in the race problem, if we can only untie the psychological knot and take off the somber Sociological wrappings.

Always I think, or rather hope, the later art of the Negro will be true to original qualities of the folk temperament, though it may not perpetuate them in readily recognizable form. For the folk temperament raised to the levels of conscious art promises more originality and beauty than any assumed or imitated class or national or clique psychology available. Already our writers have renewed the race temperament (to the extent there is such a thing) by finding a new pride in it, by stripping it of caricaturish stereotypes, and by partially compensating its acquired inferiority complexes. It stands today, one would say, in the position of the German temperament in Herder's day. There is only one way for it to get any further—to find genius of the first order to give it final definiteness of outline and animate it with creative universality. A few very precious spiritual gifts await this releasing touch, gifts of which we are barely aware—a technique of mass emotion in the arts, a mysticism that is not ascetic and of the cloister, a realism that is not sordid but shot through with homely, appropriate poetry. One wonders if in these sublimated and precious things anyone but the critic with a half-century's focus will recognize the folk temperament that is familiar today for its irresistibly sensuous, spontaneously emotional, affably democratic and naïve spirit. Scarcely. But that is the full promise of Negro art as inner vision sees it. That inner vision cannot be doubted or denied for a group temperament that, instead of souring under oppression and becoming materialistic and sordid under poverty, has almost invariably been able to give America honey for gall and create beauty out of the ashes.

5

ART OR PROPAGANDA?

Artistically it is the one fundamental question for us today.—
Art or Propaganda. Which? Is this more the generation of the
prophet or that of the poet; shall our intellectual and cultural
leadership preach and exhort or sing? I believe we are at that
interesting moment when the prophet becomes the poet and
when prophecy becomes the expressive song, the chant of
fulfillment. We have had too many Jeremiahs, major and
minor;—and too much of the drab wilderness. My chief objec-
tion to propaganda, apart from its besetting sin of monotony
and disproportion, is that it perpetuates the position of group
inferiority even in crying out against it. For it lives and speaks
under the shadow of a dominant majority whom it harangues,
cajoles, threatens, or supplicates. It is too extroverted for balance or poise or inner dignity and self-respect. Art in the best
sense is rooted in self-expression and whether naïve or sophisticated is self-contained. In our spiritual growth genius and talent must more and more choose the role of group expression, or
even at times the role of free individualistic expression,—in a
word must choose art and put aside propaganda.

The literature and art of the younger generation already reflects this shift of psychology, this regeneration of spirit. David
should be its patron saint: it should confront the Philistines
with its live smooth pebbles fearlessly. There is more strength
in a confident camp than in a threatened enemy. The sense of
inferiority must be innerly compensated, self-conviction must
supplant self-justification and in the dignity of this attitude a
convinced minority must confront a condescending majority.

Art cannot completely accomplish this, but I believe it can lead the way.

Our espousal of art thus becomes no mere idle acceptance of "art for art's sake," or cultivation of the last decadences of the overcivilized, but rather a deep realization of the fundamental purpose of art and of its function as a tap root of vigorous, flourishing living. Not all of our younger writers are deep enough in the subsoil of their native materials,—too many are pot-plants seeking a forced growth according to the exotic tastes of a pampered and decadent public. It is the art of the people that needs to be cultivated, not the art of the coteries. Propaganda itself is preferable to shallow, truckling imitation. Negro things may reasonably be a fad for others; for us they must be a religion. Beauty, however, is its best priest and psalms will be more effective than sermons.

To date we have had little sustained art unsubsidized by propaganda; we must admit this debt to these foster agencies. The three journals which have been vehicles of most of our artistic expressions have been the avowed organs of social movements and organized social programs. All our purely artistic publications have been sporadic. There is all the greater need then for a sustained vehicle of free and purely artistic expression. If Harlem should happily fill this need, it will perform an honorable and constructive service. I hope it may, but should it not, the need remains and the path toward it will at least be advanced a little.

We need, I suppose, in addition to art some substitute for propaganda. What shall that be? Surely we must take some cognizance of the fact that we live at the center of a social problem. Propaganda at least nurtured some form of serious social discussion, and social discussion was necessary, is still necessary. On this side: the difficulty and shortcoming of propaganda is its partisanship. It is one-sided and often prejudging. Should we not then have a journal of free discussion, open to all sides of the problem and to all camps of belief? Difficult, that,—but intriguing. Even if it has to begin on the note of dissent and criticism and assume Menckenian skepticism to escape the commonplaces of conformity. Yet, I hope we shall not remain at this negative pole. Can we not cultivate truly free and tolerant discussion, almost Socratically minded for the sake of truth? After Beauty, let Truth come into the Renaissance picture,—a later cue, but a welcome one. This may be premature, but one hopes not,—for eventually it must come and if we can accomplish that, instead of having to hang our prophets, we can silence them or change their lamentations to song with a Great Fulfillment.

6

BEAUTY AND THE PROVINCES

Of the many ways of defining the provinces, after all there is none more reliable than this—capitals are always creative centers, and where living beauty is the provinces are not. Not that capitals are always beautiful, but they are always, at the least, the meccas of the beauty seekers and the workshops of the beauty makers. Between capital and province, many draw the distinction merely of pomp and power: for them it is where the king lives, where the money barons thrive, where the beau monde struts. While this is superficially true, after all a capital that is not a center of culture is no capital at all, and must look to its laurels if it cannot buy or borrow sufficient talent to become so. One of the first missions of a new metropolis is the quest for genius; it is as inevitable as the passion of sudden wealth for jewels. In a country like ours that still lives primarily on borrowed culture, the metropolis becomes the marketplace for genius and its wares, and with its tentacles of trade and traffic captures and holds the prize.

It was those same forces that have made New York the culture-capital of America, which made Harlem the mecca of the New Negro and the first creative center of the Negro Renaissance. Older centers of what was thought to be culture resented the parvenu glory of careless, congested, hectic Harlem. But though many a hometown ached to be robbed of the credit for its village Homer, it was inevitable. It was also just. For oftener than not genius was starved, despised, and even crucified in the hometown, but by the more discerning judgment and quickened sensibilities of the capital was recognized, stimulated, imitated, even though still perhaps half-starved. In this way more than one Negro community has been forced to pay its quota of talent as tribute, and then smart under the slur of being lumped with the provinces. There has been only one way out—and that, to compete for creative talent and light a candle from the central torch. Even the hill towns of Italy, veritable nests of genius, had to yield first to Florence and then to Rome.

The current cultural development of Negro life has been no exception. But now as the movement spreads and beauty invades the provinces, it can be told—at least without offense. Chicago, Philadelphia, Boston, Washington, Nashville, Atlanta—is this the order, or shall we leave it to the historian?—have in turn had their awakening after nightmares of envy and self-delusion. For culture, in last analysis, is a matter not of consumption but of production. It is not a matter of degrees and diplomas, or even of ability to follow and appreciate. It is the capacity to discover and to create. Thereby came the illusion which has duped so many who cannot distinguish between dead and living culture, between appreciation and creativeness, between borrowed spiritual clothes and living beauty—even if living beauty be a bit more naked.

For the moment, we are only concerned with Washington—that capital of the nation's body which is not the capital of its mind or soul. That conglomeration of Negro folk which basks in the borrowed satisfactions of white Washington must someday awake to realize in how limited a degree Washington is the capital of the nation. A double tragedy, this of the city of magnificent distances, tragically holding to its bosom the illusion that it is not provincial. In spite of its title, its coteries, its avenues, it is only a candidate for metropolitan life, a magnificent body awaiting a soul. And but for the stultification of borrowed illusions, Negro Washington would have realized that it contains more of the elements of an intellectual race capital proportionately than the Washington of political fame and power. It is in its way a greater and more representative aggregation of intellectual and cultural talent. Had this possibility been fully realized by the Washington Negro intelligentsia a decade or so ago, and constructively striven after, Washington would have outdistanced Harlem and won the palm of pioneering instead of having merely yielded a small exodus of genius that went out of the smug city with passports of persecution and returned with visas of metropolitan acclaim.

One may pardonably point with pride—with collective pride and not too ironic satisfaction—to certain exceptions, among them the pioneer work of Howard University in the development of the drama of Negro life and the Negro Theater. Close beside it should be bracketed the faith of which this little magazine is a renewed offshoot—the pioneer foundation at Howard University in 1913 of The Stylus, a group for creative writing, with the explicit aim at that comparative early date of building literature and art on the foundation of the folk-roots and the race tradition. Since then over a score of such drama and writing groups have sprung up—the Writers Guild of New York, Krigwa of New York and elsewhere, the Scribblers of Baltimore, the Gilpins of Cleveland, the Quill Club of Boston, the Philadelphia group that so creditably publishes *Black Opals*, the several Chicago groups from the Ethiopian Folk Theatre to the most promising drama group of the present "Cube Theater," the Writers' Guild of Fisk, the Dixwell Group of New Haven, the Ethiopian Guild of Indianapolis, the recently organized Negro company of the Dallas Players in far Texas. The very enumeration indicates what has been accomplished in little more than a decade. The provinces are waking up, and a new cult of beauty stirs throughout the land.

But it is not enough merely to have been a pioneer. The Stylus and the Howard Players must carry on—vitally, creatively. The University, at least, can be—should be—a living center of culture; both of that culture which is the common academic heritage and of that which alone can vitalize it, the constant conversion of our individual and group experiences in creative thought, and the active distillation of our hearts and minds in beauty and art. The path of progress passes through a series of vital centers whose succession is the most significant line of human advance. A province conscious of its provinciality has its face turned in the right direction, and if it follows through with effort can swerve the line of progress to its very heart.

7

THE NEGRO IN
THE THREE AMERICAS

It seems fitting that our final consideration of the Negro in American life should be set in the broadest possible perspective, and so I propose as our final subject, "The Negro in the Three Americas." Even should we discover no further common denominators—though I think we shall—there will be at least two of great contemporary concern and importance,—Pan-Americanism and democracy, with both of which the general situation of the American Negro has, as we shall try to show, some vital and constructive connection. Our opening lecture, indeed, suggested that the furtherance of democracy in this Western hemisphere was bound up crucially with basic social and cultural policies upon which Negro life and its problems had direct bearing. It is incumbent upon us to justify such statements.

But before coming to the discussion either of theory or policies, let us first consider facts. In the United States of North America, we are well aware, sometimes painfully so, that the very presence of a Negro population of nearly ten percent of the total population constitutes a race problem of considerable proportions. I am aware, of course, that under an Anglo-Saxon regime of race relations ten percent may constitute, indeed does constitute, more of an active problem than a considerably larger population ratio would generate under the more tolerant Latin code of race which culturally predominates in Central and South America. However, what may show up very clearly on the surface of our North American society as a race problem may to a degree also be present under the surface of large areas of Latin American society as a class problem, as we shall later see. At any rate, as to the facts, a larger proportion of the Caribbean and South American populations is of Negro racial stock than even our North American ten percent. On a mass statistical average, by conservative estimates, the Negro population ratio of the Western hemisphere, the USA included, is 14 percent, and the closer we come to the mid-zone of the hemisphere the higher that proportion becomes. For the Caribbean or West Indian islands, it is 46 percent, for Brazil it is estimated at the lowest as 28 percent, by some as high as 36 percent. Colombia is more than one-sixth Negro, Ecuador fourteen, and Venezuela more than eight percent. The Central American republics, except Costa Rica, have their considerable Negro admixtures, Panama especially. Indeed of all the American nations, only Chile, the Argentine, and Canada can be said to have a negligible concern in this particular issue of race relations. Indeed when we superimpose the figures of the Indian population—so considerable an element in all Central and South American countries—and then the large East Indian or Hindu populations of Trinidad and British Guiana, we begin to realize and appreciate more the polyracial character of our Continent and the fact that this phase of human group relations is more crucial and critical in our intercontinental life and its progressive development than in even our respective national societies.

Fortunately, although different specific measures may be required, the same basic attitudes and principles of fully democratic living will resolve any of these problems, one as well as the other. They have different numerators and degrees in color differentials, but they have a common denominator of arbitrarily limited and unfulfilled cultural and economic democracy. Certainly for such a population situation, whether it be upon the basis of caste or of class, a hegemony of white or even the fairer elements of the population cannot be made to spell real or effective democracy. Nor can the group attitudes involved be forged into any really unified and durable hemispheric solidarity. It is in this way, to anticipate our analysis somewhat, that these matters condition Pan-Americanism almost as critically as they limit expanding democracy.

It is the common historic denominator of slavery which despite all other differences of national culture and social structure has determined both the similarity of condition and the basic identity of the problems which still so seriously affect the Negro population groups of the American hemisphere. For they are all the cultural consequences and economic aftermath of slavery, and like slavery itself they must eventually be completely liquidated just as that institution was itself abolished. Slavery in America was, of course, eliminated at different times and in quite different ways: here in Haiti, that came about by means of a slave rebellion; with us in the United States, it was Civil War; in still other American nations the process was legal emancipation, in some cases gradual, in others, immediate. But the lives of most persons of Negro blood and descent in America directly or indirectly, in one fashion or another or one degree or another are still seriously affected by the cultural, social, and economic consequences of slavery. By an approximate estimate this involves at least 35 millions of human beings among the total American population of 266 millions, among these the 13 million Negroes of the United States, the 12 or more million Negroes in Brazil, and the 8 or more million Negroes of the Caribbean.

To be sure, a considerable and an encouraging number of these Negroes have already attained the average level of cultural status, and a certain few have raised themselves considerably above the average levels of their respective cultures. But it should be clearly recognized that so long as the masses of these Negro groups comprise, even in part as a consequence of slavery, so heavy a percentage of those who are illiterate, undernourished, ill-housed, underprivileged, and in one way or another subject to social discrimination, just so long will it be necessary to give serious consideration both to the special causes and the specific remedies of such conditions, and to take stock, as well, of the undemocratic social attitudes and the antidemocratic social policies which invariably accompany these conditions.

Having now before us the fundamental historical reasons why so large a proportion of American Negroes enjoy less than their proper share of democracy, whether we take stock of the situation in Baltimore or Bahia, in São Paulo or in San Antonio, let us consider some basic common reasons why they must eventually share more fully and equitably in democracy's benefits than they do at present. The reasons which we have in mind to consider are not the uncontested and incontestable arguments of moral principle and abstract justice—important as these may be—but certain very particular and realistic reasons which it seems wise and opportune to stress at this critical hour of human history and social development. Doing so concretely, and on a hemispheric rather than a narrow nationalistic basis, may reinforce their timeliness and urgency. One nation cannot directly solve the other's problems, but certain important international dimensions have lately come into the general area of these problems which should prove mutually reinforcing and helpful. It is profitable also to see the Negro position and its claims in the same perspective.

In the first place, in every one of the countries where he constitutes a considerable proportion of the population, the Negro represents a conspicuous index by which the practical efficiency and integrity of that particular country's democracy can readily be gauged and judged. For the same high visibility which internally makes possible ready discrimination against Negroes makes the domestic practices of race externally all the more conspicuous and observable in the enlarging spotlight of international relations. However fundamental the domestic issues of race may be, today and for the future we must all be particularly concerned about their international consequences. This holds in general on a world scale. Here the American treatment of the Negro can have and already has had serious repercussions on enlightened Asiatic and African public opinion and confidence. Or, for that matter, so will our treatment of any racial minority such as the treatment of the American segments of the Hindu or the Chinese resident among us. But this situation holds with intensified force as between the American and with particular reference to the widely distributed American groups of Negro and mixed Negro descent. For historical and inescapable reasons, the Negro has thus become a basic part and a conspicuous symbol of the cause of democracy in our Western hemisphere.

For the United States, especially interested in and committed to a program of broader and closer Caribbean cooperation as well as to a thoroughgoing furtherance of Pan-American solidarity, the foreign frontier of race, so to speak, has become more critical even than the domestic. Fortunately this is being seen and realized with increasing force and frequency by enlightened liberal opinion in the United States. Farsighted statesmen and progressive race leaders alike realize that sounder and more consistently democratic practices of race at home are necessary for the successful prosecution of these important foreign programs and essential as well to complete conviction and moral confidence in our democratic professions and intentions. The "Good Neighbor" policy has worked a miracle of political and economic rapprochement between the Americas, but democratic race equality and fraternity, as its morally inescapable corollaries, are practically necessary reinforcements of the "Good Neighbor" policy and principle.

This situation, as an acute observer has recently stated, is not altogether unilateral. Latin America has its part to play in the developing American democracy of race. This observer, my colleague, Dr. E. Franklin Frazier, has this penetrating view of the situation to offer on return from a year's study and observation of the Caribbean and Latin America. Although he finds that the race barrier to American solidarity stands to the credit side of the more favorable and democratic character of the typical Latin attitudes toward race, he also observes that Latin America has her important part to play in the achievement of racial democracy. "Differences between North and Latin America," he says, in their attitudes toward race constitute one of the real barriers to American solidarity. This is a question that has not been faced frankly in most discussions of Pan-Americanism. "But," continues Dr. Frazier, "one might add that on the part of Latin Americans as well as of North Americans there has been a tendency to evade the issue, though their conflicting attitudes toward racial mixture are the basis of a real distrust and lack of mutual respect. In their dealings with North Americans, our Latin neighbors have often been careful not to offend our feelings with regard to color caste. This has been facilitated by the fact that the ruling classes, with some few exceptions, have been of predominantly light complexion. But (and I stress this but), as the masses of these countries begin to rise and as there is greater intercourse between the Latin-American countries and North America, such evasions in the long run will be impossible."

Professor Frazier has put his finger on the crux of the issue, but in a practical and constructive as well as acutely diagnostic way. For if at times class differentiation and its prejudices have contrived to aid and abet outright color caste prejudice, there is the obvious necessity of reinforcing democracy from both sides of this as yet admittedly unsolved social and cultural situation. The situation on either side needs and ultimately must undergo considerable democratizing. Almost all America, one way or the other and to one degree or another, suffers yet from the unhappy consequences of slavery, which in one situation has left us an undemocratic problem of class and in another, an even less democratic situation of color caste. We shall discuss this situation again a little further on, but it is worthwhile in passing to note the disastrous negation of democracy possible if, by way of the shortcomings of democracy either in the South or the North, fascism and its attendant racism should gain firm rootage in American soil. For then, as has been said already, racial and minority disabilities will have become a majority predicament and a general democratic catastrophe.

We must now hurry on, since ours is the constructive motive and interest, to sketch what favorable cultural trends are today coming to the aid of the cause of race democracy. But since slavery is the common root of our present difficulties, North as well as South, and in the Caribbean most especially, let us take one final backward glimpse at slavery itself in its most fundamental relationship to the whole American social scene. In the first place, it is salutary to recall that it was only historical accident that a white indentured servant class did not bear the brunt of the labor load of the European settlement of this continent, and thus become the victims, if not of slavery, certainly of its close equivalent. One need only remember the indentured servants, the convict debtors of the early United States colonies or the Jamaican Irish similarly imported as a laboring caste. However, through slavery and the slave trade, this hard fortune but constructive contribution fell to the lot of the Negro. In so doing slavery did two peculiar and significant things which have determined the course of American history and influenced the character of American civilization: *first*, American Slavery, since it was of the domestic variety, planted the Negro in the very core of the dominant white civilization, permitting not only its rapid assimilation by the Negro but its being, in turn, deeply and continuously counter-influenced culturally by the Negro; and *second*, it also planted the Negro—and that holds true for today as well as for the past—at the moral and political core of a basically democratic society, so that around him and his condition wherever there are undemocratic inconsistencies, must center the whole society's struggle for the full and continuous development of freedom.

As we shall more and more realize, the extension of American democracy must involve the reversal and eradication of these historical consequences of slavery, and it is more than appropriate, indeed it is morally inevitable that a historical American ill should have, in the long run, a typical and successful American cure. This is what I was thinking forward to when I said in the third lecture of this series that the majority stakes in the solution of the American race problem were nearly as great as the Negro minority's, and in the first lecture hinted that it would appear that the cause of the American Negro still had a constructive contribution to make to our current crusade for democracy.

We now come to some concluding considerations of ways and means. Especially important, it seems, are cultural developments, since they throw bridges of understanding and sympathy over the crevasses of the slow filling in of social reform and the still slower upbuilding of economic progress. They are essential, too, to the right and ready understanding of whatever group progress is being made along any other line. For some time now, undoubtedly, we have been aware of great Negro progress in our respective national areas, and have been taking national stock and pride in it. Now however, it seems high time to become more aware of it, as of other aspects of our American life, in an inter-American perspective.

All along it has been the tragedy of Negro talent and accomplishment to be considered and discounted in its full meaning as a matter of exception. It is only when added up and dramatically collated that its proper significance is arrived at and its legitimate social effect brought to full realization. The cultural achievements and contributions of American Negroes, startling enough within their national boundaries, are from the approach of the whole hemisphere more than trebly inspiring and reassuring. In 1818 a French libertarian, Abbé Grégoire, inspired incidentally in great part by the galaxy of Haitian heroes of your Wars for Independence, wrote a small book on *De la littérature des Nègres*, which proved one of the most influential documents of the anti-slavery campaign. For to the conviction of the Negro's moral right to freedom, it added in intellectual circles the demonstration that he had the capacity to fully use freedom's advantages. For so, in their brief day and as exceptions, these cases had previously been dismissed after the customary nine days' wonderment. But Grégoire added up a convincing total when he placed beside Toussaint Louverture and Phillis Wheatley and Benjamin Banneker, the Maryland inventor, mathematician, and almanac maker of Jefferson's day, the lesser known figures of Juan Latino, the sixteenth-century Spanish African poet, Pareja and Gómez, the Negro painter-apprentices of Velázquez and Murillo, Capitein, the Dutch African theologian, Gustavus Vassa, the English African essayist. Together they were convincing justification of the Negro's possibilities and rights.

Though needing, let us hope, no such extreme conversion today, the intelligent and forward thinking public of the Americas needs reinforcing evidence of the present cultural attainments and growing cultural influence of the American Negro.

It must come, too, with that overwhelming effect that can only derive from corroborative evidence from every quarter and from every one of the American nations having any considerable Negro contingent. Certainly such evidence is rapidly coming in, and it seems to reflect only our naturally limited information if such cultural progress seems to be more developed in North or South or Mid-America. Someday, and as soon as possible, it is to be hoped the general record will be compiled in its hemispheric rather than just a narrow nationalistic scope. Someday, too, and as soon after the conclusion of the war as possible, it is also to be hoped that inter-American exhibits and visits will make wider known and reciprocally appreciated the contemporary personalities and contributions of this cultural advance of the various contingents of American Negro life.

Here only in barest outline can we begin to indicate them. But even that should prove enlightening and stimulating. Again, but this time on an inter-American scale, let us glance briefly at the Negro in music, art, folklore, literature, and social leadership. Surprise is in store for any persistent student of the subject: I vividly recall my own, even after some years of reading, when I received unexpectedly the two volume study of Ildefonso Pereda Valdés of Uruguay on the influence of the Negro in the Plata Valley region, and again when Captain Romero turned up in Washington under the auspices of the Division of Cultural Relations of our State Department as an interested authority on the Negro in Peru.

To commence we may quote from a passage of Manuel Gonzalez, a statement that could easily be generalized to include also much of the Caribbean: "In Brazil, Cuba, Venezuela and other tropical localities, the Negro is the preponderant non-European race. The Negro is here, it is true, being slowly absorbed, but his deep inroads in the culture of these countries are today tantamount to a national characteristic and will persist for many generations to come."

In music, paralleling the North American developments with which we're now already familiar, there are, of course, those rich Negro contributions of Brazil, Cuba, Trinidad, and the French Antilles. Blending with Spanish, French, and Portuguese elements, they have produced an extraordinary crop both of folk and sophisticated American music. First, we encounter pure or almost pure African folk forms, manifested in rhythmic forms accompanied by percussion instruments or drums only. Then came what Gonzalez calls "the mulatto expression"—the hybrid "Creole" forms which are mostly of popular appeal and significance, diverting and useful as he says in the widespread service of dance and popular music. In this field today the outstanding creator is the Cuban Ernesto Lecuona, a close analogue of our North American Gershwin. Finally we have what for the future is perhaps most important, the symphonic developments based on Negro motives and rhythms, but harmonized and orchestrated with all the skill of the modern European tradition. Here, it is hard to say whether Brazil or Cuba is outstanding, for in the one we have the important work of Villa-Lobos, Fernández, and Revueltas while in Cuba we have Amadeo Roldán, Caturla, Pedro Sanjuán, and perhaps greatest of all, Gilberto Valdés. The Brazilian group combines Indian and Negro sources, but the Cuban work reflects, of course, predominantly Negro idioms. Indeed some think that serious Afro-Cuban music is one of the most promising strands of our whole contemporary American musical development, and it certainly would have already been so but for the untimely deaths of Roldán and Caturla. Most of these composers cannot, of course, be claimed as Negroes, though several have mixed ancestral strains. That is not, indeed, the emphasis of our discussion: we are speaking primarily of the power and influence of the Negro materials. However, the situation does from time to time also yield a great Negro musician, like Gomez, or the Jamaican Reginald Forsythe, or one of the present musical lights of London, the Guiana Negro composer-conductor, Rudolph Dunbar. Add to this considerable accomplishment that of the North American Negro, and one has some idea of this incontestable domination for several generations both of American popular and serious music by Negro musical elements.

The situation in the field of art is also most interesting and promiseful. In the States we have undoubtedly among sculptors of front rank Richmond Barthé, and of second magnitude Henry Bannarn and William Artis. The Cuban Negro Teodoro Ramos Blanco is by general agreement one of Cuba's leading contemporary sculptors as is also his mulatto colleague, Florencio Gelabert. Professor of sculpture at the Havana School of Fine Arts, Ramos Blanco is known both for his strong delineations of peasant and Negro themes and for his happy memorializations of Cuban heroes, among them his famous statue to the great patriot Maceo. Before an untimely death, Alberto Peña shared acclaim with Ramón Loy—companion figures in the sphere of Cuban painting. Indeed we may expect much of the development of the Negro subject and theme in Latin American art, whether it realizes itself in terms of the Negro artist or not. For already in Mexico, Rivera and Orozco have considerably emphasized the theme as has also Portinari, perhaps Brazil's leading painter. Gone completely, under the wide influence of these artists, is the over-Europeanization of sculpture and painting in progressive art circles in Latin America, and that automatically means the glorification of the indigenous types and instead of cosmopolitan emphasis, the people's norms of beauty. In countries where the classical tradition still hangs on, and where the native artists are convention-bound and timid, as once indeed were the North American Negro artists, that subject matter holdback may be expected slowly to disappear. With it always comes a freeing of technique and stronger and maturer accents of self-expression. Under the double leadership of North American and Mexican art that cultural revolution has already begun, and an art truly expressive of the polyracial elements in Latin America, the Negro among them, may shortly be expected to show the effects of such influence.

It is in the field of letters that the Negro contribution has most generally expressed its unusual force in the Antilles and Latin America. Haiti, with its high and almost continuous tradition of authorship in belles lettres, with its successive schools of poets, usually far above provincial caliber and reputation, hardly needs to be told about this. Yet few of us, if any, realize the range and extent of the Negro's literary influence throughout the hemisphere, if for no other reason than the limited view imposed by four different major languages. But the record is formidable when we add up the Haitian, Cuban, Brazilian, and North American contributions. Pereira Valdes's *Anthology of Negro American Poetry* adds even an Argentinian, Eusebio Cardozo, and Casildo Thompson and the Uruguayan Polar Barrios and Carlos Ferreira. Most general readers do know of Brazil's leading contemporary novelist, Mário de Andrade, and can also name such first magnitude Brazilian writers as the poet and abolitionist Luis Gama, Manuel Alvarenga, Tobias Barreto, one of Brazil's greatest poets, Cruz e Sousa, and Machado de Assis, founder of realism in Brazilian literature. We need only in passing mention the brilliant North American contingent of Paul Laurence Dunbar, James Weldon Johnson, Countee Cullen, Langston Hughes, Dr. Du Bois, and Richard Wright, to mention only the first-line representatives. And when we come to Cuban literature, only a book like Guirao's *Anthology of Afro-Cuban Poesie* will reveal the wide extent of the racial influence on both popular and academic poetry. But in addition, one has to take into account in the history of Cuban letters, Gabriel Valdés, better known as "Plácido," Manzano, and especially the contemporary literary genius of Nicolás Guillén. With Marcelino Arozarena and Regino Pedroso, the almost dominates the present output of Cuban verse of distinction; surely, if we consider that the movement of folklorist expression is the product of the initiative and labor of these three mestizos. And then comes *Canapé-Vert* to swell the ranks of this growing current trend of literary interest and emphasis.

Nor has this creative literary expression lacked for critical support and backing. For years now in Brazil, Arthur Ramos and Gilberto Freyre have been issuing their scholarly studies of the Negro historical and cultural backgrounds, and similarly since 1906 in Cuba that tireless champion of Negro culture in Cuba's history and folklore—Fernando Ortiz, founder of the Society of Afro-Cuban Studies. For many of these years, too, Dr. Ortiz has been promoting an even more important project—the closer relation of Afro-Brazilian and the Afro-Cuban studies. In this way, then, the new American criticism is actively promoting the appreciation of the indigenous aspects of our American culture, Indian as well as Negro, and laying the foundation for a much more democratic cultural outlook.

Best of all, Cuba and Mexico have both marshaled the reforms of their educational systems behind this movement, to the extent that in addition to a policy of wider public education, they admit the right of the people's culture to a recognized place in the program of studies. From such trends the various folk cultures must inevitably find greater representation in literature and the arts. So, if the folk yields have been as considerable as they have already been in spite of the discouragement of official philosophies of culture unfavorable to them, now that these policies have been reversed in their favor, they are doubly assured of enhanced influence and prestige.

Another factor needs, finally, to be noted. The cultural traffic that in the past has run so steadily from all our respective capitals back and forth to Europe now has swung around to a continental axis North and South. In these cultural interchanges, the native folk products and their representatives must be expected to play an increasingly important part. They are both more interesting, distinctive, and novel and, from the democratic viewpoint, more representative of the majority of the people. By the traditional exchanges in terms of the stereotyped European models, we got only to know our outstanding artists as individual talents; now if they come bringing the folk culture, we shall, in addition, really for the first time be able to foster sound international and interracial understanding. And I cannot emphasize too strongly that these interchanges must be interracial as well as international, if they are to bring about the calculated democratic result. Elsie Houston and Olga Coehlo, for example, have really brought Brazil to New York in bringing their marvelous renditions of the Afro-Brazilian folk songs: almost for the first time do we feel that we have sampled the distinctive flavor of the national culture. Marian Anderson at this moment is making her first Mexican tour, another happy augury. And certainly one of the greatest needs in the situation is the one we have been prosecuting together so pleasantly and helpfully, for Haitian-American rapprochement is both an interracial as well as international undertaking, happily so—not only for the two nations concerned, but for enlarging the democracy of the American mind throughout the entire American continent.

We might, indeed, close on this point of the radiant prospects for inter-American cultural democracy, but for a final, and let us say at the outset, more problematic point. Here, we must ask ourselves, finally, that other important question—what are the prospects for larger social democracy? Surely no one will claim that democracy can be complete or fully satisfactory without it!

Here the realism of the situation forces us to admit that unlike our cultural differences, which may even attract, our differences of social culture really do, in most instances, seriously divide. We know full well that there are great differences between the Anglo-Saxon and the Latin codes of race and the social institutions and customs founded on each. Not only do we have this as a matter of divergence between the Northern and the Southern segments of the hemisphere, but in the West Indies, we have these divergent traditions facing each other across the narrow strips of the Caribbean. But let us face the facts. Is there any way of looking at these differences constructively? Can we in any way relate them for the constructive reinforcement of democracy in America? At least, let us try.

The Latin tradition of race has, certainly, a happy freedom from a priori prejudice, looking at the individual first, and conceding him as an individual a reasonably fair chance. Triple heritage of the French Revolution, of Catholic universalism, and of Latin social tolerance, this is surely a basic democratic trait. The early and outstanding accomplishments of individual Negroes and their ready acceptance according to merit in Latin American societies could never have taken place except on this foundation.

On the other hand, it is equally evident that the Anglo-Saxon code of race does base itself on a priori prejudice, and really, as the term itself indicates, prejudges the individual on the arbitrary basis of the mass status of his group. It makes its exceptions grudgingly and as exceptions, and often cruelly forces the advancing segments of the group back to the level and limitations of the less advanced. Certainly no one would say it was justifiable either in principle or practice, no one that is who believes basically in democracy. Nor can one say that it is democratic in intention: far from it.

However—and here I ask your patience for a moment, not as an apologist, God forbid, but as a philosopher—this hard code has had some unintended democratic consequences. In forcing the advance guard of a people back upon the people, it has out of the discipline of solidarity forged mass organization for group progress. The successful individual in the majority of cases, still linked to the common lot, is not an elite released and removed from the condition of the rest of his people, but becomes as he advances an advance guard threading through an increasingly coherent mass following. I am not condoning the circumstances which have brought this fact about; I repeat, I am merely describing objectively what has historically transpired.

Now let us put these separate pictures stereoscopically together, to see if we can get a more three-dimensional view both of the situation and its prospects. The Latin American code of race does more justice and offers less harm to the individual, but at the historical price of an unhappy divorce of the elite from the masses. The Anglo-Saxon practice of race seriously handicaps the individual and his chances for immediate progress, but forges, despite intentions to the contrary, a binding bond of group solidarity, an inevitable responsibility of the elite for the masses, a necessary though painful condition for mass progress. From the practical point of view, the more liberal tradition concedes but divides, while the other refuses to concede piecemeal, but by unifying, cannot possibly in the long run divide and conquer. This seems paradoxical, and is. But for one further moment, let us look at the history of the matter.

Both of these social policies of race, the Latin as well as the

Anglo-Saxon, were laid down by slave-owning societies before the abolition of slavery. One saw in the more favorable condition and freedom of the mulatto a menacing advance that must be arbitrarily blocked by a solid wall of prejudice. The other for the most part, saw in the differential treatment of the mestizo the strategy of a buffer class, granting it considerably more than was allowed the blacks but always somewhat less than was standard for the privileged whites. Neither was democratic in intention or in the long run in basic historical effect. One produced an out-and-out race problem, the other, a tangential conversion of a large part of it into a class problem. Each respective group experience has something to teach, and the first common lesson is that you cannot expect to get democracy out of slavery or the institutional inheritances of slavery. We shall get along further and faster by the realization that democracy, as it must fully develop in America, cannot be developed either within the arbitrary and undemocratic traditions of color caste or fully within the less arbitrary but still undemocratic system of a racial elite split off, largely on the basis of a color class, from the race proletariat. Neither of these social race patterns of society is blameless, and to be fully democratic each needs radical improvement.

Obvious common sense teaches us that we shall only achieve fuller democracy in practice by democratizing further whichever system we have by historical accident inherited. However, in these days of international intercourse and collaboration, there are just as obviously mutual lessons which can be constructively learned and applied. One system, the Latin, has vindicated a basic essential of social democracy—the open career for talent and unhampered mobility and recognition for rising individual achievement. The other, the Anglo-Saxon, has taught an increasingly important essential of a democratic social order—the responsibility of the elite for the masses. The basic necessity of the latter, even within the Latin American framework has been distinctly corroborated by the organization in 1931 in Brazil—a country where there is almost no race problem as far as the individual is concerned—of a National Union of Men of Color for the improvement of the well-being of the Negro mass population. It is this organization, which sponsored the notable Second Afro-Brazilian Congress in 1937, and which, incidentally, in 1941–42 played an important political role in Brazil's anti-Axis alignment against Nazi racism and fascism.

Instead of heightened partisanship over our differences of race codes and practices, it is quite within the range of possibility that, looking at matters more broadly and objectively, we shall move forward in our democratic efforts with a sense of collaboration and a common ultimate objective. For the more democracy becomes actually realized, the closer must our several societies approach a common norm.

Slavery is one of the oldest human institutions, nearly as old as man and nearly as universal. But the longest, the most extensive, and the most cruel chapter in the history of human slavery is that dark African chapter of the transatlantic slave trade precipitated by the colonial settlement of the Americas. We must never forget how substantially it helped to make the colonial conquest of the New World possible, thus laying the foundation of that American civilization which we all enjoy today. The slave trade involved the Three Americas. It has affected permanently both the population and the culture of the Americas; especially Mid-America. It has influenced the life of the Americas both for good and evil, and almost everywhere in America, to one degree or another, the shadow of slavery's yet incomplete undoing still clouds the possibilities of a fully democratic American society. Not only for the sake of the Negro, but for the sake of that democracy, these consequences must be overcome. It is fitting and necessary that the inequities and human disabilities which came into our Western world by way of the exigencies of its colonial settlement should be liquidated through our collaborative efforts today to count as a representative American contribution to human freedom and democracy. That the Negro's situation in this hemisphere has this constructive contribution to make to the enlargement of the practice of democracy has been the main conviction and contention of these discussions. All segments of the Negro experience, that of the Latin as well as that of Anglo-Saxon society, must be focused clearly and convincingly if America is to learn effectively the lessons which the Negro's history, achievements, and social experience have it in their power to teach. And if the two wings of that experience teach that the open career for talent and the responsibility of the elite for the masses are both necessary for the full solution of the aftermaths of slavery, then the wisdom and uplifting force of both these principles must be effectively joined to enable democracy to rise and soar.

Only so can our whole American society, completely unshackled, fulfill our American institutions of freedom and equality. This, as I see it, is the constructive significance of the Negro to present-day America.

Again I thank all those who have so aided and added to the success of this series of lectures, but especially I thank those of you whose collaboration as a patient and responsive audience has given me such needed and welcome help and inspiration. It has been a great pleasure to have been among you and a great privilege to have been able to bring this message. All happiness, progress, and prosperity to Haiti. Au revoir!

LITERACIES

8

PAUL LAURENCE DUNBAR

I should like to thank Mr. Cudle and you for the opportunity. I appreciate it very much indeed, especially as I am to have the pleasure and privilege of talking about one whom I am very much interested in and in whom, I trust, you too will find something of interest and significance. There is at least this much of interest and significance in Dunbar that it is now nearly a year ago since he died and no one has yet taken his place as a representative Negro poet. And I only hope I am not bringing coals to Newcastle if I come bringing you some estimate of what Dunbar was as a representative Negro poet—and what, in my opinion, he should be to a literary society such as I am told yours is.

I am not going to weary you with details about Dunbar's life—he was as most of you know born of slave parents and poverty—and for these regions a true child of his people. And there came to him the birthright of a race tradition, just as there comes to every one of us a birthright, and my point is, ladies and gentlemen, that he did not sell it when he sold his time and labor running an elevator in Dayton, Ohio—when he was discovered as a literary man by the Dean of American Literature, William D. Howells. He did not in his justifiable pride forget this birthright, but accepted it as both an opportunity and at the same time a limitation. Dunbar might like many another peasant genius have written of times and classes and traditions which were not his by birth and inheritance. His was the tradition of the Negro, of slavery, of poverty, of a hopeful and improved optimism and it is to his lasting credit that he never forgot them, that he was eager to express them in literature as a tribute to his people. I say it is a great thing, an unfailing sign of a sterling personality neither to forget nor despise its origin. Whatever else Dunbar may have sold I care not—at least he did not sell the birthright of greater price, his race tradition. This then is all I desire to call to your attention, that Dunbar devoted his life to expressing his race tradition in literature. Dr. Du Bois says, "A man works with his hands not with his complexion, with his brains not with his facial angle." Dunbar need not have written of Negro life and emotion, nor even if he wrote of them did he need to write of them as one of them, and my point is that he did.

First then let me remind you of a few things he accomplished, and then after that of the great unaccomplished and what that means for you and for me in the light of Dunbar's example.

There have been greater writers than Dunbar of Negro extraction. Dumas in France, Robert Browning in England are said to have had a Negro strain in their ancestry—one of the great Russian poets of the last century was also of Negro descent—I refer to the celebrated Pushkin, and in France there has recently died José Maria de Heredia, a Negro poet of more than temporary worth and an accepted leader in contemporary French literature. But these men have not been American and so have not been representative of the Afro-American, nor have they written as exponents of race tradition. Dunbar, I would have you understand, I believe to be a minor poet, but a minor poet of very great significance because he was the first man of free Negro descent who obtained literary recognition as an exponent of the American Negro life in poetry. And I should like to talk over with you briefly what he has done in this. First there are the poems of Negro dialect—glimpses of true Negro life and emotion pathetically portrayed. It's generally the life of the southern Negro, the lyrical Negro—and by that I mean the man who remembers and is not ashamed to remember the days of slavery. Before Dunbar the southern Negro had been exploited by many other writers, particularly in the southern novels and stories of men like Joel Chandler Harris [and] Thomas Nelson Page and against the dark background of Aunt and Uncle Remus, the highlights of their novels are brought out in excellent and effective contrast—but in all that has been written about the Negro since *Uncle Tom's Cabin*, and even in that to a certain extent, the true Negro has been conspicuous by his absence.

Now why do I lay such emphasis on the fact and insist as if it needed no proof that the Negro must reveal himself if the true instincts and characteristics of the race are ever to find place in literature? In Ireland now some of the greatest literary men of our time are hard at work, visiting the humble cabins of the Irish peasants, collecting their folk tales, their stories and writing them into literature. They realize nowadays that all literature, especially lyric and ballad poetry, is a nation or race product. And in the primitive emotions and traditions of humble people men are today finding new material and new inspiration for literature. And the more a people has suffered, the more they have been isolated and left to themselves out of the blurring contact of an education that substitutes a written for a spoken tradition, the closer that people has been left to richer soil and the outdoor life which agriculture demands, the more does this folk tradition develop.

Dunbar has gone direct to this which I would have you consider the priceless warehouse of our race, as the one great compensation of the days of oppression and slavery. You were then uneducated, you couldn't express what you felt so you sang—and the slave hymns, your songs of sorrow as "I'm a goin' through an unfriendly world," your songs of hope, your "Swing Low Sweet Chariot" and the rest are in the sense that only is ours which we make or buy with our own exertions. And when Dunbar writes a stanza like this: "It's mighty troublesome lying round / this sorrow laden empty ground / and often I thinks / it would be a sweet thing to do / and go long home" or "de trees is bending in the storm / the rain done hid the mountains / I's am in distress / but listen dats a voice I been / a say in to me, loud and clear / Babylon in de wilderness." I say when Dunbar writes such poetry as that he is expressing you and you should recognize your race tradition in it, and first be humbled, and then thankful, and then be proud.

I do not want to keep you overlong but I must show what Dunbar has done for you. As a race we all have our share in a debt of grateful memory—that to Lincoln—most of us cannot express our gratitude, we are tongue-tied with the fullness of the heart. And if any of you feel as I do, you will appreciate what I mean when I say Dunbar paid your debt for you. Or again a teacher of mine once told me no race can succeed without its heroes, its martyrs, and whoever lifts up a true man of your race to your admiration and imitation has done you a just service. I am not going to tell those of you who do not know to whom this next section refers, but I say that there is cause for congratulation if any man of our race can be spoken of with truth as Dunbar speaks of this man—and still more if our petty jealousies do not blind us to the real truth of men.

And then do I need to tell you that throughout all his poetry, Dunbar is an exponent of race tradition—in the poems not written in the Negro dialect quite as much as in those written in dialect? It is because with the Negro farm hand he could say, "Standin' at de winder / feelin' kind of glum / listening to de rain drops / play de little drum / field and road and medder / swimming like a sea / Lord a mercy on us / whats de good of me."

I say it is because the Negro farmer could say that and Dunbar entered into his emotion that he would write such true poetry as what I am about to read, poetry that can take its stand with the best of English lyrics, poetry not doggerel, clear worded not tongue-tied with dialect, but nevertheless expressive of Negro sentiment.

> Heart of my heart the day is chill
>   The mist hangs low over the wooded hill
> The soft white mist and the heavy cloud
>   The sun and the face of the heavens shroud
> The birds are thick in the dripping trees
>   That drop their pearls to the beggar breeze
> No songs are rife when songs are wont
>   Each singer crouches in his haunt

Now when Dunbar takes the crude thoughts of a Negro farmhand, and refines and expresses them so that they may in certain instances take their place in English literature, and take that place not only as a contribution but as a representation of the Negro, he has been of some service to you and me. Why, you ask? You speak the English language, you have and are receiving through that medium the benefits of civilization—moreover you speak that English language after your own fashion, for your own needs—you owe it a debt. And I am sure that I can appeal to whomever of you may be so practical minded as to think poetry of little worth and value, when I say that the only way to repay that debt is to repay it in kind—you can't pay for civilization except by becoming civilized, you can't pay for the English language and its benefits except by contributing to it in a permanent endowment of literature. Dunbar is our first contribution, and however small in intrinsic worth he may be, however far down in the scale of literary values he may stand (and you must remember that that scale is set by such standards as Shakespeare and Milton) he is significant—very significant to me—for surely it is more blessed to give than to receive.

One more point and I will have finished. I said in the beginning that Dunbar didn't sell his birthright—the tradition of his race. Now at the risk of seeming impertinent I shall make one practical application of the practical significance of Dunbar to each and every one of us. I hope I shall not seem to be moralizing, it is not seemly for a young man to preach sermons, but I do want to impress upon myself as well as you this fact: If we are a race we must have a race tradition, and if we are to have a race tradition, we must keep and cherish it as a priceless—yes as a holy thing—and above all not be ashamed to wear the badge of our tribe. And I do not refer so much to outward manifestations or aggressiveness. I do not think we are Negroes because we are of varying degrees of black, brown, yellow, nor do I think it is because we do or should all act alike. We are a race because we have a common race tradition, and each man of us becomes such just in proportion as he recognizes, knows, and reverences that tradition. And I would above all have this opinion of Dunbar in your minds—that he was one among dozens of cultivated Negroes who devoted himself to perpetuating the tradition of the American Negro. He was interested in all of it—from the Negro's love for dancing and music . . . And even in so small a detail as the plantation Negro's love for molasses and water. He was interested in preserving the old traditions. The old styles, those that are gradually vanishing and that the younger generation seem so anxious to forget. This is the most discouraging feature of our problem to me—the younger generation want to forget, they want to forget the slavery, the plain simple useful religion, the staunch probity—yes they would forget them quite as quickly as they would forget the petty faults, the love of watermelon and chicken, the banjo and the barn dances. They seem as anxious to forget the great virtues, the instructive traits drilled into the race as all such must be drilled into any race, by suffering and experience. And the vital question is: In forgetting this tradition are they not forgetting the lessons their fathers and grandfathers learned before them? Is the dance hall in the city as innocent an amusement as the plantation dance in the corncrib? Is the grandfather who has been a slave a family disgrace or a family pride? Is the cheerful hopeful optimism of the forefathers a thing unknown and undesired by their children? I shall not answer these questions because from my limited experience I cannot answer them favorably. But I can say this: If we do not sell our birthright we will keep this tradition. If we keep this tradition we will reverence Dunbar as one of the few who have taught us to reverence and cherish it. If we reverence Dunbar we shall not claim he is a great poet, but we shall say that we need more like him—his place needs to be filled, for his task is very unfinished. I hope we have not come this far in the wanderings of thought without having reached a definite, yes a practical conclusion. Here is my argument in a nutshell—a race to advance must accept the experience of one generation as a starting point for the next—race tradition is the means of handing down that experience—literature, race literature is necessary to preserve that tradition, especially when by means of social conditions the unwritten tradition is weakening. Dunbar, finally as a pioneer in the expression in preservation of race tradition in literature is for us a very significant and important person. I said in the beginning Dunbar did not sell his birthright; here is his practical lesson to each and every one of us. Some of us have more birthright than others, some of us have lost more than others, at any rate do not let us discard that one which we all possess in common, which is, to my thinking, the most important in all, our race tradition.

This is what I call race pride. It is a very humble pride and therefore justifiable. Moreover these few remarks that I bring to you are my interpretation of what I mean when I say we should be proud of Dunbar yet humbly proud withal, for he was no great genius, nor is his task at all complete, but he was of us and was proud to be of us.

9

THE ETHICS OF CULTURE

I am to speak to you on the ethics of culture. Because I teach the one and try to practice the other, it may perhaps be pardonable for me to think of them together, but I hope at least not to leave you without the conviction that the two are in a very vital and immediate way connected. In my judgment, the highest intellectual duty is the duty to be cultured. Ethics and culture are usually thought out of connection with each other—as, in fact, at the very opposite poles. Particularly for our country, and the type of education which generally prevails, is this so. Quite unfortunately, it seems, duty toward the beautiful and the cultural is very generally ignored, and certainly, beauty as a motive has been taken out of morality, so that we confront beautiless duty and dutiless beauty. In an issue like this, it behooves education to try to restore the lapsing ideals of humanism, and to center more vitally in education the duty to be cultured.

It follows if there is any duty with respect to culture, that it is one of those that can only be self-imposed. No one can make you cultured, few will care whether you are or are not, for I admit that the world of today primarily demands efficiency— and further the only reward my experience can offer you for it is the heightened self-satisfaction which being or becoming cultured brings. There is, or ought to be, a story of a lad to whom some rather abstract duty was being interpreted who is said to have said, "If I only owe it to myself, why then I really don't owe it at all." Not only do I admit that culture is a duty of this sort, but I claim that this is its chief appeal and justification. The greatest challenge to the moral will is in the absence of external compulsion. This implies, young ladies and gentlemen, that I recognize your perfect right not to be cultured, if you do not really want to be, as one of those inalienable natural-born privileges which so-called "practical minded," "ordinary" Americans delight to claim and exercise. As a touchstone for the real desire and a sincere motive, the advocates of culture would not have it otherwise.

The way in which duty comes to be involved in culture is this: culture begins in education where compulsion leaves off, whether it is the practical spur of necessity or the artificial rod of the schoolmaster. I speak to a group that has already chosen to be educated. I congratulate you upon that choice. Though you have so chosen for many motives and with very diverse reasons and purposes. I fear that education for most of you means, in last practical analysis, the necessary hardship that is involved in preparing to earn a better living, perhaps an easier living. It is just such narrowing and truncating of the conception of education, that the ideals and motives of culture are effective to remove or prevent. Education should not be so narrowly construed, for in the best sense, and indeed in the most practical sense, it means not only the fitting of the man to earn his living, but to live and to live well. It is just this latter and higher function of education, the art of living well, or, if I may so express it, of living up to the best, that the word *culture* connotes and represents. Let me offer you, if I may, a touchstone for this idea. A sure test of its presence. Whenever and wherever there is carried into education the purpose and motive of knowing better than the practical necessities of the situation demand, whenever the pursuit of knowledge is engaged in for its own sake and for the inner satisfaction it can give, culture and the motives of culture are present. I sense immediately that you may have quite other and perhaps more authoritative notions of culture in mind. Culture has been variously and beautifully defined. But I cannot accept for the purpose I have in view even that famous definition of Matthew Arnold's, "Culture is the best that has been thought and known in the world," since it emphasizes the external rather than the internal factors of culture. Rather is it the capacity for understanding the best and most representative forms of human expression, and of expressing oneself, if not in similar creativeness, at least in appreciative reactions and in progressively responsive refinement of tastes and interests. Culture proceeds from personality to personality. To paraphrase Bacon, it is that, and only that, which can be inwardly assimilated. It follows, then, that, like wisdom, it is that which cannot be taught, but can only be learned. But here is the appeal of it, it is the self-administered part of your education, that which represents your personal index of absorption and your personal coefficient of effort.

As faulty as is the tendency to externalize culture, there is still greater error in over-intellectualizing it. Defining this aspect of education, we focus it, I think, too much merely in the mind, and project it too far into the abstract and formal. We must constantly realize that without experience, and without a medium for the absorption and transfer of experience, the mind could not develop or be developed. Culture safeguards the educative process at these two points, and stands for the training of the sensibilities and the expressional activities. Mentioning the former as the neglected aspect of American education, former President Eliot contends that, since it is the business of the senses to serve the mind, it is reciprocally the duty of the mind to serve the senses. He means that properly to train the mind involves the proper training of the sensibilities, and that, without a refinement of the channels through which our experience reaches us, the mind cannot reach its highest development. We too often expect our senses to serve us and render nothing back to them in exchange. As a result they do not serve us half so well as they might: coarse channels make for sluggish response, hampered impetus, wastage of effort. The man of culture is the man of trained sensibilities, whose mind expresses itself in keenness of discrimination and, therefore, in cultivated interests and tastes. The level of mentality may be crowded higher for a special effort or a special pursuit, but in the long run it cannot rise much higher than the level of tastes. It is for this reason that we warrantably judge culture by manners, tastes, and the fineness of discrimination of a person's interests. The stamp of culture is, therefore, no conventional pattern, and has no stock value; it is the mold and die of a refined and completely developed personality. It is the art medallion, not the common coin.

On this very point, so necessary for the correct estimation of culture, most of the popular mistakes and misconceptions about culture enter in. Democracy and utilitarianism suspect tastes because they cannot be standardized. And if I should not find you over-interested in culture or over-sympathetic toward its ideals, it is because of these same prejudices of puritanism and materialism, which, though still typically American, are fortunately no longer representatively so. Yet it is necessary to examine and refute some of these prevalent misconceptions about culture. You have heard and will still hear culture derided as *artificial, superficial, useless, selfish, over-refined*, and *exclusive*. Let us make inquiry into the reasons for such attitudes. It is not the part of loyal advocacy to shirk the blow and attack of such criticism behind the bastions of dilettantism. Culture has its active adversaries in present-day life, indeed the normal tendencies of life today are not in the direction either of breadth or height of culture. The defense of culture is a modern chivalry, though of some hazard and proportional glory.

The criticism of culture as artificial first concerns us. In the mistaken name of naturalism, culture is charged with producing artificiality destructive of the fine original naturalness of human nature. One might as well indict civilization as a whole on this point; it, too, is artificial. But perhaps just a peculiar degree of artificiality is inveighed against—to which our response must be that it is just that very painful intermediate stage between lack of culture and wholesomeness of culture which it is the object of further culture to remove. All arts have their awkward stages; culture itself is its own cure for this. Closely associated, and touched by the same reasoning, is the argument that culture is superficial. Here we encounter the bad effect of a process undertaken in the wrong order. If the polished surface is, so to speak, the last coat of a consistently developed personality, it lends its final added charm to the total worth and effect. If, on the contrary, beginning with the superficial as well as ending with the superficial, it should be merely a veneer, then is it indeed both culturally false and artistically deceptive. No true advocacy of an ideal involves the defense or extenuation of its defective embodiments. Rather on the contrary, culture must constantly be self-critical and discriminating, and deplore its spurious counterfeits and shallow imitations.

More pardonable, especially for our age, is the charge of uselessness. Here we need not so much the corrective of values as that of perspective. For we only need to appreciate the perennial and imperishable qualities of the products of culture to see the fallacy in such depreciation. Fortified in ideas and ideals, culture centers about the great human constants, which, though not rigidly unchangeable, are nevertheless almost as durable as those great physical constants of which science makes so much. Indeed, if we count in the progressive changes of science through discovery, these are the more constant—the most constant then of all the things in human experience. Moreover, there is their superior representativeness by which posterity judges each and every phase of human development. Through their culture-products are men most adequately represented; and by their culture-fruits are they known and rated. As we widen our view from the standpoint of momentary and partial judgment, this fact becomes only too obvious.

I take seriously, and would have you, also, the charge that culture is selfish. Being unnecessarily so is to be unduly so. Yet there is a necessary internal focusing of culture because true culture must begin with self-culture. Personality, and to a limited extent character also, are integral parts of the equation. In the earlier stages of the development of culture there is pardonable concentration upon self-cultivation. Spiritual capital must be accumulated; indeed, too early spending of the meager resources of culture at an early stage results in that shallow and specious variety which means sham and pretense at the start, bankruptcy and humiliation at the finish. Do not begin to spend your mental substance prematurely. You are justified in serious self-concern and earnest self-consideration at the stage of education. And, moreover, culture, even when it is rich and mature, gives only by sharing, and moves more by magnetic attraction than by transfer of material or energy. Like light, to which it is so often compared, it radiates, and operates effectively only through being self-sufficiently maintained at its central source. Culture polarizes in selfhood.

Finally we meet the criticism of exclusiveness, over-selectness, perhaps even the extreme of snobbery. Culture, I fear, will have to plead guilty to a certain degree of this: it cannot fulfill its function otherwise. Excellence and the best can never reside in the average. Culture must develop an elite, must maintain itself upon the basis of standards that can move forward but never backward. In the pursuit of culture one must detach himself from the crowd. Your chief handicap in this matter as young people of today is the psychology and "pull" of the crowd. Culturally speaking, they and their point of view define vulgarity. As Professor Palmer says, "Is this not what we mean by the vulgar man? His manners are not an expression of himself, but of somebody else. Other men have obliterated him." There is no individuality in being ordinary: it is the boast of sub-mediocrity. Who in the end wishes to own that composite of everybody's average qualities, so likely to be below our own par? Culture's par is always the best: one cannot be somebody with everybody's traits. If to be cultured is a duty, it is here that that element is most prominent, for it takes courage to stand out from the crowd. One must, therefore, pay a moral as well as an intellectual price for culture. It consists in this: "Dare to be different—stand out!" I know how difficult this advice will be to carry out: America's chief social crime, in spite of her boasted freedoms, is the psychology of the herd, the tyranny of the average and mediocre; in other words, the limitations upon cultural personality. Strive to overcome this for your own sake and, as Cicero would say, "for the welfare of the Republic."

I am spending too much time, I fear, in pointing out what culture is when I would rather point out the way to its attainment. I must not trespass, however, upon the provinces of my colleagues who are to interpret culture more specifically to you in terms of the art of English speech, the fine arts, and music. I content myself with the defense of culture in general, and with the opportunity it gives of explaining its two most basic aspects—the great amateur arts of personal expression— conversation and manners. These personal arts are as important as the fine arts; in my judgment, they are their foundation. For culture without personal culture is sterile—it is that insincere and hypocritical profession of the love of the beautiful which so often discredits culture in the eyes of the many. But with the products of the fine arts translating themselves back into personal refinement and cultivated sensibilities, culture realizes itself in the fullest sense, performs its true educative function and becomes a part of the vital art of living. We too often estimate culture materialistically by what has been called "the vulgar test of production." On the contrary, culture depends primarily upon the power of refined consumption and effective assimilation; it consists essentially in being cultured. Whoever would achieve this must recognize that life itself is an art, perhaps the finest of the fine arts—because it is the composite blend of them all.

However, to say this is not to commit the man of culture to hopeless dilettantism, and make him a Jack of the arts. Especially for you, who for the most part work toward very practical professional objectives and who lack as Americans of our time even a modicum of leisure, would this be impossible. But it is not necessary to trouble much about this, for, even were it possible, it would not be desirable. There are, of course, subjects which are primarily "cultural" and subjects which are not, but I am not one of those who bewail altogether the departure from the old-fashioned classical program of education and the waning appeal of the traditional "humanities." Science, penetratingly studied, can yield as much and more culture than the humanities mechanically studied. It lies, I think, more in the point of view and the degree of intrinsic interest rather than in the special subject matter or tradition of a subject. Nevertheless, to be sure of culture, the average student should elect some of the cultural studies; and, more important still, in his outside diversions, should cultivate a steady and active interest in one of the arts, aiming thereby to bring his mind under the quickening influence of cultural ideas and values. Not all of us can attain creative productiveness and skill in the arts, though each of us has probably some latent artistic temperament, if it only expresses itself in love and daydreaming. But each of us can, with a different degree of concentration according to his temperament, cultivate an intelligent appreciation of at least one of the great human arts, literature, painting, sculpture, music, or whatnot. And if we achieve a high level of cultivated taste in one art it will affect our judgment and interest and response with respect to others.

May I at this point emphasize a peculiarly practical reason? In any community, in any nation, in any group, the level of cultural productiveness cannot rise much higher than the level of cultural consumption, cannot much outdistance the prevalent limits of taste. This is the reason why our country has not as yet come to the fore in the production of culture-goods. And as Americans we all share this handicap of the low average of cultural tastes. As educated Americans, we share also and particularly the responsibility for helping raise this average. A brilliant Englishman once characterized America as a place where everything had a price, but nothing a value, referring to the typical preference for practical and utilitarian points of view. There is a special need for a correction of this on your part. As a race group we are at the critical stage where we are releasing creative artistic talent in excess of our group ability to understand and support it. Those of us who have been concerned about our progress in the things of culture have now begun to fear as the greatest handicap the discouraging, stultifying effect upon our artistic talent of lack of appreciation from the group which it represents. The cultural par, we repeat, is always the best, and a group which expects to be judged by its best must live up to its best so that that may be truly representative. Here is our present dilemma. If the standard of cultural tastes is not rapidly raised in the generation which you represent, the natural affinities of appreciation and response will drain off, like cream, the richest products of the group, and leave the mass without the enriching quality of its finest ingredients. This is already happening: I need not cite the painful individual instances. The only remedy is the more rapid development and diffusion of culture among us.

It follows from this that it is not creditable nor your duty to allow yourselves to be toned down to the low level of average tastes. Some of you, many of you, I hope, will be making your life's work in sections of this country and among groups that are fittingly characterized as "Saharas of culture," that know culture neither by taste nor sight. You betray your education, however, and forego the influence which as educated persons you should always exert in any community if you succumb to these influences and subside to the mediocre level of the vulgar crowd. Moreover, you will find that, like knowledge or technical skill, culture to be maintained must be constantly practiced. Just as we saw that culture was not a question of one set of subjects, but an attitude which may be carried into all, so also we must realize that it is not a matter of certain moments and situations, but the characteristic and constant reaction of a developed personality. The ideal culture is representative of the entire personality even in the slightest detail.

I recall an incident of visiting with a friend a celebrated art connoisseur for his expert judgment upon a painting. He examined with a knife and a pocket magnifying glass a corner of the canvas. I perhaps thought for a moment he was searching for a signature, but it was not the signature corner. Without further scrutiny, however, he gave us his judgment: "Gentlemen, it is not a Holbein." The master painter puts himself into every inch of his canvas, and can be told by the characteristic details as reliably, more reliably even than by general outlines. Culture likewise is every inch representative of the whole personality when it is truly perfected. This summing up of the whole in every part is the practical test which I want you to hold before yourselves in matters of culture. Among cultivated people you will be judged more by your manner of speech and deportment than by any other credentials. They are meant to bear out your training and your heritage, and more reliably than your diplomas or your pedigree will they represent you or betray you. Manners are thus the key to personal relations, as expression is the key to intellectual intercourse. One meets that element in others which is most responsively tuned to a similar element in ourselves. The best fruits of culture, then, are the responses it elicits from our human environment. And should the environment be limited or unfavorable, then, instead of compromising with it, true culture opens the treasuries of art and literature, and lives on that inheritance.

Finally I must add a word about that aspect of culture which claims that it takes several generations to produce and make the truly cultured gentleman. Exclusive, culture may and must be, but seclusive culture is obsolete. Not all that are wellborn are well-bred, and it is better to be well-bred. Indeed, one cannot rest satisfied at any stage of culture: it has to be earned and re-earned, though it returns with greater increment each time. As Goethe says, "What thou hast inherited from the fathers, labor for, in order to possess it." Thus culture is inbred—but we ourselves are its parents. With all of the possible and hoped for spread of democracy, we may say that excellence of this sort will always survive. Indeed, when all the other aristocracies have fallen, the aristocracy of talent and intellect will still stand. In fact, one suspects that eventually the most civilized way of being superior will be to excel in culture.

This much, then, of the ideals of humanism must survive; the goal of education is self-culture, and one must hold it essential even for knowledge's own sake that it be transmuted into character and personality. It must have been the essential meaning of Socrates's favorite dictum—"Know thyself"—that to know, one must be a developed personality. The capacity for deep understanding is proportional to the degree of self-knowledge, and by finding and expressing one's true self, one somehow discovers the common denominator of the universe. Education without culture, therefore, ignores an important half of the final standard, "a scholar and a gentleman," which, lest it seem obsolete, let me cite in those fine modern words which former President Eliot used in conferring the arts degree, "I hereby admit you to the honorable fellowship of educated men." Culture is thus education's passport to converse and association with the best.

Moreover, personal representativeness and group achievement are in this respect identical. Ultimately a people is judged by its capacity to contribute to culture. It is to be hoped that as we progressively acquire in this energetic democracy the common means of modern civilization, we shall justify ourselves more and more, individually and collectively, by the use of them to produce culture-goods and representative types of culture. And this, so peculiarly desirable under the present handicap of social disparagement and disesteem, must be for more than personal reasons the ambition and the achievement of our educated classes. If, as we all know, we must look to education largely to win our way, we must look largely to culture to win our just reward and recognition. It is, therefore, under these circumstances something more than your personal duty to be cultured—it is one of your most direct responsibilities to your fellows, one of your most effective opportunities for group service. In presenting this defense of the ideals and aims of culture, it is my ardent hope that the Howard degree may come increasingly to stand for such things—and especially the vintage of 1926.

10

REVIEW OF
THE WEARY BLUES

I believe there are lyrics in this volume which are such contributions to pure poetry that it makes little difference what substance of life and experience they were made of, and yet I know no other volume of verse that I should put forward as more representatively the work of a race poet than *The Weary Blues*. Nor would I style Langston Hughes a race poet merely because he writes in many instances of Negro life and consciously as a Negro; but because all his poetry seems to be saturated with the rhythms and moods of Negro folk life. A true 'people's poet' has their balladry in his veins; and to me many of these poems seem based on rhythms as seasoned as folk songs and on moods as deep-seated as folk-ballads. Dunbar is supposed to have expressed the peasant heart of his people. But Dunbar was the showman of the Negro masses; here is their spokesman. The acid test is the entire absence of sentimentalism; the clean simplicity of speech, the deep terseness of mood. Taking these poems too much merely as the expressions of a personality, Carl Van Vechten in his debonair introduction wonders at what he calls "their deceptive air of spontaneous improvization." The technique of folk song and dance are instinctively there, giving to the individual talent the bardic touch and power. Especially if Hughes should turn more and more to the colloquial experiences of the common folk whom he so intimately knows and so deeply loves, we may say that the Negro masses have found a voice, and promise to add to their natural domain of music and the dance the conquest of the province of poetry. Remember—I am not speaking of Negro poets, but of Negro poetry.

Poetry of a vitally characteristic racial flow and feeling then is the next step in our cultural development. Is it to be a jazz-product? The title poem and first section of *The Weary Blues* seem superficially to suggest it. But let us see.

> *And far into the night he crooned that tune.*
> *The stars went out and so did the moon.*

Or this:

> *Sing your Blues song,*
> *Pretty baby.*
> *You want lovin'*
> *And you don't mean maybe.*
>
> *Jungle lover. . . .*
> *Night black boy. . . .*
> *Two against the moon*
> *And the moon was joy.*

Here,—I suspect yet uncombined, are the two ingredients of the Negro poetry that will be truly and beautifully representative: the rhythm of the secular ballad but the imagery and diction of the Spiritual. Stranger opposites than these have fused to the fashioning of new beauty. Nor is this so doctrinaire a question as it seems, when considering a poet who has gone to the cabaret for some of his rhythms and to the Bible for others.

In the poems that are avowedly racial, Hughes has a distinctive note. Not only are these poems full of that passionate declaration and acceptance of race which is a general characteristic of present-day Negro poets, but there is a mystic identification with the race experience which is, I think, instinctively deeper and broader than any of our poets has yet achieved.

"The Negro Speaks of Rivers" catches this note for us most unmistakably:

I've known rivers;
I've known rivers ancient as this world and older than
the flow of human blood in human veins.

My soul has grown deep like the rivers.

I bathed in the Euphrates when dawns were young.
I built my hut near the Congo and it lulled me to sleep.
I looked upon the Nile and raised the pyramids above it.
I heard the singing of the Mississippi when Abe Lincoln
went down to New Orleans, and I've seen its muddy
bosom turn all golden in the sunset.

I've known rivers;
Ancient, dusky rivers.
My soul has grown deep like the rivers.

Remembering this as the basic substratum of this poetry, we may discriminatingly know to what to attribute the epic surge underneath its lyric swing, the primitive fatalism back of its nonchalance, the ancient force in its pert colloquialisms, the tropic abandon and irresistibleness of its sorrow and laughter.

No matter how whimsical or gay the poet may carry his overtones after this, or how much of a bohemian or happy troubadour he may assume to be, we will always hear a deep, tragic undertone pulsing in his verse. For the Negro experience rightly sensed even in the moods of the common folk is complex and paradoxical like the Blues which Hughes has pointed out to be so characteristic, with their nonchalant humor against a background of tragedy; there is always a double mood, mercurial to the artist's touch like an easily improvised tune. As our poet himself puts it:

In one hand
I hold tragedy
And in the other
Comedy,—
Masks for the soul.

Laugh with me,
You would laugh!
Weep with me,
Would you weep!

Tears are my laughter.
Laughter is my pain.
Cry at my grinning mouth,
If you will.
Laugh at my sorrow's reign.

AMERICAN LITERARY TRADITION AND THE NEGRO

I doubt if there exists any more valuable record for the study of the social history of the Negro in America than the naïve reflection of American social attitudes and their changes in the literary treatment of Negro life and character. More sensitively, and more truly than the conscious conventions of journalism and public debate, do these relatively unconscious values trace the fundamental attitudes of the American mind. Indeed, very often public professions are at utter variance with actual social practices, and in the matter of the Negro this variance is notably paradoxical. The statement that the North loves the Negro and dislikes Negroes, while the South hates the Negro but loves Negroes, is a crude generalization of the paradox, with just enough truth in it, however, to give us an interesting cue for further analysis. What this essay attempts must necessarily be a cursory preliminary survey: detailed intensive study of American social attitudes toward the Negro, using the changes of the literary tradition as clues, must be seriously undertaken later.

For a cursory survey, a tracing of the attitude toward the Negro as reflected in American letters gives us seven stages or phases, supplying not only an interesting cycle of shifts in public taste and interest, but a rather significant curve for social history. And more interesting perhaps than the attitudes themselves are the underlying issues and reactions of class attitudes and relationships which have been basically responsible for these attitudes. Moreover, instead of a single fixed attitude, sectionally divided and opposed, as the popular presumption goes, it will be seen that American attitudes toward the Negro have changed radically and often, with dramatic turns and with a curious reversal of role between the North and the South according to the class consciousness and interests dominant at any given time. With allowances for generalization, so far as literature records it, Negro life has run a gamut of seven notes,—heroics, sentiment, melodrama, comedy, farce, problem-discussion, and aesthetic interest—as, in their respective turns, strangeness, domestic familiarity, moral controversy, pity, hatred, bewilderment, and curiosity have dominated the public mind. Naturally, very few of these attitudes have been favorable to anything approaching adequate or even artistic portrayal; the Negro has been shunted from one stereotype into the other, but in this respect has been no more the sufferer than any other subject class, the particular brunt of whose servitude has always seemed to me to consist in the fate of having their psychological traits dictated to them. Of course, the Negro has been a particularly apt social mimic, and has assumed protective coloration with almost every change— thereby hangs the secret of his rather unusual survival. But of course a price has been paid, and that is that the Negro, after three hundred years of residence and association, even to himself, is falsely known and little understood. It becomes all the more interesting, now that we are verging for the first time on conditions admitting anything like true portraiture and self-portrayal, to review in retrospect the conditions which have made the Negro traditionally in turn a dreaded primitive, a domestic pet, a moral issue, a ward, a scapegoat, a bogey and pariah, and finally what he has been all along, could he have been seen that way, a flesh and blood human, with nature's chronic but unpatented varieties.

Largely because Negro portraiture has rarely if ever run afoul of literary genius, these changes have rather automatically followed the trend of popular feeling, and fall almost into historical period stages, with very little overlapping. Roughly we may outline them as a Colonial period attitude (1760–1820), a pre-Abolition period (1820–45), the Abolitionist period (1845–65), the Early Reconstruction period (1870–85), the late Reconstruction period (1885–95), the Industrial period (1895–1920), and the Contemporary period since 1920. The constant occurrence and recurrence of the Negro, even as a minor figure, throughout this wide range is in itself an indication of the importance of the Negro as a social issue in American life, and of the fact that his values are not to be read by intrinsic but by extrinsic coefficients. He has dramatized constantly two aspects of white psychology in a projected and naïvely divorced shape—first, the white man's wish for self-justification, whether he be at any given time anti-Negro or pro-Negro, and, second, more subtly registered, an avoidance of the particular type that would raise an embarrassing question for the social conscience of the period; as, for example, the black slave rebel at the time when all efforts were being made after the abatement of the slave trade to domesticate the Negro; or the defeatist fiction types of 1895–1920, when the curve of Negro material progress took such a sharp upward rise. There is no insinuation that much of this sort of reflection has been as conscious or deliberately propagandist as is often charged and believed; it is really more significant as an expression of "unconscious social wish," for whenever there has been direct and avowed propaganda there has always been awakened a reaction in public attitude and a swift counter-tendency. Except in a few outstanding instances, literature has merely registered rather than molded public sentiment on this question.

Through the Colonial days and extending as late as 1820, Negro life was treated as strange and distant. The isolated instances treat the Negro almost heroically, with an exotic curiosity that quite gaudily romanticized him. At that time, as in the more familiar romantic treatment of the American Indian, there was registered in the emphasis upon "savage traits" and strange ways a revulsion to his social assimilation. The typical figure of the period is a pure blood, often represented as a "noble captive," a type neither fully domesticated nor understood, and shows that far from being a familiar the Negro was rather a dreaded curiosity. Incidentally, this undoubtedly was a period of close association between the more domesticated Indian tribes and the Negroes—an almost forgotten chapter in the history of race relations in America which the heavy admixture of Indian blood in the Negro strain silently attests; so the association of the two in the public mind may have had more than casual grounds. Two of the most interesting features of this period are the frank concession of ancestry and lineage to the Negro at a time before the serious onset of miscegenation, and the hectic insistence upon Christian virtues and qualities in the Negro at a time when the Negro masses could not have been the model Christians they were represented to be, and which they did in fact become later. As James Oneal has pointed out in an earlier article, the notion of the boon of Christianity placated the bad conscience of the slave traders, and additionally at that time there was reason at least in the feeling of insecurity to sense that it was good social insurance to stress it.

By 1820 or 1825 the Negro was completely domesticated, and patriarchal relations had set in. The strange savage had become a sentimentally humored peasant. The South was beginning to develop its "aristocratic tradition," and the slave figure was the necessary foil of its romanticism. According to F. P. Gaines, "the plantation makes its first important appearance in American literature in John Pendleton Kennedy's *Swallow Barn* (1832) and William Caruther's *The Cavaliers of Virginia* (1834)." As one would expect, the really important figures of the regime are discreetly ignored,—the mulatto house servant concubine and her children; the faithful male body-servant, paradoxically enough, came in for a compensating publicity. In fact, the South was rapidly developing feudal intricacies and their strange, oft-repeated loyalties, and was actually on the verge of a golden age of romance when the shadow of scandal from Northern criticism darkened the highlights of the whole regime and put the South on the defensive. It is a very significant fact that between 1845 and 1855 there should have appeared nearly a score of plays and novels on the subject of the quadroon girl and her tragic mystery, culminating in William Wells Brown's bold exposé *Clotel; or, The*

President's Daughter (1853), as the caption of the unexpurgated English edition of this black Abolitionist's novel read. Southern romance was chilled to the marrow, and did not resume the genial sentimental approach to race characters for over a generation.

With the political issues of slave and free territory looming, and the moral issues of the Abolitionist controversy coming on, Negro life took on in literature the aspects of melodrama. The portraiture which had started was hastily dropped for exaggerated types representing polemical issues. The exaggerated tone was oddly enough set by the Negro himself, for long before *Uncle Tom's Cabin* (1852) the lurid slave narratives had set the pattern of Job-like suffering and melodramatic incident. Apart from its detailed dependence on Josiah Henson's actual story, Mrs. Stowe's novel simply capitalized a pattern of story and character already definitely outlined in 1845–50, and in some exceptional anticipations ten years previous. Of course, with this period the vital portrayal of the Negro passed temporarily out of the hands of the South and became dominantly an expression of Northern interest and sentiment. In its controversial literature, naturally the South responded vehemently to the Abolitionist's challenge with the other side of the melodramatic picture,—the Negro as a brute and villain. But the formal retaliations of Reconstruction fiction were notably absent; except for a slight shift to the more docile type of Negro and peasant life further removed from the life of the "big house," G. P. James and others continued the mildly propagandist fiction of the patriarchal tradition,—an interesting indication of how the impending danger of the slave regime was minimized in the mass mind of the South. *Uncle Tom's Cabin*, of course, passes as the acme of the literature of the Abolitionist period, and it is in relation to its influence upon the issues involved. But as far as literary values go, *Clotel* by Wells Brown and *The Garies and Their Friends* by Frank J. Webb were closer studies both of Negro character and of the Negro situation. Their daring realism required them to be published abroad, and they are to be reckoned like the Paris school of Russian fiction as the forerunners of the native work of several generations later. Especially Webb's book, with its narrative of a sophisticated and cultured group of free Negroes, was in its day a bold departure from prevailing conventions. Either of these books would have been greater still had it consciously protested against the melodramatic stereotypes then in public favor; but the temptation to cater to the vogue of *Uncle Tom's Cabin* was perhaps too great. The sensational popularity of the latter, and its influence upon the public mind, is only another instance of the effect of a great social issue to sustain melodrama as classic as long as the issue lives. The artistic costs of all revolutions and moral reforms is high.

The Early Reconstruction period supplied the inevitable sentimental reaction to the tension of the war period. The change to sentimental genre is quite understandable. If the South could have resumed the portrayal of its life at the point where controversy had broken in, there would be a notable Southern literature today. But the South was especially prone to sugarcoat the slave regime in a protective reaction against the exposures of the Abolitionist literature. Northern fiction in works like the novels of Albion Tourgée continued its incriminations, and Southern literature became more and more propagandist. At first it was only in a secondary sense derogatory of the Negro; the primary aim was self-justification and romantic daydreaming about the past. In the effort to glorify the lost tradition and balm the South's inferiority complex after the defeat, Uncle Tom was borrowed back as counterpropaganda, refurbished as the devoted, dependent, happy, carefree Negro, whom the South had always loved and protected, and whom it knew "better than he knew himself." The protective devices of this fiction, the accumulative hysteria of self-delusion associated with its promulgation, as well as the comparatively universal acceptance of so obvious a myth, form one of the most interesting chapters in the entire history of social mind. There is no denying the effectiveness of the Page-Cable school of fiction as Southern propaganda. In terms of popular feeling it almost recouped the reverses of the war. The North, having been fed only on stereotypes, came to ignore the Negro in any intimate or critical way through the deceptive influence of those very stereotypes. At least, these figures Southern fiction painted were more convincingly human and real, which in my judgment accounted in large part for the extraordinary ease with which the Southern version of the Negro came to be accepted by the Northern reading public, along with the dictum that the South knows the Negro.

But the false values in the situation spoiled the whole otherwise promising school—Chandler Harris excepted—as a contrast of the later work of Cable or Page with their earlier work will convincingly show. Beginning with good genre drawing that had the promise of something, they ended in mediocre chromographic romanticism. Though the genteel tradition never fully curdled into hatred, more and more hostilely it focused upon the Negro as the scapegoat of the situation. And then came a flood of flagrantly derogatory literature as the sudden rise of figures like Thomas Dixon, paralleling the Vardamans and Tillmans of political life, marked the assumption of the master-class tradition by the mass psychology of the "poor-whites." Reconstruction fiction thus completed the swing made quite inevitable by the extreme arc of Abolitionist literature; the crudities and animus of the one merely countered the bathos and bias of the other. In both periods the treatment of Negro life was artistically unsatisfactory, and subject to the distortions of sentiment, propaganda, and controversy. The heavy artillery of this late Reconstruction attack has shambled its own guns; but the lighter fusillade of farce still holds out and still harasses those who stand guard over the old controversial issues. But the advance front of creative effort and attack has moved two stages further on.

As a result of the discussion of the Late Reconstruction period, "White Supremacy" had become more than a slogan of the Southern chauvinists; it became a mild general social hysteria, which gave an almost biological significance to the race problem. It is interesting to note how suddenly the "problem of miscegenation" became important at a time when there was less of it than at any period within a century and a quarter, and how the mulatto, the skeleton in the family closet, suddenly was trotted out for attention and scrutiny. From 1895 or so on, this problem was for over a decade a veritable obsession; and from William Dean Howells's *Imperative Duty* to Stribling's *Birthright* the typical and dominant figure of literary interest is the mulatto as a symbol of social encroachment, and the fear of some "atavism of blood" through him wreaking vengeance for slavery. While serious literature was discussing the mulatto and his problem, less serious literature was in a subconscious way no less seriously occupied with the negative side of the same problem;—namely, extolling the unambitious, servile, and "racially characteristic" Negro who in addition to presenting diverting humor represented no serious social competition or encroachment. The public mind of the whole period was concentrated on the Negro "in" and "out of his place;" and the pseudoscientific popularizations of evolutionism added their belabored corollaries. But the real basic proposition underlying it all was the sensing for the first time of the serious competition and rivalry of the Negro's social effort and the failure of his social handicaps to effectively thwart it.

Many will be speculating shortly upon the reasons for the literary and artistic emancipation of the Negro, at a time when his theme seemed most hopelessly in the double grip of social prejudice and moral Victorianism. Of course, realism had its share in the matter; the general reaction away from types was bound to reach even the stock Negro stereotypes. Again, the local color fad and the naturally exotic tendencies of conscious aestheticism gave the untouched field of Negro life an attractive lure. The gradual assertion of Negro artists trying at first to counteract the false drawing and values of popular writers, but eventually in the few finer talents motivated by the more truly artistic motives of self-expression, played its additional part. But in my judgment the really basic factor in the sharp and astonishing break in the literary tradition and attitude toward the Negro came in the revolt against puritanism. This seems to me to explain why current literature and art are for the moment so preoccupied with the primitive and pagan and emotional aspects of Negro life and character; and why suddenly something almost amounting to infatuation has invested the Negro subject with interest and fascination. The release which almost everyone had thought must come about through a change in moral evaluation, a reform of opinion, has actually and suddenly come about merely as a shift of interest, a revolution of taste. From it there looms the imminent possibility not only of a true literature of the Negro but of a Negro Literature as such. It becomes especially interesting to watch whether the artistic possibilities of these are to be realized, since thrice before this social issues have scotched the artistic potentialities of Negro life, and American literature is thereby poorer in the fields of the historical romance, the period novel, and great problem drama than it should be. But the work of Waldo Frank, Jean Toomer, Walter White, Rudolph Fisher, and DuBose Heyward promises greatly; and if we call up the most analogous case as a basis of forecast,—the tortuous way by which the peasant came into Russian literature and the brilliant sudden transformation his advent eventually effected, we may predict, for both subject and its creative exponents, the Great Age of this particular section of American life and strand in the American experience.

THE NEGRO'S CONTRIBUTION TO AMERICAN ART AND LITERATURE

There are two distinctive elements in the cultural background of the American Negro: one, his primitive tropical heritage, however vague and clouded over that may be, and second, the specific character of the Negro group experience in America both with respect to group history and with regard to unique environing social conditions. As an easily discriminable minority, these conditions are almost inescapable for all sections of the Negro population, and function, therefore, to intensify emotionally and intellectually group feelings, group reactions, group traditions. Such an accumulating body of collective experience inevitably matures into a group culture which just as inevitably finds some channels of unique expression, and this has been and will be the basis of the Negro's characteristic expression of himself in American life. In fact, as it matures to conscious control and intelligent use, what has been the Negro's social handicap and class liability will very likely become his positive group capital and cultural asset. Certainly whatever the Negro has produced thus far of distinctive worth and originality has been derived in the main from this source, with the equipment from the general stock of American culture acting at times merely as the precipitating agent; at others, as the working tools of this creative expression.

CULTURAL HISTORY

The cultural history of the Negro is as unique and dramatic as his social history. Torn from his native culture and background, he was suddenly precipitated into a complex and very alien culture and civilization, and passed through the fierce crucible of rapid, but complete adaptation to its rudiments, the English language, Christianity, the labor production system, and Anglo-Saxon mores. His complete mental and spiritual flexibility, his rapid assimilation of the essentials of this new culture, in most cases within the first generation, is the outstanding feat of his group career and is almost without parallel in history. Costly as it was, it was complete and without reservations. And yet from the earliest efforts at crude self-expression, it was the African or racial temperament, creeping back in the overtones of his half-articulate speech and action, which gave to his life and ways the characteristic qualities instantly recognized as peculiarly and representatively his.

The materials were all American, but the design and the pattern were different,—in speech, social temper, song, dance, imagination, religious attitude. Some of these reactions were so vivid and so irresistible that they communicated themselves by contagious though condescending imitation to the general community and colored the temper and mores of the Southern whites. This generally unacknowledged influence was the Negro's first and perhaps most basic contribution to American culture. It is a fallacy that the overlord influences the peasant and remains uninfluenced by him; and in this particular case, with the incorporation of the Negro into the heart of the domestic life of the South, the counter-influence became particularly strong.

In humor, emotional temper, superstitions, nonchalance, amiability, sentiment, illogicality,—all of which were later to find expression in forms of folk literature and art,—the Negro colored the general folkways of the South. The Negro has exerted in no other way since so general an influence, but in passing, we must note a near approach to a similar influence,

nationwide though more superficial, in our own generation,—
the contagious influence of the "jazz-spirit," a corrupt hybrid
of the folk-spirit and modern commercialized amusement and
art. Both these influences, we shall see, have direct relevance
to formal art and literature, but have had their profoundest effect on the general background of life outside the boundaries
of formal expression. It is on another plane, but it is just as important, perhaps more so, to color the humor of a country, or
to influence its tempo of life and feeling, or to mold its popular
song, dance, and folktale, as it is to affect its formal poetry or
art or music. This point will need to be borne in mind when,
later, without detracting from his literary skill and service, we
call Joel Chandler Harris a "kindly amanuensis for the illiterate Negro peasant." For Uncle Remus created himself, so to
speak, and the basic imaginative background of his tales was
African.

It was inevitable that the peculiar experiences of the American Negro should sooner or later find artistic expression. The
history of the situation is that they did not wait for a control of
the formal, civilized means of expression. They expressed
themselves first in folkways and folk arts. Notably, the folk
dance, folk song, both the spirituals and the less known but
equally abundant seculars, and the folktale and proverb,—the
latter going over into colloquial modifications too rapidly for
exact tracing. More and more, especially as the younger contemporary American and Afro-American artists turn back to
this mine of folk material for artistic ore, we are coming to a
new appreciation of its extent, quality, and originality. Paradoxically enough, it may be that in slavery the Negro made
American civilization permanently his spiritual debtor.

The cultural history of the Negro himself in America may
be broadly traced as falling into two periods,—a long period
of sustained but unsophisticated expression at the folk level
dating from his introduction to this country to half a generation after Emancipation, and a shorter period of expression at
the cultural, articulate level, stretching back in exceptional
and sporadic instances to 1787, but becoming semi-literary

with the anti-slavery controversy from 1835–1860, and literary in the full sense only since 1890.

Between these two levels there is a gap, transitional only in the historical sense, when the main line of Negro expression was motivated by the conscious imitation of general American standards and forms, and reacted from the distinctive racial elements in an effort at cultural conformity. This was inevitable and under the circumstances normal; but the position of cultural conformity has since been reversed,—first by the dialect-folklore school of Negro expression of which Paul Laurence Dunbar was the leading exponent, and more lately still by the younger contemporary school of "racial self-expression,"—the so-called "New Negro movement," which, growing in volume since 1917, has in a decade produced the most outstanding formal contribution of the Negro to American literature and art. Among the latter are to be enumerated both the "race-realists" who follow the general technical trend of American realism, developing on the basis of local color the native distinctiveness of Negro life, and the "race-symbolists" who have made a cult of the revival of the traits of the race temperament, its philosophy of life, and the re-expression on the cultural level of the folk-spirit and folk-history, including the half-forgotten African background. The importance of this latter movement is not to be underestimated: for, apart from its own creative impulse, it has effected a transformation of race spirit and group attitude, and acted like the creation of a national literature in the vernacular upon the educated classes of other peoples, who also at one or another stage of their cultural history were not integrated with their own particular tradition and folk-background.

AMERICAN ATTITUDE

The general history of white American attitude toward the Negro cultural traits and elements may be similarly traced in broad outline. First a long period of unconscious absorption and exchange, beginning in sentimental curiosity and growing with institutionalized slavery into a sentimental, condescending disdain. Then a transitional period of formal revulsion, in part a natural reaction, in part a definite accompaniment of the Slavery-Anti-slavery controversy. This was an attempt to insulate the Negro culturally, to "put him in his place" culturally as well as socially,—the last hectic throes of which can be seen in the "Reconstruction" school of fiction of Cable, Thomas Nelson Page, and to a modified extent even Joel Chandler Harris.

Finally after a gap of disinterest, there began about 1895 in American literature a new more objective interest in the Negro which, with the growth of American realism, has since 1918 resulted in a serious preoccupation of many of the leading American novelists, dramatists, story-writers, musicians, and folklorists with the Negro folk-themes and materials. This movement, amounting at times to definite exploitation of this now highly prized material, has paralleled the Negro cultural movement described above, has given it from time to time encouragement, objective vindication (in the sense that majority attitudes always influence minority attitudes) and developed new points of cooperative contact between the intellectuals and artists of both races.

Some of the best expressions of Negro life in formal American art have in this decade come from such outside sources, like Eugene O'Neill's plays of Negro life, DuBose Heyward's *Porgy*, Mrs. Peterkin's *Green Thursday* and *Black April*, Gershwin's adapted "jazz," the University of North Carolina studies in Negro folk song and folklore, to mention some outstanding examples.

The more the cultural rather than the sociological approach to the Negro matures, the more it becomes apparent, both to white and black observers, that the folk-products of the peasant Negro are imperishably fine, and that they constitute a national asset of the first rank. They have survived precariously; much has been lost. Modern research may retrieve some. But Uncle Remus tales and the "Spirituals" are enough to assure one of the quality of the simon-pure product, and of the pity that the generation of 1840 to 1880 was blind to their value.

The folk-story background was rescued by Thomas Cable and Joel Chandler Harris, but modern scholarship has yet to winnow out the sentimental additions which glossed over the real folkiness of the originals. The spirituals and other aspects of folk song and dance were saved by the Negroes themselves, beginning with the movement of the Fisk Jubilee Singers for the preservation and vindication of the folk music. Their effort, beginning in 1878, has culminated since 1900 in the work of Negro musicians like Harry T. Burleigh, S. Coleridge-Taylor, Rosamond Johnson, Carl Diton, Nathaniel Dett, Lawrence Brown, Edward Boatner, Grant Still, C. S. Ballanta, and others; some in careful arrangement of the Negro folk song in unvarnished transcription, others in more elaborate formal composition based upon its themes.

Meanwhile the secular Negro music, after a period of sentimental treatment culminating in the melodies of Stephen Foster, and one of minstrel balladry commencing about 1850 and climaxing in the eighties and nineties, has finally, as jazz in the contemporary period, exerted a constant, and at times, dominating influence on American popular music, light entertainment, and popular dance figures. All of these popularizations have been somewhat debased versions of their original folk derivatives, even in the hands of their Negro professional exponents. The authentic things themselves, in surviving such treatment, prove their sterling worth; and modern scholarship is now coming to their rescue. Such work as Odum and Johnson's *The Negro and His Songs*, Krehbiel's *Afro-American Folksongs*, Weldon Johnson's prefaces to the *First and Second Book of Negro Spirituals*, Weldon Johnson's transcriptions of Negro antebellum folk-sermons in his *Seven Negro Sermons in Verse (God's Trombones)*, Ballanta's *St. Helena Island Spirituals* enable us now to judge the genuine worth and tone of the Negro folk-product. Finely representative as they are in their historical time and setting, they are now regarded as even more precious in their potential worth as material for fresh artistic development.

The modern scholar is, therefore, reverent where the older generation were patronizing, and painstakingly scientific where we were once sentimentally amateurish. We have learned to appreciate the poetic imagination as well as the music of

> Bright sparkles in de churchyard
> Give light unto de tomb

and the serene faith of "Dese bones gwine to rise again" and "De mornin'-star was a witness too." And grateful as we are for his farsighted preservation of the most organic body of Negro folktale that American literature possesses, we cannot help wishing that Joel Chandler Harris had been a more careful and less improvising amanuensis of the mid-Georgian Negro peasant whom he knew and liked so well. Imperfect as the documentation is, emotionally the antebellum Negro has left, however, a satisfactory picture of his spirit. Slavery, which a brilliant ex-slave called "the graveyard of the mind," did not prove to be a tomb of the spirit; the Negro soul broke through to two ideals,—heaven and freedom,—and expressed these hopes imperishably. Although this was an expression of his own particular situation and his specific reactions, it was so profoundly intense as to become universalized; spiritually there are no finer expressions of belief in freedom and immortality, or of the emotional side of Christianity native to the American soil than these Negro folk utterances.

EFFECTS OF SLAVERY ON LITERATURE

If slavery molded the emotional life of the Negro, it was the anti-slavery struggle that gradually developed his intellect and brought him to articulate expression. The pivot of thought and focus of inspiration with the two first Negro writers, both poets,—Jupiter Hammon (1787) and Phillis Wheatley (1773),—was freedom, and the inconsistency of slavery, both with American revolutionary ideals and Christianity. There was in prose an anonymous arraignment of slavery by "Othello" as early as 1799, followed by Walker's famous "Appeal" in 1829. From this point on the growing anti-slavery movement developed necessarily the second-rate literature of controversy. Yet in this and the allied field of oratory, the Negro contribution was exceptional and at times up to the level of contemporary white talent, Garrison, Jay, Gerrit Smith, Sumner Phillips, as a critical comparison of the orations and essays of Martin Delany, James McCune Smith, Thomas Remond, Ringgold Ward, Henry Highland Garnet, Edward Wilmot Blyden, the West Indian scholar and abolitionist, and the greatest popular figure of the group, Frederick Douglass, will show.

These men all developed stages beyond literacy to forceful and polished oratory, and occasionally into matured scholarship. A synoptic view of their half-forgotten writings, such as Carter Woodson's carefully edited *Negro Orators and Their Orations* affords, shows their contribution to American literature of this type and period to have been surprising in volume and quality, and also reveals the intellectual Negro in the role of an active and valuable collaborator throughout the whole range of the anti-slavery movement and its activities, 1831–1859.

From the literary point of view, anti-slavery literature by both white and black writers is admittedly second-rate, but no one can deny its representativeness of its historical period. In the main throughout this period the Negro was a conformist imitator; here and there characteristic notes cropped out, but not dominantly. The most original products of this period, therefore, are the so-called "slave-narratives,"—life stories of fugitive slaves, all of them picturesquely, some of them forcefully, written. Frederick Douglass's *Narrative of "A Fugitive Slave"* (1845), afterward expanded into his autobiography, was one of the best known, Josiah Henson's life story (1858) was taken orally by Mrs. Stowe as the basis of her *Uncle Tom's Cabin* for characterization and a large part of the plot. The really most distinctive of these narratives are the early ones (1830–40), less known but also less tinctured with the tractate appeal of those later inspired directly by Abolitionist patrons, like Moses Roper's wonderful narrative of his escape (1837) or the story of Henry Bibb (1849). During this period there were two anti-slavery poets,—George Horton, a talented slave retainer of the University of North Carolina, who sold love lyrics to the Beau Brummel students at twenty-five cents a poem, and whose poems, *The Hope of Liberty*, were published in 1829 by friends to raise funds for the purchase of his freedom; and a more versatile and trained person, Frances Ellen Watkins Harper of Baltimore, whose verses in the style of Dorothea Hemans made her really one of the most popular and best-selling poets of her day. (*Forest Leaves*, 1855; *Collected Poems*, 1854.)

Against the background of the naïve and winsome folk-expressions, and the powerfully self-contained "Sorrow-songs," these painfully self-conscious effusions of sentimental appeal and moral protest are tame, feeble, and only historically interesting. But they were the first necessary stage of articulate expression: they did open up the mastery of the whole range of the English language and bring the Negro mind out into the mainstream of practical and cultural contacts. In this period, too, there was considerable production of belles lettres apart from that more practical polemical and propagandist work which, however, absorbed the major effort of the talented tenth who might otherwise have produced more creatively. Foremost among these more literary things were the essays of Martin Delany and Henry Highland Garnet, the commentaries of William Wells Brown, and the novels of Frank J. Webb (1857–59). Many of these works, like Phillis Wheatley's Poems, were first published in London.

The Civil War in one sense drained the energies of the anti-slavery campaign; in another sense gave it a specious satisfaction. In this and the early Reconstruction period little was produced by the Negro intellectuals. The practical emergencies of emancipation and reconstruction absorbed their time and attention. Shortly after 1875, reconstruction fiction by white writers began to appear, and took the form of sentimental glorification of the old antebellum regime, with little protest or counter-statement by white Northern writers,—there was the notable exception of the prolific Albion Tourgée. Negro writers meanwhile were absorbed writing revisions of slave autobiographies or propounding panaceas for the solution of the race question. Memoirs and amateurish histories were the vogue, but a huge mass of valuable historical data got itself written down, beginning with Samuel Nell's *Colored Patriots of the American Revolution*, and *The Services of Colored Americans in the Wars of 1776 and 1812*, published in 1852–55, running through work like Frederick Douglass's *Life and Times* (1882) and Simmon's *Men of Mark* (1887), and culminating in 1883 with George Williams's epoch-making, two-volume *History of the Negro Race from 1619–1880*.

Meanwhile, in literature the Southern protagonists had their innings in an uncontested field,—the enthusiasm of the North having spent itself in the furious and embittered campaign of Anti-slavery. Reconstruction literature was in its first stage sentimentalist, and created the stereotypes by which the Negro is still popularly known in America; and then after Cable, Harris, and Nelson Page, indeed before the end of their writing careers, became still more violently propagandist and caricaturist in its treatment of the Negro,—this phase culminating in the work of Thomas Dixon.

RECOVERY OF LITERARY EFFORT

Only in the late eighties did Negro literary effort recover itself, to succeed really only with two figures, Charles Waddell Chesnutt, the novelist and story writer, and Paul Laurence Dunbar, known as a dialect poet, but also considerably versatile as sentimental lyric poet, story writer, and novelist. Chesnutt modeled his story style and technique upon Cable and Bret Harte, and achieved a real success in the *Atlantic Monthly*, which led to a series of publications by Houghton Mifflin and Scribner's. Stories like the "Conjure Woman," and "The Wife of His Youth" represent the modern breaking-through of the Negro man of letters after the gap of Reconstruction; but Mr. Chesnutt's more ambitious work has been the writing of period novels to counter the distorted picture of the Southern regime given by the Nelson Page school of fiction. Two of these, *The House Behind the Cedars* (1900) and *The Marrow of*

Tradition (1901), are of documentary as well as literary importance.

Paul Laurence Dunbar is in the popular mind the outstanding Negro writer. This is because his poetry, heralded by William Dean Howells, started that increasingly popular school of Negro dialect poetry, about which there has been such controversy. There is no question about the representativeness of Dunbar's happy-go-lucky, self-pitying peasant; it is only a matter of realizing two things,—that he stands for the race at a certain stage of its history and a certain class at that stage. The Negro abolitionists were lecturing in Europe and J. C. Pennington preaching at the University of Heidelberg at the same time that Sam, Malindy, Dinah, and Joe were making the plantation cookhouse merry and the front porch gayer. Braithwaite, the critic, has the vital word on this question: "Dunbar was the articulate end of a régime, and not the beginning of a tradition, as most careless critics, both white and colored, seem to think. His work reflected chiefly the life of the typical Negro during the era of Reconstruction and just a little beyond, the limited experience of a transitional period, the rather helpless and still subservient era of testing freedom, of adjusting in the masses a new condition of relationship to the social, economic, civil and spiritual fabric of American civilization." Dunbar himself rebelled against this overemphasis upon his dialect poetry, and thought more both of his legitimate English lyrics and his fiction, in both of which fields he is not a negligible figure. In his "Ode to Ethiopia" and the sonnets to Robert Gould Shaw, Frederick Douglass, and Booker Washington, Dunbar reflected another side of the Negro soul than that delightfully rendered in "When Malindy Sings" or "When de Co'n Pone's Hot."

It was in this period (1895–1905) that the peasant cause and the mind of the Negro intellectuals became temporarily estranged because of a controversial feud over race programs and objectives. The cause of the masses found its protagonist in Booker T. Washington and his program of economic development, industrial education, and political and cultural laissez-faire. His autobiography, *Up from Slavery*, since becoming an accepted American classic, made this wing of Negro thought articulate. *The Souls of Black Folk*, by Dr. W. E. B. Du Bois, equally a classic though not so generally recognized, articulated the other cause of equal civic and educational and undifferentiated cultural ideals for the Negro.

The dialect school of poetry and all other strictly realistic arts were innocently caught in the dilemma of this controversy and aligned on the "segregationist" side. A considerable amount of controversial literature sprang up about this issue, most of it second-rate and negligible. Its effect was to delay pure art expression, to motivate Negro art temporarily upon an attempt to influence white opinion, and to retard the study of folk forms and tradition,—since the intellectuals capable of such study were for the time being out of sympathy with native and peculiarly indigenous things. A strain of dialect poetry trickled on, led by the ever-increasing popularity of Dunbar, but Du Bois was followed by the majority of the talented class and himself undertook a semi-propagandist school of social document fiction, of which *The Quest of the Silver Fleece* (1911) is representative, and sentimental belles lettres of which *Darkwater* is the classic expression. This literature of assertion and protest did perform a valuable service, however, for it encouraged and vindicated cultural equality, and at the price of much melodramatic sentimentalism, did induce a recovery of morale for purely cultural pursuits and self-expression. Meanwhile, the vogue of the school of Dunbar wrote into American literature, about a decade behind the general vogue of local-color sentimentalism, the important genre figure of the Negro peasant and troubadour-minstrel.

Then from 1912–15 on, with poetry of the intellectual school leading, a new phase of Negro self-expression gradually began. Previously, we must recall, except as singer or rhymester poet, the Negro as artist was not taken seriously. In this new phase, important as was the influence of Du Bois, perhaps even more influential was the indirect effect of the career and standing of William Stanley Braithwaite, who, in addition to his own verse publications in Pre-Raphaelite and symbolist veins, became, by his scholarly anthologies and his advocacy of modern American verse, a figure in the general literary world. The effect upon the cause, poetry and art for art's sake among Negroes, cannot be overestimated; the "legitimate" poets took heart and the dialect school became obsolescent. James Weldon Johnson published *Fifty Years and After* in 1917, facing Dunbar in one direction and away from him in another. Later Mr. Johnson declared for a new interpretation of the dialect school, "for the idioms of the folk imagination" rather than the broken jingle of Negro patois, in his "Creation" published in 1920 (later expanded into *Seven Negro Sermons in Verse, "God's Trombones"* (1927)). Fenton Johnson, Charles Bertram Johnson, Roscoe Jamison, Georgia Douglas Johnson, and most important of all, Claude McKay, began to publish, so that between 1917 and 1922 a revival of first-class artistic production had set in.

The Negro experience was now taken as the starting point, but universalized and for the most part treated in traditional poetic forms and symbols. Real virtuoso technique was sought and in cases achieved. Part of this output continued in a more dignified way the note of social protest, as in Claude McKay's "America":

> Although she feeds me bread of bitterness,
> And sinks into my throat her tiger's tooth,
> Stealing my breath of life, I will confess
> I love this cultured hell which tests my youth.
> Her vigor flows like tides into my blood,
> Giving me strength against her hate,
> Her bigness sweeps my being like a flood.
> Yet as a rebel fronts a king in state.
> I stand within her walls with not a shred
> Of terror, malice, not a word of jeer,
> Darkly I gaze into the days ahead.
> And see her might and granite wonders there,
> Beneath the touch of Time's unerring hand,
> Like priceless treasures sinking in the sand.

Another part, now the dominant note of the newer poetry, is a glorification of the racial background and of racial types of beauty, as in the same poet's lyric to "The Harlem Dancer":

> Applauding youths laughed with young prostitutes
> And watched her perfect, half-clothed body sway;
> Her voice was like the sound of blended flutes
> Blown by black players on a picnic day.
> She sang and danced on gracefully and calm,
> The light gauze hanging loose about her form;
> To me she seemed a proudly-swaying palm
> Grown lovelier through passing through a storm.

Some of this new crop of poetry indeed is quite general without reference to race situations or moods, which is particularly true of many poems by the three outstanding Negro women poets, Georgia Douglas Johnson, Angelina Grimké, and Anne Spencer, who range in technique from sentimental lyricism to ultramodern free verse.

POETRY AND MUSIC

Obviously Negro artists had by this stage outgrown the fault of allowing didactic emphasis and propagandist motives to choke their sense of artistry. In music the same growth took place with a rediscovery of the artistic possibilities of the Spirituals and other folk music forms. Harry Burleigh, Rosamond Johnson, Carl Diton, Nathaniel Dett, and others led this advance of the Negro musician to classic control and general recognition. In fiction and drama realistic folk portrayal was being taken up, by imitation in the last two instances of such pioneering experiments with a purely artistic treatment of Negro themes by modernist white American artists as Stribling, Shands, Clement Wood, Ellen Glasgow, Julia Peterkin, DuBose Heyward in the field of the novel and short story, and Ridgley Torrence, Eugene O'Neill, and Paul Green in the drama. From the Negro side and point of view, however, the main motivation, instead of being a new realistic cult of utilizing native materials in American art, has established itself in a new desire for representative group expression, paralleling the quickening of the group life which increased education and economic prosperity have given. Additionally there were the factors of migration from the farms and the South generally, rapid urbanization, intensification of group feeling growing out of the World War, and a general resurgence of race-consciousness and group-pride.

In 1924–25, after it had focused itself in advanced centers of culture like the Harlem Negro colony in New York, and somewhat in other centers like Chicago and Washington, and as it was running subconsciously in the veins of the youngest school of Negro poets, the present writer articulated these trends as a movement toward racial self-expression and cultural autonomy, styling it the New Negro movement (Harlem issue, *Survey Graphic*, March, 1925). Since then the accumulated spiritual momentum of one knows not how many generations has suddenly precipitated in a phenomenal burst of creative expression in all the arts, poetry and music leading as might be expected, but with very considerable activity in the fields of fiction, race drama, Negro history, painting, sculpture, and the decorative arts. It is a sound generalization to say that three-fourths of the total output is avowedly racial in inspiration and social objective, that a good part of it aims at the capitalization of the folk materials and the spiritual products of the group history; and equally safe to assert that more worthwhile artistic output and recognition have been achieved in less than a decade than in all the range of time since 1619.

Coming concurrently with a distinct attention on the part of American writers and artists to the artistic possibilities of Negro life, this recent movement is momentous. And since it is based on a conscious revival of partly lapsed tradition and experience, particularly with reference to the African past, it is not ineptly termed "the Negro Renaissance." Its general social and cultural effects will not be apparent for half a generation yet, but in its literary and artistic course it has all the earmarks of other recent folk revivals like that of the Celtic tradition in the Irish Renaissance or of the Bohemian history and folk arts in the Czechoslovakian developments still more contemporaneously. And as a result already accomplished, we have a general acceptance of the Negro today as a contributor to national culture and a potential collaborator in national self-expression.

Since 1920, four Negro poets have appeared who, in addition to their significant extension of the gamut of Negro life and experience artistically expressed, must also be reckoned in any fair survey of leading contemporary American poets,— Claude McKay, Jean Toomer, Countee Cullen, and Langston Hughes. Their poetry is racial on the whole, but in a new way. As Charles S. Johnson has aptly put it:

> The new racial poetry of the Negro marks the birth of a new racial consciousness, and the recognition of difference *without the usual implications of disparity*. It lacks apology, the wearying appeals to pity, and the conscious philosophy of defense. In being itself it reveals its greatest charm. In accepting this life it invests it with a new meaning.

And in evidence he quotes the manifesto of Langston Hughes, whose poetry he rightly claims as

> without doubt the finest expression of this new Negro poetry: "We younger Negro artists who create now intend to express our individual dark-skinned selves without fear or shame. If white people are pleased we are glad. If they are not, it doesn't matter. We know we are beautiful. And ugly, too. If colored people are pleased we are glad. If they are not, their displeasure doesn't matter either. We build our temples for tomorrow, strong as we know how, and we stand on the top of the mountain, free within ourselves."

A declaration of cultural independence, this—and a charter of spiritual emancipation.

Yet as a cursory glance at Mr. Cullen's anthology of the younger Negro poets, *Caroling Dusk*, will show, the field of poetic expression has at the same time so broadened technically as to have produced competent exponents of practically all the stylistic trends of contemporary poetry. Within the same period interest in Negro drama has also developed; on the metropolitan stage as a distinct Broadway vogue for serious acting by Negroes and for plays by and about Negroes, of which *Emperor Jones*, *In Abraham's Bosom*, and *Porgy* deserve outstanding mention. But Negro drama has still more importantly advanced in the direction of a movement for the development of a Negro theater and a repertory of plays based on the folk tradition. Similarly in art, where five years ago one or two painters and sculptors of general note like Henry O. Tanner, Meta Warrick Fuller, May Howard Jackson were isolated exceptions, now centers like Chicago or New York can muster for special exhibit the work of younger Negro artists in all the media from illustration and applied art to formal painting, and count on a dozen to a score of contributing artists; among whom Archibald Motley, Aaron Douglas, William Edouard Scott, Laura Wheeler, Hale Woodruff, Edwin Harleston, Palmer Hayden,— painters, and the sculptors Augusta Savage, Sargent Johnson, and Richmond Barthé must be mentioned. The work of some of these artists is in the general field, but much is racially interpretative, with some as a portrayal of folk types, with others as an attempt to base color and design somewhat more originally on the motives and technical originalities of primitive African sculpture and decoration.

FICTION

More significant still, sociologically, is the field of fiction. Here arrival at maturity represents more than emotional or technical control, resting as it does on the capacity for social analysis and criticism. Viewed in contrast with such masterfully objective and balanced portrayals of Harlem life as Rudolph Fisher's *The Walls of Jericho* and Claude McKay's *Home to Harlem*, the Negro novel of ten or even five years back seems generations less mature. For the work of Du Bois, *The Quest of the Silver Fleece*, and even his recent novel *Dark Princess*,

Jessie Fauset's *There Is Confusion*, and Walter White's *Fire in the Flint* and *Flight* are all essentially in the category of problem literature, and gain half or more of their value as "social documents." But the work of the younger generation stands artistically self-sufficient and innerly controlled. Beginning with the reaction from social interpretation in the pioneer artistic novel, Jean Toomer's *Cane* (1923),—a brilliant performance, and gaining momentum with some very competent short story portrayals by Fisher, John Matheus, Zora Hurston, and Eric Walrond,—the younger school have swung round finally to an artistically unimpeachable combination of social and aesthetic interpretation. In technical control and poise, we can now match the best contemporary writers of fiction in this field,—Van Vechten, Mrs. Peterkin, DuBose Heyward,—and promise shortly to overtake the same handicap in the field of drama, where as yet writers like Paul Green and Eugene O'Neill hold the preeminence. And this newly acquired mastery, in combination with the advantage of inside emotional touch with the facts and feelings of Negro experience, ought to give the young Negro writer and artist undisputed priority, though fortunately for American art as a whole, not an uncontested monopoly in this rich new field of the purely artistic expression of Negro life.

On the basis of evidence of this sort, it is warrantable to conclude that the advance guard of Negro life has either reached or nearly reached cultural maturity after a hard and inauspicious transplanting; and it is difficult to know in advance which effects will be more far-reaching and important, those of the direct artistic products, or those of the cultural and social by-products. Apart from the great actual and potential effects of this self-expression upon group morale and inner stimulation, there is that equally important outer effect which may possibly bring about a new cultural appraisal and acceptance of the Negro in American life.

America, in fact, has never psychologically spurned the Negro or been cold to the spiritual elements of his temperament; it is simply a question now of what reactions their expression on a new and advanced level will generate in a situation where both products and producer must together be accepted or rejected, deprecated or recognized. The initial re-actions to this phase are promising, which is in itself a signifi-cant and hopeful fact. In view of the dramatic yet integral character of the Negro's life with that of the dominant major-ity, and especially in view of the complementary character of the dominant Negro traits with those of the Anglo-Saxon Nordic, it would seem to be a situation of profitable exchange and real cultural reciprocity. For the Negro's predisposition toward the artistic, promising to culminate in a control and mastery of the spiritual and mystic as contrasted with the me-chanical and practical aspects of life, makes him a spiritually needed and culturally desirable factor in American life. How-ever, for the general working out of such a delicate interaction of group psychologies we cannot predict, but can only await the outcome of what is historically and sociologically a unique situation. All that we can be sure of in advance is the positive and favorable internal effect of such recent cultural develop-ment upon the course of Negro group life itself.

13

STERLING BROWN

The New Negro Folk-Poet

Many critics, writing in praise of Sterling Brown's first volume of verse, have seen fit to hail him as a significant new Negro poet. The discriminating few go further; they hail a new era in Negro poetry, for such is the deeper significance of this volume (*Southern Road*, Sterling A. Brown, Harcourt Brace, New York, 1932). Gauging the main objective of Negro poetry as the poetic portrayal of Negro folk-life true in both letter and spirit to the idiom of the folk's own way of feeling and thinking, we may say that here for the first time is that much-desired and long-awaited acme attained or brought within actual reach.

Almost since the advent of the Negro poet public opinion has expected and demanded folk-poetry of him. And Negro poets have tried hard and voluminously to cater to this popular demand. But on the whole, for very understandable reasons, folk-poetry by Negroes, with notable flash exceptions, has been very unsatisfactory and weak, and despite the intimacy of the race poet's attachments, has been representative in only a limited, superficial sense. First of all, the demand has been too insistent. "They required of us a song in a strange land." "How could we sing of thee, O Zion?" There was the canker of theatricality and exhibitionism planted at the very heart of Negro poetry, unwittingly no doubt, but just as fatally. Other captive nations have suffered the same ordeal. But with the Negro another spiritual handicap was imposed. Robbed of his own tradition, there was no internal compensation to counter the external pressure. Consequently the Negro spirit had a triple plague on its heart and mind—morbid self-consciousness, self-pity, and forced exhibitionism. Small wonder that so much poetry by Negroes exhibits in one degree or another the blights of bombast, bathos, and artificiality. Much genuine poetic talent has thus been blighted either by these spiritual faults or their equally vicious overcompensations. And so it is epoch-making to have developed a poet whose work, to quote a recent criticism, "has no taint of music-hall convention, is neither arrogant nor servile"—and plays up to neither side of the racial dilemma. For it is as fatal to true poetry to cater to the self-pity or racial vanity of a persecuted group as to pander to the amusement complex of the overlords and masters.

I do not mean to imply that Sterling Brown's art is perfect, or even completely mature. It is all the more promising that this volume represents the work of a young man just in his early thirties. But a Negro poet with almost complete detachment, yet with a tone of persuasive sincerity, whose muse neither clowns nor shouts, is indeed a promising and a grateful phenomenon.

By some deft touch, independent of dialect, Mr. Brown is able to compose with the freshness and naturalness of folk balladry—"Maumee Ruth," "Dark O' the Moon," "Sam Smiley," "Slim Greer," "Johnny Thomas," and "Memphis Blues" will convince the most skeptical that modern Negro life can yield real balladry and a Negro poet achieve an authentic folk-touch.

Or this from "Sam Smiley":

> The mob was in fine fettle, yet
> The dogs were stupid-nosed, and day
> Was far spent when the men drew round
> The scrawny wood where Smiley lay.
>
> The oaken leaves drowsed prettily,
> The moon shone benignly there;
> And big Sam Smiley, King Buckdancer,
> Buckdanced on the midnight air.

This is even more dramatic and graphic than that fine but more melodramatic lyric of Langston Hughes:

> Way down South in Dixie
> (Break the heart of me!)
> They hung my black young lover
> To a cross-road's tree.

With Mr. Brown the racial touch is quite independent of dialect; it is because in his ballads and lyrics he has caught the deeper idiom of feeling or the peculiar paradox of the racial situation. That gives the genuine earthy folk-touch, and justifies a statement I ventured some years back: "The soul of the Negro will be discovered in a characteristic way of thinking and in a homely philosophy rather than in a jingling and juggling of broken English." As a matter of fact, Negro dialect is extremely local—it changes from place to place, as do white dialects. And what is more, the dialect of Dunbar and the other early Negro poets never was on land or sea as a living peasant speech; but it has had such wide currency, especially on the stage, as to have successfully deceived half the world, including the many Negroes who for one reason or another imitate it.

Sterling Brown's dialect is also local, and frankly an adaptation, but he has localized it carefully, after close observation and study, and varies it according to the brogue of the locality or the characteristic jargon of the milieu of which he is writing. But his racial effects, as I have said, are not dependent on dialect. Consider "Maumee Ruth":

> Might as well bury her
> And bury her deep,
> Might as well put her
> Where she can sleep. . . .
>
> Boy that she suckled
> How should he know,
> Hiding in city holes
> Sniffing the "snow"?

And how should the news
Pierce Harlem's din,
To reach her baby gal
Sodden with gin?

Might as well drop her
Deep in the ground,
Might as well pray for her,
That she sleep sound.

That is as uniquely racial as the straight dialect of "Southern Road":

White man tells me—hunh—
Damn yo' soul;
White man tells me—hunh—
Damn yo' soul;
Got no need, bebby,
To be tole.

If we stop to inquire—as unfortunately the critic must—into the magic of these effects, we find the secret, I think, in this fact more than in any other: Sterling Brown has listened long and carefully to the folk in their intimate hours, when they were talking to themselves, not, so to speak, as in Dunbar, but actually as they do when the masks of protective mimicry fall. Not only has he dared to give quiet but bold expression to this private thought and speech, but he has dared to give the Negro peasant credit for thinking. In this way he has recaptured the shrewd Aesopian quality of the Negro folk-thought, which is more profoundly characteristic than their types of metaphors or their mannerisms of speech. They are, as he himself says,

Illiterate, and somehow very wise,

and it is this wisdom, bitter fruit of their suffering, combined with their characteristic fatalism and irony, which in this book gives a truer soul picture of the Negro than has ever yet been

given poetically. The traditional Negro is a clown, a buffoon,
an easy laugher, a shallow sobber, and a credulous Christian;
the real Negro underneath is more often an all but cynical fa-
talist, a shrewd pretender, and a boldly whimsical pagan; or
when not, a lusty, realistic religionist who tastes its nectars
here and now.

> Mammy
> With deep religion defeating the grief
> Life piled so closely about her

is the key picture to the Negro as Christian; Mr. Brown's
"When the Saints Come Marching Home" is worth half a dozen
essays on the Negro's religion. But to return to the question of
bold exposure of the intimacies of Negro thinking—read that
priceless apologia of kitchen stealing in the "Ruminations of
Luke Johnson," reflective husband of Mandy Jane, tromping
early to work with a great big basket, and tromping wearily
back with it at night laden with the petty spoils of the day's
picking:

> Well, taint my business noway,
> An' I ain' near fo'gotten
> De lady what she wuks fo',
> An' how she got her jack;
> De money dat she live on
> Come from niggers pickin' cotton,
> Ebbery dollar dat she squander
> Nearly bust a nigger's back.
>
> So I'm glad dat in de evenins
> Mandy Jane seems extra happy,
> An' de lady at de big house
> Got no kick at all I say—
> Cause what huh "dear grandfawthaw"
> Took from Mandy Jane's grandpappy—
> Ain' no basket in de worl'
> What kin tote all dat away. . . .

Or again in that delicious epic of "Sporting Beasley" entering heaven:

> Lord help us, give a look at him,
> Don't make him dress up in no nightgown, Lord.
> Don't put no fuss and feathers on his shoulders, Lord.
> Let him know it's heaven,
> Let him keep his hat, his vest, his elkstooth, and everything.
> Let him have his spats and cane.

It is not enough to sprinkle "dis's and dat's" to be a Negro folk-poet, or to jingle rhymes and juggle popularized clichés traditional to sentimental minor poetry for generations. One must study the intimate thought of the people who can only state it in an ejaculation, or a metaphor, or at best a proverb, and translate that into an articulate attitude, or a folk philosophy, or a daring fable, with Aesopian clarity and simplicity—and above all, with Aesopian candor.

The last is most important; other Negro poets in many ways have been too tender with their own, even though they have learned with the increasing boldness of new Negro thought not to be too gingerly and conciliatory to and about the white man. The Negro muse weaned itself of that in McKay, Fenton Johnson, Toomer, Countee Cullen, and Langston Hughes. But in Sterling Brown it has learned to laugh at itself and to chide itself with the same broomstick. I have space for only two examples: "Children's Children":

> When they hear
> These songs, born of the travail of their sires,
> Diamonds of song, deep buried beneath the weight
> Of dark and heavy years;
> They laugh.
>
> They have forgotten, they have never known
> Long days beneath the torrid Dixie sun,
> In miasma'd rice swamps;
> The chopping of dried grass, on the third go round

In strangling cotton;
Wintry nights in mud-daubed makeshift huts,
With these songs, sole comfort.

They have forgotten
What had to be endured—
That they, babbling young ones,
With their paled faces, coppered lips,
And sleek hair cajoled to Caucasian straightness,
Might drown the quiet voice of beauty
With sensuous stridency;

And might, on hearing these memories of their sires,
Giggle,
And nudge each other's satin-clad
Sleek sides.

Anent the same broomstick, it is refreshing to read "Mr. Samuel and Sam," from which we can only quote in part:

Mister Samuel, he belong to Rotary,
Sam, to de Sons of Rest;
Both wear red hats like monkey men,
An' you cain't say which is de best. . . .

Mister Samuel die, an' de folks all know,
Sam die widout no noise;
De worl' go by in de same ol' way,
And dey's both of 'em po' los' boys.

There is a world of psychological distance between this and the rhetorical defiance and the plaintive, furtive sarcasms of even some of our other contemporary poets—even as theirs, it must be said in all justice, was miles better and more representative than the sycophancies and platitudes of the older writers.

In closing it might be well to trace briefly the steps by which Negro poetry has scrambled up the sides of Parnassus from the ditches of minstrelsy and the trenches of race propaganda. In complaining against the narrow compass of dialect poetry (dialect is an organ with only two stops—pathos and humor), Weldon Johnson tried to break the Dunbar mold and shake free of the traditional stereotypes. But significant as it was, this was more a threat than an accomplishment; his own dialect poetry has all of the clichés of Dunbar without Dunbar's lilting lyric charm. Later in the *Negro Sermons* Weldon Johnson discovered a way out—in a rhapsodic form free from the verse shackles of classical minor poetry, and in the attempt to substitute an idiom of racial thought and imagery for a mere dialect of peasant speech. Claude McKay then broke with all the moods conventional in his day in Negro poetry, and presented a Negro who could challenge and hate, who knew resentment, brooded intellectual sarcasm, and felt contemplative irony. In this, so to speak, he pulled the psychological cloak off the Negro and revealed, even to the Negro himself, those facts disguised till then by his shrewd protective mimicry or pressed down under the dramatic mask of living up to what was expected of him. But though McKay sensed a truer Negro, he was at times too indignant at the older sham, and, too, lacked the requisite native touch—as of West Indian birth and training—with the local color of the American Negro. Jean Toomer went deeper still—I should say higher—and saw for the first time the glaring paradoxes and the deeper ironies of the situation, as they affected not only the Negro but the white man. He realized, too, that Negro idiom was anything but trite and derivative, and also that it was in emotional substance pagan—all of which he convincingly demonstrated, alas, all too fugitively, in *Cane*. But Toomer was not enough of a realist, or patient enough as an observer, to reproduce extensively a folk idiom.

Then Langston Hughes came with his revelation of the emotional color of Negro life, and his brilliant discovery of the flow and rhythm of the modern and especially the city Negro, substituting this jazz figure and personality for the older plantation stereotype. But it was essentially a jazz version of Negro life, and that is to say as much American, or more, as Negro; and though fascinating and true to an epoch this version was surface quality after all.

Sterling Brown, more reflective, a closer student of the folk-life, and above all a bolder and more detached observer, has gone deeper still, and has found certain basic, more sober and more persistent qualities of Negro thought and feeling; and so has reached a sort of common denominator between the old and the new Negro. Underneath the particularities of one generation are hidden universalities which only deeply penetrating genius can fathom and bring to the surface. Too many of the articulate intellects of the Negro group—including sadly enough the younger poets—themselves children of opportunity, have been unaware of these deep resources of the past. But here, if anywhere, in the ancient common wisdom of the folk, is the real treasure trove of the Negro poet; and Sterling Brown's poetic divining rod has dipped significantly over this position. It is in this sense that I believe *Southern Road* ushers in a new era in Negro folk-expression and brings a new dimension in Negro folk-portraiture.

14

PROPAGANDA— OR POETRY?

As the articulate voices of an oppressed minority, one would naturally expect the work of Negro poets to reflect a strongly emphasized social consciousness. That is the case, if gauged by their preoccupation with the theme of race. But whereas the race consciousness factor has been strong for obvious reasons, more generalized social-mindedness has been relatively weak in Negro poetry, and until recently the form of it which we know today as class consciousness has been conspicuously absent.

Before broaching an interpretation, let us look at the facts. Negro expression from the days of Phillis Wheatley was pivoted on a painfully negative and melodramatic sense of race. Self-pity and its corrective of rhetorical bombast were the ground notes of the Negro's poetry for several generations. The gradual conversion of race consciousness from a negative sense of social wrong and injustice to a positive note of race loyalty and pride in racial tradition came as a difficult and rather belated development of spiritual maturity. This and its group analogue—a positively toned morale of group solidarity—was the outstanding feature of Negro development of the post–World War period. I would not recant my 1925 estimate of this, either as a symptom of cultural maturity or as a sign of a significant development in the Negro folk consciousness. However, I would not confuse this upsurging of race consciousness with a parallel maturing of social consciousness, such as seems recently to be taking place. I do think, however, that the Negro could only be spurred on to the development of social consciousness in his creative expression through the previous intensification and change of tone of his racial consciousness.

But for a long while it was quite possible for the Negro poet and writer to be a rebel and protestant in terms of the race situation and a conforming conventionalist in his general social thinking. Just as it was earlier possible for many Negroes to be anti-slavery but Tory, rather than Whig, in their general politics. The average Negro writer has thus been characteristically conservative and conformist on general social, political, and economic issues, something of a traditionalist with regard to art, style, and philosophy, with a little salient of racial radicalism jutting out in front—the spear-point of his position. Many forces account for this, chief among them the tendency the world over for the elite of any oppressed minority to aspire to the conventionally established values and court their protection and prestige. In this the Negro has been no exception, but on that very score is not entitled to exceptional blame or ridicule.

There is an additional important factor in accounting for the lack of social radicalism in the Negro's artistic expression. This comes from the dilemma of racialism in the form in which it presents itself to the American Negro. Let me state it, with grateful acknowledgments, in the words of Rebecca Barton's admirable but little known study, *Race Consciousness and the American Negro.*

"The Negroes have no distinctive language to help foster their uniqueness. Their religion is the same fundamentally as that of the white group. There is no complete geographical isolation or centralization in one part of the country. On leaving their particular community they find themselves in a white world which suggests that the only claim they have for being a distinctive group is their color, and that this is nothing to arouse pride. Their manners, habits and customs are typically American, and they cannot escape from a certain economic and cultural dependence on the white people. They have not as much inner content to nurture their separate group life in America as national groups composed of immigrants from the Old World. Too great insistence upon withdrawing into their race would be an unhealthy escape, and would damage the chances of group efficiency by a balanced adjustment to the larger environment. . . . On the other hand, race values are too important not to preserve, and if the Negroes tried to identify themselves completely with white America, they feel that there would be a cultural loss. The skepticism as to any uniqueness of race temperament which has biological roots may be justified, but there is plenty in the distinctive social experience of the group to account for it and to give it tangible substance. The solution becomes one of being both a Negro and an American. It is the belief of many that this middle course can be taken, that the Negro can still be his individual self and yet cooperate in American life. If the building up of some group tradition is encouraged only as long as it is harmonious with fuller participation in national culture, then it can be a center from which creative activity can radiate. From this point of view, 'the racialism of the Negro is no limitation or reservation with respect to American life; it is only a constructive effort to build the obstructions in the stream of his progress into an efficient dam of social energy and power.'"

It is this flaming dilemma that has narrowed and monopolized the social vision of the Negro artist. Race has been an obsession with him, and has both helped and hampered his spiritual progress. However, it is absurd to expect him to ignore it and cast it aside. Any larger social vision must be generated from within the Negro's race consciousness, like the adding of another dimension to this necessary plane of his experience. The deepening social consciousness of Negro poets actually follows this expected course, from its earliest beginning even to the present.

As early as 1914, Fenton Johnson flared out with a mood of emotional revolt and social indictment that was half a generation ahead of its time. Johnson went much further than the usual rhetorical protest against social injustice; he flung down a cynical challenge and a note of complete disillusionment with contemporary civilization. His contemporaries were too startled to catch the full significance of "Tired" and "The Scarlet Woman."

TIRED

I am tired of work; I am tired of building up somebody else's civilization.

Let us take a rest, M'Lissy Jane.

I will go down to the Last Chance Saloon, drink a gallon or two of gin, shoot a game or two of dice and sleep the rest of the night on one of Mike's barrels.

You will let the old shanty go to rot, the white people's clothes turn to dust, and the Calvary Baptist Church sink to the bottomless pit.

You will spend your days forgetting you married me and your nights hunting the warm gin Mike serves the ladies in the rear of the Last Chance Saloon.

Throw the children into the river; civilization has given us too many. It is better to die than it is to grow up and find out that you are colored.

Pluck the stars out of the heavens. The stars mark our destiny. The stars marked my destiny.

I am tired of civilization.

THE SCARLET WOMAN

Once I was good like the Virgin Mary and the Minister's wife.

My father worked for Mr. Pullman and white people's tips; but he died two days after his insurance expired.

I had nothing, so I had to go to work.

All the stock I had was a white girl's education and a face that enchanted the men of both races.

Starvation danced with me.

So when Big Lizzie, who kept a house for white men, came to me with tales of fortune that I could reap for the sale of my virtue I bowed my head to Vice.

Now I can drink more gin than any man for miles around.

Gin is better than all the water in Lethe.

Claude McKay's vibrant protests of a few years later deserve mention, although in social philosophy they are no more radical because the indignation is fired by personal anger and the threat of moral retribution. McKay was a rebel, but an individualistic one. And so, for the most part was Langston Hughes, except in his later phase of deliberate proletarian protest. In his earlier poetry, Hughes has a double strain of social protest; the first, based on a curious preoccupation (almost an obsession) with the dilemma of the mulatto, and the other, a passionate description of the suppressed worker. But in both, Hughes's reaction is that of an ironic question mark or the mocking challenge of a folk laughter and joy which cannot be silenced or suppressed. "Loudmouthed laughers in the hands of Fate:" Hughes throws his emotional defiance into the teeth of oppression. He rarely extends this mood to systematic social criticism or protest, often suggests, instead of a revolutionary solution, emotional defiance and escape—as in

CROSS

My old man's a white old man
And my old mother's black.
If ever I cursed my white old man
I take my curses back.

If ever I cursed my black old mother
And wished she were in hell,
I'm sorry for that evil wish
And now I wish her well.

My old man died in a fine big house.
My ma died in a shack.
I wonder where I'm gonna die,
Being neither white nor black?

and

BRASS SPITTOONS

A bright bowl of brass is beautiful to the Lord.
Bright polished brass like the cymbals
Of King David's dancers,
Like the wine cups of Solomon.
Hey, boy!
A clean spittoon on the altar of the Lord. . . .
At least I can offer that.

This is hardly more socialistic than Countee Cullen's well-turned epigram

FOR A LADY I KNOW

She even thinks that up in Heaven,
Her class lies late and snores,
While poor black Cherubs rise at seven
To do celestial chores.

or Waring Cuney's

THE RADICAL

Men never know
What they are doing.
They always make a muddle
Of their affairs,
They always tie their affairs
Into a knot
They cannot untie.
Then I come in
Uninvited.

They do not ask me in;
I am the radical,
The bomb thrower,

I untie the knot
That they have made,
And they never thank me.

These were the moods of 1927–31; and though they are not
Marxian or doctrinal, their emotional logic is significantly
radical. They have one great advantage over later, more doctrinal versification—they do have poetic force and artistry.

Right here we may profitably take account of an unfortunate
insistence of proletarian poetry on being drab, prosy, and inar-
tistic, as though the regard for style were a bourgeois taint and
an act of social treason. Granted that virtuosity is a symptom of
decadence, and preciosity a sign of cultural snobbishness, the
radical poet need not disavow artistry, for that is a hallmark of
all great folk art. The simplicity, calm dignity, and depth of folk
art have yet to be constructively considered by the bulk of the
proletarian exponents of our present scene. This decline in poetic force, terseness, and simplicity is noticeable in the majority
of the overtly radical Negro poetry. In his later poems that more
directly espouse the cause of the masses, Langston Hughes, for
example, is much less of a poet; he is often merely rhetorical and
melodramatic rather than immersed in the mood. *Scottsboro
Limited* (1932) marks with him the definite transition from the
folk concept to the class concept. But instead of the authentic
folk note, the powerful and convincing dialect, the terse moving
rhythm of his lyric and his "blues" period, or the barbed and
flaming ironies of his earlier social challenge, we have turgid,
smoldering rhetoric, rimed propaganda, and the tone of the
ranting orator and the strident prosecutor. I have two criticisms
in passing, made in the interests of effective expression of the
very reactions in question and the radical objectives themselves.
The fire of social protest should flame, not smolder; and any expression on behalf of the Negro masses should exhibit the characteristic Negro folk artistry.

That is why we should scan the horizon for the appearance
of a true spokesman for the black masses, an authentic voice
of the people. As yet, he seems not at hand. But a succession of
younger poets points in his direction. Richard Wright, Frank

Marshall Davis, Sterling Brown show a gradually nearer approach to the poetry that can fuse class consciousness with racial protest, and express proletarian sentiment in the genuine Negro folk idiom. And with this we approach a really effective and probably lasting poetry. Even Hughes moves on between 1933 and 1935, from the turgid tractate drawl of his "Letter to the Academy" (1933):

"But please—all you gentlemen with beards who are so wise and old, and who write better than we do and whose souls have triumphed (in spite of hungers and wars and the evils about you) and whose books have soared in calmness and beauty aloof from the struggle to the library shelves and the desks of students and who are now classics—come forward and speak upon The subject of the Revolution.

We want to know what in the hell you'd say?" to the terser, homelier, more effective "Ballad of Roosevelt:"

> The pot was empty,
> The cupboard was bare.
> I said, Papa
> What's the matter here?
> "I'm waitin' on Roosevelt, son,
> Roosevelt, Roosevelt,
> Waitin' on Roosevelt, son."
>
> But when they felt those
> Cold winds blow
> And didn't have no
> Place to go—
> Pa said, "I'm tired
> O' waitin' on Roosevelt,
> Roosevelt, Roosevelt,
> Damn tired o' waitin' on Roosevelt."

Similarly, much of Richard Wright's poetry is mere strophic propaganda, little better for being cast in the broken mold of free verse than if it were spoken in plain pamphlet prose. Of course, this is not always so. "I Have Seen Black Hands," for all its obvious Whitman derivation, is powerful throughout, and, in several spots, is definitely poetic. The final strophe, lifted out of the descriptive potpourri of the earlier sections by a really surging rhapsodic swell, is convincing and exceeds propagandist dimensions:

> "I am black and I have seen black hands
> Raised in fists of revolt, side by side with the white fists
>   of white workers,
> And some day—and it is only this which sustains me—
> Some day, there will be millions and millions of them,
> On some red day in a burst of fists on a new horizon!"

But Wright is capable of the still finer, though entirely non-racial note of

> "Everywhere,
>   On tenemented mountains of hunger,
>   In ghetto swamps of suffering,
>   In breadline forest of despair,
>   In peonized forest of hopelessness
>   The red moisture of revolt
>   Is condensing on the cold stones of human need."

Frank Marshall Davis, of Chicago, for all that he boasts of a "perch on Parnassus" and confesses an urge "to take little, pale, wan, penny-apiece words and weave them into gay tapestries for beauty's sake," has an etcher's touch and an acid bite to his vignettes of life that any "proletarian poet" or Marxian critic might well envy and emulate. For he speaks of

> Black scars disfigure the ruddy cheeks of new mornings
>   in Dixie
>   (lynched black men hanging from green trees)
> Blind justice kicked, beaten, taken for a ride and left for dead
>   (have you ever heard of Scottsboro, Alabam?)

Your Constitution gone blah-blah, shattered into a thousand
   pieces like a broken mirror
Lincoln a hoary myth
   (how many black men vote in Georgia?)
Mobs, chaingangs down South
Tuberculosis up North
—so now I am civilized
What do you want, America?. . . .
Kill me if you must, America
All at once or a little each day
It won't matter. . . .

Yet today is today
Today must be emptied like a bucket before it dries into
   history
Today is an eagle, lingering a while, ready to fly into eternity,
Today I live
Today I tell of black folk who made America yesterday,
   who make America now
Today I see America clawing me like a tiger caged with a hare
Today I hear discords and crazy words in the song America
   sings to black folk
So today I ask—
What do you want, America?

How different, even in the similarity of theme, is this from
James Weldon Johnson's pale rhetoric of yesterday:

> "How would you have us—
>   As we are,
>   Our eyes fixed forward on a star?
>   Or clanking chains about your feet?"

No more apt illustration could be given of the change in the
last fifteen years of the tone and gamut of the Negro poet's social consciousness. But let us follow Frank Davis a step further
in his social analysis which is as accurate as his social description is trenchant: from his "Georgia's Atlanta:"

As omnipresent as air
are the Complexes
reminding white folk of superiority
keeping black folk subdued.
God
it so happens
either sleeps in the barn
or washes dishes for the Complexes.

Black Shirts—B.Y.P.U.'s
Ku Klux Klan—Methodist Conventions
Colleges—chaingangs
Millionaires—Breadlines
and taxes for the poor
(out of every dollar. . . .
take twenty-five cents
to feed the Complexes
who keep white folk, black folk separate).

"Yas suh—Yas suh"
"You niggers ain't got no business bein' out past midnight"
"I know it's so . . . a white man said it"
"That black gal you got there, boy, is good enough for any
    white man. Is she youah wife or youah woman? . . ."
"S'cuse me, Boss"
"You niggers git in th' back of this streetcah or stand up"
"We's got seats reserved for you white folks at ouah church
    Sunday night"
"He's a good darky"
"I know'd mah whitefolks'd git me outa dis mess from
    killin' dat no good nigguh"
"I've known one or two of you Nigras who were highly
    intelligent."

These, in case you don't know, are extracts from the official
book on race relations as published by the Complexes.

Is it necessary to call attention to the evenhanded, unsparing chastisement meted out to white and black alike? Or to the

unanswerable realism? Or to the devastating irony, or the calm courage? For all its sophisticated underpinning, I construe this as more instinctively and idiomatically an expression of Negro social protest than an officially proletarian screed. It comes from the vital heart of the Negro experience and its setting; it smacks neither of Marx, Moscow, nor Union Square.

Similarly undoctrinated, and for that reason, in my judgment, more significant and more effective, are Sterling Brown's recent poems of social analysis and protest. The indictment is the more searching because of its calm poise and the absence of melodramatic sweat and strain. Not all of Mr. Brown's poems reach this altitude, but the best do. So that where the earlier Negro poetry of protest fumes and perorates, these later ones point, talk, and reveal: where the one challenges and threatens, the other enlightens and indicts. Today it is the rise of this quieter, more indigenous radicalism that is significant and promising. Doubly so, because along with a leftist turn of thought goes a real enlargement of native social consciousness and a more authentic folk spokesmanship. Judged by these criteria, I find today's advance point in the work of Sterling Brown. Without show of boast or fury, it began in the challenge of "Strong Men:"

> "Walk togedder, chillen, Dontcha git weary. . . .
> They bought off some of your leaders.
> You stumbled, as blind men will . . .
> They coaxed you, unwontedly soft-voiced . . .
> You followed a way
> Then laughed as usual.
> They heard the laugh and wondered;
> Uncomfortable;
> Unadmitting a deeper terror . . .
> The strong men keep a-comin' on
> Gittin' stronger. . . ."

Later there was the unconventional appeal of "Strange Legacies" to the folk hero, unconquered in defeat:

"John Henry, with your hammer;
John Henry, with your steel driver's pride,
You taught us that a man could go down like a man,
Sticking to your hammer till you died. Brother, . . .
You had what we need now, John Henry.
Help us get it."

But in yet unpublished poems, the proletarian implications of "Mr. Samuel and Sam" become more explicit as the color line and its plight are definitely linked up with the class issue:

"Listen, John Cracker:
Grits and molasses like grease for belts
Coffee-like chicory and collards like jimson,
And side-meat from the same place on the hog
Are about the same on both sides of the track.

Listen, John, does Joe's riding ahead in the 'Jimmy'
Sweeten so much the dull grits of your days?
When you get where you're going, are you not still
John, the po' cracker, Joe, the po' nig?"

And profounder, still, the calm indictment of his "Decature Street," entirely within the black Ghetto physically, but underscoring it as but a segment of a common American tragedy:

The picture of content should be complete
I sing the happy pickaninnies
Underneath the Georgia moon. . . .

M'ole man is on de chaingang
Muh mammy's on relief

Down at the Lincoln Theatre, little Abe is set free again,
Hears music that gets deep-down into his soul:
"Callin' all cars,—callin' all cars," and the prolonged hiss—
"Black Ace, Black Ace!" And his thin voice screams
When the tommy-guns drill and the bodies fall,

"Mow them down, mow them down—gangsters or "G" men
So long as folks get killed, no difference at all,
So long as the rattling gun-fire plays little Abe his song.

And the only pleasure exceeding this
Will come when he gets hold of the pearl-handled gat
Waiting for him, ready, at Moe Epstein's.
Gonna be the Black Ace hisself before de time ain't long.

Outside the theatre he stalks his pa'dner,
Creeps up behind him, cocks his thumb,
Rams his forefinger against his side,
"Stick 'em up, damn yuh," his treble whines.

The squeals and the flight
Are more than he looked for, his laughter peals.
He is just at the bursting point with delight.
Black Ace. "Stick 'em up, feller . . . I'm the Black Ace."

Oh to grow up soon to the top of glory, With a glistening
     furrow on his dark face, Badge of his manhood, pass-key
     to fame.
"Before de time ain't long," he says,
"Lord, before de time ain't long."

The young folks roll in the cabins on the floor
And in the narrow unlighted streets
Behind the shrouding vines and lattices
Up the black, foul allies, the unpaved roads
Sallie Lou and Johnnie Mae play the spies.
Ready, giggling, for experiments, for their unformed bodies
To be roughly clasped, for little wild cries,
For words learned of their elders on display.
"Gonna get me a boy-friend," Sallie Lou says.
"Got me a man already," brags Johnnie Mae.

This is the schooling ungrudged by the state,
Short in time, as usual, but fashioned to last.

The scholars are apt and never play truant.
The stockade is waiting . . . and they will not be late.

Before, before the time ain't very long.

In the stockade: "Little boy, how come you hyeah?"
"Little bitty gal, how old are you?"
"Well, I got hyeah, didn't I?—Whatchu keer!"
"I'm goin' on twelve years old."

Say of them then: "Like Topsy, they just grew."

It is not enough to think of this as a modern equivalent of "the slave in the dismal rice-swamp" and the Abolitionist moral threat of "Woe be unto ye!" For here it is the question of a social consciousness basic, mature, fitted not to the narrow gauge of the race problem but to the gauge and perspective of our whole contemporary scene. In such a mold poetic and artistic expression can be universal at the same time that it is racial, and racial without being partial and provincial.

A recent writer, of doctrinaire Marxist leanings, insists that as a matter of strict logic the racial note and the class attitude are incongruous. So the proletarian poet should not be a racialist; and the common denominator of the art of our time is to be the "class angle." I think, in addition to documenting some notable changes in the social consciousness of recent Negro poets, the burden of this evidence is against such a doctrinaire conclusion and in favor of a high compatibility between race-conscious and class-conscious thought. The task of this younger literary generation is not to ignore or eliminate the race problem, but to broaden its social dimensions and deepen its universal human implications. And on the whole, at least so far, the more moving expression seems to have come from the side of the racial approach broadened to universality than from the poetry conceived in doctrinaire Marxist formulae and applied, like a stencil, to the racial problem and situation. The one has the flow and force of reality and the vital tang of life itself; the other, the clank and clatter of propaganda, and for all its seriousness, the hollow echoes of rhetoric. The Negro poet has not so long outgrown the stage of rhetoric; let us hope that the new social philosophy will not stampede our artists into such a relapse. Especially, since the present prospects are that some of the finest and most effective expressions of social protest in contemporary art will come from the younger Negro poet and his colleagues.

DRAMA

15

STEPS TOWARD
THE NEGRO THEATER

Culturally we are abloom in a new field, but it is yet decidedly a question as to what we shall reap—a few flowers or a harvest. That depends upon how we cultivate this art of the drama in the next few years. We can have a Gilpin, as we have had an Aldridge—and this time a few more—a spectacular bouquet of talent, fading eventually as all isolated talent must; or we can have a granary of art, stocked and stored for season after season. It is a question of interests, of preferences:—are we reaping the present merely or sowing the future? For the one, the Negro actor will suffice; the other requires the Negro drama and the Negro theater.

The Negro actor without the Negro drama is a sporadic phenomenon, a chance wayside flower, at mercy of wind and weed. He is precariously planted and still more precariously propagated. We have just recently learned the artistic husbandry of race drama, and have already found that to till the native soil of the race life and the race experience multiplies the dramatic yield both in quality and quantity. Not that we would confine the dramatic talent of the race to the fence-fields and plant-rooms of race drama, but the vehicle of all sound art must be native to the group—our actors need their own soil, at least for sprouting. But there is another step beyond this which must be taken. Our art in this field must not only be rescued from the chance opportunity and the haphazard growth of native talent, the stock must be cultivated beyond the demands and standards of the marketplace, or must be safe somewhere from the exploitation and ruthlessness of the commercial theater and in the protected housing of the art-theater flower to the utmost perfection of the species. Conditions favorable to this ultimate development, the established Negro Theater will alone provide.

In the past, and even the present, the Negro actor has waited to be born; in the future he must be made. Up till now, our art has been patronized; for the future it must be endowed. This is, I take it, what we mean by distinguishing between the movement toward race drama and the quite distinguishable movement toward the Negro Theater. In the idea of its sponsors, the latter includes the former, but goes further and means more; it contemplates an endowed artistic center where all phases vital to the art of the theater are cultivated and taught— acting, playwriting, scenic design and construction, scenic production and staging. A center with this purpose and function must ultimately be founded. It is only a question of when, how, and where. Certainly the time has come; everyone will admit that at this stage of our race development it has become socially and artistically imperative. Sufficient plays and sufficing talent are already available; and the awakened race consciousness awaits what will probably be its best vehicle of expansion and expression in the near future.

Ten years ago it was the theory of the matter that was at issue; now it is only the practicabilities that concern us. Then one had constantly to be justifying the idea, citing the precedents of the Irish and the Yiddish theaters. Now even over diversity of opinion as to ways and means, the project receives the unanimous sanction of our hearts. But as to means and auspices, there are two seriously diverse views; one strenuously favoring professional auspices and a greater metropolitan center like New York or Chicago for the Negro Theater; another quite as strenuously advocating a university center, amateur auspices, and an essentially educational basis. Whoever cares to be doctrinaire on this issue may be: it is a question to be decided by deed and accomplishment—and let us hope a question not of hostility and counter-purpose, but of rivalry and common end.

As intended and established in the work of the Department of the Drama at Howard University, however, the path and fortunes of the latter program have been unequivocally chosen. We believe a university foundation will assure a greater continuity of effort and insure accordingly a greater permanence of result. We believe further that the development of the newer forms of drama has proved most successful where laboratory and experimental conditions have obtained and that the development of race drama is by those very circumstances the opportunity and responsibility of our educational centers. Indeed, to maintain this relation to dramatic interests is now an indispensable item in the program of the progressive American college. Through the pioneer work of Professor Baker, of Harvard, the acting and writing of plays has become the natural and inevitable sequence, in a college community, of the more formal study of the drama. Partly through the same channels, and partly as a result of the pioneer work of Wisconsin, college production has come to the rescue of the art drama, which would otherwise rarely get immediate recognition from the commercial theater. And finally in its new affiliation with the drama, the American college under the leadership of Professor Koch, formerly of North Dakota, now of the University of North Carolina, has become a vital agency in community drama, and has actively promoted the dramatization of local life and tradition. By a threefold sponsorship, then, race drama becomes peculiarly the ward of our colleges, as new drama, as art-drama, and as folk-drama.

Though concurrent with the best efforts and most significant achievements of the new drama, the movement toward Negro drama has had its own way to make. In addition to the common handicap of commercialism, there has been the singular and insistent depreciation to stereotyped caricature and superficially representative but spiritually misrepresentative force. It has been the struggle of an artistic giant in art-engulfing quicksands; a struggle with its critical period just lately safely passed. Much of this has been desperate effort of the "bootstrap-lifting kind," from the pioneer advances of Williams, Cole, Cook, and Walker, to the latest achievements of *Shuffle Along*. But the dramatic side has usually sagged, as might be expected, below the art level under the imposed handicap. Then there has been that gradual investment of the legitimate stage through the backdoor of the character role; the hard way by which Gilpin came, breaking triumphantly through at last to the major role and legitimate stardom. But it is the inauguration of the Negro art drama which is the vital matter, and the honor divides itself between Burghardt Du Bois, with his *Star of Ethiopia*, staged, costumed, and manned by students, and Ridgley Torrence, with his *Three Plays for a Negro Theatre*. In the interim between the significant first performances and the still more significant attempts to incorporate them in the Horizon Guild and the Mrs. Hapgood's Players, there was organized in Washington a Drama Committee of the NAACP which sponsored and produced Miss Grimké's admirable pioneer problem-play, *Rachel*, in 1917. Between the divided elements of this committee, with a questionable paternity of minority radicalism, the idea of the Negro Theater as distinguished from the idea of race drama was born. If ever the history of the Negro drama is written without the scene of a committee wrangle, with its rhetorical climaxes after midnight—the conservatives with their wraps on protesting the hour; the radicals, more hoarse with emotion than effort, alternately wheedling and threatening—it will not be well-written. The majority wanted a performance; the minority, a program. One play no more makes a theater than one swallow, a summer.

The pariah of the committee by the accident of its parentage became the foundling and subsequently the ward of Howard University. In its orphan days, it struggled up on the crumbs of the University Dramatic Club. One recalls the lean and patient years it took to pass from faculty advice to faculty supervision and finally to faculty control; from rented costumes and hired properties to self-designed and self-executed settings; from hackneyed "stage successes" to modern and finally original plays; and hardest of all progressions, strange to relate, that from distant and alien themes to the intimate, native, and racial. The organization, under the directorship of Professor

Montgomery Gregory, of a Department of Dramatics, with academic credit for its courses, the practical as well as the theoretical, and the fullest administrative recognition and backing of the work have marked in the last two years the eventual vindication of the idea. But from an intimacy of association second only to that of the director, and with better grace than he, may I be permitted to record what we consider to be the movement's real coming of age? It was when simultaneously with the production of two original plays on race themes written in course by students, staged, costumed, and manned by students, in the case of one play with the authoress in role, there was launched the campaign for an endowed theater, the successful completion of which would not only give the Howard Players a home, but the Negro Theater its first tangible realization.

As will already have been surmised from the story, the movement has, of course, had its critics and detractors. Happily, most of them are covered by that forgiveness which goes out spontaneously to the opposition of the shortsighted. Not they, but their eyes, so to speak, are to blame. Rather it has been amazing, on the other hand, the proportion of responsiveness and help that has come, especially from the most prominent proponents of the art drama in this country; names too numerous to mention, but representing every possible section of opinion—academic, non-academic; northern, southern, western; conservative, ultramodern; professional, amateur; technical, literary; from within the university, from the community of Washington; white, black. Of especial mention because of special service, Gilpin, O'Neill, Torrence, Percy MacKaye, Du Bois, Weldon Johnson, and the administrative officers of the University; and most especially the valuable technical assistance for three years of Cleon Throckmorton, technical director of the Provincetown Players, and for an equal time the constant and often self-sacrificing services of Miss Marie Forrest in stage training and directing, services recently fitly rewarded by appointment to a professorship in the department. But despite the catholic appeal, interest, and cooperation it is essentially as a race representative and race-supported movement that we must think of it and that it must ultimately become, the best possible self-expression in an art where we have a peculiar natural endowment, undertaken as an integral part of our higher education and pursuit of culture.

The program and repertoire of the Howard Players, therefore, scarcely represent the full achievement of the movement; it is the workshop and the eventual theater and the ever-increasing supply of plays and players that must hatch out of the idea. The record of the last two years shows in performances:

1920-21—

Tents of the Arabs—Lord Dunsany.
Simon the Cyrenian—Ridgley Torrence.
The Emperor Jones—Guest performance with Charles Gilpin at the Belasco; student performance at the Belasco.

COMMENCEMENT PLAY, 1921-22—

The Canterbury Pilgrims—Percy MacKaye. Repetition of first bill in compliment of the delegates to the Washington conference on Limitation of Armaments.
Strong as the Hills (a Persian play)—Matalee Lake.

ORIGINAL STUDENT PLAYS—

Genefrede,—a play of the Life of Toussaint Louverture—Helen Webb.
The Yellow Tree—DeReath Irene Busey.

COMMENCEMENT PLAY—

Aria da Capo—Edna St. Vincent Millay.
The Danse Calinda—a Creole Pantomime Ms. performance— Ridgley Torrence.

A movement of this kind and magnitude is, can be, the monopoly of no one group, no one institution, no paltry decade.

But within a significant span, this is the record. The immediately important steps must be the production of original plays as rapidly as is consistent with good workmanship and adequate production, and the speedy endowment of the theater, which fortunately, with the amateur talent of the university, means only funds for building and equipment. I am writing this article at Stratford-on-Avon. I know that when stripped to the last desperate defense of himself, the Englishman with warrant will boast of Shakespeare, and that this modest Memorial Theatre is at one and the same time a Gibraltar of national pride and self-respect and a Mecca of human civilization and culture. Music in which we have so trusted may sing itself around the world, but it does not carry ideas, the vehicle of human understanding and respect; it may pierce the heart, but does not penetrate the mind. But here in the glass of this incomparable art there is, for ourselves and for the world, that which shall reveal us beyond all propaganda on the one side, and libel on the other, more subtly and deeply than self-praise and to the confusion of subsidized self-caricature and ridicule. "I saw Othello's visage in his mind," says Desdemona explaining her love and respect; so might, so must the world of Othello's mind be put artistically to speech and action.

STRATFORD-ON-AVON, AUGUST 5, 1922.

16

THE NEGRO AND THE
AMERICAN STAGE

In the appraisal of the possible contribution of the Negro to the American theater, there are those who find the greatest promise in the rising drama of Negro life. And there are others who see possibilities of a deeper, though subtler influence upon what is after all more vital, the technical aspects of the arts of the theater. Certainly the Negro influence upon American drama has been negligible. Whereas even under the handicaps of secondhand exploitation and restriction to the popular amusement stage, the Negro actor has considerably influenced our stage and its arts. One would do well to imagine what might happen if the art of the Negro actor should really become artistically lifted and liberated. Transpose the possible resources of Negro song and dance and pantomime to the serious stage, envisage an American drama under the galvanizing stimulus of a rich transfusion of essential folk arts and you may anticipate what I mean. A race of actors can revolutionize the drama quite as definitely and perhaps more vitally than a coterie of dramatists. The roots of drama are after all action and emotion, and our modern drama, for all its frantic experimentation, is an essentially anemic drama, a something of gestures and symbols and ideas and not overflowing with the vital stuff of which drama was originally made and to which it returns for its rejuvenation cycle after cycle.

Primarily the Negro brings to the drama the gift of a temperament, not the gift of a tradition. Time out of mind he has been rated as a "natural born actor" without any appreciation of what that statement, if true, really means. Often it was intended as a disparaging estimate of the Negro's limitations, a recognition of his restriction to the interpretative as distinguished from the creative aspect of drama, a confinement, in terms of a second order of talent, to the status of the mimic and the clown. But a comprehending mind knows that the very life of drama is in dramatic instinct and emotion, that drama begins and ends in mimicry, and that its creative force is in the last analysis the interpretative passion. Welcome then as is the emergence of the Negro playwright and the drama of Negro life, the promise of the most vital contribution of our race to the theater lies, in my opinion, in the deep and unemancipated resources of the Negro actor, and the folk arts of which he is as yet only a blind and hampered exponent. Dramatic spontaneity, the free use of the body and the voice as direct instruments of feeling, a control of body plastique that opens up the narrow diaphragm of fashionable acting and the conventional mannerisms of the stage—these are indisputably strong points of Negro acting. Many a Negro vaudevillian has greater store of them than finished masters of the polite theater. And especially in the dawn of the "synthetic theater" with the singing, dancing actor and the plastic stage, the versatile gifts of the Negro actor seem peculiarly promising and significant.

Unfortunately it is the richest vein of Negro dramatic talent which is under the heaviest artistic impediments and pressure. The art of the Negro actor has had to struggle up out of the shambles of minstrelsy and make slow headway against very fixed limitations of popular taste. Farce, buffoonery, and pathos have until recently almost completely overlaid the folk comedy and folk tragedy of a dramatically endowed and circumstanced people. These gifts must be liberated. I do not narrowly think of this development merely as the extension of the freedom of the American stage to the Negro actor, although this must naturally come as a condition of it, but as a contribution to the technical idioms and resources of the entire theater.

To see this rising influence one must of course look over the formal horizons. From the vantage of the advanced theater, there is already a significant arc to be seen. In the sensational successes of *The Emperor Jones* and *All God's Chillun Got Wings* there have been two components, the fine craftsmanship and clairvoyant genius of O'Neill and the unique acting gifts of Charles Gilpin and Paul Robeson. From the revelation of the emotional power of the Negro actor by Opal Cooper and Inez Clough in the Ridgley Torrence plays in 1916 to the recent half successful experiments of Raymond O'Neill's Ethiopian Art Theatre and the National Ethiopian Art Theatre of New York, with Evelyn Preer, Rose MacClendon, Sidney Kirkpatrick, Charles Olden, Francis Corbie, and others, an advanced section of the American public has become acquainted with the possibilities of the Negro in serious dramatic interpretation. But the real mine of Negro dramatic art and talent is in the subsoil of the vaudeville stage, gleaming through its slag and dross in the unmistakably great dramatic gifts of a Bert Williams, a Florence Mills, or a Bill Robinson. Give Bojangles Robinson or George Stamper, pantomimic dancers of genius, a Bakst or an expressionist setting; give Josephine Baker, Eddie Rector, Abbie Mitchell, or Ethel Waters a dignified medium, and they would be more than a sensation, they would be artistic revelations. Pantomime, that most essential and elemental of the dramatic arts, is a natural forte of the Negro actor, and the use of the body and voice and facile control of posture and rhythm are almost as noteworthy in the average as in the exceptional artist. When it comes to pure registration of the emotions, I question whether any body of actors, unless it be the Russians, can so completely be fear or joy or nonchalance or grief.

With his uncanny instinct for the theater, Max Reinhardt saw these possibilities instantly under the tawdry trappings of such musical comedies as *Eliza*, *Shuffle Along,* and *Runnin' Wild*, which were in vogue the season of his first visit to New York. "It is intriguing, very intriguing," he told me, "these Negro shows that I have seen. But remember, not as achievements, not as things in themselves artistic, but in their possibilities, their tremendous artistic possibilities. They are most modern, most American, most expressionistic. They are highly original in spite of obvious triteness, and artistic in spite of superficial crudeness. To me they reveal new possibilities of technique in drama, and if I should ever try to do anything American, I would build it on these things."

We didn't enthuse—my friend Charles Johnson of *Opportunity* and myself, who were interviewing Mr. Reinhardt. What Negro who stands for culture with the hectic stress of a social problem weighing on the minds of an over-serious minority could enthuse. *Eliza, Shuffle Along, Runnin' Wild*! We had come to discuss the possibilities of serious Negro drama, of the art-drama, if you please. Surely Director Reinhardt was a victim of that distortion of perspective to which one is so liable in a foreign land. But then, the stage is not a foreign land to Max Reinhardt; he has the instinct of the theater, the genius that knows what is vital there. We didn't outwardly protest, but raised a brow already too elevated perhaps and shrugged the shoulder that carries the proverbial racial chip.

Herr Reinhardt read the gestures swiftly. "Ah, yes—I see. You view these plays for what they are, and you are right; I view them for what they will become, and I am more than right. I see their future. Why? Well, the drama must turn at every period of fresh creative development to an aspect which has been previously subordinated or neglected, and in this day of ours, we come back to the most primitive and the most basic aspect of drama for a new starting point, a fresh development and revival of the art—and that aspect is pantomime, the use of the body to portray story and emotion. And your people have that art—it is their special genius. At present it is prostituted to farce, to trite comedy—but the technique is there, and I have never seen more wonderful possibilities. Yes, I should like to do something with it."

With the New Russian Theatre experimenting with the "dynamic ballet" and Meyerhold's improvising or Creative actor, with Max Reinhardt's own recently founded International Pantomime Society inaugurated at the last Salzburg Festival, with the entire new theater agog over "mass drama," there is at least some serious significance to the statement that the

Negro theater has great artistic potentialities. What is of utmost importance to drama now is to control the primitive language of the art, and to retrieve some of the basic control which the sophisticated and conventionalized theater has lost. It is more important to know how to cry, sob, and laugh, stare and startle than to learn how to smile, grimace, arch, and wink. And more important to know how to move vigorously and with rhythmic sweep than to pirouette and posture. An actor and a folk art controlling the symbolism of the primary emotions has the modern stage as a province ripe for an early and easy conquest. Commenting on the work of the players of the Ethiopian Art Theatre, discerning critics noticed "the freshness and vigor of their emotional responses, their spontaneity and intensity of mood, their freedom from intellectual and artistic obsessions." And almost every review of Paul Robeson's acting speaks of it as beyond the calculated niceties, a force of overwhelming emotional weight and mastery. It is this sense of something dramatic to the core that flows movingly in the blood rather than merely along the veins that we speak of as the racial endowment of the Negro actor. For however few there may be who possess it in high degree, it is racial, and is in a way unique.

Without invoking analogies, we can see in this technical and emotional endowment great resources for the theater. In terms of the prevalent trend for the serious development of race drama, we may expect these resources to be concentrated and claimed as the working capital of the Negro Theater. They are. But just as definitely, too, are they the general property and assets of the American Theater at large, if once the barriers are broken through. These barriers are slowly breaking down both on the legitimate stage and in the popular drama, but the great handicap, as Carl Van Vechten so keenly points out in his "Prescription for the Negro Theatre," is blind imitation and stagnant conventionalism. Negro dramatic art must not only be liberated from the handicaps of external disparagement, but from its self-imposed limitations. It must more and more have the courage to be original, to break with established dramatic convention of all sorts. It must have the courage to develop its own idiom, to pour itself into new molds; in short, to be experimental. From what quarter this impetus will come we cannot quite predict; it may come from the Negro theater or from some sudden adoption of the American stage, from the art-theater or the commercial theater, from some home source, or first, as so many things seem to have come, from the more liberal patronage and recognition of the European stage. But this much is certain—the material awaits a great exploiting genius.

One can scarcely think of a complete development of Negro dramatic art without some significant artistic reexpression of African life, and the tradition associated with it. It may seem a far cry from the conditions and moods of modern New York and Chicago and the Negro's rapid and feverish assimilation of all things American. But art establishes its contacts in strange ways. The emotional elements of Negro art are choked by the conventions of the contemporary stage; they call for freer, more plastic material. They have no mysterious affinity with African themes or scenes, but they have for any life that is more primitive and poetic in substance. So, if, as seems already apparent, the sophisticated race sense of the Negro should lead back over the trail of the group tradition to an interest in things African, the natural affinities of the material and the art will complete the circuit and they will most electrically combine. Especially with its inherent color and emotionalism, its freedom from body-hampering dress, its odd and tragic and mysterious overtones, African life and themes, apart from any sentimental attachment, offer a wonderfully new field and province for dramatic treatment. Here both the Negro actor and dramatist can move freely in a world of elemental beauty, with all the decorative elements that a poetic emotional temperament could wish. No recent playgoer with the spell of Brutus Jones in the forest underbrush still upon his imagination will need much persuasion about this.

More and more the art of the Negro actor will seek its materials in the rich native soil of Negro life, and not in the threadbare tradition of the Caucasian stage. In the discipline of art playing upon his own material, the Negro has much to gain. Art must serve Negro life as well as Negro talent serve art. And no art is more capable of this service than drama. Indeed the surest sign of a folk renascence seems to be a dramatic flowering. Somehow the release of such self-expression always accompanies or heralds cultural and social maturity. I feel that soon this aspect of the race genius may come to its classic age of expression. Obviously, though, it has not yet come. For our dramatic expression is still too restricted, self-conscious, and imitative.

When our serious drama shall become as naïve and spontaneous as our drama of fun and laughter, and that in turn genuinely representative of the folk spirit which it is now forced to travesty, a point of classic development will have been reached. It is fascinating to speculate upon what riotously new and startling may come from this. Dramatic maturings are notably sudden. Usually from the popular subsoil something shoots up to a rapid artistic flowering. Of course, this does not have to recur with the American Negro. But a peasant folk art pouring out from under a generation-long repression is the likeliest soil known for a dramatic renascence. And the supporters and exponents of Negro drama do not expect their folk temperament to prove the barren exception.

17

THE DRAMA OF NEGRO LIFE

Despite the fact that Negro life is somehow felt to be particularly rich in dramatic values, both as folk experience and as a folk temperament, its actual yield, so far as worthwhile drama goes, has been very inconsiderable. There are many reasons behind this paradox; foremost of course the fact that drama is the child of social prosperity and of a degree at least of cultural maturity. Negro life has only recently come to the verge of cultural self-expression, and has scarcely reached such a ripening point. Further than this, the quite melodramatic intensity of the Negro's group experience has defeated its contemporaneous dramatization; when life itself moves dramatically, the vitality of drama is often sapped. But there have been special reasons. Historical controversy and lowering social issues have clouded out the dramatic colors of Negro life into the dull mass contrasts of the Negro problem. Until lately not even good problem drama has been possible, for sentiment has been too partisan for fair dramatic balancing of forces and too serious for either aesthetic interest or artistic detachment. So although intrinsically rich in dramatic episode and substance, Negro life has produced for our stage only a few morally hectic melodramas along with innumerable instances of broad farce and low comedy. Propaganda, pro-Negro as well as anti-Negro, has scotched the dramatic potentialities of the subject. Especially with the few Negro playwrights has the propaganda motive worked havoc. In addition to the handicap of being out of actual touch with the theater, they have had the dramatic motive deflected at its source. Race drama has appeared to them a matter of race vindication, and pathetically they have pushed forward their moralistic allegories or melo-dramatic protests as dramatic correctives and antidotes for race prejudice.

A few illuminating plays, beginning with Edward Sheldon's *Nigger* and culminating for the present in O'Neill's *All God's Chillun Got Wings*, have already thrown into relief the higher possibilities of the Negro problem-play. Similarly, beginning with Ridgley Torrence's *Three Plays for a Negro Theatre* and culminating in *The Emperor Jones* and *The No 'Count Boy,* a realistic study of Negro folk-life and character has been begun, and with it the inauguration of the artistic Negro folk play. The outlook for a vital and characteristic expression of Negro life in drama thus becomes immediate enough for a survey and forecast of its prospects and possibilities. Of course, in the broad sense, this development is merely the opening up of a further vein in the contemporary American drama, another step in the path of the dramatic exploration and working out of the native elements of American life. At the same time, es-pecially in the plan and effort of the Negro dramatist, it be-comes a program for the development of the Negro drama as such and of a Negro Theater. Fortunately this special motive in no way conflicts with the sectional trend and local color emphasis of American drama today with its Wisconsin, Hoo-sier, Carolina, and Oklahoma projects. It is this coincidence of two quite separate interests that has focused the attention of both white and Negro artists upon the same field, and al-though we should naturally expect the most intimate revela-tions to come from the race dramatist, the present situation sustains a most desirable collaboration in the development of this new and fertile province. Indeed the pioneer efforts have not always been those of the Negro playwright and in the list of the more noteworthy recent exponents of Negro drama, Shel-don, Torrence, O'Neill, Howard Culbertson, Paul Green, Burghardt Du Bois, Angelina Grimké, and Willis Richardson, only the last three are Negroes.

The development of Negro drama at present owes more to the lure of the general exotic appeal of its material than to the special program of a racial drama. But the motives of race drama are already matured, and just as inevitably as the Irish, Russian, and Yiddish drama evolved from the cultural programs of their respective movements, so must the Negro drama emerge from the racial stir and movement of contemporary Negro life. Projects like the Hapgood Players (1917–18), The Horizon Guild (1920), The Howard Players (1921–24), The Ethiopian Art Theatre (1923), The National Ethiopian Art Theatre founded in Harlem last year, and The Shadows, a Negro "Little Theater" just started in Chicago, though short-lived and handicapped for an adequate and competent repertory, are nevertheless unmistakable signs of an emerging Negro drama and the founding of a Negro Theater.

But the path of this newly awakened impulse is by no means as clear as its goal. Two quite contrary directions compete for the artist's choice. On the one hand is the more obvious drama of social situation, focusing on the clash of the race life with its opposing background; on the other the apparently less dramatic material of the folk life and behind it the faint panorama of an alluring race history and race tradition. The creative impulse is for the moment caught in this dilemma of choice between the drama of discussion and social analysis and the drama of expression and artistic interpretation. But despite the present lure of the problem play, it ought to be apparent that the real future of Negro drama lies with the development of the folk play. Negro drama must grow in its own soil and cultivate its own intrinsic elements; only in this way can it become truly organic, and cease being a rootless derivative.

Of course the possibilities of Negro problem drama are great and immediately appealing. The scheme of color is undoubtedly one of the dominant patterns of society and the entanglement of its skeins in American life one of its most dramatic features. For a long while strong social conventions prevented frank and penetrating analysis, but now that the genius of O'Neill has broken through what has been aptly called "the last taboo," the field stands open. But for the Negro it is futile to expect fine problem drama as an initial stage before the natural development in due course of the capacity for self-criticism. The Negro dramatist's advantage of psychological intimacy is for the present more than offset by the disadvantage of the temptation to counter partisan and propagandist attitudes. The white dramatist can achieve objectivity with relatively greater ease, though as yet he seldom does, and has temporarily an advantage in the handling of this material as drama of social situation. Proper development of these social problem themes will require the objectivity of great art. Even when the crassest conventions are waived at present, character stereotypes and deceptive formulae still linger; only genius of the first order can hope to penetrate to the materials of high tragedy—and, for that matter, high comedy also—that undoubtedly are there. For with the difference that modern society decrees its own fatalisms, the situations of race hold tragedies and ironies as deep and keen as those of the ancient classics. Eventually the Negro dramatist must achieve mastery of a detached, artistic point of view, and reveal the inner stresses and dilemmas of these situations as from the psychological point of view he alone can. The race drama of the future will utilize satire for the necessary psychological distance and perspective, and rely upon irony as a natural corrective for the sentimentalisms of propaganda. The objective attack and style of younger contemporary writers like Jean Toomer, who in "Kabnis" has written a cryptic but powerful monologue, promise this not too distantly.

The folk play, on the other hand, whether of the realistic or the imaginative type, has no such conditioned values. It is the drama of free self-expression and imaginative release, and has no objective but to express beautifully and colorfully the folk life of the race. At present, too, influenced perhaps by the social drama, it finds tentative expression in the realistic genre plays of Paul Green, Willis Richardson, and others. Later no doubt, after it learns to beautify the native idioms of our folk life and recovers the ancestral folk tradition, it will express itself in a poetic and symbolic style of drama that will remind us of Synge and the Irish Folk Theatre or Ansky and the Yiddish Theatre. There are many analogies, both of temperament, social condition, and cultural reactions, which suggest this. The life which this peasant drama imperfectly reflects is shot page through with emotion and potential poetry; and the soggy, somewhat sordid realism of the plays that now portray it does not develop its full possibilities. The drabness of plays like Culbertson's *Jackey* and *Goat Alley* and of *Granny Boling* and *White Dresses* is in great part due to the laborious effort of first acquaintance. They are too studied, too expository. Even in such a whimsical and poetically conceived folk comedy as Paul Green's *No 'Count Boy*, with which the Dallas Little Theatre group won a recent amateur dramatic contest in New York, there is this same defect of an over-studied situation lacking spontaneity and exuberant vitality. It seems logical to think that the requisite touch must come in large measure from the Negro dramatists. It is not a question of race, though, but of intimacy of understanding. Paul Green, for example, is a close student of, almost a specialist in, Negro folk life, with unimpeachable artistic motives and a dozen or more Negro plays to his credit. But the plays of Willis Richardson, the colored playwright, whose *Chip Woman's Fortune* was the first offering of the Chicago Ethiopian Art Theatre under Raymond O'Neill, are very much in the same vein. Though the dialogue is a bit closer to Negro idiom of thought and speech, compensating somewhat for his greater amateurishness of technique and structure, there still comes the impression that the drama of Negro life has not yet become as racy, as gaily unconscious, as saturated with folkways and the folk spirit as it could be, as it eventually will be. Decidedly it needs more of that poetic strain whose counterpart makes the Irish folk drama so captivating and irresistible, more of the joy of life even when life flows tragically, and even should one phase of it remain realistic peasant drama, more of the emotional depth of pity and terror. This clarification will surely come as the Negro drama shifts more and more to the purely aesthetic attitudes. With life becoming less a problem and more a vital process for the younger Negro, we shall leave more and more to the dramatist not born to it the dramatization of the race problem and concern ourselves more vitally with expression and interpretation. Others may anatomize and dissect; we must paint and create. And while one of the main reactions of

Negro drama must and will be the breaking down of those false stereotypes in terms of which the world still sees us, it is more vital that drama should stimulate the group life culturally and give it the spiritual quickening of a native art.

The finest function, then, of race drama would be to supply an imaginative channel of escape and spiritual release, and by some process of emotional reinforcement to cover life with the illusion of happiness and spiritual freedom. Because of the lack of any tradition or art to which to attach itself, this reaction has never functioned in the life of the American Negro except at the level of the explosive and abortive release of buffoonery and low comedy. Held down by social tyranny to the jester's footstool, the dramatic instincts of the race have had to fawn, crouch, and be amusingly vulgar. The fine African tradition of primitive ritual broken, with the inhibitions of puritanism snuffing out even the spirit of a strong dramatic and mimetic heritage, there has been little prospect for the development of strong native dramatic traits. But the traces linger to flare up spectacularly when the touch of a serious dramatic motive once again touches them. No set purpose can create this, only the spontaneous play of the race spirit over its own heritage and traditions. But the deliberate turning back for dramatic material to the ancestral sources of African life and tradition is a very significant symptom. At present just in the experimental stage, with historical curiosity the dominating motive, it heralds very shortly a definite attempt to poetize the race origins and supply a fine imaginative background for a fresh cultural expression. No one with a sense for dramatic values will underestimate the rich resources of African material in these respects. Not through a literal transposing, but in some adaptations of its folklore, art-idioms and symbols, African material seems as likely to influence the art of drama as much as or more than it has already influenced some of its sister arts. Certainly the logic of the development of a thoroughly racial drama points independently to its use just as soon as the Negro drama rises to the courage of distinctiveness and achieves creative independence.

MUSIC

18

ROLAND HAYES

An Appreciation

One of the most accepted of the Viennese musical critics writes in a recent issue of the *Mittags-Zeitung*: "Roland Hayes, heralded before his first concert as a sensation and artistic curiosity because of his color, had already before this last one quite disillusioned the curiosity-seekers and chastened the gossip-mongers. Not as a Negro, but as a great artist, he captured and moved his audience. And our prophecy of April last, that he would always be welcomely heard in Vienna, was fulfilled yesterday. An audience that filled the Konzerthaus to capacity was again enthralled by the magic of his really wonderful mezza voice, was once more astounded by the matchless diction and interpretation of his German songs, and was made to realize the deep religious inspiration and poetic feeling of the Negro spirituals. Indeed, these admirably simple but unfortunately not too happily harmonized songs were among the best that the artist had to offer."

By the time this article is in print, Mr. Hayes will have sung as soloist with the Boston Symphony Orchestra and will be in the midst of a concert tour of America that will be epoch-making with regard to the recognition by the general American public of a Negro singer. As outstanding and commendable as this is as an artistic achievement, it has still more considerable significance—it should serve—it will serve—two timely purposes: it will educate the American public out of one of its worst and most unfair provincialisms (and in this respect, we must remember that the native-born and native-trained artist, white or black, has had great handicaps in America); and then too it will mark a very singular vindication of indisparagable ambition and courage, which would not accept the early rewards of the double standard so often temptingly imposed upon Negro talent by well-meaning but shortsighted admirers of both races. For these reasons, I write this comment—though of course, artistically, racially, and personally I was happy that the circumstances of travel made me a companion and witness of Mr. Hayes's almost triumphant recent tour of Austria, Hungary, and Czechoslovakia.

Vienna is the music capital of Europe—the Viennese critics are the most exacting and the Viennese public one of the most musically enlightened bodies in the world. The acclaim of Vienna is therefore the ambition of the greatest artists, and the tradition of success here opens all doors; especially that which leads to the historical recognition of posterity. It is perhaps not becoming for a friend to chronicle over-laboriously the details of such a success—I mention as mere suggestions, that the audience cheered about the stage in semi-darkness for quite a half hour after the regular program; that several critics missed Jeritza's annual leave-taking of the Opera to attend; that Madame Arnoldson Fischoff, the prima donna who has sung with the greatest tenors of two musical generations from Tamagno to Battistini, requested an Italian aria as an encore and declared it "perfectly sung"; that the creator of the role of Parsifal declared very generously that he would have given half his career for such mastery of the mezza-voice; that occasional Americans of the foreign colony spoke with pride of "our American artist" whom until recently they could never have heard without condescension and in some parts of our country, proscription and segregation. How shall we best appraise this triumph—as personal, as artistic, or racially? In each of these respects, it is significant and exceptional.

Personally, it represents the triumph of a particularly high and farsighted ambition. Just when his admirers in America were on the verge of flattering him into the fatal success of mediocrity, Mr. Hayes began in a fresh field to study and conquer the higher interpretative technique of his art. Indefatigable

work, a large part of it is the cultural background so often neglected by musicians, has made a seasoned artist out of a
gifted, natural-born singer. We have as a group more artistic
talent and fewer artists than any other; nature has in music
done too much for us—so that in this musical generation we
have produced but two artists whose equipment can challenge
the international standard—Roland Hayes and Hazel Harrison. There will be many more when the lesson of their careers is sufficiently impressed upon the younger generation of
race talent. Race talent in all fields is in the quicksands of the
double standard—our own people through shortsighted partisanship and pardonable provincialism, white Americans
through sentimental partiality or through haughty disparagement, make it doubly difficult. The turning point of Mr.
Hayes's career was when he refused to accept an assured success of this sort, and risked failure for the single standard of
musical Europe. Success there has opened doors otherwise
closed in America, not only for Mr. Hayes but for all qualified
talent in the future. As he himself told me, "I hope to leave
open behind me every door that I open—my ultimate intention in coming to Europe, in appealing to European judgment,
was eventually to widen opportunity for the Negro artist in
America." So an Acropolis has been captured by the shrewd
strategy of a flank attack.

Artistically Mr. Hayes, through the very intelligent pedagogy of Mr. Hubbard of Boston and Dr. Lierhammer of London, has cultivated his voice on its own pattern. It is not an
imitation of other models, however great, but an intensive cultivation of a voice that had its natural limitations—especially
that of medium volume. Through building up the intrinsic resources of the voice, there has been produced a lyric song-
tenor of unique quality and flawless technique—a voice that
would really be over-refined and too subtle except for the peculiarly fine rhapsodic flow which Mr. Hayes has taken over
from the primitive race gift in the art of song. The combination has created a rare medium which satisfies the most critical
and sophisticated, without losing the primary universal appeal
of simplicity and directly apprehensible beauty. So that a critic

can say, "This Negro singer adds a new contribution to the tenor-mystery in producing sensuous effects. It is old traditional culture taken hold of by a new temperament."

Without losing its individuality, the voice adapts itself to every language, to all schools and periods—because of its essential naturalness and freedom. Critical France is satisfied with the interpretation of its best modern music, and the German school with the interpretations of Bach, Schumann, Schubert, Strauss, and Wolf, whereas the Italian literature, especially of the older seventeenth and eighteenth centuries, is sung with a flow that qualifies according to the best traditions of bel canto. "Perhaps it comes through the deeper naturalness of tone-expression," suggests the same critic—no less than the dean of Viennese critics, Korngold, "that from each phrase, though technically perfectly rendered, a primitive sort of feeling wells up." No better artistic lesson can be taught than that of escaping from the limitations of one school and style of singing by the arduous endeavor to be sincere, genuine, and original—in other words, to be throughout all oneself and wholesomely natural. Refined but unaffected, cultivated but still simple—it is a voice of artistic paradoxes, and for that reason, unique.

Racially? Is there race in art? Mr. Hayes attributes his success to his racial heritage, which fortunately he cannot disown, if he would. Contrary to the general impression, it has not been an easy matter to make musical Europe accept and understand upon an art-plane the Negro spirituals which Mr. Hayes has always insisted upon as part of his program. Accompanists have often failed to interpret them properly, critics have been condescending toward them while nevertheless wholly favorable to other classical numbers, orchestrations have had to be expressly made and orchestral traditions broken to allow them as part of several programs. That which might have been expected to make Mr. Hayes's career easier upon the basis of a novelty has really, to my knowledge, been a difficult crusade, that but for tact and insistence would have failed. The result has been of peculiar value in giving a new cultural conception of the Negro to important circles of Euro-

pean society—a work that has made the artist a sort of ambas-
sador of culture in our behalf. At first they excite only curiosity
and the reaction—why does he sing them? Then a few catch
the seriousness of the interpretation and eventually the few
understand. "Mr. Hayes sang the spirituals with dignity, pen-
etrated by his mission," says one. "We should not forget that
of the three wise men who were guided by the star on their
quest, one was a Negro, and that the Negro today is able in
the cool, peculiar beauty of these spirituals to tell of Him so
vividly and touchingly that one might forget much that, had
the wise men lived long enough to experience, might bitterly
have disappointed them," says another. And not to rest upon
the testimony of others, I will venture the opinion that here in
this side of Mr. Hayes's work, we have had an artistic mis-
sioner of the highest effect and importance—a racial vindication and appraisal that could not have come in any better way,
being all the more effective through being expressed through
the international speech of melody and insinuated into the
mind through the channels of feeling and the heart. The Negro
as a group has lived Christianity in a peculiar way and exceptional degree. It has saved him—saved him in this world—
saved his heart from corrosion under the acid of persecution,
enabled him to survive through optimism and hope when despair and cynicism would have added the last sinking ounce of
weight—and in this near future of racial vindication, it is to be
one of the most potent mediums of interpretation and vindication.

"The highest tribute we can offer Mr. Hayes is to say that
while singing these, he might have been a statue shaped by the
hands of his own race through long centuries, for the ultimate
purpose of transmitting the soul of the race. It was the soul of
his race which sang through him in these childlike yet tragic
spirituals; sang of barbarities committed and endured, and of
a faith running like a golden thread through the gloomy web
of wrongs." To have elicited such recognition from the stranger
is a tribute to interpretative art of the highest character. A similar impression was no doubt made upon the sensitive mind of
Mr. Glyn Philpot, whose portrait of *Roland Hayes Singing* is

more the expression of a race symbol than of an individual—
the attempt to translate a spiritual message and give the social
rather than the personal note in art. The effect is, in every such
instance, reciprocal; the people gain through the art; the art
gains in vitality and in spirituality from its background in the
people.

Mr. Hayes has given this racial material a balanced background by which it has commanded more respect than when
separately and overexploited as has been the case with many
other European presentations of our songs. "I will never sing
spirituals without classics, or classics without spirituals, for
properly interpreted they are classics,"—this is Mr. Hayes's
artistic platform—and he is right and will be eventually justified. From this challenging comparison with other classical
song material has come not always an admission of equal
value—that could not be expected—but always there has been
conceded a seriousness of purpose and mission and loyalty to
self that has commanded admiration and respect.

No better instance of the soundness of this procedure can
be given than the transfer from these simple folk songs to
Bach, through an affinity of religious feeling, of a religious
quality which makes Mr. Hayes's interpretation of Bach songs
a delight to all connoisseurs of that great master. And then, finally, their inclusion has demonstrated to the very apprehend-
ing the true school of Mr. Hayes's art. It has folk-parentage—it
is the mother-art that through intense and sincere and quite
religious feeling has given rare capacity in evoking the spirituality which lies back of all great music, but the sense of which
comes not so much from the technique and discipline of art,
but from the discipline of life itself, and most often from that
side of it which we racially have so deeply tasted under the necessities of hardship. To capitalize these spiritual assets, especially in and through art, ought to be one of the main objectives
and missions of the younger, more happily circumstanced,
generations.

19

EXCERPT FROM
THE NEGRO AND HIS MUSIC

"From Jazz to Jazz Classics: 1926–1936"

From Jazz to "Jazz Classics."—For many persons, "classic" is a highbrow stick with which to spank so-called "lowbrow" music, because traditional music is more grown-up and authoritative. But let us listen to what may be said from the side of *jazz* in self-defense; and then realize, perhaps, that the important distinction is not between *jazz* and classical music but between the good, mediocre, and bad of both varieties. Jazz has its classics; and the classical tradition has its second, third, and fourth raters. By such standards a fine bit of writing or playing in the popular idiom and forms should outrate a mediocre attempt in the "classical" forms.

Louis Armstrong puts the case for good jazz plainly and sensibly. "Swing musicians worked hard for a quarter of a century, and against odds, to bring swing to the top; and swing musicians today have their work cut out for them to carry their art forward, to develop swing music into a broad and rich American music. . . . The way I look at swing music as it stands today is that it is America's second big bid to bring forth a worthwhile music of its own. The first big attempt was in the early days of jazz. We can now look back and see the mistakes and see about where *jazz* got side-tracked. We won't have many excuses to make if we let today's swing music go the same way. Jazz lost its originality and freshness and stopped growing. It stopped early. Jazz went down the easiest road where the big money was. . . . The writers of jazz have not "developed jazz music much during all these years, although a few men must be given credit. But for the most part, the new songs that have been coming out of 'Tin Pan Alley,' which is Broadway's music publishing district, are really not new at all. They are the same old melodies and rhythms just twisted around in a different way and with different words. Coarse beats or sticky-sweet phrases, and all that, year after year. It makes a good musician tired, for they are the very ones who are doing most to break up these worn-out patterns. The reason swing musicians insist upon calling their music 'swing music' is because they know how different it is from the stale brand of jazz they've got so sick of hearing. But in the early days, when jazz was born, jazz wasn't that way at all."

So what we have said and quoted in defense and praise of jazz is by no means meant for the cheap low-browed jazz that is manufactured for passing popular consumption. But embedded in this mass of mediocrity and trash are many compositions and versions of compositions that may justly be styled "jazz classics." One version of a song or dance tune may be cheap, trite, and stereotyped and another version distinguished, original, and highly musical. It depends on who "arranges" or recomposes it, and also upon who plays it. Some clownish rendition of "It Don't Mean a Thing" or crooner's wail of "Stormy Weather" will be musical trash, while an Ethel Waters or a Duke Ellington version must really be rated a "jazz classic," both for technical musicianship and for typically racial or "pure" style. It may take the connoisseur or expert to point it out to us, but after that, the difference is easily recognized.

Jazz has now developed its serious devotees and critics. They collect records, classify periods of style, trace developments of new technique, have their critical quarrels over favorites, have their special journals and their occasional "Jazz Recitals." Thus the nameless musical foundling of the slums and dance halls has, within less than a decade, acquired musical respectability, a pedigree, and such standing in serious musical circles as in previous musical history no popular music has ever received. Later we shall quote several of the most authoritative jazz critics,—Henry Prunières and Robert Goffin of Paris, Constant Lambert, the English composer. In passing, it will be enough to refer to Hugues Panassié's book,—*Le Jazz Hot*,—recently translated, which traces and analyzes jazz like a combined encyclopedia and hallmarking guild register.

The Title.—However, the most convincing praise of jazz will not come from the "jazz fans," but must come from the ranks of the orthodox musicians. And it is from such sources that jazz of the better sort has received great consideration. Kreisler, Rachmaninoff, Koussevitzky, and Stokowski are certainly names authoritative enough. "Jazz," says Serge Koussevitzky, famous conductor of the Boston Symphony, "is an important contribution to modern musical literature. It has an epochal significance—it is not superficial, it is fundamental. Jazz comes from the soil, where all music has its beginning." And Leopold Stokowski, of the Philadelphia Orchestra, says more pointedly: "Jazz has come to stay because it is an expression of the times, of the breathless, energetic, super-active times in which we are living,—it is useless to fight against it. . . . Already its new vigor, its new vitality is beginning to manifest itself. . . . America's contribution to the music of the past will have the same revivifying effect as the injection of new, and in the larger sense, vulgar blood into dying aristocracy. Music will then be vulgarized in the best sense of the word, and will enter more and more into the daily lives of people. . . . The Negro musicians of America are playing a great part in this change. They have an open mind and unbiased outlook. They are not hampered by conventions or traditions, and with their new ideas, their constant experiment, they are causing new blood to flow in the veins of music. The jazz players make their instruments do entirely new things, things finished musicians are taught to avoid. They are pathfinders into new realms."

We have to reckon with two types of worthwhile jazz, as distinguished from the trashy variety. First that which, rising from the level of ordinary popular music, usually in the limited dance and song-ballad forms, achieves creative musical excellence. This we may call the "jazz classic;" and will consider it in this chapter. The other is that type of music which successfully transposes the elements of folk music, in this case jazz idioms, to the more sophisticated and traditional musical forms. This latter type has become known as "classical jazz," and will be considered in due course. Both the jazz classic and classical jazz are examples of the serious possibilities of the Negro's music, and both have been vital contributions to the new modernistic music of our time.

Jazz Contributions.—Jazz has thus seriously influenced modern music in general. It has educated the general musical ear to subtler rhythms, unfinished and closer harmonies, and unusual cadences and tone qualities. It has also introduced new systems of harmony, new instrumental techniques, novel instrumental combinations, and when fully developed, may lead to a radically new type of orchestra and orchestration. Thus jazz has been a sort of shock troop advance, which the regular line advance of modernistic music has entrenched and consolidated. In accounting for its originality and force, Mr. Stokowski has already referred to the Negro jazz musician's freedom from the shackles of musical conventionality. But he could also have mentioned another factor. Much of the musical superiority and force of jazz comes from the fact that the men who play it create it. In the typical Negro jazz band, the musicians compose as a group under the leadership of a conductor who is also a composer or at least an arranger. The music comes alive from the activity of the group, like folk music originally does, instead of being a mere piece of musical execution. There is the story that Rossini, the great Italian composer, often composed in bed, and that when a manuscript slipped down to the floor on the wall-side, he would think up another melody because it was easier than picking up the strayed manuscript. Improvising is an essential trait of the genuine jazz musician: with the assurance that "there is plenty more where it came from," he pours his music out with a fervor and freshness that is unique and irresistible. This titanic originality of the jazz orchestras has only to be harnessed and seriously guided to carry jazz to new conquests.

The Jazz Orchestra.—With all the changes of style and all the feverish experimenting, the jazz orchestra has remained relatively stable in its makeup. Usually a combination of from eleven to fourteen musicians, it is composed usually of three trumpets, two or three trombones, three or four saxophones, one or two clarinets, interchangeable with bassoon, a bass fiddle, guitar, violin, or banjo, and the two basic instruments, a piano and the "traps" or drums and percussion. The conductor traditionally is the pianist, though not always, and usually plays or alternates between conducting "in front" or at the piano, although more and more, the vogue is calling for the dangerous theatricality of the virtuoso or stunt conductor. Usually the Negro combinations are smaller and less formally organized than the white jazz orchestras, and get similar or greater effects with fewer musicians.

Of course, their number is legion. Even to mention the outstanding organizations is difficult; but no jazz fan would omit Fletcher Henderson, Earl Hines, Luis Russell, Claude Hopkins, "Fats" Waller, Cab Calloway, Louis Armstrong, Don Redman, Jimmie Lunceford, or Duke Ellington from the list of great Negro jazz combinations. Similarly, experts single out among the great white jazz groups, the 1926 orchestra of Jean Goldkette, Paul Whiteman's early aggregation, Ben Pollack's, Red Nichols's, Ted Lewis, the Casa Loma Orchestra, Jimmy Dorsey, and finally Benny Goodman. Many a popular and lucrative jazz combination is omitted, but they are the vendors of diluted and hybrid jazz, which the experts frown on as mere popular amusement music lacking real jazz character and distinction.

And when it finally comes to the blue ribbon of the fraternity, Ellington's band has usually received the expert's choice, although for a racier taste, Louis Armstrong has always had his special praise and rating. The Continental critics, with the advantage perhaps of distance, always argue Ellington versus Armstrong warmly, generally to conclude that Armstrong is the most phenomenal jazz player of today but that Duke Ellington is the greatest jazz composer.

Duke Ellington.—Constant Lambert, himself a modern

composer of note and one who has used jazz idioms in his own compositions like the symphonic suite "The Rio Grande," has this to say about jazz in general and Ellington and Armstrong in particular:

An artist like Louis Armstrong, who is one of the most remarkable virtuosi of the present day, enthralls us at first hearing, but after a few records one realizes that all his improvisations are based on the same restricted circle of ideas. . . . The best records of Duke Ellington, on the other hand, can be listened to again and again because they are not just decorations of a familiar shape but a new arrangement of shapes. Ellington, in fact, is a real composer, the first jazz composer of distinction, and the first Negro composer of distinction. His works, apart from a few minor details, are not left to the caprice or ear of the instrumentalist; they are scored and written out . . . and the best American records of his music may be taken definitively like a full score, and they are only jazz records worth studying for their form as well as their texture. Ellington, himself being an executant of second rank, has probably not been tempted to interrupt the continuity of his texture with bravura passages for the piano, and although his instrumentalists are of the finest quality, their solos are rarely demonstrations of virtuosity for its own sake.

The real interest of Ellington's records lies not so much in their color, brilliant though it may be, as in the amazingly skillful proportions in which the color is used. I do not only mean skillful as compared with other jazz composers, but as compared with so-called highbrow composers. I know of nothing in Ravel so dexterous in treatment as the varied solos in the middle of the ebullient "Hot and Bothered!" and nothing in Stravinsky more dynamic than the final section. The combination of themes at this moment is one of the most ingenious pieces of writing in modern music. It is not a question, either, of setting two rhythmic patterns working against each other in the mathematical Aaron Copland manner—it is genuine melodic and rhythmic counterpoint which, to use an old-fashioned phrase, "fits perfectly." . . .

He has crystallized the popular music of our time and set up a standard by which we may judge not only other jazz composers, but also those highbrow composers, whether American or European, who indulge in what is roughly known as "symphonic jazz."

Extravagant and eccentric as such praise might seem coming from only a single voice, however distinguished, it becomes something quite different when echoed here and there independently by the most competent European and American critics and composers. On such a basis, I think we must agree that in addition to being one of the great exponents of pure jazz, Duke Ellington is the pioneer of super-jazz and one of the persons most likely to create the classical jazz toward which so many are striving. He plans a symphonic suite and an African opera, both of which will prove a test of his ability to carry native jazz through to this higher level. Many of his more spectacular competitors have changed their style repeatedly, proof of musical versatility, but Ellington's has developed more solid maturity, especially as shown by the lately published four-part *Reminiscing in Tempo*. Critics had said previously: "His one attempt at a larger form, the two-part *Creole Rhapsody* is not wholly successful, although it does develop and interweave a larger number of themes than usual in his work. It is here that Ellington has most to learn." The later record proves that he has learned or is learning. So one can agree with Robert Goffin that "the technique of jazz production has been rationalized by Ellington" and that "he has gradually placed intuitive music under control."

Jazz has been as fickle a medium as acting, and but for recording would have vanished in thin air. Its most extraordinary achievement, as has been said, is "the dissociation of interpretation from a stenographic execution of a work," to "improvise upon a given rhythmic theme with changes of tone, combinations of voices, and unexpected counterpoints (spontaneous interpolations)." Someone had to devise a technique for harnessing this shooting geyser, taming this wild well. R. D. Darrell's tribute to Ellington is probably an anticipation of what the future critics will judge. He says:

"The larger works of Gershwin, the experiments of Copland and other serious composers are attempts with new symphonic forms stemming from jazz but not of it. Not forgetting a few virtuoso or improvisatory solos (by Zez Confrey, J. Venuti and Lang, Jimmie Johnson, and others), one can truthfully say that a purely instrumental school of jazz has never grown beyond the embryonic stage . . . Ellington's compositions gravitate naturally toward two types, the strongly rhythmed pure dance pieces ('Birmingham Breakdown,' 'Jubilee Stomp,' 'New Orleans Low Down,' 'Stevedore Stomp') or the slower paced lyrical pieces with less forcefully rhythmed dance bass ('Mood Indigo,' 'Take it Easy,' 'Awful Sad,' 'Mystery Son,' etc.) Occasionally the two are combined with tremendous effectiveness, as in the 'East St. Louis Toodle-O,' 'Old Man Blues,' or 'Rocking in Rhythm.' The most striking characteristic of all his works, and the one that stamps them as ineradicably his own, is the individuality and unity of style that weld composition, orchestration, and performance into one inseparable whole. . . . Within an Ellington composition there is a similar unity of style of the essential musical elements of melody, rhythm, harmony, color, and form. Unlike most jazz writers, Ellington never concentrates undue attention on rhythm alone. . . . Delightful and tricky rhythmic effects are never introduced for sensational purposes, rather they are developed and combined with others as logical part and parcel of the whole work. . . . Harmonically Ellington is apt and subtle, rather than obvious and striking, and in the exploitation of new tone and coloring, he has proceeded further than any other composer—popular or serious, of today."

Such praise would be too much if it were entirely true of Ellington (as a wise caution spoken by the same critic will show in a moment), or if it were not partly true of many other of the great jazz composers and "arrangers" like Don Redman, Benny Carter, Sy Oliver, in their best but often too fragmentary passages. It is quoted as much in praise of jazz and its correct appreciation as in praise of Ellington. Jazz is in constant danger from the commercialization of the money changers who exploit it and the vulgarization of the immense public that consumes it.

Thus the word of caution, which Darrell offers to Ellington, ought to be stressed for all who come into the dangerous zone of commercially controlled popular music. Darrell says: "He may betray his uniqueness for popularity, be brought down to the level of orthodox dance music, lose his secure footing and intellectual grasp in the delusion of grandeur. Most of his commercial work evidences just such lapses. But he has given us, and I am confident will give us again [Darrell wrote this in 1932], more than a few moments of the purest, the most sensitive revelations of feeling in music today." All this is the common enemy of the jazz musician, white and black. But the artistic loss would be irreparable for the Negro musician, whose spirit-child jazz is, and whose artistic vindication its sound development must be. If these musicians can accomplish what they have, with commercial chains on and hampered by the straitjacket of popular dance tempo and pattern, they must seek to break through these limitations or else yield the future possibilities of jazz to the modernistic musicians who are trying "symphonic" jazz. There is enough genius, however, in the ranks of the professional jazz musicians to do the job independently.

The present vogue of "swing music," and the development of groups like the "Hot Clubs" for the serious study and support of undiluted jazz, true to the Negro idiom, comes at a strategic time. Already this support has rejuvenated the old-guard veterans like Ellington, Armstrong, Fletcher Henderson, Noble Sissle, "Fats" Waller, Earl Hines, "Chick" Webb, and Don Redman, who are returning to their original traditions. They must try to minimize the empty tricks of eccentric jazz on the one hand and thus get over the minstrel dangers of the "scat period" of popular jazz, and on the other, avoid the musical shallows of diluted, sentimental "sweet jazz," still popular but by the testimony of every expert neither racially or musically very significant. Behind the "old guard" organizations mentioned stand the promising younger Negro bands:

Luis Russell's merger with Louis Armstrong, the Claude Hopkins orchestra, the Blue Rhythm group of "Lucky" Millinder, and most especially the band of Jimmie Lunceford, that is composed almost exclusively of musicians of high technical and cultural training. Shoulder to shoulder with these exponents of "real" jazz stand such white musical organizations as the orchestras of "Red" Nichols, "Red" Norvo, the Dorsey brothers, and the now favorite "swing" group of Benny Goodman, who, by the way, uses principally Fletcher Henderson's arrangements, and has in his group the sensational young Negro jazz pianist, Teddy Wilson.

20

SPIRITUALS

Ladies and gentlemen, nothing quite so subtly or characteristically expresses a people's group character than their folk music, and so tonight we turn to that, to discover if we can sense, the essence of what is Negro, or if we cannot do that, at least to sample the heart of the Negro's racial experience. It is fitting, too, from the musical point of view, that we turn to the folk to render them their just due as the prime sources of our musical and spiritual heritage. I shall speak of the spirituals, and my esteemed friends and colleagues Sterling Brown and Alan Lomax will speak of the even wider problems of the secular folk music, showing you how deep and varied this folk experience has been and how many-sided is the folk character.

But I think we would all agree that the spirituals symbolize, as nothing else can do, our racial past. They are as well the taproot of our folk music. Certainly in terms of the historic occasion which this festival thoughtfully and reverently commemorates, the slave songs have a particular place and significance. It is that dark but rich and worthy side of the people's past which gives at one and the same time the most illuminating background of our present race accomplishment, the true perspective of our future hopes and ambition, and most important of all for us at this moment, the sampling of the mother soil of our creative genius.

For the musical talent that has grown up and flowered so distinctively to the extent that it is original has its basic rootage there. That soil of folk experience it is, which gives the special taste and tang, form and flavor, to what we are proud to claim as typically Negro in art and poetry and music. That, too, we must remember, lends its substance by a spiritual chemistry which men cannot curb or control into that other precious and representative cultural product which we are also proud to call American.

The spirituals are [the] taproot of our folk music—stemming generations down from the core of the group experience, in the body and soul suffering slavery and expressing for the race, the nation, for the world, the spiritual fruitage of that hard experience. But they are not merely slave songs or even Negro folk songs. The very elements that make them spiritually expressive of the Negro make them at the same time deeply representative of the soil that produced them. They constitute a great, and now increasingly appreciated, body of regional American folk song and music. As unique spiritual products of American life they've become nationally, as well as racially, characteristic. They also promise to be one of the profitable wellsprings of the native idiom in serious American music. In that sense they belong to a common heritage and, properly appreciated and used, can be, should be, will be part of the cultural tie that binds.

While this is true to a degree of all of our folk music, it is eminently true of the spirituals. For just before and immediately after the Civil War, they were the first Negro folk songs to be discovered and collected. Again, in 1871, through the Fisk Jubilee Singers, they were the first to gain serious musical attention—nationally and internationally. Still again, in 1894, through Dvořák and others, they were the first native folk idioms proposed as the base for a nationally representative American music. We still hear, those of us who were present last night, the beautiful echoes of the Dvořák quartet on American themes, which more convincingly even than the *New World Symphony* brought them that musical tribute and vindication. Finally, the spirituals in these glorious times of Roland Hayes, Paul Robeson, Marian Anderson, and Dorothy Maynor, and others have brought our interpretive artists a welcome opportunity, after mastery of the great universal language, to pay their racial homage to the native source of their artistic skill and spiritual strength, and to express their artistic indebtedness to the singing generations behind them and to the peasant geniuses who were, in James Weldon Johnson's apt phrase, "the black and unknown bards" of long ago.

To these humble folk roots we now turn as directly as we can through recordings of contemporary survivals from the folk song archives of the Library of Congress and with the talented assistance of a group of folk singers and musicians close to these roots. They, with their vital and very racial art, give us a comforting assurance that these folk sources are still alive in our generation even though we shall never again hear the spirituals in their original fervor and intensity. Since slavery was their historic setting, we can gladly dispense with that. Even the primitive religion which was their other root is lapsing fast, and both the emotional and musical patterns of so deep a group experience have survived, much to our musical and spiritual gain. Indeed, the contemporary composition of spirituals is still in occasional occurrence as the singers will illustrate in due course, by a rendition of one of their own making. Such, however, is sharply to be distinguished from that modern concoction of artificial, so-called spirituals, with superficial imitations of the folk idioms, that to the trained student of folk music, are misrepresentative caricatures of the deeply sincere and noble tradition. For the spirituals are, even when lively in rhythm and folky in imagination, always religiously serious in mood and conception. That does not even exclude humor of a sort—but the true spiritual is always the voice of a naïve unshaken faith for which the things of the spirit are as real as the things of the flesh.

This naïve and spirit-saving acceptance of Christianity is the hallmark of the true spiritual. Other factors have entered in, otherwise we should have merely dialect versions of evangelical Protestant hymns. First and foremost, there is the primary ingredient of a strong peasant soul with its naïve faith—a literal believing and soul-saving faith which preserved the emotional sanity of the Negro and kept his spirit somewhat above the fate of his body. Then there was, even out of a mass illiteracy, some great intuitive understanding of his own experience, in terms of a grand and inspiring analogy with the

Bible narratives. From which came all those inspiring parallels that kept hope alive, hope and faith alive in even the humblest Negro souls, and formed the basis of the dramatic part of the spirituals. The backbone of their narrative tradition is just such Bible parallels and they were selected on the basis of their closeness to the slaves' experience—own spiritual experience.

There was, too, borne out of the emotional fire of the group, a folk imagination that transposed the already glowing King James texts into real folk poetry. These have given us—and I wish I had more time to illustrate the poetic side of the spirituals—these have given us gems like "I lay in the grave and stretch out my arms, I lay this body down, I go to the judgment in the evening of the day when I lay this body down—when I lay this body down and my soul and your soul meet the day I lay this body down." Or, again, things like that spiritual which Roland Hayes sings so beautifully—"My Lord is so high, you can't get over him. My Lord is so low you can't get under him—you must come in and through the Lamb."

And finally there is the music itself—that great literacy of musical speech towering up over the dialect and the broken, sometimes feeble words to make an instinctive welding of all this into an amalgam of music that shades every meaning and evokes a mood almost independently of the words. This, it seems to me, is that blend of factors which makes the Negro spiritual and makes it so unique.

Now many of them, the purest of them, the oldest of them, it seems to me, must have been pure prayer songs, definitely coming out of the context of a worshiping band with a leader. And, it must have been, of course, somebody as a leader improvising a lead line and a lead idea, but that thing spreading from some kind of contagion that became instinctive as the tradition grew into a song in which finally the lead line and the burden of the refrain merged with the whole body to make it a great choral improvisation. And it's these things that, though not dated, we can judge by their purity to this tradition, which one might call the core spirituals. And these things, although they have been treated in many ways and have a first- and second- and third-generation attitude toward them, certainly in their origin are among the purest and best examples of religious feeling and emotion, and they communicate that feeling and emotion not just for the participants, but even those who do not share the naïve peasant literal beliefs.

Now, these songs have been treated in many ways, but they essentially, of course, call for choral rendition. And their style also calls for, not a set form, but an improvisation of feeling and of singing idiom according as the spirit moves. And they are best represented when they are sung that way, although it's difficult in these days, of course, to even closely imitate the sincere simple conditions out of which these beautiful folk songs sprang. When I hear them as art songs—and they are great as that—I always sort of feel that like that contrast of the Bach cantata, when toward the end after all his great exercise of composition, contrapuntal skill—the great master takes off his hat to what he recognizes as a still greater musical thing and pays that tribute in the simple playing of German choral to the faith of the people and to the folk song from which the whole thing grew.

Now, there was a double meaning in a great deal of spirituals, even to the illiterate Negro, because of this way in which they symbolized their own experience. And we find it even in as old a spiritual as the one that the singers are going to start with, where we think, those of us who look back on it, we see not just merely the feeling of a group of slaves stealing out to worship—for even at that early time worship was something of a . . . [inaudible] . . . from their toil, but that they symbolized in this song also their feeling that there was something ahead of them, most of them thought it was after the grave and after crossing Jordan, but others of them probably thought also that it was over the river toward Canada, toward the North Star, toward the freedom that sometimes so precariously they set out for. The group will sing "Steal Away."

There's a bolder note in some of this music, a note probably that crept in as their enthusiasm rose and as they distanced, in the fervor of their religious excitement, the slave world that they had left behind. And we want to give you shortly, next, one of the instances of this, that expresses the jubilance of the slave in the midst of his religious ecstasy. A good deal of this has a different tone from the prayer song. It verges on the spiritual shout, and it probably, in its original context, had impromptu extemporizations of the sort that we can find half-duplicated probably in some of the cults today.

It has always interested me greatly the frequency of a reference to Jordan. And while I know the importance of that in the Christian tradition and the way in which it would naturally fasten itself on the mind of slave groups, especially that were used to the ritual of baptism, I personally think that there is back of this some of that primitive carry-over of water symbolism of West African religions. But whatever it is, it's something very, very deep that you can immediately feel whenever the mention of Jordan comes in the spirituals or whenever this question of the water ritual comes up. It was symbolic to them, of course, of many things, but particularly of that spiritual purification that they thought was their only salvation within reach, and frequently, again and again, you have it in that reference to Jordan that chose the body but not the soul. The group will sing "Wade in the Water."

Another side of this tradition probably crystallized around the dramatic sermon, which was the illiterate or semiliterate preacher's version—dramatic version of—or expansion of his testament text. But very soon this narrative balladry, which probably was running along concurrently in the secular songs, spread into the field of the spirituals, and we have a whole group of these so-called narrative spirituals retelling dramatically and effectively the Bible stories, the picturesque ones; there are any number of them, but we all, of course, recall "The Walls of Jericho," and "Ezekiel in Heaven," and that very dramatic, and I think for the Negro, symbolic one of "David and Goliath," and one that we are later to hear about Moses. But there is one which the singers are to sing that represents another most favorite theme and story of the Negro peasant imagination—the story of Noah where, of course, again, Noah's experience symbolized to them the promise and the fulfillment after hard trials. This particular spiritual is given in a version that originates with the Golden Gate Quartet. It's "Noah."

I surely don't blame the audience, but as the timekeeper I'm afraid we must hurry on. In fact, we are having to telescope the next two numbers, both of which symbolize the mounting confidence and optimism of the Negro as it is nourished on this spiritual food. You find this triumphant note creeping in, in spite of all the suffering and sorrow. It's most inspiring and I'm sure you'll be very glad to listen to a short, joint rendering of the next two spirituals, "I'm So Glad (Trouble Don't Last Always)" and "We're Climbing Jacob's Ladder."

It's a commonplace that this accommodation of circumstances and this Christian tradition set the slave's and the Negro's eye on the other world, and gave him perhaps an otherworldly, and, in these days, what we call an escapist philosophy. But we must remember that the slave really, always had his eye on freedom of the body, as well as the soul. There was that frequent phenomenon of the slave rebellion, and of the still more frequent phenomenon of the fugitive slave, and I think this escapist tradition of which we complain is perhaps more typical of the Reconstruction than really of the slave period itself. Because during the Reconstruction we had this rather cruel blocking of the hopes of full freedom and the great disappointment that came from that.

Now, of course, the slave didn't get his democracy from the Bill of Rights. He got it from his reading of the moral justice of the Hebrew prophets and his concept of the wrath of God. And, particularly, his mind seized on the experience of the Jews in Egypt and of the figure of Moses, the savior of the people, leading them out from bondage, and, therefore, there is not only no more musically beautiful spiritual, but no more symbolic spiritual than "Go Down Moses."

As freedom came nearer historically, the slave sensed it probably through that great institution of theirs—the grapevine—and their hope for freedom became more pronounced and their songs for freedom really became more triumphant or at least anticipating triumph and release, and the group is now going to sing together two of those, the famous "Freedom, freedom over me, before I be slave I be buried in my grave and go home to my Master, be free" and "Pharoah's Army Got Drowned."

The power of the spiritual looms more and more as they stand the test of time. They outlived the particular generation and the peculiar conditions that produced them; they have survived, in turn, the contempt of the slave owners, the cold conventionalizations of formal religion, the artistic repressions of puritanism, the cheap corruption of sentimental balladry, the neglect and disdain of second-generation respectability, and now, the tawdry exploitation of Tin Pan Alley and our musical marketplaces. They've escaped the lapsing conditions and fragile vehicle of folk art, and come firmly under the protection of the skillful music folklorists a little late, but not too late to capture some of their fading original beauty. Only classics survive such things.

And now, finally, the quartet will give us one of their own original contemporary spirituals on the theme, a rather characteristic one, that death—that everyone has to die—that assertion of a democracy of death which must have meant so much to the Negro peasants in their own thin satisfactions in life. The quartet will close with "Travelin' Shoes."

ART

21

A NOTE ON AFRICAN ART

The significance of African art is incontestable; at this stage it needs no apologia. Indeed no genuine art ever does, except when it has become encumbered with false interpretations. Having passed, however, through a period of neglect and disesteem during which it was regarded as crude, bizarre, and primitive, African art is now in danger of another sort of misconstruction, that of being taken up as an exotic fad and a fashionable amateurish interest. Its chief need is to be allowed to speak for itself, to be studied and interpreted rather than to be praised or exploited. It is high time that it was understood, and not taken as a matter of oddness and curiosity, or of quaint primitiveness and fantastic charm.

This so-called "primitive" Negro art in the judgment of those who know it best is really a classic expression of its kind, entitled to be considered on a par with all other classic expressions of plastic art. It must be remembered that African art has two aspects which, for the present at least, must be kept rigidly apart. It has an aesthetic meaning and a cultural significance. What it is as a thing of beauty ranges it with the absolute standards of art and makes it a pure art form capable of universal appreciation and comparison; what it is as an expression of African life and thought makes it an equally precious cultural document, perhaps the ultimate key for the interpretation of the African mind. But no confusing of these values as is so prevalent in current discussions will contribute to a finally accurate or correct understanding of either of these. As Guillaume Apollinaire aptly says in "A propos de l'art des Noirs" (Paris, 1917), "In the present condition of anthropology one cannot without unwarranted temerity advance definite and final assertions, either from the point of view of archeology or that of aesthetics, concerning these African images that have aroused enthusiastic appreciation from their admirers in spite of a lack of definite information as to their origin and use and as to their definite authorship."

It follows that this art must first be evaluated as a pure form of art and in terms of the marked influences upon modern art which it has already exerted, and then that it must be finally interpreted historically to explain its cultural meaning and derivation. What the cubists and post-expressionists have seen in it intuitively must be reinterpreted in scientific terms, for we realize now that the study of exotic art holds for us a serious and important message in aesthetics. Many problems, not only of the origin of art but of the function of art, wait for their final solution on the broad comparative study of the arts of diverse cultures. Comparative aesthetics is in its infancy, but the interpretation of exotic art is its scientific beginning. And we now realize at last that, scientifically speaking, European art can no more be self-explanatory than one organic species intensively known and studied could have evolved in the field of biology the doctrine of evolution.

The most influential exotic art of our era has been the African. The article of M. Paul Guillaume, its ardent pioneer and champion, is in itself sufficient witness and acknowledgment of this. But apart from its stimulating influence on the technique of many acknowledged modern masters, there is another service which it has yet to perform. It is one of the purposes and definite projects of the Barnes Foundation, which contains by far the most selected art collection of Negro art in the world, to study this art organically, and to correlate it with the general body of human art. Thus African art will serve not merely the purpose of a strange new artistic ferment, but will also have its share in the construction of a new broadly comparative and scientific aesthetics.

Thus the African art object, a half a generation ago the most neglected of curios, has now become the cornerstone of a new and more universal aesthetic that has all but revolutionized the theory of art and considerably modified its practice. The movement has a history. Our museums were full of inferior and relatively late native copies of this material before we began to realize its art significance. Dumb, dusty trophies of imperialism, they had been assembled from the colonially exploited corners of Africa, first as curios then as prizes of comparative ethnology. Then suddenly there came to a few sensitive artistic minds realization that here was an art object, intrinsically interesting and fine. The pioneer of this art interest was Paul Guillaume, and there radiated from him into the circles of postimpressionist art in Paris that serious interest which subsequently became an important movement and in the success of which the art of African peoples has taken on fresh significance. This interest was first technical, then substantive, and finally, theoretical. "What formerly appeared meaningless took on meaning in the latest experimental strivings of plastic art. One came to realize that hardly anywhere else had certain problems of form and a certain manner of their technical solution presented itself in greater clarity than in the art of the Negro. It then became apparent that prior judgments about the Negro and his arts characterized the critic more than the object of criticism. The new appreciation developed instantly a new passion, we began to collect Negro art as art, became passionately interested in corrective reappraisal of it, and made out of the old material a newly evaluated thing."

There is a curious reason why this meeting of the primitive with the most sophisticated has been so stimulating and productive. The discovery of African art happened to come at a time when there was a marked sterility in certain forms of expression in European plastic art, due to generations of the inbreeding of idiom and style. Restless experimentation was dominant. African images had been previously dismissed as crude attempts at realistic representation. Then out of the desperate exhaustion of the exploiting of all the technical possibilities of color by the Impressionists, the problem of form and decorative design became emphasized in one of those natural reactions which occur so repeatedly in art. And suddenly with

the substitution in European art of a new emphasis and technical interest, the African representation of form, previously
regarded as ridiculously crude, suddenly appeared cunningly
sophisticated. Strong stylistic associations had stood between
us and its correct interpretation, and their breaking down had
the effect of a great discovery, a fresh revelation. Negro art
was instantly seen as a "notable instance of plastic representation." . . . "For western art the problem of representation of
form had become a secondary and even mishandled problem,
sacrificed to the effect of movement. The three-dimensional interpretation of space, the ground basis of all plastic art, was
itself a lost art, and when, with considerable pains, artists
began to explore afresh the elements of form perception, fortunately at that time African plastic art was discovered and it
was recognized that it had successfully cultivated and mastered the expression of pure plastic form."

It was by such a series of discoveries and revaluations that
African art came into its present prominence and significance.
Other articles in this issue trace more authoritatively than the
present writer can the attested influence of Negro art upon
the work of Matisse, Picasso, Modigliani, and Soutine among
the French painters, upon Max Pechstein, Irma Stern among
German painters, upon Modigliani, Archipenko, Epstein, Lipchitz, and Lehmbruck among sculptors. This much may be regarded, on the best authority, as incontestable. The less direct
influence in music and poetry must be considered separately,
for it rests upon a different line both of influence and of evidence. But in plastic art the influence is evident upon direct
comparison of the work of these artists with the African sculptures, though in almost every one of the abovementioned cases
there is additionally available information as to a direct contact with Negro art and the acknowledgement of its inspiration.

The verdict of criticism was bound to follow the verdict of
the creative artists. A whole literature of comment and interpretation of "exotic art" in general, and Negro art in particular has sprung up, especially in Germany. Most diverse
interpretations, from both the ethnographic and the aesthetic

points of view, have been given. On good authority much of this is considered premature and fantastic, but this much at least has definitely developed as a result,—that the problems raised by African art are now recognized as at the very core of art theory and art history. Ethnographically the most promising lines of interpretation are those laid down in Joyce and Torday's treatise on the Bushongo and by A. A. Goldenweiser in the chapter on art in his book entitled *Early Civilization*. Aesthetically, the most authentic interpretations are those of Paul Guillaume, who from his long familiarity with this art is selecting the classical examples and working out a tentative stylistic and period classification, and that of the accomplished critic Roger E. Fry, from whose chapter on Negro sculpture (*Vision and Design*, 1920) the following is quoted: "We have the habit of thinking that the power to create expressive plastic form is one of the greatest of human achievements, and the names of great sculptors are handed down from generation to generation, so that it seems unfair to be forced to admit that certain nameless savages have possessed this power not only in a higher degree than we at this moment, but than we as a nation have ever possessed it. And yet that is where I find myself. I have to admit that some of these things are great sculpture,— greater, I think, than anything we produced even in the Middle Ages. Certainly they have the special qualities of sculpture in a higher degree. They have indeed complete plastic freedom, that is to say, these African artists really can see form in three dimensions. Now this is rare in sculpture. All archaic European sculpture, Greek and Romanesque, for instance— approaches plasticity from the point of view of bas-relief. The statue bears traces of having been conceived as the combination of back, front, and side bas-reliefs. And this continues to make itself felt almost until the final development of the tradition. Complete plastic freedom with us seems only to have come at the end of a long period, when the art has attained a high degree of representational skill and when it is generally already decadent from the point of view of imaginative significance. Now the strange thing about these African sculptures is that they bear, as far as I can see, no trace of this process. . . .

So,—far from clinging to two dimensions, as we tend to do, he (the Negro artist) actually underlines, as it were, the three-dimensionalness of his forms. It is in some such way that he manages to give to his forms their disconcerting vitality, the suggestion that they make of being not mere echoes of actual figures, but of possessing an inner life of their own. . . . Besides the logical comprehension of plastic form which the Negro shows, he has also an exquisite taste in his handling of material."

Equally important with this newer aesthetic appreciation is the newer archeological revaluation. Negro art is no longer taken as the expression of a uniformly primitive and prematurely arrested stage of culture. It is now seen as having passed through many diverse phases, as having undergone several classical developments, and as illustrating several divergent types of art evolution. The theory of evolution has put art into a scientific straitjacket, and African art has had to fit in with its rigid preconceptions. It is most encouraging therefore to see an emancipated type of scientific treatment appearing, with Torday and Joyce's historical interpretation of art in terms of its corresponding culture values, and in Goldenweiser's rejection of the evolutionary formula which would make all African art originate from crude representationalism, that is to say, naïve and non-aesthetic realism. For Goldenweiser, primitive art has in it both the decorative and the realistic motives, and often as not it is the abstract principles of design and aesthetic form which are the determinants of its stylistic technique and conventions. Of course this is only another way of saying that art is after all art, but such scientific vindication of the efficacy of pure art motives in primitive art is welcome, especially as it frees the interpretation of African art from the prevailing scientific formulae. Thus both the latest aesthetic and scientific interpretations agree on a new value and complexity in the art we are considering.

Perhaps the most important effect of interpretations like these is to break down the invidious distinction between art with a capital A for European forms of expression and "exotic" and "primitive" art for the art expressions of other peoples.

Technically speaking an art is primitive in any phase before it has mastered its idiom of expression, and classic when it has arrived at maturity and before it has begun to decline. Similarly art is exotic with relation only to its relative incommensurability with other cultures, in influencing them at all vitally it ceases to be exotic. From this we can see what misnomers these terms really are when applied to all phases of African art. Eventually we will come to realize that art is universally organic, and then for the first time scientifically absolute principles of art appreciation will have been achieved.

Meanwhile as a product of African civilization, Negro art is a peculiarly precious thing, not only for the foregoing reasons, but for the additional reason that it is one of the few common elements between such highly divergent types of culture as the African and the European, and offers a rare medium for their fair comparison. Culture and civilization are regarded too synonymously: a high-grade civilization may have a low-grade culture, and a relatively feeble civilization may have disproportionately high culture elements. We should not judge art too rigidly by civilization, or vice versa. Certainly African peoples have had the serious disadvantage of an environment in which the results of civilization do not accumulatively survive, so that their non-material culture elements are in many instances very much more mature and advanced than the material civilization which surrounds them. It follows then that the evidence of such elements ought to be seriously taken as factors for fair and proper interpretation.

Indeed the comparative study of such culture elements as art, folklore, and language will eventually supply the most reliable clues and tests for African values. And also, we may warrantably claim, for the tracing of historical contacts and influences, since the archeological accuracy of art is admitted. Comparative art and design have much to add therefore in clearing up the riddles of African periods and movements. Although there are at present no reliable conclusions or even hypotheses, one can judge of the possibilities of this method by a glance at studies like Flinders Petrie's "Africa in Egypt" (*Ancient Egypt*, 1916) or G. A. Wainwright's "Ancient Survivals in Modern Africa,"—*Bulletin de la Société de Géographie*, Cairo, 1919–20.) Stated more popularly, but with the intuition of the artist, we have the gist of such important art clues in the statement of Guillaume Apollinaire to the effect that African sculptures "attest through their characteristic style an incontestable relationship to Egyptian art, and contrary to current opinion, it seems rather more true that instead of being a derivative of Egyptian art, they, (or rather we would prefer to say, their prototypes) have on the contrary exerted on the artists of Egypt an influence which amply justifies the interest with which we today regard them."

But for the present all this is merest conjecture, though we do know that in many cases the tradition of style of these African sculptures is much older than the actual age of the exemplars we possess. Paul Guillaume, who has been the first to attempt period classification of this art, has conjecturally traced an Early Sudan art as far back as the Vth or VIth century, and has placed what seems to be its classic periods of expression as between the XIIth and the XIVth centuries for Gabon and Ivory Coast art, the XIth and XIIth for one phase of Sudan art, with another high period of the same between the XIVth and the XVth centuries. There are yet many problems to be worked out in this line—more definite period classification, more exact ethnic classification, especially with reference to the grouping of the arts of related tribes, and perhaps most important of all, the determination of their various genres.

A new movement in one of the arts in most cases communicates itself to the others, and after the influence in plastic art, the flare for things African began shortly to express itself in poetry and music. Roughly speaking, one may say that the French have been pioneers in the appreciation of the aesthetic values of African languages, their poetry, idiom, and rhythm. Of course the bulk of the scientific and purely philological interpretation is to the credit of German and English scholarship. There were several decades of this, before scholars like René Basset and Maurice Delafosse began to point out in addition the subtlety of the expressive technique of these languages. Attracted finally by the appeal of Negro plastic art to the studies of these men, poets like Guillaume Apollinaire and Blaise Cendrars brought the creative mind to the artistic re-expression of African idiom in poetic symbols and verse forms. So that what is a recognized school of modern French poetry professes the inspiration of African sources,—Apollinaire, Reverdy, Salmon, Fargue and others. The bible of this school has been Cendrars's *Anthologie nègre*, now in its sixth edition.

The starting point of an aesthetic interest in Negro musical idiom seems to have been H. A. Junod's work,—*Les chants et les contes des Ba-Rongas* (1897). From the double source of African folk song and the quite serious study of American Negro musical rhythms, many of the leading modernists of French music have derived much inspiration. Bérard, Satie, Poulenc, Auric, Honegger, are all in diverse ways affected, but the most explicit influence is upon the work of Darius Milhaud, who is an avowed propagandist of the possibilities of Negro musical idiom. The importance of the absorption of this material by all of the major forms of art, some of them relatively independently of the others, is striking and ought really be considered as a quite unanimous verdict of the creative mind upon the values, actual and potential, in this yet unexhausted reservoir of art material.

Since African art has had such a vitalizing influence in modern European painting, sculpture, poetry, and music, it becomes finally a natural and important question as to what artistic and cultural effect it can or will have upon the life of the American Negro. It does not necessarily follow that it should have any such influence. Today even in its own homeland it is a stagnant and decadent tradition, almost a lost art, certainly as far as technical mastery goes. The sensitive artistic minds among us have just begun to be attracted toward it, but with an intimate and ardent concern. Because of our Europeanized conventions, the key to the proper understanding and appreciation of it will in all probability first come from an appreciation of its influence upon contemporary French art, but we must believe that there still slumbers in the blood something which once stirred will react with peculiar emotional intensity toward it. If by nothing more mystical than the sense of being ethnically related, some of us will feel its influence at least as keenly as those who have already made it recognized and famous. Nothing is more galvanizing than the sense of a cultural past. This at least the intelligent presentation of African art will supply to us. Without other more direct influence even, a great cultural impetus would thus be given. But surely also in the struggle for a racial idiom of expression, there would come to some creative minds among us, from a closer knowledge of it, hints of a new technique, enlightening and interpretative revelations of the mysterious substrata of feeling under our characteristically intense emotionality, or at the very least, incentives toward fresher and bolder forms of artistic expression and a lessening of that timid imitativeness which at present hampers all but our very best artists.

22

HARLEM TYPES

Portraits by Winold Reiss

Here and elsewhere throughout this number, Winold Reiss presents us a graphic interpretation of Negro life, freshly conceived after its own patterns. Concretely in his portrait sketches, abstractly in his symbolic designs, he has aimed to portray the soul and spirit of a people. And by the simple but rare process of not setting up petty canons in the face of nature's own creative artistry Winold Reiss has achieved what amounts to a revealing discovery of the significance, human and artistic, of one of the great dialects of human physiognomy, of some of the little understood but powerful idioms of nature's speech. Harlem, or any Negro community, spreads a rich and novel palette for the serious artist. It needs but enlightenment of mind and eye to make its intriguing Problems and promising resources available for the stimulation and enrichment of American art.

Conventions stand doubly in the way of artistic portrayal of Negro folk; certain narrowly arbitrary conventions of physical beauty, and as well, that inevitable inscrutability of things seen but not understood. Caricature has put upon the countenance of the Negro the mask of the comic and the grotesque, whereas in deeper truth and comprehension, nature or experience have put there the stamp of the very opposite, the serious, the tragic, the wistful. At times, too, there is a quality of soul that can only be called brooding and mystical. Here they are to be seen as we know them to be in fact. While it is a revealing interpretation for all, for the Negro artist, still for the most part confronting timidly his own material, there is certainly a particular stimulus and inspiration in this redeeming vision. Through it in all likelihood must come his best development in the field of the pictorial arts, for his capacity to express beauty depends vitally upon the capacity to see it in his own life and to generate it out of his own experience.

Winold Reiss, son of Fritz Reiss, the landscape painter, pupil of Franz von Stuck of Munich, has become a master delineator of folk character by wide experience and definite specialization. With ever-ripening skill, he has studied and drawn the folk-types of Sweden, Holland, of the Black Forest and his own native Tyrol, and in America, the Blackfoot Indians, the Pueblo people, the Mexicans, and now, the American Negro. His art owes its peculiar success as much to the philosophy of his approach as to his technical skill. He is a folklorist of the brush and palette, seeking always the folk character back of the individual, the psychology behind the physiognomy. In design also he looks not merely for decorative elements, but for the pattern of the culture from which it sprang. Without loss of naturalistic accuracy and individuality, he somehow subtly expresses the type, and without being any the less human, captures the racial and local. What Gauguin and his followers have done for the Far East, and the work of Ufer and Blumenschein and the Taos school for the Pueblo and Indian, seems about to be done for the Negro and Africa: in short, painting, the most local of arts, in terms of its own limitations even, is achieving universality.

23

TO CERTAIN OF
OUR PHILISTINES

Of all the arts, painting is most bound by social ideas. And so, in spite of the fact that the Negro offers, in the line of the human subject, the most untouched of all the available fields of portraiture, and the most intriguing, if not indeed the most difficult of technical problems because of the variety of pigmentation and subtlety of values, serious painting in America has all but ignored him. As far as my knowledge and judgment go, the best that has been done by reputable American masters in this line is work like Winslow Homer's *Gulf Stream* or his *Sunday Morning in Virginia* and the "Pickaninny" of Robert Henri. All of this work is in the vein and mood of the traditional "Study in Brown"—the half-genre, half study-sketch in which so many a master hand has satisfied its artistic curiosity without exerting its full command either of interpretation or expression. Negro artists, themselves victims of the academy-tradition, have had the same attitude, and have shared the blindness of the Caucasian eye. Nothing above the level of a genre study or more penetrating than a Nordicized transcription has been done. Our Negro-American painter of the best academic technique, though in his youth and into his mature period a professed type—realist devoted to the portrayal of Jewish Biblical types, has never maturely touched the portrayal of the Negro subject.

Facts shouldn't be regretted: they should be explained. Social conventions stand closer guard over painting than most of the other arts. It is for that reason that a new school and idiom of Negro portraiture is particularly significant. As might be expected, it began in Europe, and because of the American situation has had to be imported. Portraiture is too controlled by social standards for it to be otherwise. But its really promising and vital development will be American, and, at least we hope, in large part the work of Negro artists. The latter cannot be predicted with as great confidence as the former—for the American Negro mind, in large sections, suffers as yet from repressions which make the idioms of the new school less welcome than the genre-peasant portraiture to which we have become accustomed, and almost as objectionable as the caricature conventions from which our "touchy" reactions have been developed. Too many of us still look to art to compensate the attitudes of prejudice, rather than merely, as is proper, to ignore them. And so, unfortunately for art, the struggle for social justice has put a pessimism upon a playing-up to Caucasian type-ideals, and created too prevalently a half-caste psychology that distorts all true artistic values with the irrelevant social values of "representative" and "unrepresentative," "favorable" and "unfavorable"—and threatens a truly racial art with the psychological bleach of "lily-whitism." This Philistinism cannot be tolerated. Already on the wane in our social life, after a baneful career, it cannot be allowed this last refuge in art. To rid ourselves of this damaging distortion of art values by color-line, we shall have to draw the culture-line sharply and without compromise, and challenge, without hope or expectation of quarter, our own Philistines.

Meanwhile, until we can find or create a considerable body of appreciative support for the new art, the painting of the Negro subject will have to rely upon the boldly iconoclastic stand of the convinced and purposefully original artist. The work of Winold Reiss, represented in the Harlem number of the *Survey Graphic,* and more elaborately in the exhibition of the original color pastels at the Harlem branch of the New York Public Library, was deliberately conceived and executed as a pathbreaker in the inevitable direction of a racially representative type of art. In idiom, technical treatment, and social angle, it was meant to represent a new approach, and constructively to break with the current tradition. In the first place, it breaks as European art has already done, with the limited genre treatment of the Negro subject. Next, it recognizes what is almost a law of development, that a new subject requires a new style, or at least a fresh technique. The Negro physiognomy must be freshly and objectively conceived on its own patterns if it ever is to be seriously and importantly interpreted. Art must discover and reveal the beauty which prejudice and caricature have obscured and overlaid. Finally it must reinforce our art with the dignity of race pride and the truly cultural judgment of art in terms of technical and not sentimental values.

Awed by a name, the Philistines will accept in a Holbein or a van Eyck or a Rubens qualities which they bray at in this logical application in contemporary work. All vital art discovers beauty, and opens our eyes to beauty that previously we could not see. And no great art will impose alien canons of beauty upon its subject matter. But it is harder to discover beauty in the familiar—and that may perhaps be why our own Negro artists may be the last to recognize the new potentialities, technical and aesthetic, of our racial types.

Modern art happily has already discovered them: Mr. Reiss is simply a pioneer in the application of this discovery to the American Negro subject. Already Max Slevogt, Pechstein, Elamic Stein, von Ruckteschell, Lucie Cousturier, Neville Lewis, F. C. Gadell, and most especially the Belgian, Auguste Mambour, have looked upon the African scene and the African countenance and discovered there a beauty that calls for a distinctive idiom both of color and of modeling. Their work should even now be the inspiration and the guideposts of a younger school of American Negro artists. Mambour's canvases at the International Art Show at Venice impressed me as standing out among the most preeminent work of the entire exhibition, not merely the Belgian section. Not that we would have all our young painters ultramodernists of this or that

European cult or coterie, but that the lesson of an original and bold approach is just that which must be learned to start any vital art development among us.

We have a right to expect and demand two things of the cultural expression of the Negro, that it should be vital and that it should be contemporary. This isn't the creed of being new-fangled for the sake of being so—let others who have more cause to be decadent and blasé than we, be eccentric and bizarre for the sheer need of new sensations and renewed vigor. But for another more vital and imperative reason the artistic expression of Negro life must break through the stereotypes and flout the conventions—in order that it may be truly expressive at all—and not a timid, conventional, imitative acceptance of the repressions that have been heaped upon us by both social persecution and by previous artistic misrepresentation. Artistically we shall have to fight harder for independence than for recognition, and this we cannot achieve either through slavish imitation, morbid conventionalism, or timid conservatism.

Let us take as a concrete instance, the much criticized Reiss drawing entitled *Two Public School Teachers*. It happens to be my particular choice among a group of thirty more or less divergently mannered sketches; and not for the reason that it is one of the most realistic but for the sheer poetry and intense symbolism back of it. It happens to represent my own profession, about which I may be presumed to know something. I am far from contending that there is an orthodox interpretation of any art—many minds, many reactions—but this at least is my reaction. I believe this drawing reflects in addition to good type portraiture of its sort, a professional ideal, that peculiar seriousness, that race redemption spirit, that professional earnestness and even sense of burden which I would be glad to think representative of both my profession and especially its racial aspects in spite of the fact that I am only too well aware of the invasion of our ranks in some few centers by the parasitic, society-loving "flapper." I do not need to appeal to race pride, but only to pride of profession to feel and hope that *Two Public School Teachers* in addition to being "good drawing" is finely representative. The young Negro artist, when he comes, will conquer this opposition in his own, unique way; but at any rate, here is the smoothest pebble we can find—ready for David's sling.

THE ART OF
AUGUSTE MAMBOUR

Our main story is about Auguste Mambour and his brilliant contribution to the art expression of Negro types—but the news has just come of the death of Lucie Cousturier. We must mix our bay with laurel and grieve as well as praise. Elsewhere in this issue, as is most appropriate, René Maran—friend, comrade, fellow-crusader, pays the fuller tribute of which he alone is capable. But it is impossible to speak of the artistic revolution which has invested Negro types with their own inherent beauty and given them their classic tradition and place in art without homage to Lucie Cousturier, whose pioneer vision was such a discovering genius in this field. Intimate human understanding, and a universalizing conviction of kinship without reservation or forced doctrinizing gave the author of *Des inconnus chez moi* and *Mes inconnus chez eux* a moral and spiritual penetration into African life as well as a technical and artistic insight. Madame Cousturier was one of the discoverers of the Negro soul—and painting but one of her avenues of approach. But, despite her fervent interest in literature portraiture, she recognized its supreme importance as a channel of revelation for the direct enlightenment of the masses. Certainly this seemed her philosophy of the new social vision for which she so ardently worked and hoped as she arose by a desperate effort of will from her couch that single afternoon when I was privileged to see her, to receive us, René Maran, some West Coast students from the Normal College at Bordeaux then on vacation in Paris, and myself. "To see, one must have vision—to understand, one must have more sympathy than curiosity, more understanding than sympathy, more love than understanding." With the peculiar hectic fever of her disease reinforcing the ardor of the adventuresome reformer and traveler, it was a memory-searing scene and experience. That was what made Madame Cousturier more than a technical experimenter, or a delver in the exotic: she loved and understood what others have merely used and exploited.

Auguste Mambour's grasp upon the Negro subject is deeper than that of a marvelous technical control, and to that extent he, with many others, is a debtor of one to whom he owes no direct artistic technical debt or influence. Mambour's control is technical, his chief significance is as the painter who of all the many now interested in the portrayal of African types has achieved the most distinctively original idiom of style and color, but back of that lies an intimate sympathy and understanding of his subject. Ed Jaloux in *La revue belge* singles out "the striking originality of a man who would go to study in the Congo when others were going to Rome." It is no middle-aged quest for fresh fields after the exhaustion of the traditional that brought Mambour to his subject. He is yet counted among the younger generation of Belgian painters. But deeper even than his own strong Walloon tradition, the types of his own Liégeois, is his hold upon African types and scenes. Six of the eight canvases selected to represent him at the International Art Exhibit at Venice were Negro in subject, and Sander Pierron in his review of the Belgian exhibit, also in *La revue belge,* credits the Congo with having given him his characteristic atmosphere,—a 'brutally contrasting, almost overwhelming color scheme, weighted down in spite of its brilliance with a heavy, quite tropical melancholy and fatalism.' The reproductions show the forceful stylization of Mambour,—a modelling of masses that is truly sculptural and particularly suited to the broad, massive features of the African countenance— surely mere line and contour treatment can never be the technique for the classical treatment of Negro types—but to this masterful handling of mass and light and shade in bold but subtle planes, there must in imagination be added the striking illumination of the rich browns and vivid greens of a tropical color scheme, and a sense of dripping sunlight from the high-lights of the canvas. It is not to be wondered at, then, that these were among the most startling works of the entire exhi-bition. Mambour has an originality of technique which he owes largely to his early interest, and his deep study, of things African.

It will take still another article to prove the quite invariable originality of the influence in European painting. The work of Bonnard, Georges Rouault, Kees van Dongen will especially have to be noticed, but Mambour alone even ought to be a rev-elation to the eye unaccustomed to seeing pure beauty in alien molds. For the Negro artist must consider work like this as basic, both from the point of view of technique as well as of interpretation. It is a principle of all art, that each body of ma-terial has, so to speak, its own inherent idioms, that are only to be derived through letting the material dictate its own ex-pression. In this sense, Keats's ideal that "Beauty is Truth, Truth, Beauty" becomes almost a dictum of technique. The spirit of African life is maintained, and not merely the external form and feature. That is what differentiates such work from the merely exotic renderings of so many colonial painters. Mambour is at home with his subject psychologically rather than just physically there. Where others rely on theatrical ef-fect, and draw an attention that they cannot sustain, Mam-bour's art has an arresting quality that converts curiosity into understanding. A single Mambour may eventually do more for the modern status of African and Negro material than scores of academic studies or reams of critical argument. For, after all, the justification in art is beauty,—nothing more or less, and here is beauty made immediately convincing.

The *Marche funèbre* has appropriately been acquired by the Colonial Museum at Tervuren. But Mambour is still largely in the private collections of his fellow countrymen, and at Liège. His significance however is international, and his influence should be made so. On sheer technical merit, he ranks with the leaders of his nation's art, Jakob Smits, Lucien Rion, Georges Latinis, and almost with the contemporary Belgian masters Laermans and Rik Wouters. M. G. D. Perier, that zealous exponent of the Negro tradition in modern colonial art, has used Mambour almost as effectively as text as he has the indigenous native art itself. Belgian criticism is thus almost as actively enlightened in the interest of this important phase of modern art development as France, with its Madame Cousturier, its Guillaume Janneau, and its Paul Guillaume. As soon as reproductions are available, it will be interesting to supplement these Mambour illustrations with some of the other material that documents this material as part of a vital art movement rather than shows them as isolated instances of an ephemeral fad. The influence goes beyond the narrow confines of the original subject matter, as was the case also with the influence of the native African art. Indeed in both phases, it has been an influence full of the greatest subtleties—things primitive have had far from a primitive influence and effect in modern art. It was Madame Cousturier who said in a symposium upon the value of African art to European art in *Le bulletin de la vie artistique*,—"When our art discovers the real values of Negro art, and our museums open their doors to it, they will find not merely a supplementing addition but will discover their basic common factor." And though Auguste Mambour is the greater artist, it honors his art to be in the context of such ideals of human universality.

25

A COLLECTION OF
CONGO ART

Intermittently since the de Zayas exhibition of 1916, African art has been called to our attention both as an art object and as an art influence—in ways more calculated, however, to impress us with its importance than its inner significance. For our approach, even in the presence of the primitive originals, has been for the most part secondary, since Negro art has come to our notice principally as an ingredient of contemporary European modernism, and thus has been seen and admired more in the mirror of its influence than valued and understood in the reality of its own intrinsic beauty. To possess African art permanently and not merely as a passing vogue, we shall have to go beyond such reflected values and their exotic appeal and study it in its own context, link it up vitally with its own cultural background, and learn to appreciate it as an organic body of art.

Toward this, the prime prerequisite is the availability of the original material in collections sufficiently extensive to present a representative unit yet selective enough to make an exclusive appeal as art. This is a combination that is unfortunately rare—rarest of all in America—for there are few collections of African art that do not sacrifice either the scientific interest to the artistic or the artistic to the scientific. In the one case, cultural representativeness is lost in the attempt to cull out the objects of superior beauty and workmanship, with the result that we get a mere exotic hodgepodge of uncorrelated samples, widely separated in type, period, and provenance. In the other, in the search for museum completeness, with no rigid principle of artistic selection, this art is allowed to lapse back to the dead level of the ethnographic curiosity, from the dry dust of which the modernists resurrected some of its buried beauty.

The Blondiau collection, now brought to America permanently under the auspices of *Theatre Arts*, and at present on exhibition at the galleries of the New Art Circle in New York, is notable for combining the artistic and the scientific approach to African art. It is a collection drawn from the extensive and varied region of the Belgian Congo, selected over a period of twenty-five years on a rather rigid standard of line workmanship, yet sufficiently inclusive as to the various types and intensive as to regional representativeness to give a really organic impression of one of the great schools of primitive Negro art. Its acquisition is therefore a valuable supplementation of our sources for the study and appreciation of this art; for even with the Ward collection of the Smithsonian in Washington, the Barnes Foundation collection at Merion, the University of Pennsylvania Museum collection, and those in New York at the Brooklyn Museum and the Museum of Natural History, our resources are very meagre in comparison with the great special collections of France, Germany, England, and Belgium. And of all these, Belgium, with its concentration on so rich a province as the Congo, and its palatial special government museum of the Congo at Tervuren, has almost uniquely these important combined qualities of scientific completeness and artistic excellence, which on a much smaller scale this distinctive private Belgian collection typically reflects.

The art of the Congo region, despite the conceded craftsmanship of the work of the Bushongo, has yet to come into its proper due of recognition and esteem. In contrast with the art of the coastal regions, which has been seen and appraised in terms of spectacularly beautiful specimens of single outstanding types, Congo art has usually been seen only in its poorer and more rustic examples. Consequently the current reputation of Benin, Ivory Coast, and Guinea Coast art is much higher.

Further, the obvious craft basis of Congo art has led us to judge most of it under what is for us the subordinate category of applied art. In this we fail to see how irrelevant such a distinction is for a culture where fine and decorative art have never been separated out, and where things can be superlatively beautiful and objects of utility at the same time. Indeed it is on this point that African art offers our art its greatest challenge and possible inspiration, as an art that never has been divorced from the vital context of everyday life. Its vindication of one of the soundest and most basic of aesthetic principles—beauty in use—and its distinction in a field where we usually encounter and tolerate the commonplace, entitle it to the most serious consideration and study apart from all its other values, and nowhere do we find more of this vital organic quality than in the arts and crafts of the Congo. Here we have the most intact sample of the old characteristic African culture, work in all possible art media and art forms—large and small-scale carving in ivory, horn, and wood, forged and decorated work in iron and other metals, metal inlay work, carved and appliqué masks, pottery, woven and decorated textiles, all existing side by side, each in a relatively high state of artistic development.

The additional fact that this level of development has been maintained over the span of three or four centuries at the least, with stability of types and patterns and without perceptible signs of decadence until the recent breakup of the indigenous culture under European influences, gives convincing evidence of a tradition of exceptional richness and vigor. Torday, the Belgian explorer, reports that among the artistic tribes not only has every design motif its proper name and association, but also every pattern variant, that there is such a diffusion of art appreciation that the average child is taught to draw the patterns in the sand endlessly, that there is a definite tradition of the introduction of particular crafts in certain dynasties, and that these traditions are so settled that the making of raffia cloth, after three hundred years of use, is still regarded as relatively an innovation.

Incontestably, then, we have here one of the great parent

branches of African art, which further comparative study may prove to be one of the main sources, if not the great ancestral reservoir. Many other regions have in single lines more outstanding and distinctive art, but there is no denying Herbert Ward's original impression that the Congo epitomizes Africa, that its culture is one of the oldest and most typical, and that nowhere else do we find an equivalent or more characteristic flowering of the several handicrafts.

The Blondiau-Theatre Arts collection represents all important aspects of Congo art, and though particularly rich in Bakuba and Baluba work—the most developed of the Bushongo schools—includes numerous fine examples of Bangongo, Bayaka, Kasai, Bena Lulua, and Azandé specimens, and fine bits of Basonge pottery. Thus both the art of the dominant Bantu and of the subjugated non-Bantu stocks are represented. In several types such as the Bakuba figure cups, the Bushongo decorative bowls and cups, and Azandé lutes and other musical instruments there are interesting series, displaying almost every known variation of type.

Indeed it is from the comparison of such series rather than from the examination of single exceptional specimens that one gets the most convincing proof of a really great art tradition. From the minute variation in the use of highly stereotyped patterns, by the skillful balance between originality and tradition, in the clever transposition of design motifs from one medium to another with scrupulous regard for the limitations and peculiar appropriateness of the material, one can gauge the high artistry of these craftsmen. For instance, a pattern that originated as a woven under-and-over raffia design will be stippled dot and dash on metal, surface-grooved on pottery, surface raised and conventionally broken short at the crossovers in wood, and in ivory so rigidly stylized as to be scarcely recognizable at first glance. Generations of familiarity with the materials have bred an instinctive feeling for the right thing. None of that naturalistic imitation in alien materials, which a contemporary critic satirizes as "the artiness of withered oak leaves rendered in wrought iron," that is of such painful frequency in our own art; but instead almost always a logical and clean adjustment of motive, design, and material. Always too, a quite ingenious observance of surface spacing, gradation of finish to natural texture, and the like—points of artistic value to us so abstract, but to the African artist, so immediate and obvious. Take as an example the group of carved buffalo drinking horns, where the natural curvatures have been arbitrarily set, and observe the striking unity of the added patterns with both surface curvature and outline, and then note in addition, as with almost every bit of African carving, the obvious working out of effective design from every possible visual approach to the object.

But most persons are disposed to concede to African art its characteristic virtuosity of surface ornament and design. That is incontestable. But in the larger plastic technique, and the recognition of its values, there is often hesitancy, especially for Congo works. The high forms of Bushongo art seem to be the sculptural heads combined with ornamental forms, the fetish statuettes, and the semi-portraitistic figurines that are supposed to have reached their artistic acme in the eighteenth century. The two head goblets shown on this page and the next are admittedly exceptional for this or any other general collection. But they show power in the handling of sculptural mass and surface quite of the highest order. Particularly surprising in view of prevalent conceptions, is the subtle, placid tone and smooth flow of surface, and the austere economy of decorative elements. One of the head cups might pass as early Buddhist in its quality of austerity and mystic restraint. Clearly they belong to a seasoned and classic tradition, and could stand almost without commentary as sufficient contradiction of a recent dictum about Congo art that "the vast majority of objects produced here are unimpressive plastically, tending either to extreme crudity of workmanship, to unimaginative naturalism, or to overcrowding with superficial decoration." It is just the exact opposites of these that constitute the special sophisticated strength and conscious power of these particular specimens. Really they exemplify, along with a number of ceremonial objects, scepters, staffs of office and other insignia, jewel boxes and articles of fine personal adornment, an apparent aristocratic strain in Congo art, with a characteristic refinement and subtlety that marks it, for all the diversity of the objects themselves, as a distinct tradition in itself—a proud art of the ruling and conquering caste.

At the courts of the Bushongo chiefs special artisans are reserved for the chiefs, and the wood-carvers are given precedence over all other craftsmen. This same tradition works itself out in the superfine, almost delicate elaborateness of the ceremonial knives and swords, of which no finer examples exist in all Africa than the Bushongo types.

In marked contrast to this, we have two other quite distinct styles in Congo art, running consistently through the characteristic tribal differences, a bizarre and grotesque strain and another, crudely rustic and realistic. The former as a style dominates most of the strictly religious objects,—the fetish images, the dance and ceremonial masks, and particularly the miniature ivory masks and talismans. These latter, particularly the small circumcision masks of ivory and the body fetishes, are of exquisite workmanship, linking up with the sophisticated court style, but the large masks are for the most part broad and powerful in treatment, and achieve their effect more through emotional than plastic appeal. The Congo seems more likely to become famous for the great variety than for the beauty of its masks; only a few are comparable in stunning originality and artistic effect to those of the Fang, Mpongwe, Gabon, and Ivory Coast tribes. The plain mask reproduced is rather exceptional in its stark beauty. There are several fine examples of composite masks with elaborate appliqué decoration in beads, cowrie shells, and other contrasted ornamentation,—principally of the familiar Kasai, Bapende, and Baluba types, but with three rare specimens of unusual Bayaka and Bakette forms.

The Congo masks are in the main more grotesque than beautiful in form, but this is often compensated by unusual decorative values in color and surface contrasts. Strangely enough the accessory articles and accoutrements of the dramatic and ritual ceremonies in which they are used seem to be of greater artistic distinction and beauty. Anklets, collars, rings, pendants, rattles, gongs, whistles, divining-blocks, drums, and other musical instruments are so finely conceived and executed that their sheer beauty and abstract decorative appeal lift them quite out of the class of the minor arts. From our point of view they seem almost too fine for practical purposes, yet they are structurally sound and utilize their most essential lines and features as the path of their artistic appeal. Take for example, the drum, lute, and double dance-gong in the collection; they exceed in beauty almost anything of their kind. In bewilderment one wonders why such beauty in accessories with such grotesque starkness and crudity in the masks and costume ensemble. The only explanation plausible is that symbolic requirements and the religious and ceremonial necessity for evoking terror and awe dictate the latter, but that in subordinate details the inhibited instinct for pure beauty seizes upon its only opportunity for free play.

Finally, we come to those crude, heavy, squat, and sensuous things which in the popular mind typify the Congo exclusively. As a matter of fact, characteristic as they are, they represent but one strand in Congo art, a rustic and somewhat peasant strain in the culture. These things smack of the jungle, and reflect its crude, primitive realities. And while they doubtless have in them the special idioms of some of the less culturally developed stocks, they know no tribal barriers and exist side by side with the refined and sophisticated work we have already noticed. Here again the best explanation is that of a special controlling tradition, dictating the peculiar style. We find a valuable clue in the fact that this technique of rough bold outline and unfinished masses focuses in particular classes of objects,—the totemic fetishes, the funerary statuettes, and the nail and fertility fetishes with their direct practical appeal to sympathetic magic. Can it be that the rationale of the style is after all superstitiously motivated, and that the salient symbolism expressed at the expense of artistic balance and restraint is sensed as making the objects more potent and effective? One cannot be certain of this, of course, until fuller studies of the cultural background of African art become available. Certain it is, however, that many things in this style could have been rendered more expertly, and even as it is, some of them achieve absolute beauty in spite of the first impression which they give of crudity and weirdness.

Oddly enough it is this most primitive strain in the Congo art which is its weakest and least stable tradition. It is the first to yield to the infiltration of European idioms, as is shown by the many examples of this style registering in ludicrous combinations the superimposing of European hats, boots, and whatnot upon African fundamentals. A few such impossibles have their place in any representative collection, but it is a tragedy to see the easy corruption and degeneracy of the most indigenous and possibly one of the earliest of the African styles. And yet perhaps it is not so certain that this cruder style is the earliest and most basic. That is merely a European assumption. The crude styles may just as well be themselves degenerated strains, or more possibly even, with the crisscrossings of endless tribal warfare, parallel ethnic strands of other tribal traditions, and not the basis from which the fine tradition built itself up.

What is quite certain both by internal and external evidence is that Bushongo and other varieties of African art reached a classic stage of expression very early indeed, and then remained stable over many generations. Certain types have persisted for centuries. Dated both by the registration of early European influences and by the dynastic dates of the Bantu chronicles,—those of the Bushongo record a succession of a hundred and twenty–odd chieftains—even the acme of Congo art must be placed back from three to six hundred years. Even when the particular pieces are comparatively recent, since with a stereotyped art like this it is a matter of copying fresh examples over and over, the type forms are exceedingly ancient.

The most important issue about African art is then not that of the dating of the piece itself, but of the dating of the type; it is only in a rapidly evolving culture like ours that copies become so swiftly deteriorations of their originals and lower in creative force. It is possible then in the case of African art to determine roughly the period of the type when it is impossible to determine the age of the particular example, and what is most to be desired in a collection is that it should contain representative examples of standard and classic forms.

We must remember that the enthusiasts of the generation of Matisse who discovered African art and incorporated it into their new aesthetic were by no means in a position to be connoisseurs of African art. To the artistically wise the striking hints of a few examples were sufficient, and the basic characteristics of the African sculpture could be gotten from relatively poor specimens. They but introduced us to its strange values and generalized upon its idioms. But now that the first phase of the technical absorption of the principles of African art has taken place, and the tradition has grown more subtle and complicated in the developments of modern Cubism, Expressionism, and *Surrealisme*, we are thrown back on a more intensive study of African art in its first principles. We need to do more than intuit its values and feel its inspiration, we must understand it, and that sufficiently to know how it came to have such an influence.

Modern art in taking up African art into its own substance then has given it a new lease of life, and made it doubly necessary to understand it. Indeed just as the Renaissance rejuvenated and universalized classical antiquity, modernism has permanently revitalized these and all other primitives. It becomes necessary today to understand the arts formerly alien and exotic to our cultural tradition in thoroughness of historical and theoretical grasp, because they are now organically correlated with our own tradition. Seeking only for a Northwest Passage in style, the modernists have opened up whole new continental areas of art, and have made it necessary and possible to take the entire range of human art upon the broad basis of its universal factors and underlying common principles.

With this significant instance of the perennial vitality of beauty, how absurd it is to pronounce any art officially dead or lost. African art is, to be sure, no longer a novelty—its first influences and the faddist flare of interest which it excited have already passed—but neither is it yet fully understood nor have we exhausted its full potentialities. There is one particularly intriguing possibility of further influence which is only beginning to open up, and which gives particular bearing and point to the movement for bringing African art to fuller attention and understanding in America. The importation of representative collections will have a vital effect on our own art apart even from the general modernist trend if, as may reasonably be expected, African art should once more event a new influence in quickening the artistic development of the American Negro. With the particular appeal of a rediscovered race heritage, it cannot fail to stimulate a generation of artists who are already in the swing of a program to express their racial life and experience in intimate and original ways. Strangely enough until now the artistic development of the American Negro, significant as it has been in music and poetry, has lagged in the field of the plastic and decorative arts, the very forte of his original ancestry. One can of course think of no stronger or more promising stimulus than this which has already influenced contemporary art so notably, but which would have in this particular field of influence such strong additional appeals of intimate force and pull. It is one of the prime motives back of the project that brings the Blondiau-Theatre Arts collection to us, that through this channel especially, African art should be made a vital influence for the creation of fresh sources of beauty in America.

26

THE AMERICAN NEGRO
AS ARTIST

Between Africa and America the Negro, artistically speaking, has practically reversed himself. In his homeland, his dominant arts were the decorative and the craft arts—sculpture, metalworking, weaving—and so the characteristic African artistic virtuosities are decoration and design. But in America, the interpretive, emotional arts have been the Negro's chief forte, because his chief artistic expression has been in music, the dance, and folk poetry. One single strand alone has connected the ancestral and the new-world art—the age-old virtuosity in dance and pantomime. Except for this, the American Negro as an artist is completely different from his African prototype.

Why should this be? There is a historical reason. Slavery not only transplanted the Negro, it cut him off sharply from his cultural roots and his ancestral heritage, and reduced him to cultural zero by taking away his patterns and substituting the crudest body labor with only the crudest tools. Thus slavery severed the trunk-nerve of the Negro's primitive skill and robbed him of his great ancestral gift of manual dexterity. Alexandre Jacovleff, the Russian artist whose drawings of African types are to date unsurpassed, has well said of Africa—"A continent of beautiful bodies, but above all of beautiful hands." This fact is really a symbol: with virtuosity of muscle has gone a coordination resulting in great beauty. But the hardships of cotton and rice-field labor, the crudities of the hoe, the axe, and the plow, reduced the typical Negro hand to a gnarled stump, incapable of fine craftsmanship even if materials, patterns, and incentives had been available.

In a compensatory way the artistic urges of the American Negro flowed toward the only channels left open—those of song, movement, and speech, and the body itself became the Negro's prime and only artistic instrument. Greatest of all came the development of the irrepressible art of the voice, which is today the Negro's greatest single artistic asset. Thus the history of generations is back of the present lopsidedness in the Negro's art development, and the basis of his handicap in the graphic, pictorial, and decorative arts explains, as well, his proficiency in the emotional arts. No comment on the contemporary advance of the Negro in the plastic and pictorial arts would be sound without this historical perspective. For in his latest developments in formal fine art, the Negro artist is really trying to recapture ancestral gifts and reinstate lost arts and skill.

Considering this, the early advent of American Negro artists in painting and sculpture was all the more remarkable. As might be expected, however, this early art was of a purely imitative type, but not without technical merit. The two pioneer instances were Edward M. Bannister of Providence, Rhode Island, a landscapist of considerable talent, and founder, oddly enough, of the Providence Art Club; and Edmonia Lewis, our first sculptor, who studied in Rome in the early seventies and executed many very acceptable portrait busts in the current pseudo-classic style. And another pioneer instance is R. S. Duncanson, of Cincinnati, figure painter, landscapist, and historical painter, who achieved considerable recognition between 1863 and 1866 in London and Glasgow. It is characteristic of this period, 1860 to 1890, that the Negro artists were isolated and exceptional individuals, imitative though, judged by contemporary American standards, not mediocre and almost entirely lacking in race consciousness. They were artists primarily and were incidentally Negroes.

The next generation also lived and worked as individuals, but despite their academic connections and ideals, with a sentimental shadow of race hanging over them. The outstanding

talents that matured during this period (1895–1915) were
Henry O. Tanner, William Edouard Scott, painters; and Meta
Warrick Fuller and May Howard Jackson, sculptors. Of these,
of course, Mr. Tanner is by far the best known and recognized. However varied their talents as artists of this transitional generation, they have much in common. All of them
products of the best American academies, their talents were
forced into the channels of academic cosmopolitanism not
merely by the general trend of their time, but also by the pressure and restrictions of racial prejudice. So they not only matured under French instruction and influence—three of them
were products of Julian's Academy—but have received their
earliest and widest recognition abroad. Instead of being the
challenging influence and special interest that it is for the
Negro artist of today, race, by reason of circumstances beyond
their control, was for them a ghetto of isolation and neglect
from which they must escape if they were to gain artistic freedom and recognition. And so, except for occasional sentimental gestures of loyalty, they avoided it as a motive or theme in
their art.

Because of her more completely American experience, May
Howard Jackson, the sculptress, was first to break away from
academic cosmopolitanism to frank and deliberate racialism.
She was followed about 1907 (largely because of her commission to do commemorative Negro historical reliefs for the
Jamestown Exposition) by Mrs. Fuller, who has continued
since to work in the double vein of her earlier Rodinesque style
and a very stylized idealization of Negro types, more exotic
and Egyptian than realistically racial. The career of Mr. Tanner, professionally successful as it has been, is in this respect
at least typical of the tragedy of this generation of Negro artists. Beginning under the realistic influence of his American
teacher, Thomas Eakins, Tanner's early work showed marked
interest and skill in painting Negro and Norman and, later,
Jewish peasant types. It was the heyday of the regional school
and but for his exile and the resentment of race as an imposed
limitation, Tanner's undoubted technical genius might have
added a significant chapter to the Jules Breton, Jozef Israëls

school of the half-romantic, half-realistic glorification of peasant life. Instead Tanner's work became more and more academic in treatment and cosmopolitan in theme; while for a
treatment of Negro types in the style of this period we have to
rely on sporadic canvases by white American painters like
Winslow Homer, Wayman Adams, Robert Henri.

But this generation, Tanner especially, did have, after all, a
constructive influence upon the American Negro artist though
not in the direction of the development of a special province of
Negro art. They were inspiring examples to the younger generation and convincing evidence to a skeptical public opinion
of the technical competence and artistic capacity of the Negro
artist when given the opportunity of contact with the best traditions and academic training. This is taken for granted now,
but largely as a result of their pioneer effort and attainment.

But the younger generation of Negro artists since 1915 have
a new social background and another art creed. For the most
part, the goal of the Negro artist today projects an art that
aims to express the race spirit and background as well as the
individual skill and temperament of the artist. Not that all
contemporary Negro artists are conscious racialists—far from
it. But they all benefit, whether they choose to be racially expressive or not, from the new freedom and dignity that Negro
life and materials have attained in the world of contemporary
art. And, as might be expected, with the removal of the cultural stigma and burdensome artistic onus of the past, Negro
artists are showing an increasing tendency toward their own
racial milieu as a special province and in their general work
are reflecting more racially distinctive notes and overtones. In
1920, the One Hundred and Thirty-Fifth Street Branch, in
Harlem, of the New York Public Library began special exhibits of the work of Negro artists, which, having continued to
date, have given showing to over a hundred young artists. In
1927, public-spirited citizens of Chicago pioneered with a special "Negro in Art Week" series of talks and exhibitions of the
work of Negro artists, a program that has been repeated at
centers as far south as Atlanta and Nashville, as far north as
Boston and Rochester, and as far west as San Diego and Los

Angeles. Most influential of all, the Harmon Foundation has, by a five-year series of prize awards for Negro artists, with an annual New York show and extensive traveling exhibition of a considerable section of the same throughout the country, not only stimulated a new public interest in the Negro artist, but incubated more young talent in these last five years than came to maturity in the last twenty. As has been aptly said, "The public consciousness of Negro art has grown to be nationwide and practically worldwide in the last decade."

And so, at present, the Negro artist confronts an interested public, and that public faces an interesting array of productive talent. Without undue violence to individualities, these contemporary Negro artists may be grouped in three schools or general trends: the Traditionalists, the Modernists, and the Africanists, or Neo-Primitives, with the latter carrying the burden of the campaign for a so-called "Negro Art." Even among the traditionalists, there is considerable of the racial emphasis in subject matter, but without the complementary adoption of any special stylistic idioms, directly racial or indirectly primitive. But conservatism on this point seems doomed, since the young Negro artist has a double chance of being influenced by Negro idioms, if not as a deliberate racialist or conscious "Africanist," then at least at secondhand through the reflected influence of Negro idioms on general modernist style.

Noteworthy among the traditionalists are William Edouard Scott, of Indianapolis, portrait and mural painter; William Farrow, of Chicago, landscapist and etcher; Laura Wheeler Waring, of Philadelphia, landscapist and type-portraitist of considerable distinction; Palmer Hayden, of New York and Paris, marine painter of talent; Albert A. Smith, of New York; and the late Edwin A. Harleston, of Charleston, South Carolina, whose genre studies of Southern Negro peasant types have competently filled an important niche in Negro painting. His prize canvases of *The Bible Student* and *The Old Servant* are permanent documents by reason of their double artistic and social significance, and it is much to be regretted that his talent expired just at the point of maturity and recognition.

The work of four women sculptors, Meta Warrick Fuller, May Howard Jackson, Elizabeth Prophet, and Augusta Savage, despite individual variation in competence and style, would all fall in the conservative category, with a common attitude of heavily idealized and sentimentalized portrayal of racial types and character.

It is this saccharine, romantic quality that has given the younger modernists their foil; they aim at hard realism and verge at times on the grotesque and the satirical. The *Old Snuff Dipper* of Archibald Motley, or the *Self-Portrait* of Lillian Dorsey, or *Meditation* of Malvin Gray Johnson shows these new notes boldly and unmistakably. In this attitude, they have reinforcement from their young modernist contemporaries, but it represents a peculiar psychological reaction and achievement when a persecuted group breaks through the vicious circle of self-pity or compensatory idealization and achieves objectivity. Apart from the artistic merit of the work—which is considerable—the social significance of the recent canvases of William H. Johnson tells an interesting story. Born in Florence, South Carolina, this dock-working night-school student of the National Academy of Design, protégé of Charles Hawthorne and George Luks, disciple of French ultramodernism with strong influences of Rouault and Soutine, came back from four years in Europe to paint in his hometown. The result is a series of landscapes and portrait studies that reek with irony and satire and that probably will not get local appreciation till long after he has put his birthplace on the artistic map. His ironic picture of the town hotel paints the decadence of the old regime, and his quizzical portrait study of *Sonny*, a Negro lad with all the dilemma of the South written in his features, is a thing to ponder over, if one believes that art has anything important to say about life.

The other two modernists of note and promise are Hale Woodruff, of Indianapolis, now painting in France; and James Lesesne Wells, of New York, this year's Harmon award winner. Mr. Woodruff paints landscapes of originality, and his color has a warm beauty that, in spite of abstract formalism, seems characteristically racial. Mr. Wells, on the other hand, has a pronounced mystical lean, which makes his ultramodern style all the more unusual and attractive. Some of his work has recently been acquired by the Phillips Memorial Gallery, and in terms of accomplishment and promise, Mr. Wells must be rated as one of the most promising of the younger Negro artists.

His work in design and decorative black-and-white media is strong and original. But, as a black-and-white artist, Mr. Wells is a conscious "Africanist." That is, he goes directly to African motives and principles of design for his inspiration. Another of the younger decorative painters, Aaron Douglas, does also; in fact, he has been doing so since 1925 and therefore deserves to be called the pioneer of the African Style among the American Negro artists. His book illustrations have really set a vogue for this style, and his mural decorations for Club Ebony, New York, the Sherman Hotel, Chicago, and the symbolic murals of the Fisk University Library are things of fine originality. It is in sculpture, though, that the neo-primitivism of an attempted Negro style has to date most clearly expressed itself; in fact it is my opinion that sculpture will lead the way in this direction. So the work of our two younger sculptors, Richmond Barthé and Sargent Johnson, takes on more than individual significance. Both are consciously racial, with no tendency to sentimentalize or over-idealize, and their style emphasizes the primitive. Barthé's *West Indian Girl* has a proud, barbaric beauty that matches Claude McKay's glorification of the primitive in the lines:

> To me she seemed a proudly swaying palm Grown lovelier for passing through a storm.

Sargent Johnson's bust *Chester* is particularly striking; it has the qualities of the African antique and recalls an old Baoulé mask. It is a long stretch from an isolated Negro sculptor living and working in California to the classic antiques of bygone Africa, but here it is in this captivating, naïve bust for even the untutored eye to see.

Single instances do not make a style, nor can propaganda

re-create lost folk arts, but it is significant that directly in proportion as the younger Negro talent leaves the academic and
imitative vein, it becomes stronger; and that the more particu-
laristic and racial it becomes, the wider and more spontaneous
is its appeal. And so, the immediate future seems to be with
the racialists, both by virtue of their talent and their creed.

However, a truly representative racial style and school of art
are as yet only in the making. Reviewing a recent exhibit of
the work of Negro artists, Cyril Kay-Scott comments on its
imitative and derivative character, saying "it is almost purely
Parisian and New York art done by Negroes, with almost
nothing of the simplicity and directness of folk art, and little
assimilation or use of the African primitive art, which has
so profoundly affected the great European modernists." Mr.
Scott is right in wishing that some American Negro artists
would delve "into the marvelous and beautiful background
which is their racial heritage." He is very probably right in
thinking that should they do so, "they could make to their age
a contribution that would be unique" and which would "sur-
pass the enthusiastic and conscientious efforts of even the great
men of our time who have made such splendid use of the inspiration of Negro art."

But this provocative criticism by the director of the Denver
Museum of Art overlooks one explanatory and extenuating
fact: the young American Negro artist must evolve a racial
style gradually and naturally. A sophisticated or forced exoticism would be as ridiculous at the one extreme as the all-too-
prevalent servile imitation is at the other. Moreover, most
American Negro artists have not yet been exposed to the influence of African art. Their European contemporaries have
been, and likewise the European-trained American artist. As
recently as 1927, the first attempt was made to bring the Negro
artist and the lay public in direct contact with African art.
After an exhibition of the Blondiau-Theatre Arts Collection of
sculpture and metal work from the Belgian Congo, part of this
collection was purchased as the permanent and traveling collection of the Harlem Museum of African Art, organized at
that time, and has since been housed in the exhibition rooms

of the One Hundred and Thirty-Fifth Street Branch of the New York Public Library. The project was organized to preserve and interpret the ancestral arts and crafts of the African Negro, and to make them effective as fresh inspiration for Negro art expression and culture in America. Though yet so recent and meager a contact, the work of several contemporary Negro artists has begun to reflect African influences. There are marked traces in the motives and design structure of the work of Aaron Douglas; reflected idioms—through European exposure—in the work of William H. Johnson and Hale Woodruff; and definite suggestions, as we have already noticed, in the sculptures of Richmond Barthé and Sargent Johnson.

These are good omens for the development of a distinctively racial school of American Negro art. Naturally not all of our artists will confine their talents to race subjects or even to a racial style. However, the constructive lessons of African art are among the soundest and most needed of art creeds today. They offset with equal force the banalities of sterile, imitative classicism and the empty superficialities of literal realism. They emphasize intellectually significant form, abstract design, formal simplicity, restrained dignity, and the unsentimental approach to the emotions. And more important still, since Africa's art creed is beauty in use, they call for an art vitally rooted in the crafts, uncontaminated with the blight of the machine, and soundly integrated with life.

Surely we should expect the liberating example of such an aesthetic to exert as marked an influence on the work of the contemporary Negro artist as it has already exerted on leading modernists like Picasso, Modigliani, Matisse, Epstein, Lipchitz, Brâncuşi, and others. Indeed we may expect even more with a group of artists becoming conscious of a historical and racial bond between themselves and African art. For them, rather than just a liberating idiom or an exotic fad, African art should act with all the force of a rediscovered folk art, and give clues for the repression of a half-submerged race soul. The younger generation seem to have accepted this challenge to recapture this heritage of creative originality and this former mastery of plastic form and decorative design and are attempting to carry them to distinctive new achievement in a vital and racially expressive art. One of the advances evident in a comparison of the five successful annual shows of the works of Negro artists, sponsored by the Harmon Foundation, along with marked improvement in the average technical quality, has been the steadily increasing emphasis upon racial themes and types in the work submitted. Thus the best available gauge records not only a new vitality and maturity among American Negro artists, but a pronounced trend toward racialism in both style and subject. In this downfall of classic models and Caucasian idols, one may see the passing of the childhood period of American Negro art, and with the growing maturity of the young Negro artist, the advent of a representatively racial school of expression, and an important new contribution, therefore, to the whole body of American art.

27

EXCERPT FROM *NEGRO ART: PAST AND PRESENT*

The Negro as Artist.—When a few American Negroes, less than three generations ago, began to paint and model and aspire to be "artists," it was not only thought strange and unusually ambitious, but most people, even they themselves, thought it was the Negro's first attempt at art. Art in fact, in those days was thought to be the last word in culture; the topmost rung of the ladder of civilization. For the Negro, it was thought to be a little presumptuous, like beginning with poetry instead of a "blue-back speller." The Western world had yet to learn, to its amazement, that primitive civilization not only had its artists but had produced a great art, and that of the many types of primitive art now known but then yet to be discovered, that of the Negro in Africa was by all odds the greatest and the most sophisticated. Yes,—believe it or not, the most sophisticated; at least it is the most sophisticated modern artists and critics of our present generation who say so. And even should they be wrong as to this quality of African art, the fact still remains that there is an artistic tradition and skill in all the major craft arts running back for generations and even centuries, among the principal African tribes, particularly those of the West Coast and Equatorial Africa from which Afro-Americans have descended. These arts are wood and metal sculpture, metal forging, wood carving, ivory and bone carving, weaving, pottery, skillful surface decoration in line and color of all these crafts, in fact everything in the category of the European fine arts except easel painting on canvas, marble sculpture, and engraving and etching, and even here the technique of the two latter is represented in the surface carving of much African art. So we must entitle our booklet: *Negro Art: Past and Present*. The pioneer American Negro artists were, really, unbeknown to themselves, starting the Negro's second career in art and unconsciously trying to recapture a lost artistic heritage.

How the Heritage was Lost.—The reader will naturally ask: Why should this be? How was this heritage lost? There is one great historical reason; incidentally one that, tragically enough, explains much about the Negro. Slavery is the answer. Slavery not only physically transplanted the Negro, it cut him off sharply from his cultural roots, and by taking away his languages, abruptly changing his habits, putting him in the context of a strangely different civilization, reduced him, so to speak, to cultural zero. And no matter how divided one may be as to the relative values of human civilizations, no one can intelligently think that the African stood, after centuries of living and a long intertribal history, at cultural zero. One of the high points in African civilization, like all primitive cultures, was dexterity of hand and foot and that coordination of eye and muscle which constitutes physical skill. This expressed itself in elaborate and fine native crafts, the traditions of which had been built up on generations of trial and error experience. These patterns were lost in the nakedness and horror of the slave-ship, where families, castes, tribes were ruthlessly scrambled. When subsequently slavery substituted the crudest body labor with only the crudest tools, it finally severed this bruised trunk nerve of the Negro's technical skill and manual dexterity. Alexandre Jacovleff, the Russian artist whose drawings of African types are today unsurpassed, has well said of Africa: "It is a continent of beautiful bodies, but above all, of beautiful hands." This fact is really a symbol: life in Africa required a skill of hand and foot and almost perfect coordination of nerve and muscle. And as with all nature peoples, this skill that could throw a weapon accurately and weave or tie with accuracy brought with it an art that could carve, scrape, or trace to a nicety. Nature had molded out of the primitive artisan a primitive artist.

We will never know and cannot estimate how much technical African skill was blotted out in America. The hardships of cotton and rice-field labor, the crudities of the hoe, the axe, and the plow reduced the typical Negro hand to a gnarled stump, incapable of fine craftsmanship even if materials, patterns, and artistic incentives had been available. But we may believe there was some memory of beauty; since by way of compensation, some obviously artistic urges flowed even with the peasant Negro toward the only channels of expression left open,—those of song, graceful movement, and poetic speech. Stripped of all else, the Negro's own body became his prime and only artistic instrument; dance, pantomime, and song were the solace for his pent-up emotions. So it was environment that forced American Negroes away from the craft arts and their old ancestral skills to the emotional arts of song and dance for which they are known and noted in America. When a few Negroes did get contact with the skilled crafts, their work showed that here was some slumbering instinct of the artisan left, for especially in the early colonial days, before plantation slavery had become dominant, the Negro craftsmen were well-known as cabinetmakers, marquetry setters, wood carvers, and ironsmiths as the workmanship of many colonial mansions in Charleston, New Orleans, and other colonial centers of wealth and luxury will attest.

II

The Negro Artist and Negro Art

Somehow, too, in this dislocating process of being transplanted from Africa to America, Negro art and the Negro artist got separated. It was generations before they got together again. Meanwhile, we had African art forgotten and discredited; the Negro theme and subject matter neglected by American artists generally, and many Negro artists who themselves regarded Negro art as a Ghetto restriction from which they fled in protest and indignation. All this has changed and today the exact opposite is largely true. African art today is widely recognized and highly prized; in fact for the last twenty years has been a great inspiration for the best and most original modern painters and sculptors. Gradually American artists have come to treat the Negro subject as something more than a passing and condescending side interest; the portrayal of Negro types with serious dignity and understanding has become a major theme in the program for developing a "native American art." And still more importantly, the younger generation Negro artists now regard it as one of their main objectives and opportunities to interpret the Negro and to develop what is now called "Negro art." For although the Negro as a vital part of the American scene is the common property of American artists, black and white, he is certainly the special property and a particular artistic interest and asset of the Negro artist. However, this could come about only after African art and the Negro theme had acquired artistic dignity through the recognition of master artists and world critics. Before that the shadow of prejudice clouded the Negro in the mirror of art almost as darkly as prejudice and social discrimination hampered and clouded his real life.

Art, in fact, always mirrors social ideals and values. If the history books were all lost or destroyed, we could almost rewrite history from art. A keen eye could tell from the way in which art painted him just what the Eighteenth, Nineteenth and Twentieth Centuries thought of the Negro,—or for that matter any other class, race, or type. And whenever there has been a significant change of social attitude, it has either been reflected in the mirror of art or sometimes even, this sensitive medium has registered the change before it has become generally apparent in the conventional attitudes of society at large. By this token, for example, we may reliably judge that for the Seventeenth Century, the Negro was an unfamiliar figure exciting curiosity and romantic interest, and that this attitude shown first in the blackamoor figures of the Negro king in the three legendary magi who came to Bethlehem with their gold, myrrh, and frankincense continued into the tradition of the Eighteenth Century, when most Negroes painted, though personal attendants of notables, were fancy-dress favorites obviously as personally intimate as court jesters, only more prized and petted because of their rarity. Few portraits of the courtesans of the Empire and Pompadour period were complete without this traditional figure of the black page or personal attendant, dressed elegantly as a pet possession. And of course, we must not forget the occasional black notable or scholar, whose idealized portrait reflected the admiration and sentimental interest of the Eighteenth Century in the Negro. As literary examples, characters like "Oronooko" by Mrs. Aphra Behn, or "Rasselas, Prince of Ethiopia" by Voltaire, are typical. These men, like Juan Latino, the Spanish Negro scholar, Gomez Parera, the apprentice disciple of Velázquez, Capitein, the black Dutch theologian, down to Samuel Brown, the learned servant of Samuel Johnson, sat for the best painters and engravers of their day, and thus from this tradition we have the occasional but important Negro figure portrait of a Velázquez, Rembrandt, Rubens, Goya, Reynolds, or a Hogarth.

Such a tradition even carried over into early colonial America, wherever the aristocratic tradition was strong. We see it unmistakably in the portrait of George Washington's family, where the dark brown, elegantly groomed Lee is a prominent figure in the group. In fact, there is scarcely a grotesque or carelessly painted Negro figure in art before the beginning of the Nineteenth Century, which coincides exactly with the Negro's lapse into chattel slavery and plantation bondage. Then it was, that the social stigma was branded from which it has taken more than a century to free him; and from which he is only now slowly emerging. For a time, the Negro completely disappears from the canvas of art, and when he makes his reappearance it is in the background corner as a clownish, grotesque object setting off the glory of his master or as the comic subject of his amused condescension. The "old faithful uncle,"—later Uncle Tom, Uncle Ned, and Uncle Remus, the broad expansive "mammy" from Aunt Chloe to Aunt Jemima,

the jigging plantation hands in tattered jeans and the sprawl-
ing pickaninnies all became typical stereotypes, and scarcely
any Nineteenth Century art show was without its genre portrait study of one or more of these types or its realistically
painted or sketched portrayal of "The Plantation Quarters" or
"Ole Virginia Life" or some such glorification of the slave system. The tradition was so strong that it lasted forty years at
least after the nominal fall of chattel slavery; and it has been
and still is one of the mainstays of the literary and artistic defense of the "lost cause" of the Confederacy. In fact the clever-
est argument for the slave system was this misrepresentation
of the Negro as happy, content, and "naturally in place" in
such a romanticized presentment of the patriarchal regime of
the Southern plantation. It was from this that American art
had to react in the latter decades of the Nineteenth Century,
and it was this tradition that made the Negro artist, during all
that period, dread and avoid the Negro subject like the black
plague itself.

Few were able to remember that the Negro subject had been
treated with dignity and even romantic touch in the previous
century; and no one dared to resume it against so strong and
flourishing a stereotype of Nordic pride and prejudice. A
Negro figure not obviously a peasant or servant, decently clad,
with decent clothes and without a counterfoil of his overlord
to show his inferior social status was a rarity; a book in a
Negro hand instead of a serving tray would have been an intolerable heresy. Oddly enough, the few Negro painters and
sculptors did not realize that at this juncture it was their duty
and opportunity to furnish the antidote to this social poison.
For the most part, instead of counteracting it, they, too,
shunned the Negro subject. Gradually this fixed tradition
began to lapse. It was undermined for artistic rather than social reasons, and for the most part by pioneering white artists.
As we shall see in more detail later on, while a few Negro
painters were proving that Negroes could become competent
and recognized artists, pioneering realists and "American-
ists," were developing a realistic art of native types including
a new and almost revolutionizing portrayal of the Negro

subject. Some of them began, like Winslow Homer, with sketches of the exotic Negro of the West Indies, less familiar and therefore less subject to the American stereotype; others started with one foot in the plantation school, like Wayman Adams, but the other rather firmly in the advance ground of true type portraiture. Finally, with the great American realists, like Robert Henri and George Luks at the turn of the Twentieth Century, Negro types took on the technical thoroughness of a major artistic problem, and finally reflected the dignity of an entirely changed artistic approach and social attitude. Now with contemporary artists like George Bellows, John Steuart Curry, James Chapin, Julius Bloch, Thomas Benton, and many others, the Negro subject has become a matter of a major interest and reached dignified, sympathetic portrayal, even, at times, spiritual interpretation.

But this is just a favorable beginning. Now that the Negro subject has become artistically respectable and important again, it is the duty and opportunity of the Negro artist to develop this province of American art as perhaps only he can. Certainly from the point of view of spiritual values and interpretation, the Negro painter and sculptor and graphic artist ought to be able to advance an additional message, if not add the last word. Although one-tenth of the population, one trembles to think what posterity would have thought of us had some Vesuvius buried us under or tidal wave washed us out in 1920. The archeologists of the next age of civilization, digging out the evidences of American art, would not only have had a sorry idea of the Negro but no clue as to his factual bulk or cultural character. By only the narrow margin of a little over a decade, then, are we safe from such a serious misrepresentation.

There is a double duty and function to Negro art,—and by that we mean the proper development of the Negro subject as an artistic theme—the role of interpreting the Negro in the American scene to America at large is important, but more important still is the interpretation of the Negro to himself. Frankness compels the admission and constructive self-criticism dictates the wisdom of pointing out that the Negro's own conception of himself has been warped by prejudice and the common American stereotypes. To these there is no better or effective antidote than a more representative Negro art of wider range and deeper penetration. Not an art artificially corrective or self-pluming; but at least one that aims to tell the whole truth, as the artist sees it, and tells it, as all good art must, with an accent of understanding or beauty, or both.

Negro art, then, is an important province of American art, and a vital challenge to the Negro artist.

28

ADVANCE ON
THE ART FRONT

The recent advances in contemporary Negro art remind me of nothing so much as a courageous cavalry move over difficult ground in the face of obstacles worse than powder and shell—silence and uncertainty. I have only read one book on military strategy, and remember only one or two sentences. But these happen to be appropriate. One said: "It's not the ground you gain but the ground you can hold that counts"; the other: "Even retreat, organized, is safer than disorganized advance." So, sobering though it may be, before we lose our heads and handkerchiefs in hysterical hurrahs for the brave lads who press forward, let us look at the cold strategy of our art situation and ask a few pertinent questions.

After all, we cannot win on the art front with just a thin advance line of pioneering talent or even the occasional sharp salient of genius; we must have behind this talent and this genius the backing of solid infantry and artillery support and the essential lifelines of supply and communication. In short, we must have for the most effective use of our art proper public appreciation, adequate financial support, competent and impersonal criticism, and social and cultural representativeness. We must first of all support our artists, or our art will fail—fail outright or what is quite as bad, fail to represent us. We must consolidate our art gains or their accumulative effect will be lost as mere individual and "exceptional" achievement. Finally, we must capitalize our art, for it is, after all, as the most persuasive and incontrovertible type of group propaganda, our best cultural line of defense.

Surely after the recent Marian Anderson case this is self-evident. But why should we wait upon a mis-maneuver of the enemy or hang precariously on a fumble of the opposition? The essence of strategy is planned action and the tactics of internally organized resources. As illustration, imagine the educative public effect of a permanently organized traveling exhibit of the work of contemporary Negro artists. Or visualize the social dividends on such a representative collection as part of the Golden Gate Exposition or of the New York World's Fair. I heard the subject debated for months pro and con, and in the end, I believe, positive action was impaled on the horns of the usual dilemma. That old dilemma of the persecuted which the successful always dare to ignore! Imagine confronting a Polish artist with the alternative of a national *or* an international showing; if he had as few as two pictures the answer would be "one in each." At the World's Fair practically every nation is reinforcing its share in the international showing with special national collections under its own auspices; and the Union of South Africa, including as a prominent part of its art exhibit the rock drawings of the prehistoric Hottentots and Bushmen, makes it seem as though consistency was the enforced virtue of the disinherited.

So while we rejoice over a few well-earned inclusions of the works of some of our younger artists in the exhibit of contemporary American art at the Fair, let us frankly lament and take the blame for the lack of a representative unit collection of the best work of contemporary Negro artists. And while we glow over the increasing number of one-man shows by Negro painters and sculptors, let us regret that thus far no comprehensive and representative permanent collection of the work of Negro artists exists.

Too, I have heard Negro artists and critics in some strange befuddlement question the relevance of African art to our cultural tradition. Try to buy, beg, borrow, or steal that prehistoric African art from the state collections of the Union of

South Africa! Question, if you must quibble on something, the relevance of the African art in the imperial museums and colonial expositions the world over or the often concealed transfusion of African style in contemporary modernist art. Art belongs where it is claimed most or where it functions best. Bohemian art was in strange and sad succession Bohemian, German, Polish, Austrian, Czechoslovakian and now, I daresay will become "German" all over again. Art doesn't die of labels, but only of neglect—for nobody's art is nobody's business.

Negro art is and should be primarily our business, and deserves to be our glory to the extent that it has been our concern. Happily enough, as in the art of Miss Anderson, the more deeply representative it is racially, the broader and more universal it is in appeal and scope, there being for truly great art no essential conflict between racial or national traits and universal human values.

Within the field we are reviewing two illustrations will clinch this point. The intuitive genius of a New York lad, using the Haitian historical materials of the Schomburg Collection in the 135th Street Branch Library, reinterprets in forty-one modernistic tempera panels the life of Toussaint Louverture and the whole course of the Haitian Revolution. It would be hard to decide which cause owed the greater debt to Jacob Lawrence's talents, Haitian national history, Negro historical pride, expressionism as an appropriate idiom for interpreting tropical atmosphere and peasant action and emotion, or contemporary Negro art. As a matter of fact, all scored simultaneously when this brilliant series of sketches was exhibited in a special gallery at the Baltimore Museum of Art's recent showing of Negro artists.

Or again, let us take the *Mother and Son* group exhibited for the first time in the recent one-man show of Richmond Barthé's sculptures at the Arden Gallery in New York, and now to be shown at the World's Fair. Here is a subject racial to the core—a Negro peasant woman kneeling and mournfully cradling in her arms the limp, broken-necked body of her lynched son. But striking enough to be more potent anti-lynching propaganda than an armful of pamphlets, this statue group is properly, as a work of art, universalized, and would move with pity a spectator who had never heard of lynching or an art critic merely interested in the problems of sculptural form and tradition that have come down to us from the days of classic sculpture.

What should concern us primarily, then, is how to encourage and support our artists, assuring them that artistic freedom which is their right, but buttressing their creative effort with serious social and cultural appreciation and use so that their powerful influence is widely felt.

As for the present, if it had not been for the Federal Art Project and its direct and indirect support, almost all of our art gains would have been snuffed out in the last few years. More power to this project, but in addition, we need the reinforcements of voluntary and sacrificial outside support, such as that of the Harlem Citizen's Sponsors Committee that guarantees rental and materials for the Harlem Community Art Center, or that admirable initiative of the Baltimore Negro Citizens' Art Committee that was back of the Baltimore Municipal Museum of Art's exhibit of *Contemporary Negro Art*, or that pioneer offer of Le Moyne College of quarters for the Federal Art Gallery in Memphis, or the creditable commission of the Amistad murals for the new Savery Library building of Talladega College. These things, let us hope, are the beginnings of a movement for the popular support of the Negro artist who is beginning to take his place as one of the forceful factors in our cultural advance.

On the artists' part, there have been signs of remarkable activity. In Boston one-man shows of the work of Allan Crite and of Loïs Jones have been held recently; in Philadelphia, at the A.C.A. Galleries, Sam Brown exhibited a striking series of watercolors—most of them from Nassau, the Bahamas—in a joint show with Hen Jones, who exhibited a new series of oil landscapes and figure studies in a successful modernistic change of style. The same gallery later had an exhibit of the black-and-whites and lithographs of one of our most skillful technicians in these media, Dox Thrash. In New York, the Labor Club recently held a stimulating exhibit of the work of younger Negro artists, and at the Harlem Art Center under the enterprising direction of Gwendolyn Bennett a whole series of exhibitions has been held, culminating in interest, from our point of view, in the third annual group exhibit of the Harlem Artists Guild. Here in this group we have probably the nucleus of the younger Negro art movement, for in rapid sequence it has brought forward the talents of promising young artists like Georgette Seabrook, Norman Lewis, Sara Murrell, Ernest Crichlow, Vertis Hayes, William Blackburn, Ronald Joseph, and Jacob Lawrence.

The New York season has also seen one-man showings of the work of William H. Johnson at the Artists Gallery and of Aaron Douglas at the A.C.A. Gallery. Each of these somewhat older artists has modified his earlier style, Mr. Johnson by moving somewhat extremely to the artistic left of disorganized expressionism and Mr. Douglas by a retreat from his bold earlier style to mild local-color impressionism, which though technically competent, gives little distinctively new or forceful either in his Negro type studies or his series of Haitian landscapes.

Then on the general front there have come credible inclusions for Sam Brown and Lois Jones in the Philadelphia Academy Water Color Show, for Florence Purviance, Allan Crite, and Lois Jones in the Corcoran Clarke Biennial, and for Hale Woodruff and several others in the World's Fair Contemporary American Show. Miss Savage's much publicized commission statue, *Lift Every Voice and Sing*, has back of it a magnificently dramatic idea, and if its execution carries through the force of the conception it will be a notable exhibit and noteworthy representation in a situation which, as we have previously said, the Negro artist and Negro art as such have pitifully inadequate representation.

But certainly the outstanding artistic events of the season thus far have been the Baltimore Museum of Art's well-chosen and brilliantly arranged show and the equally well arranged and unusually comprehensive one-man sculpture show of the work of Richmond Barthé. Barthé, by his industrious application, has developed a seasoned technical proficiency: thirty-seven subjects in five media ranging from portrait commission busts to heroic figure compositions like *Mother and Son* and the forty-foot bas reliefs of *Exodus and Dance* for the Harlem River Housing Project attest to original talent and steadily maturing artistic stature. Critics, both conservative and modernistic, agreed in their praise because of undeniable proficiency and versatility. This adaptation of style to subject is Barthé's forte. Always seeking for a basic and characteristic rhythm and for a pose with a sense of suspended motion, there is an almost uncanny emphasis, even in his heads, of a symbolic type of line, like the sinuous patterned curves of the Kreutzberg figure, the sensuous ecstatic posture of *The African Dancer*, the sagging bulbous bulk of *The Stevedore*, the medieval medallion-like faces and figures of the *Green Pastures Exodus* scene, or the lilting lift of *Benga*, the sophisticated African dancer. Carl Van Vechten is right in his statement that Barthé is actually seeking "the spiritual values inherent in moving figures." This sensitiveness to moods and temperaments makes Barthé an excellent character portraitist, as his portrait busts of John Gielgud, Maurice Evans, Kreutzberg, Jimmie Daniels, and Rose MacClendon show unmistakably. However, it is as a figure sculptor of racial types that his talent, released from surface realism, expresses itself most capably and with greater promise of making a unique contribution to Negro art.

The Baltimore Museum show was in many respects the Negro art event of the year. In the first place, it represented the first regular showing of Negro art in a Southern municipal museum, in which several factors played a role of progressive collaboration: the timely initiative of the Baltimore Negro Citizens' Art Committee under the chairmanship of Mrs. Sarah C. Fernandis, the new liberal policy of the Museum management under the leadership of Mr. Henry Triede, the cooperation of the Harmon Foundation, the pioneer organization in the exhibition of the work of Negro artists; and the selective taste of the Museum's acting director, Mr. R. C. Rogers. As a combined result, there ensued a selective showing of the advance front of Negro art with a decided emphasis on modernism in style and technical maturity. Black and white, oils and sculpture were well represented, with the emphasis on the graphic media. Among the sculptors, Sargent Johnson, Barthé, and Henry Bannarn were well represented, together with the first American showing of a strong newcomer, the Jamaican-born modernist sculptor Ronald Moody. Moody's work, even though influenced by cosmopolitan expressionism, has a healthy primitivism about it, especially in figures like *Une Tête* and *Midonz*, which makes him a welcome adjunct to the growing group of representative Negro sculptors. His talent would undoubtedly benefit from closer contact with racial types, either West Indian or American.

In painting we have already mentioned the sensational series of Jacob Lawrence's Haitian tempera sketches, which attracted favorably both lay and professional attention. Archibald Motley was well represented by a competent series in his later style, Elton Clay Fax had a strong self-portrait and three competent oils, *Coal Hoppers, Steel Worker,* and *Lunchtime*; Palmer Hayden had two vigorously naïve racial interpretations, *Midsummer Night in Harlem* and *The Janitor Who Paints*; and Sam Brown, several abstractionist watercolors of clever conception and deft execution.

But the chief attraction in the oils section was a most carefully selected group of the work of the late Malvin Gray Johnson that was an object lesson in direct and sincere approach and convincing evidence of what contemporary Negro art lost in the premature death of this young genius. Whether Virginia landscapes or rural Negro types or rural labor themes, all of Gray Johnson's pictures in oil and watercolor were done with sincerity and power, hinting at that decline among our artists of both imitativeness and derivative exhibitionism which is the main hope for the future of the younger generation of Negro artists. Miss Florence Purviance, a Baltimore artist, made a creditable debut, and in the black-and-white section James

Lesesne Wells, Hale Woodruff, Dox Thrash, Robert Blackburn, and most especially Wilmer Jennings gave evidence of maturing powers of technical execution and conceptual grasp. With a request invitation for this show from the Dallas, Texas, Museum, we may justifiably say that Negro art has inaugurated a new phase of public influence and service.

29

UP TILL NOW

A representative overview of the work of the contemporary Negro artist, such as this exhibition opportunely offers, achieves, like the proverbial "two birds with one stone," two objectives with a single effort. It documents, in the first place, the quite considerable contribution which the younger Negro is making to contemporary American art. But it also demonstrates, both in its competence and originality as well as by its wide diversity of style, the happy and almost complete integration of the Negro artist with the trends, styles, and standards of present-day American art. The Albany Institute of History and Art is to be congratulated upon having assembled, without benefit of special appeal or double standard of values, what is at one and the same time a representative and challenging cross-section of contemporary American art and, additionally, convincing evidence of the Negro's maturing racial and cultural self-expression in painting and sculpture.

Such achievement represents, naturally, a long and arduous struggle against cultural as well economic odds. This has required generations, and a brief panoramic background of the history of the Negro as an artist in this country is necessary for proper perspective and appreciation of the present. Few persons are today aware of how early and noteworthy the pioneer instances are which vindicated the right of the Negro to be an artist. Though not represented in this exhibition, these instances must be cited both for their individual attainment and for their precedent-breaking cultural effect. Naturally, however, much of this early art of Negroes began as did our own colonial art in imitative and derivative European styles.

Joshua Johnston (c. 1770–1830) of Baltimore was a practicing portraitist of considerable skill and note in the accepted style of his day; so much so that several of his paintings were for years attributed to Rembrandt Peale. Edmonia Lewis (1845–1890) of Boston, pioneer Negro woman sculptor, a protégé of the Storey family, studied and practiced her art in Rome, winning prizes at home and abroad for her competent but not overly original neoclassical figures and figure groups. Edward Mitchell Bannister (1828–1901) was a leading and accepted member of the Providence, RI art group and a landscapist and marine painter of considerable ability. With even greater talent and success, Robert Duncanson (1821–1871) was similarly an accepted member of the Cincinnati art group in the late '60s and '70s. After study in Edinburgh and outstanding success in London art circles, he returned before his death to Cincinnati, there to execute commission portraits and murals for the leading art patrons of that vicinity.

But obviously such exceptional developments by no means established the Negro either as a generally accepted or an integrated artist. Even the next stage of development achieved but one of these desirable goals; and that at the sacrifice of the other. As in so many other artistic fields, owing to the obstacles and discounts of prejudice, the Negro artist was forced to bid first for foreign opportunity and recognition. At that time also, American art generally, by way of outgrowing its early provincialism, was cosmopolitan in focus and outlook. Partly by way of sharing this Parisian orientation, and partly to avoid the handicaps of race, the next generation of Negro artists were divorced both from their own racial backgrounds as well as from the American scene. This went so far with some as an unfortunate but understandable avoidance of racial subject matter for fear of being insidiously labeled. The outstanding Negro artists of this period accordingly contributed little either to the development of Negro expression in art or to the development of native American art. But they did contribute importantly to the single-standard acceptance of the Negro as artist, first in international recognition and later by national acceptance. This, in addition to their individual contribution, was the significant accomplishment of such outstanding artists as Meta Warrick Fuller, pupil of Rodin in sculpture, and Henry O. Tanner (1859–1937), the internationally known painter. They and a few lesser lights like Wm. Harper, Wm. E. Scott, May Howard Jackson, demonstrated complete assimilation of the best academic tradition and style, and beyond that, with Tanner and Mrs. Fuller, creative power and originality.

Trends around 1910, some arising from the external pressures of American realism and others from internal urges for racial self-expression, raised sentimentally at first the basic issue of racial representation in and through art. For a while it divided our artists into two camps of thought, even threatening some with split artistic personalities as they oscillated between the urge to be "racial" and the desire to be "universal" in their art. Not all the landscape, marine and still-life painting of this transitional period was pure preoccupation with form, color, and technical problems. Some was escapist, avoiding this ever-recurring issue. Finally in the mid-Twenties the combined weight of realism, Americanism and cultural racialism won dominance and we experienced our first group-conscious school of "Negro art." A few traditionalists as May Howard Jackson, Archibald Motley, Laura Wheeler Waring, yielded to the trend while pioneering talents as Aaron Douglas, Sargent Johnson, Richmond Barthé, Palmer Hayden, Wm. H. Johnson and especially Hale Woodruff, Malvin Gray Johnson, broke through to the avowed acceptance of racial self-portraiture and self-expression as the primary goal of the Negro artist. The Negro artist thus found his place beside the poets and writers of the "New Negro" movement, which in the late Twenties and through the Thirties galvanized Negro talent to strong and freshly creative expression.

All during this critical period the Negro artist had helpful allies. First and foremost was the sustaining example of such non-Negro artists as Thomas Eakins, Robert Henri, George Luks, Henry Bellows, James Chapin, Julius Bloch, and others who were raising the Negro subject from the level of trivial or sentimental genre to that of serious type study and socially sympathetic portrayal. Then, too, there was the considerable

influence of successful self-expression by Negroes in the kindred arts during this period. Of particular importance and
help also were the annual exhibits and prize awards of the
Harmon Foundation between 1928 and 1935 for the work of
Negro artists. Finally there was the culminating lift of the
Federal Arts Project, which greatly multiplied the art contacts
and horizons of both this and a younger generation of artistically ambitious Negroes.

By this time fairly coherent groups of young Negro artists
were flourishing not only in New York's Harlem, but in Chicago, Cleveland, Boston, Philadelphia, Hampton, Atlanta. It is
this crop, largely, whose work is the core of the present exhibition. Flanked by the figures already mentioned are such talents
as Charles Alston, Wm. Artis, Romare Bearden, Henry Bannarn, Wm. Carter, Elizabeth Catlett, Ernest Crichlow, Eldzier
Cortor, Fred Flemister, Rex Goreleigh, Jacob Lawrence, Norman Lewis, Edward Loper, Charles Sebree, Charles White,
Ellis Wilson, James Lesesne Wells,—to call a partial but significant roll. These, with that exceptional older but modernis-
tically abstract talent of Horace Pippin, constitute what can
confidently be described as the Negro's contemporary contribution to American art. For it is a notable contribution both in
content and in style.

Important as it is to gauge the extent to which the Negro
group experience has ripened and flowered artistically, it is
even more important to realize how proper and inevitable it is
that this work be viewed and accepted as an integral and representative segment of our native American art. Indeed it runs
the gamut of practically every well-known variety of modern
art approach and style. It therefore has basic common denominators with the art of our time and has found fruitful fellowship with its fellow American artists. That is to be construed
as a happy and necessary coming of age for the Negro artist.

But in spite of such wide divergence of style and art approach, there seem to be many subtle and significant common
traits. Some reflect, no doubt, a natural commonality of time
and place,—the authentic American flavor and touch. Other
overtones suggest, however, common emotional factors of

racial life and experience. Certainly among these, one can note to an unusual degree strength and virtuosity of color and rhythm and vivid originality of imagination. This work, too, is on the whole vigorous and vital even when sophisticated: and a surprising amount of it will be found sophisticated by those who expected a predominant naïveté. Especially in view of the extreme youth of a number of these artists, most of them in their late twenties and early thirties and four under twenty-five, one can confidently anticipate from the young Negro artist in the near future as distinctive creative originality as many have conceded only to the race in music.

Further, the social message of the younger Negro artist is particularly noticeable and noteworthy. Whether treating his theme realistically or symbolically, the artist is obviously keenly alive and sensitive to social documentation and achieves forcefulness in expressing both social sympathy and social protest. These artists have this trait partly of course as products of the depression and latterly the war era, but one feels that they also have drawn on the emotional depths of their racial experience and derived therefrom unusual penetration of social understanding and insight.

Yet the thread of social documentation and commentary is but one strand in this art. There is just as evident a strong decorative interest in design, color, and the technicalities of their art, with indications of more than average capacity to find strong and original solutions for the more technical aesthetic problems of painting and sculpture. But what I find most significant, especially in the canvasses of the youngest talents like those of Crichlow, Lawrence, Catlett, Norman Lewis, Charles White, and John Wilson, is an ability to blend the somewhat conflicting approaches of a social message with the abstractly aesthetic into a balanced, mutually reinforcing synthesis. This, among others, is a development to be watched for its obvious future promise as these younger artists come to maturity; for exceptional power in these respects in the Negro artist could warrantably be regarded as likely and legitimate dividends from his racial inheritance of group experience.

Such warmly human but piercing social irony is an oft-repeated note in the work of Crichlow, Bearden, William Johnson, Norman Lewis, Charles White, Elizabeth Catlett, and others. Particularly characteristic is it of Jacob Lawrence's fertile and powerful talent, more apparent in his *Harriet Tubman, John Brown, Negro Migration*, and *Harlem* series even than in individual subjects. Horace Pippin, especially in his moving *John Brown* series, has the same in his own naïvely forceful way. There can be no doubt of the increasingly important place of the Negro artist in the social commentary vein that is becoming so characteristic of much recent American art. That with the Negro artist it is expressed with such broad human sympathy and controlled restraint is fortunate for its increased social effectiveness, apart even from its praiseworthy artistic propriety. With great temptation in that direction, the Negro artist is seldom the crude or even overt propagandist.

Much of this work, however, must be judged by absolute standards and abstract criteria; which is only to say again that today the Negro artist is in the first instance an artist and only incidentally Negro. More and more as the present integration spreads will this be the case, and more and more must it become also the general public approach and attitude. By stages, it seems, we are achieving greater democracy in art,—and let us hope, through art.

One phase of this growing democracy in American art has broken the limiting stereotypes through which we traditionally saw Negro life and the Negro. Another has freed the Negro artist alike from the limiting avoidance of Negro subject matter and later led him to more objective and effective self-portrayal. Still another has brought forward the common denominators of a truly representative native American art, which logically has included the serious interpretation of the Negro elements in the national whole. This democratically shared interest has brought the Negro artist into closer rapport and collaboration with his fellow American artists.

Finally, as a combined result of the new attitude toward the Negro theme and subject and of the increasing maturity of the Negro artist the double standard of performance and judgment is fading out of the national art picture. In the last five years the number of practicing Negro artists of accepted merit has about doubled. Their work is appearing increasingly in general exhibitions and recognized galleries, both in mixed and one-man showings: one of the leading New York galleries devoted especially to American art has by choice of its director and the associated artists two Negro painters in its roster of twenty. The present exhibit, it is to be confidently expected, will have widespread enlightening influence. If the gains of the last five years are matched by the next five, by 1950 we shall have realized almost complete democracy in American art, which will be as significant and valuable an achievement for the national culture as for the Negro.

RETROSPECTIVE
THINKING

30

1928: A RETROSPECTIVE
REVIEW

The year 1928 represents probably the flood-tide of the present Negrophile movement. More books have been published about Negro life by both white and Negro authors than was the normal output of more than a decade in the past. More aspects of Negro life have been treated than were ever even dreamed of. The proportions show the typical curve of a major American fad, and to a certain extent, this indeed it is. We shall not fully realize it until the inevitable reaction comes; when as the popular interest flags, the movement will lose thousands of supporters who are now under its spell, but who tomorrow would be equally hypnotized by the next craze.

A retrospective view ought to give us some clue as to what to expect and how to interpret it. Criticism should at least forewarn us of what is likely to happen. In this, as with many another boom, the water will need to be squeezed out of much inflated stock and many bubbles must burst. However, those who are interested in the real Negro movement which can be discerned behind the fad, will be glad to see the fad subside. Only then will the truest critical appraisal be possible, as the opportunity comes to discriminate between shoddy and wool, fair-weather friends and true supporters, the stockbrokers and the real productive talents. The real significance and potential power of the Negro renaissance may not reveal itself until after this reaction, and the entire topsoil of contemporary Negro expression may need to be ploughed completely under for a second hardier and richer crop.

To my mind the movement for the vital expression of Negro life can only truly begin as the fad breaks off. There is inevitable distortion under the hectic interest and forcing of the present vogue for Negro idioms. An introspective calm, a spiritually poised approach, a deeply matured understanding are finally necessary. These may not, need not come entirely from the Negro artist; but no true and lasting expression of Negro life can come except from these more firmly established points of view. To get above ground, much forcing has had to be endured; to win a hearing, much exploitation has had to be tolerated. There is as much spiritual bondage in these things as there ever was material bondage in slavery. Certainly the Negro artist must point the way when this significant moment comes, and establish the values by which Negro literature and art are to be permanently gauged after the fluctuating experimentalism of the last few years. Much more could be said on this subject,—but I was requested to write a retrospective review of the outstanding literary and artistic events of 1928 in the field of Negro life.

The year has been notable particularly in the field of fiction,—a shift from the prevailing emphasis in Negro expression upon poetry. In this field there were three really important events.—Claude McKay's *Home to Harlem*, Rudolph Fisher's *Walls of Jericho*, and Julia Peterkin's *Scarlet Sister Mary*. An appraisal of the outstanding creative achievement in fiction a year ago would not have given us a majority on the Negro side. That in itself reflects a solid gain, gauged by the standard I have set,—for no movement can be a fad from the inside. Negro fiction may even temporarily lose ground in general interest, but under cover of the present vogue there has been nurtured an important new articulateness in Negro life more significant than mere creativeness in poetry. For creative fiction involves one additional factor of cultural maturity,—the art of social analysis and criticism. If *Home to Harlem* is significant, as it notably is, for descriptive art and its reflection of the vital rhythms of Negro life, *The Walls of Jericho* is notable in this other important direction,—the art of social analysis. The ironic detachment of the one is almost as welcome as the emotional saturation of the other; they are in their several ways high-water marks in fiction for the Negro artist. Those who read *Home to Harlem* superficially will see only a more authentic *Nigger Heaven*, posterity will see the peculiar and persistent quality of Negro peasant life transposed to the city and the modern mode, but still vibrant with a clean folkiness of the soil instead of the decadent muck of the city-gutter. Moreover *Home to Harlem* will stand as a challenging answer to a still too prevalent idea that the Negro can only be creatively spontaneous in music and poetry, just as Mr. Fisher's book must stand as the answer to the charge that the Negro artist is not yet ripe for social criticism or balanced in social perspective.

The scene of Harlem is of course more typical of modern Negro life than a South Carolina plantation, but the fact that the year has produced another novel from the South almost equal to *Porgy* is one of outstanding importance. *Scarlet Sister Mary*, by a veteran protagonist of the new school of Southern fiction, represents not only an acme of Mrs. Peterkin's art, but evidence that the new attitude of the literary South toward Negro life is firmly established. To be rooted deep enough for tragedy, layers beneath the usual shallowness and sentimentalism of the older Southern fiction, is of course an achievement for the literature of the South, apart even from the fact that this artistic growth has been achieved in the field of Negro fiction.

Indeed this new attitude of the white writer and artist toward Negro life has now become an accepted attitude, it registers more than the lip service of realism, for it is equally a tribute to the deeper human qualities of black humanity. Dr. Odum's *Rainbow Round My Shoulder* is another case in point. Paul Green's more recent plays and stories reinforce the same motive. Even *Black Sadie* by T. Bowyer Campbell, of the Far South, almost achieves the same respectful approach and the evenhandedness of treatment which spells the banishment of propaganda from art.

Of course, it is the problem novel which is the acid test for propaganda. *Dark Princess*, marking the reappearance in

fiction of the versatile Dr. Du Bois, for all its valuable and
competent social portraiture, does not successfully meet this
test, but falls an artistic victim to its own propagandist am-
bushes. This novel by the veteran must on this account cede
position in this field to the quite successful thrust of the novice,—Nella Larsen's *Quicksand*. This study of the cultural
conflict of mixed ancestry is truly a social document of importance, and as well a living, moving picture of a type not often
in the foreground of Negro fiction, and here treated perhaps
for the first time with adequacy. Indeed this whole side of the
problem which was once handled exclusively as a grim tragedy
of blood and fateful heredity now shows a tendency to shift to
another plane of discussion; as the problem of divided social
loyalties and the issues of the conflict of cultures. As one
would expect, foreign fiction is showing us the way in this,
just as it previously did with the "light ironic touch and the
sympathetic charm" which is now so accepted an approach to
the Negro peasant figure. In the discussion of this social tragedy type, Mrs. Millin has again touched it masterfully this
year in *The Coming of the Lord*, it has been too melodramatically stated, though with evident seriousness, in *White Nigger*,
and rather competently handled by Esther Hyman in *Study in
Bronze*.

Even in the literature of the comic approach, stereotypes no
longer reign supreme. E. C. L. Adams's *Nigger to Nigger* actually documents the contemporary peasant Negro with real humanity and accuracy; and Roark Bradford's *Ol' Man Adam
an' His Chillun* seriously tries to emulate *Uncle Remus*. One
of the strange and not too reassuring features of the present
situation is the comparative silence of the Negro writers in the
field of humor and comic portrayal. There can never be adequate self-portrayal until some considerable section of our
own literature rings to the echo with genuine and spontaneous
Negro laughter.

After the extraordinary productiveness of the past years in
poetry, the subsidence in this field has been inevitable and is
wholesome. The gap has been filled in part by the industrious
gleanings of the anthology makers; and in another more

creative direction in the development of several important literary schools or coteries outside of the central pioneer group in New York. This movement, which I have elsewhere characterized as the spread of beauty to the provinces, is one of the most potent effects of the Negro cultural revival. Notable instances have been the formation of a literary group in Boston which has sponsored the occasional publication of the *Quill*, the revival of the younger ultra-expressionist group who published *Fire!!* and who now are publishing *Harlem*, the continued activity of the Philadelphia group that is responsible for the publication of *Black Opals*, the revival of one of the earliest founded of all these producing artistic groups, the Stylus group at Howard University, Washington, and the crystallization of several writing, dramatic, and art groups in Chicago and Indianapolis. This movement of general response to the impulses from the metropolis, has been paralleled by a general quickening of interest in the study of Negro life by white groups over a very wide area, for which two progressive centers have been largely responsible—Chicago, through the sponsoring of a campaign plan of introducing Negro art and cultural achievement to the general public by a "Negro Art Week" program; and the liberal group at the University of North Carolina, who have been so consistently and effectively pursuing a constructive and valuable program of research and publication with their studies of Negro life and culture, of which the total now is nearly a score of indispensable contributions. In this connection the second issue of *The Carolina Magazine*, devoted to Negro poetry, with the projected third issue on the Negro folk play, must be mentioned as showing a parallel interest and liberal tendency on the part of the younger Southern college generation.

In the field of drama, the Theatre Guild's presentation of *Porgy* has eclipsed everything else, and warrantably. The demonstration of the power and unique effects of Negro ensemble made by this play is a contribution of importance; over and above its intrinsic delightfulness. Broadway is more anxious for Negro plays than ever before; a little too anxious, therefore an unusual list of artistic and commercial failures due primarily to half-baked plays hurried through to exploit the present vogue. Meanwhile the typical musical revue type goes merrily and profitably on, with just a crack or two in the banal stereotypes and several laudable attempts at Negro opera,— *Voodoo* and *Deep Harlem*. In the field of the amateur stage, where the hope of Negro drama still focuses, there has been a slight growth in the activity of Negro playing groups, with outstanding achievements centering this year in the work of the Karamu theater of the Gilpin Players, at Cleveland, Ohio, and the successful participation of the Dixwell Players in the Yale Theatre Tournament at New Haven. Paul Green has consolidated many of his unpublished or separately published plays in a volume *In the Valley and Other Carolina Plays*, which is almost another contribution to the Negro Theater, by reason of the fact that a majority of these plays are of Negro subject matter.

Sociological literature usually if not most technical is ephemeral: this year has exceptionally produced two books of profound interpretative value; Raymond L. Buell's two-volume survey of the racial situations of colonial Africa, *The Native Problem in Africa*, and the volume just published on *The American Negro* as the special issue of *The Annals of the American Academy of Political and Social Science*. This last, for all its authoritativeness, actually succeeds in vitalizing and humanizing the large majority of its subject matter, and therefore marks a new era in the official sociology of the race problem. A third event of prime importance in this field is the publication of the extensive classified *Bibliography of the Negro*, prepared by the Tuskegee Bureau of Records under the editorship of Monroe Work.

There has been unusual activity in the field of art, stimulated in part by the Harmon Awards in this field and the institution of an annual show of the work of Negro artists. Prior to this, special shows of the work of Negro artists had been inaugurated by the management of the Harlem Library, and on a larger scale exhibits of Negro painting, sculpture, and decorative art, including exhibits of African art have been held at the Chicago Art Institute, under the auspices of the Chicago

Negro in Art Week Committee, at Fisk University, at Howard University, Hampton Institute, Rochester Memorial Gallery, San Diego, California, and at the exhibit rooms of the new Harlem Museum of African Art in the Harlem Library. The increased output of the younger Negro artists is directly attributable to the fresh stimulus of these new channels of public interest and support. An individual fact of more than individual importance was Archibald Motley's one-man show at the Ainslee Galleries, New York. Among white artists generally a new interest in Negro types has matured culminating in special exhibitions such as Winold Reiss's Penn Island series of Negro type studies, Captain Perfielieff's series of Haitian sketches, Erick Berry's North African types, Covarrubias's recent African series, Mrs. Laura Knight's studies, and Annette Rosenshine's sculpture studies; to mention only in passing such notable single things as Wayman Adams's *Foster Johnson*, James Chapin's *Negro Boxer* and Epstein's *Paul Robeson*. Indeed the reflection of another interest in the field of the fine arts than that of the casual genre study is one of the most recent and hopeful developments in the whole range of new trends.

I have reserved for brief final treatment what is in my judgment the most significant of all recent developments; the new interest in Negro origins. If there is anything that points to a permanent revaluation of the Negro, it is the thoroughgoing change of attitude which is getting established about Africa and things African. Africa has always been a subject of acute interest; but too largely of the circus variety. A sudden shift from the level of gross curiosity to that of intelligent human comprehension and sympathy is apparent in the current literature about Africa. In their several fields, recent publications like the translation of Blaise Cendrars's anthology of African folklore, *The African Saga*, Captain Canot's *Adventures of an African Slaver*, Mrs. Gollock's two informative books—*Lives of Eminent Africans* and *Sons of Africa*, Donald Fraser's *The New Africa* and Milton Staffer's symposium entitled "Thinking with Africa," the publication of the new quarterly journal of the International Institute of African Languages and

Cultures called *Africa*, and very notably, I think, J. W. Vandercook's *Black Majesty* represent in about the space of a year's time a revolutionary change not only in interest but in point of view and approach. Really this is not to be underestimated, because a revaluation of the Negro without an equivalent restatement of the Negro background could easily sag back to the old points of view. But with so thoroughgoing a transformation of opinion and an approach which implies cultural recognition to the Negro in his own intrinsic rights, no such reaction can reasonably occur; it will encounter the resistance of facts instead of the mere fluid tide of sentiment. Even when the reaction comes that was predicted at the outset of this article, there will be a vast net gain that can be counted upon as a new artistic and cultural foundation for a superstructure which it really is the privilege and task of another generation than ours to rear.

BLACK TRUTH
AND BLACK BEAUTY

*A Retrospective Review of the
Literature of the Negro for 1932*

It becomes more obvious as the years go on that in this matter of the portrayal of Negro life in American literature we must pay artistic penance for our social sins, and so must seek the sober, painful truth before we can find the beauty we set out to capture. Except in the rarest instances, in the current literature of the Negro, we continue to find more of the bitter tang and tonic of the Reformation than the sweetness and light of a Renaissance; and rarely, it seems, can truth and beauty be found dwelling, as they should, together. Yet rare instances, gleams here and there, do convince us that in the end we shall achieve the promise that was so inspiring in the first flush of the Negro awakening,—a black beauty that is truth,—a Negro truth that is purely art; even though it may not be all that we need to know. This year one volume gives us special hope, being just that single-stroke revelation of both truth and beauty. It is *Southern Road*, a volume of verse by Sterling Brown; and for that reason I count it the outstanding literary event of the year.

But again, the output of the year is predominantly prose; and not only as last year sober, fact-seeking prose, careful human document study, but this year, in many instances, sharp-edged, surgical prose, drastically probing, boldly cutting down to the quick of the Negro problem. It is as if at last in the process of problem analysis, the scalpels of the scientific and the realistic attitude had suddenly been pushed through the skin and tissues of the problem to the vital viscera in a desperate effort to "kill or cure." Fiction is as bold and revealing as sociology; and at no time have writers, black and white, seemed more willing or more successful in breaking through the polite taboos and the traditional hypocrisies to the bare and naked, and often, tender truth about this or that vital situation of the American race problem. It is a good sign and promiseful omen, even if our nerves do twitch under the shock or wince at the sudden pain. Indeed the scientific approach is revealing the condition of the Negro more and more as just a special phase or segment of the common life, and even as a problem, as but a special symptom of general social ills and maladjustment. The most significant new trend I am able to discover in this year's literature is this growing tendency not to treat the Negro entirely as a separate or special subject, but rather as part of a general situation, be it social, economic, artistic, or cultural. A score of books that cannot by any stretch be listed as "literature of the Negro," have important analyses of one aspect or another of Negro life. In *America as Seen by Americans*, three of the chapters touch vitally on the Negro, and wise editing has frankly realized it. Again, a book like Ehrlich's masterly study of John Brown,— *God's Angry Man*, treats the Negro all the more epically by putting him properly into sane but dramatic perspective. So although books like Donald Young's *American Minority Peoples* or Paul Lewinson's *Race, Class, and Party* have enough special relevance to be listed, many of the most important commentaries do not. A recent review of T. S. Stribling's novel of Reconstruction, *The Store*, makes this appropriate statement:—"In this novel, Mr. Stribling shows the consequences to both Negroes and whites by a skillful series of interactions. Any system inevitably enmeshes all its members equally though diversely." When such a basic fact is fully realized and carried out in literary and sociological practice, we shall be on the last stage of our constantly improving technique in handling the fascinating but difficult theme of Negro life. Except for folk literature and occasional "genre" studies, then, we must expect a return by both white and Negro authors to the common canvas and the large perspective.

In fiction this year, four realists, three of them white southerners, turn to the delineation of the southern scene; each with a certain measure of pioneering success. Miss Stephens, author of the well-known drama *Roseanne*, pictures the same figures, Roseanne and the erring parson, Cicero Brown, in full-length portraiture in *Glory*. Her novel is most successful in its depiction of a rural Georgia village, with its dual life; and a real advance is scored in the handling of local-color material. For Miss Stephen's picture is movingly human and true; it is only with her characterization that she has difficulties, and here only because her motivation is more melodramatic than tragic. Miss Peterkin, more seasoned, ventures forth from her beloved plantation milieu to carry the heroine of *Bright Skin* to Harlem. Here she is less at home, and naturally enough is not completely successful in her portrayal of the mulatto heroine,—Cricket. Yet withal each of these stories is a considerable step toward the triumph of the new southern realism in handling the Negro character and setting sincerely, sympathetically, and truthfully; and both writers have the right idea that Negro life must be treated with a certain amount of poetry, at the same time that sentiment is rigorously excluded. And so, step by step, southern fiction about the Negro approaches great art.

A third novel, *Amber Satyr*, introduces a bold new theme. Roy Flannagan, as a Virginian, breaks the traditional taboos and portrays the love story of Sarah, a white farmer's wife, and Luther, the mulatto hired man. It is not just a formula situation or a formula solution; even though the outraged southern gods decree a lynching. *Amber Satyr* is real, moving tragedy; and is a harbinger of what southern fiction will be when it is courageously and truthfully written. No fiction can be great on mere courage and truthfulness, however, and the possibilities of Mr. Flannagan's or Miss Stephens' subjects cannot be judged from these two first novels, any more than their own mature possibilities as writers. But these are

particularly significant beginnings. *Georgia Nigger* is the fourth
novel in this group. Here is the pure propaganda novel, but
with that strange power that propaganda takes on when it
flames with righteous indignation. This story of peonage and
the southern chain gang and prison labor system is vital fiction
for all its biting polemic; it may well be the *Uncle Tom's Cabin*
of this last vestige of the slave-system, even though David
Jackson, its black hero, will never become the household idol
that Uncle Tom became. Still John Spivak has seized on one of
the legitimate uses of fiction, and within the limits of journal-
istic virtues, has written a powerful and humanly moving
novel. It surely is a symptom of a new realism in the air, especially when we place beside it its counterpart, Harrison Kroll's
more balanced, but equally revealing story of "poor white"
peonage and plantation feudalism, *Cabin in the Cotton*. It is
evident that the reform novel is taking on a new lease of life.

Meanwhile, the Negro writer of fiction, as might be expected, leans backward, away from propaganda and problem
fiction. But the flight from propaganda does not always bring
us safely to art. In fact, when the great Negro writer of fiction
comes forward, he will probably steer head-on into what for a
lesser talent would be the most obvious and shoddy propaganda and transform it into a triumphant victory for art. For
the present, there is only one talent with a masterful touch,
and he, less successful with the novel than the short story. But
undoubtedly Claude McKay's collection of stories, *Ginger-
town*, has maturity, skill, and the universal touch. His stories
run from the tropical Jamaican village to "high Harlem,"
and then to the riverfront of Marseilles, but in all there is real
flesh and blood characterization and really human motivation,
whether the accent be tragic, comic, or as is favorite with
McKay, ironic. Nothing in the whole decade of the "Negro
awakening" is to be more regretted than the exile of this great
talent from contact with his most promising field of material;
for even from memory and at a distance, he draws more powerfully and poignantly than many who study the Harlem scene
"from life."

From right within Harlem two novels have come, neither as

successful artistically as McKay's fiction. These are Countee Cullen's first novel, *One Way to Heaven*, and Wallace Thurman's second novel, *Infants of the Spring*. Both are pathbreaking, however, as to theme. *One Way to Heaven*, the story of Sam Lucas, card gambler but professional penitent at revival meetings, is a story that just barely misses distinction. The duel in Sam's life is unfortunately external; had it been cast as a psychological conflict, there would have been high tragedy and real achievement. Mr. Cullen also ambitiously attempts to weld a low-life and a high society theme into the same story. Desirable as this is, it is a task for the seasoned writer; but as it is, Sam and Mattie's romance and tragedy do not mesh in naturally or effectively with the activities of Constancia Brandon, whose maid Mattie is, and Constancia's intellectual set. Mr. Thurman's novel also misses fire, with a capital theme to make the regret all the keener. *Infants of the Spring* is the first picture of the younger Negro intelligentsia, and was conceived in the satiric vein as a criticism of the Negro Renaissance. Here is a wonderful chance for that most needed of all styles and most needed of all attitudes: self-criticism and perspective-restoring humor are indispensable in the long run in the artistic and spiritual development of the Negro. But they are not forthcoming from Mr. Thurman's sophomoric farce and melodrama or the problem-talk that his characters indulge in. The trouble with the set whom he delineates, and with the author's own literary philosophy and outlook, is that the attitudes and foibles of Nordic decadence have been carried into the buds of racial expression, and the healthy elemental simplicity of the Negro folk spirit and its native tradition forgotten or ignored by many who nevertheless have traded on the popularity for Negro art. As the novel of this spiritual failure and perversion, Mr. Thurman's book will have real documentary value, even though it represents only the lost wing of the younger generation movement.

Finally, Rudolph Fisher turns completely away from the serious and the stereotyped to write a Harlem "mystery story," *The Conjure-Man Dies*. It is a refreshing tour de force, all the more so because one of the flaws of Negro fiction is the failing of taking itself too seriously. But the leaven of humor, and the light touch, will be even more welcome when they come in the context of the serious, literary novel of Negro life by the artist who should know it deepest and best, the young, intellectually emancipated Negro.

This difficult combination of intimacy and detachment is just what distinguishes *Southern Road* by Sterling Brown. It is no exaggeration to say that this young newcomer among the poets has introduced a new dimension into Negro folk portraiture. A close student of the folk-life, he has caught along with the intimate particularities of Negro thought and feeling, more of the hidden universalities which our other folk-poets have overlooked or been incapable of sounding. The dominant angle of sweet or humane irony has enabled this poet to see a Negro peasant humble but epic, carefree but cynical, sensual but stoical, and as he himself says, "illiterate, but somehow very wise." It is a real discovery, this new figure who escapes both the clichés of the rhetorical propagandist poets and equally those of the "simple peasant" school. Undoubtedly, it is a step in portrayal that would have been impossible without the peasant portraits of Jean Toomer and Langston Hughes, but it is no invidious comparison to point out how much further it goes in the direction of balanced spiritual portraiture.

Meanwhile, as the folk-school tradition deepens, Langston Hughes, formerly its chief exponent, turns more and more in the direction of social protest and propaganda; since *Scottsboro Limited* represents his latest moods, although *The Dream Keeper* and *Popo and Fifina* are also recent publications. The latter is a quite flimsy sketch, a local-color story of Haitian child life, done in collaboration with Arna Bontemps, while *The Dream Keeper* is really a collection of the more lyrical of the poems in his first two volumes of verse, supplemented by a few unprinted poems,—all designed to be of special appeal to child readers. The book is a delightful lyrical echo of the older Hughes, who sang of his people as "walkers with the dawn and morning," "loudmouthed laughers in the hands of fate."

But the poet of *Scottsboro Limited*, is a militant and indignant proletarian reformer, proclaiming:

> *The voice of the red world*
> *Is our voice, too.*
> *The voice of the red world is you!*
> *With all of the workers,*
> *Black or white,*
> *We'll go forward*
> *Out of the night.*

And as we turn to the sociological scene, it does seem that the conflicts of Negro life can no longer be kept apart from the general political and economic crises of the contemporary world. Even historical studies like *Race, Class, and Party* or Professor Frazier's two competent studies of Negro family life, one the free Negro family and the other, modern family adjustments, as they are taking place in a typical urban center like Chicago, point unmistakably to the Negro situations as just the symptoms and effects of general conditions and forces. Similarly a labor study like Miss Herbst's narrative of the struggle of Negro labor to organize in Chicago, or an economic study of economic power like Professor Edward's, both force home the same lesson that the Negro position is a reflex of the dominant forces in the local situation. I have already referred to this trend in several independent lines of investigation. It suggests at least a new attitude of looking beyond the narrow field of Negro life itself for our most significant explanations and more basic causes; and even suggests expecting basic remedies to come from general social movements rather than just the narrow movements of race progress, however helpful or indicative they themselves may be. Possibly the most constructive of all points of view will turn out to be that reflected in Professor Young's *American Minority Peoples*. Here we have the case of the various minorities compared against the common reactions of the dominant majority, and a tracing of common lines through their differences. Two advantages are obvious; one the broader chance of discovering basic reasons, and then also, the possibility of foreseeing the possibilities not only of minority advance, but as Professor Young farsightedly suggests, minority coalition under the stress of common persecution and suffering. To the conservative thinker or the goodwill humanitarian, such alternatives may seem to be unwelcome and unwarranted bogeys, but one of the real services of social science should be a level-headed exploration of all the possibilities in a situation under analysis. And certainly, no one with a scientific-minded or realistic approach could overlook the possibility of such developments. This will be even more apparent as the special research of the Negro question integrates itself more and more with the competent analysis of the common general problems of which the Negro problem is a traditional, but loose and unscientific conglomerate.

In the other fields, the literary output is interesting, but not of outstanding significance. For all their common focus in the rather uniquely primitive life of the St. Helena Island group, Professor Johnson's book, *Folk Culture on St. Helena Island* and Dr. Kiser's study of the breakup and change of pattern between that and migration from there to Harlem, these two studies have only descriptive virtue. Only occasionally do they reveal the mechanisms of the interesting changes or survivals which they chronicle. That deep secret still eludes the anthropologist, and one comes away from these studies only with an impression of the infinite variability and adaptability of the human animal. Decidedly more venturesome is Father Williams's provocative study of *Voodoos and Obeahs* in Haiti. He rightly distinguishes voodoo as originally a pagan survival, coming from the traditional Ashanti and West Coast cults, driven underground and fusing with black magic or Obeah, which "was originally antagonistic to Myalism or white magic, until the ban of missionarism brought them together in common outlawry." This is a really important suggestion, illustrating more than a mere "description of facts." Controversial as such interpretations must be, eventually our only scientific explanations must come from the analysis of historical roots and causes. Another promising start in true anthropological interpretation is in the volume of family genealogies and anthropometric comparison of direct descendants brought together by Mrs. Day under the auspices of Professor Hooton of Harvard University, who writes the sponsoring foreword. Here we have the very antithesis of bold and highly conjectural tracing of clues, in painstaking and detailed comparisons within limited but exhaustively controlled areas. This is a pioneer and promising approach, put forward undoubtedly more to prove and vindicate a method than to establish as final the very tentative conclusions or suggestions about mulatto trends.

Passing mention must be made of a delightful child's biography of Harriet Tubman in Mrs. Swift's *The Railroad to Freedom*, a continuation of Mrs. Gollock's school biographies of prominent African characters, this time *Daughters of Africa*, companion volume to *Sons of Africa*, and *Women Builders*, a series of life sketches of prominent Negro women, compiled by Miss Sadie Daniel, and published by the press of the Society for the Study of Negro Life and History. Professor Brawley has also added to his long list of publications another volume, *The History of the English Hymn*. But generally speaking, the field of biography and belles lettres has not been as much to the fore as usual: nor has the field of drama; in which several stage presentations have been at best only partial successes, and the only published play,—*Black Souls* by Mrs. Annie Nathan Meyer, decidedly a propaganda piece, of good intentions and laudable sympathy, but decidedly weak in dramatic conception and execution.

It would seem, then, that the year on the whole had been more notable for pathbreaking than accomplishment, with exceptions already noted. It is to the promise of their fulfillment, however, that we look forward to another year and another crop of what still has to be called "Negro Literature."

32

THE ELEVENTH HOUR
OF NORDICISM

Retrospective Review of the
Literature of the Negro for 1934

PART I

A retrospective review must needs ask the question: what have been the dominant trends in the literature of the year? I make no apology for presenting my conclusions first, although I vouch for their being conclusions and not preconceptions. Only toward the end of a long list of reading was there any semblance of dominant notes and outstanding trends. But in retrospect they were unmistakably clear; each writer somewhere along the road, no matter what his mission, creed, or race, had met the Zeitgeist, had been confronted with the same hard riddle, and had not been allowed to pass on without some answer. Even in the variety of answers, the identity of the question is unmistakable. Of course, for almost no one has it been an overt or self-conscious question: the artist is concerned with his own specific theme and knows firsthand only the problems of his own personality. But the Zeitgeist is as inescapable as that goblin of chatterbox days that wormed himself as tape through the keyhole of a bolted door to become a real ogre again as soon as he had twisted through: if the artist bars the front-gate, it slips round to the back door, and when he bolts that, up through the trapdoor of the subconscious or down the chimney of his hearth or in between the windows of his observation of life, the dominant question of the day relentlessly comes in sooner or later. It is the small-souled artist who runs and cringes; the great artist goes out to meet the Zeitgeist.

What is the riddle for 1934? Time was when it was some paradox of art, some secret of Parnassus. Today, it is a conundrum of the marketplace, a puzzle of the crossroads,—for the literary Sphinx sits there at the crossroads of civilization ceaselessly asking, "Whither, Mankind?" and "Artist, Whither goest thou?" The social question will not down, no matter what the artist's other problems. For the Negro writer, this has been:—Shall I go left or right or take the middle course; for the white writer:—Shall I stick with the Nordics or shall I desert their beleaguered citadel? It is the eleventh hour of capitalism and the eleventh hour of Nordicism, and all our literature and art are reflecting that. Naturally it is the latter which for the literature of the Negro theme is the matter of chief concern.

One wonders by what strange premonition artists are so suddenly and keenly aware of such crises, until one realizes that they are after all the spiritually sensitive, the barometers of the spirit and the sentinels of change. And now, with striking unanimity they are all agog over Nordicism. Many are for it, passionately, vehemently, but they are just as symptomatic of a present crisis and an impending change as those who are boldly and deliberately recanting it. Dominant ideas behave that way at their critical moments, and before their last relapses always have these hectic fevers and deliriums of violent assertion. Rampant fascism and hectic racialism are in themselves omens of the eleventh hour, as much and more than the rising liberal tide of repudiation and repentance. There is no millennium around the corner, art has little or no solutions, but it is reflecting the decline of a whole ideology and the rise of a new conception of humanity,—as humanity.

Until some evidence is before him, the reader may think this an unwarrantable conclusion from such a provincial segment of contemporary literature as the fiction of Negro life traditionally is. But after glancing at the list of novels on this theme, let him consider that the fiction of Negro life for the year 1934 contains five or six of the best sellers of the year's fiction crop, one prize novel, two choices of the Book-of-the-Month and two of the Literary Guild. The unquestioned prominence and popularity of the theme itself is significant. To that we must add the advance in the treatment that the year has registered. Of course, the old pattern gets itself repeated; Stark Young makes a virtue of a romantic throwback adequately exposed and criticized for *Opportunity* readers in Sterling Brown's recent review. But in the light of many another novel of the South on this same list, who would begrudge the old plantation tradition this beautiful but quavering swan song? Personally I am not as concerned as some over the persistence of the old tradition, for alongside *So Red the Rose*, and *Transient Lady*, and *Let the Band Play Dixie*, there comes also from the same South the corrective antidotes, *Stars Fell on Alabama*, and lest that be cited in spite of its evident close study as a Yankee's novel, then the work of native Southerners like Stribling's *Unfinished Cathedral*, Margaret Sperry's *Portrait of Eden*, William March's *Come in at the Door*, and Clement Wood's *Deep River*. It is true no deep vindication comes from the unusual frank realism of these novels of the new school, but for all their present defeatist denouements, they show a South in the throes of a dilemma tragic for both sides and insoluble because of the local traditions. What more can we ask of art; it is only the logic of history that can go further,—and of that such art is a prophet and forerunner.

In *Unfinished Cathedral,* Miltiades Vaiden does take a stand, even though futile, against the lynching mob, and yet fate after forcing him to taste the bitter dilemma of the lynching of his own son, confronts him once again, after the tragedy of his own daughter, with the same situation in the black side of the family escutcheon, and the curtain catches him repudiating even the sacred aristocratic tradition of patronage as he drives off his quadroon half-sister. And in *Stars Fell on Alabama*, Mr. Carmer gets down to the real folklore that Joel Chandler Harris coated over, exposes realistically its sordid rootage in the bogs of illiteracy and primitive reversions and boldly suggests that such conditions know no racial boundary. Carl Carmer anatomizes Alabama, and for all his poetic love of the primitive shows the other devastating side of the deep South.

In *Come in at the Door,* William March tells a most unusual story, that of the close psychological relationship between an impressionable white lad, Chester Hurry, and Simon Baptiste, his educated mulatto tutor, whom he unwittingly dooms and from whose spirit, in self-imposed expiation, he can never successfully disentangle his own inner life. Remembering that psychological intimacy is the last taboo, more sacrosanct than the admission of sex intimacies, we ought to see the tradition cracking to the core in a book like this, in spite of its poetic diffidence. Then in *Portrait of Eden,* we come under the bold pen of a woman writer to the most unromantic and frank portrayal of the seamy side of the South that I have yet encountered. The hero, Doctor McIntyre, working to reconstruct the almost unreconstructable, has an educated Negro colleague, who is lynched; he himself is murdered by "a cracker imbecile," and in the words of another reviewer, his enemies are "virulent Babbitry, political corruption, barbarous Fundamentalism, primitive superstition and personal feuds." Here is another South, and it is as much the South as that other one of colonels and colonel's ladies, wide porches, rambler roses, juleps, and magnolias. For one, I would not deny the South its romanticism; if realism reminds us that it is not the whole story. Even Octavus Roy Cohen in *Transient Lady* has left the banter of black servant's dialogue for the bitter feuds of the townsfolk; and only Mr. Bradford remains in the groove of the old tradition, if we except the apologetic *So Red the Rose.* Bradford's stories cannot be dismissed because of their social philosophy: they are powerful sketches based on acute though narrow vision. If he ever broadens the angle, the South will have another Uncle Remus.

Everyone realizes that *Candy,* Mrs. Alexander's much read novel, is in the Peterkin tradition, and I suppose will complain that another stereotype is forming. I suppose this is so, but why should the Negro theme be exempt from this general phenomenon of imitation for which we have yet discovered no antidote but the shifting effect of time? The day is fast approaching when no few fixed types can be generalized as portraying the sum-total substance of Negro life and character. Then and then only the invidiousness of certain types will disappear (I admit and deplore their present invidiousness). But the only remedy is the portrayal of the neglected types. And then, too, in the formula of Scarlet Sister Mary and Cricket and Candy, there is one significant strand of the recantation of Nordicism,—the genuine admiration and envy of the primitive and the reaction from puritanism. No student of the current trend of morals and convention ought to grieve too deeply over the implied slight of the amoralist mores of these South Carolina plantations; the novels of Greenwich Village and Hollywood, except for the setting, reveal the same attitudes and reactions. My complaint is that Mrs. Alexander, for all her studious effort, is no Julia Peterkin, as yet.

Finally, if it is Nordic bearbaiting that the fans call for, no partisan propagandist could have framed a more poetic-justice type of plot than Clement Wood's story of the marriage, quarrel, and reunion of a daughter of the South and Elden, the Negro concert singer, even though their private Eden has to be in exile. But *Deep River* is a provocative and not a sincerely artistic or competent novel. One regrets that a theme of such ultimate implications has been reached before the proper maturity of those tendencies we have been discussing; for the present, only irony can make them real or effective with any considerable number of readers.

And just this mechanism has been used in the more successful of the stories of the first Negro writer whose fiction we discuss, Langston Hughes in his much discussed *The Ways of White Folks*. Here is the militant assault on the citadel of Nordicism in full fury, if not in full force. Avowedly propagandist, and motivated by radical social philosophy, we have here the beginnings of the revolutionary school of Negro fiction. But though anti-bourgeois and anti-Nordic, it is not genuinely proletarian. But it is nevertheless a significant beginning, and several stories in the volume, notably "Father and Son," rise far above the general level of rhetorical protest and propagandist reversal, achieving rare irony and real tragedy. But for pure folk quality, even the sort that a proletarian school of Negro fiction must think of achieving, Zora Hurston's first novel has the genuine strain and the most promising technique. This is not surprising to those who know the careful apprenticeship she has served in the careful study of the South from the inside. John Buddy's folk talk, and later his sermons as "Rev. Pearson" are rare revelations of true Negro idiom of thought and speech, and if the plot and characterization of this novel were up to the level of its dialogue and description, it would be one of the high-water marks of Negro fiction. It is for this reason that I look forward to Miss Hurston's later work with more curiosity and anticipation than to that of any of our younger prose writers. For years we have been saying we wanted to achieve "objectivity":—here it is. John's first and last encounters with a train are little classics. "You ain't never seed nothin' dangerous lookin' lak dat befo', is yuh?" "Naw suh and hit sho look frightenin'. But hits uh pretty thing do. Whar it gwine?" "Oh eve'y which and whar." The train kicked up its heels and rattled off. John watched it until it had lost itself down its shiny road and the noise of its going was dead. And then the last encounter: "He drove on but half-seeing the railroad from looking inward. The engine struck the car squarely and hurled it about like a toy. John was thrown out and lay perfectly still. Only his foot twitched a little. . . . "Damned, if I kin see how it happened,' the engineer declared. 'God knows I blowed for him.' . . . And the preacher preached a barbaric requiem poem. So at last the preacher wiped his mouth in the final way and said, 'He wuz uh man, and nobody knowed 'im but God,'—and it was ended in rhythm."

However it is when we turn from the Southern to the African scene that we sense the full force of the anti-Nordic tide that seems to have set in. For here we have the almost unqualified worship and glorification of the primitive, combined with a deep ironic repudiation of the justifying illusions of the "white man's burden." The native now not only dominates the scene, but it is his philosophy that triumphs or at least has the last word. Fatalism and futility brood over the scene like the heat and the fever, and if anything wins, it is nature. Indeed in *Black God*, Miss Manners-Sutton suggests that it is black magic that casts the die: M'Kato waiting for years for vengeance for his maimed hands and the rape of his sister sees a pilgrimage of death overtake trader, missionary, free-booter, government officer, outcast adventurer, and eventually his long awaited enemy. The jungle everywhere exacts its expiating toll for the intrusions of white civilization; a different story from the romantic conquests in the fiction of a decade back. And only the weapon of magic, bribed from the native witch doctor, stops the avenging path of the "Black Master," native agitator and foe of the white man's power, who has undermined the Governor's self-confidence and authority and even become the paramour of his wife. It is a pity to sketch this lurid outline of melodrama, when the real charm and value of the book lies in the ironic etchings of character and description which make the substance of the book so superior to its theme and plot that one quite wishes there were no plot. Nevertheless, the justifications of our main conclusion must be pointed out.

Finally comes Emily Hahn's *With Naked Foot*, a masterpiece of observation, style, and conception. Miss Hahn has served a fine apprenticeship in *Congo Solo*,—she knows her terrain and her human subject matter perfectly. Now she has chosen a daring and a great theme and lifts the last shroud of silence from the tragedy of sex and love as it entangles the white man and the black woman, alien to each other in folkways, but not in basic emotions and common human needs. Mawa has a child by her first master-husband,—Joachim, who throughout the succession of four liaisons remains the light and hope of her life. One by one they died or went, and Mawa holds her precarious superiority over her tribesmen as the mistress of the powerful. The Portuguese shopkeeper, the fat trader, the lean, meticulous government officer, and finally the romantic American schoolteacher with a conscience; they all succumbed to Mawa's charms and the African loneliness. At last it is Adam Kent's conscience that proves her undoing, he hurt her with a kind of love of which she knew nothing and wounded her life to the quick in trying to save her child from the primitive environment to which he only partly belonged. And as he passes out of her life, Mawa or the hull of Mawa sinks back into the chattel marriage she has defied so long to become the headsman's aging concubine. Here is the compound tragedy of individuals and of the civilizations they represent, told with the swift deft touch and with ironically tempered understanding. This book will be cited years from now as one of the significant atonements for Nordicism: may it and its like provide the catharsis we have awaited so long!

One can afford to linger over the fiction of the year because of the almost complete cessation of poetry. Somehow the poetic strain has dwindled in quantity and quality; the occasional poems of Cullen and Hughes are below the level of their earlier work, and only the muse of Sterling Brown seems to mature, and then only with a satirical and somewhat sardonic twist. Evidently it is not the hour for poetry; nor should it be,—this near-noon of a prosaic, trying day. Poets, like birds, sing at dawn and dusk, they are hushed by the heat of propaganda and the din of work and battle, and become vocal only before and after as the heralds or the caroling serenaders. The poetry section of the Cunard *Anthology* for example has for the most part an iron, metallic ring; interesting as it is, it is nevertheless hot rhetoric, clanging emotion. That is indeed the dominant note of this whole remarkable volume; making it one of the really significant signs of these times. There is much of unique informational and critical value in these eight hundred pages which document both the wrongs and the achievements of the black man and capitalize for the first time adequately the race problem as a world problem. But the capital "P" is for propaganda, not poetry, and the book hurls shell, bomb, and shrapnel at the citadel of Nordicism. And again we must pause to notice that the daring initiative in so many instances comes from the white woman artist and author: strange, we say until we remember Lucretia Mott and Harriet Beecher Stowe. In passing, we must mention a noteworthy revival of John Brown by David Karsner, to goad the militancy of our day with the tonic of the militancy of our grandfathers' generation.

Still the pealing of the tocsin bell, however timely, cannot completely crowd out the old carefree romanticism and drown out entirely the strum of the guitar and the plunk of the banjo. The Lomax collection of *American Ballads* is with us to recall the immense contribution of the Negro to the balladry of the country, and George Lee's *Beale Street* comes to remind us vividly of the picturesque, swaggering, and racy origin of the "Blues." Mr. Lee knows his Beale Street from its respectable end to the river bottoms where "River George" blustered and ruled. Incidentally the story of River George is one of the gems of the book; to my mind he is a better ballad subject than John Henry. In fact I confess to liking the picaresque side of this book; the respectabilities are pitiably pompous by contrast, and one regrets often that the author has chosen to mix his narrative. Yet to leave out the strange incongruities that the ghetto policy creates on Beale Street and elsewhere in Negro life would perhaps be false to the realities of Negro life; Mr. Lee has his justification in fact, if not in the congruities of art.

Turning now to the Negro drama of the year, we find a curious mixture of primitivism and modernism. Perkins' *Dance with Your Gods* and Heywood's *Africana* obviously each tried to exploit the vogue which *Kykunkor* started. To the credit of Broadway be it said that their tawdry tinsel and melodramatic shoddy failed; where the authentic and moving vitality of *Kykunkor* succeeded. Mr. Horton, (Asadata Dafora by original name) has really made a contribution to the drama of the African theme and setting; only its difficult intricacies of dance, pantomime, chant, and drum-orchestra technique will prevent its sweeping the Negro stage with cleansing and illuminating fire. The production should by all means have a photo-sound recording; it is a classic of a new genre and will be eventually a turning point in Negro native drama.

The Broadway that is to be commended for thumbing down several specious fakes is to be chided for dooming Paul Green's *Roll Sweet Chariot*. Of course it was a cumbersome chariot, too overworked and overlaid with trappings (Mr. Green frequently overloads his plays with ideas and clogs his dramatic machinery), but the theme idea was good and significant. But for the present sound development of Negro drama, anyway, we need the tributary rather than the commercial theater. It is for such a theater obviously that Mr. Randolph Edmonds has written his *Six Plays for a Negro Theatre.* Professor Koch is right in his preface when saying: "This, so far as I know, is the first volume of its kind. [He means by a Negro playwright]. It suggests new horizons." And Mr. Edmonds is theoretically right when he calls for a few Negro plays that are not defeatist and that are pivoted on the emotions and interests of Negro audiences. But, though they may be considerably redeemed by good acting, these historical and situational melodramas are hardly the stuff of great or highly original Negro drama. But their author has the temperament and the enthusiasm necessary for hardy pioneering, and he has bravely crossed some dramatic Rubicon,—even if the Alps are still ahead.

Finally here is a play that, though it has not scaled the dramatic heights, has burrowed under. Coming into the thick of the race problem by the unusual route of the class struggle and its radical formulae, this vehicle of the Theatre Union has not only made a box-office success but has harnessed the theater to propaganda more successfully than has been done in this generation. Its clock, so to speak, strikes eleven for capitalism and Nordicism by the same pounding realistic strokes. No matter where one stands on the issues, there is no denying the force and effect of *Stevedore.* Only a driving, pertinent theme could carry such amateurish dialogue and technique; but then, *Uncle Tom's Cabin* was one of the worst plays dramatically in the long history of the American stage, but look at its record and its results, in and out of the theater! Certainly two of the most powerful issues of the contemporary scene have met in *Stevedore,* and a synthesis of race and class as a new type of problem drama may just as well be taken for granted. The applause which has greeted this play may well have national and international repercussions, and I do not envy the consternation of Nordic ears.

PART II

Where it is a question of Nordicism, sociology might reasonably be expected to be in the vanguard; however it is not so. Sociology,—at least the American brand, is a timid science on general principles and conclusions; fact-finding is its fetish. It particularly sidesteps conclusions on the race question, and Negro sociologists, fearing to break with the genteel academic tradition in this respect, have usually been more innocuous than their white confreres,—making a great virtue and parade of inconsequential fact-finding and bland assertions of inter-racialism. That this situation is finally changing after nearly two decades dominated by such attitudes is due to the influence of just a few strong dissenting influences,—the most important of which has come from the militant but unquestionably scientific school of anthropologists captained by Professor Boas. They have dared, in season and out, to challenge false doctrine and conventional myths, and were the first to bring the citadel of Nordicism into range of scientific encirclement and bombardment. An essay in itself could be written on the slow but effective pressure that now has ringed the Nordic doctrines and their advocates round with an ever-tightening scientific blockade. The gradual liberalizing of the American historians and sociologists on the race question has been largely due to the infiltration of the conclusions of cultural anthropology, with its broader perspective and its invalidation of the basic contentions of historical racialism. Yet in the face of this, Negro educators have just made a belated beginning with the study of anthropology and the application of its findings to racial history and the social analysis of contemporary racial situations. At last, however, some beginning has been made.

An item, omitted from our first list, *Race and Culture Contacts*, edited from the proceedings of the Twenty-Eighth Meeting of the American Sociological Society, aside from interesting papers on "Traditions and Patterns of Negro Family Life" by Professor E. F. Frazier and on "Negro Personality Changes in a Southern Community" by Professor Charles S. Johnson, has important theoretical papers by Professor Robert E. Park on "Race Relations and Certain Frontiers" and Professor W. O. Brown on "Culture Contact and Race Conflict." In fact for years, Professor Park has been insisting on the application of some general principles of culture contacts to the analysis of the American race problem (our most insidious and unscientific assumption has been and still is that this question is completely sui generis). Here in this paper he discusses general phenomena of racial intermixture and through an analysis of mixed blood status tries to get at the basic phenomena of ethnic conflict and change. Professor Brown undertakes more boldly (thank God for a bit of theoretical boldness occasionally) to trace "the process or natural history of race conflict," and tentatively develops a "race conflict sequence through six steps to the ultimate liquidation of conflict in the cultural assimilation and racial fusion of the peoples in contact." I suggest that even with the dangers of hasty generalization, a major interpretative contribution to the fruitful analysis of the race problem has either been made or will grow out of this approach and its comparative technique. Such work lifts the discussion immediately from that futilely academic plane of mere fact-finding upon which our best trained minds, black and white, have been considering the race question for nearly a generation. Though not devoted exclusively to our special subject, I would star this book as the most significant sociological item of the year, in this field of course, because of the promise and significance of this new approach to the scientific discussion of the race question.

From such thought-provoking viewpoints, one naturally turns with impatience to the traditional grooves of fact-finding and interracial reporting. Under the title of *Negro-White Adjustment*, Paul E. Baker makes a very exhaustive and painstaking summary of interracial work and organization, which is redeemed partially from the category of a catalogue by the attempt to analyze the platforms and classify the techniques of interracial work in America. Similarly, Mr. George R. Arthur, of the YMCA. and the Rosenwald Fund, gives an interpretive analysis and history of the welfare work of the twenty-five separate YMCAs in *The Negro Frontier,* with a deserved chronicle of Mr. Julius Rosenwald's contributions and his philosophy of their mission as "frontiers of adjustment in the urbanization of the Negro." It may seem ungrateful to label books of this type as manuals of professional interracial work, but they are in the sense that they are committed, unconsciously for the most part, to a definite philosophy of the race question and see the facts of the situation in terms of these commitments. No new light on the nature of the question or of possible new attacks and approaches need be expected under these circumstances, no matter how careful or exhaustive the analysis of the situation. Gradualism and goodwill are the dogmatic commitments of this school of social thought,— and that's that.

Shadow of the Plantation by Professor Charles S. Johnson is a triumph of recording sociology, the general limitations of which we have already discussed. Such detailed description cannot issue, as Dr. Park in his preface seems to think, in interpretative sociology, because the comparative basis and approach are lacking. For example, the conditions described in backward rural Alabama are not merely a relic of slavery and the "belated shadow of the old plantation," but a decidedly different modern deterioration, which though an aftermath of slavery, is actually the product of contemporary exploitation and the demoralization of the rural community life of the South. It is not primarily racial; but a question of a set of conditions as vividly shown by Carl Carmer's *Stars Fell on Alabama;* in this sense a better version of the situation, even in the scientific sense, though a reputed work of fiction. A more interpretative purpose and accomplishment can be credited to Weatherford and Johnson's *Race Relations,*—an elaborate and much belated textbook covering the whole range of the main historical and sociological aspects of the American race problem. The freshest contributions seem to be the discussion of "Programs Looking Toward Solution or Amelioration of Race Relations" and the chapter discussing "Can There be a Separate Negro Culture?" Rarely has either topic been put into the frame of full or objective discussion, and it is a distinct service to have done so.

Another wing of Negro scholars have definitely taken the less objective approach and philosophy; and of these Dr. Carter G. Woodson is the pioneer and leader. More and more, this erstwhile factual historian deliberately abandons that point of view and strikes boldly out for corrective criticism and the partisan encouragement of group morale. Dr. Woodson's stocktaking of *The Negro Professional Man and the Community* is weighted as much with trenchant criticism, soundly constructive for the most part, as it is with a factual report of the rise and service of the Negro professional classes. The thesis of the peculiar importance of these groups in Negro life is well sustained and explained, and the diagnosis that today we are seriously suffering from a faulty distribution of our professional group is worth immediate and serious consideration. On the whole, this is a book every Negro professional man or prospective professional should be required to read. Dr. Willis N. Huggins has compiled a useful syllabus outline of references and source materials in *African History* and the wider aspects of the color problem, conceived very much in the same school of semi-propagandist thought that Dr. Woodson is responsible for. An inevitable product of the reaction to Nordic bias, such corrective history and sociology has its definite place and value, even though such a position is difficult to universalize. Until the pseudoscience of the Nordics is completely routed, there will be a grave need for such militant history and for a critical, opinionated sociology.

In *Negro Americans, What Now?*, James Weldon Johnson tries and rather succeeds in striking a happy medium. It is an attempt at pithy, commonsense analysis of the racial situation, its alternatives, and of the major objectives of the struggle. It is neither surprising nor discrediting that in the final weighing, the NAACP platform of political and civil rights action should receive very favorable, perhaps preferential emphasis. The value of the analysis lies in the succinct way in which issues usually clouded with partisan bias and emotion are clarified and touched with the wand of common sense; oddly enough an infrequent salt in the problem loaf. One quotation I should like to risk, because it is important: "What we require is a sense of strategy as well as a spirit of determination. . . . I have implied the fact that our policies should include an intelligent opportunism; by which I mean the alertness and ability to seize the advantage from every turn of circumstance whenever it can be done without sacrifice of principle." This is one of my reasons for characterizing this book as 'glorified common-sense on the race question.' It has anticipated its radical critics by saying: "Conservatism and radicalism are relative terms. It is as radical for a black American in Mississippi to claim his full rights under the Constitution as it is for a white American in any state to advocate the overthrow of the existing national government. The black American in many instances puts his life in jeopardy, and anything more radical than that cannot reasonably be required."

Finally, attention must be called to a contribution from the distant perspective of the International Peoples College in Denmark, Rebecca Barton's *Race Consciousness and the American Negro,*—essentially a philosophical study of the psychological complications and complexes of racial consciousness as reflected in Negro literature. This is a painstaking study from a pioneer angle, and only the lack of intimate knowledge of the suppressions that do not get into the literature has prevented its being an interpretation of major and final importance. This book must be taken into consideration in the new social criticism which is just below the horizon.

The field of Negro education is at last in scholastic bloom. To chronicle this is a mild reflection on the profession, but now it can be told. Of course, the obvious handicaps of the profession and the lowered tone of a segregated fraternity have accounted for the lack of productiveness in this field. *The Journal of Negro Education* climaxes a very creditable but young career with a Yearbook on "The Physical and Mental Abilities of the Negro," a symposium that reflects not only valuable collaboration between white and Negro scholars but the interpretative focusing that only Negro auspices can give to issues that too long have had controversial discussion on uneven terms. The further historical contribution of Professor Dwight O. W. Holmes in his study, *The Evolution of the Negro College* and the analytic study of Professor Horace Mann Bond on *The Education of the Negro in the American Social Order* balance the educational field's contribution in a way that suggests providence since it is not the result of collusion. If the competent discussion of the educational problems and situations of the Negro pick up from this new start, we may anticipate a new phase of development in this numerous but somewhat stagnated and stultified profession. In Dean Holmes's book the dramatic historical role of the Negro college as the pivot of advance during Reconstruction is importantly documented, and in Dean Bond's book, the present inadequacies and injustices of public provision for Negro education are pointedly briefed and analyzed; to mention only one phase of the constructive contributions of these welcome contributions. In all, there is fortunately reflected a growing tendency not to regard the educational problems of the Negro as different in kind, but only in degree; with a definite trend toward rejoining the mainstream of educational thought after a period of regrettable but inevitable isolation, which has been the heaviest cost of the policy of educational segregation.

In the field of Africana, the contributions this year are not voluminous, but they are significant. In *Liberia Rediscovered* we have little more than a veiled justification of the Firestone policy in that sad tangle of democracy and imperialism, and in Ifor Evans's *Native Policy in Southern Africa*, we have a faint beginning at objectivity in the discussion of the worst racial situation in the world,—that of the Union of South Africa and adjacent protectorates and mandates. The significant books are those by Helser, Herskovits, and Westermann. Dr. Herskovits, this time in collaboration with his wife, resurveys the Suriname cultures of the South American Guinea Negroes after a sojourn in the original home of these cultures, West Africa. He, or rather they, find more evidence than previously for their contention that there are important transplanted survivals of African cultures in the Western hemisphere. Eventually

as the outlines of these are retraced, we may be able to reconstruct in rough outline the cultural derivations of various
groups of Negroes or various stages in the fading out of these
original traits and traditions. In addition to its serious anthropological bearings, *Rebel Destiny* is fascinating reading and
proves that sound folklore can be as entertaining as pseudo
folklore.

Helser's book on *Education of Primitive People* is primarily
an attempt to find a practical technique of missionary education based upon some sensible recognition of the place and
worth of the native tradition in such a program. Carried out a
little more thoroughly, the study would have constituted a
contribution on the part of the practice of social training in
primitive society to our own changing system of educational
aims and technique. Such a contribution must in time be made,
and when it arrives the final reversal on the missionary psy-
chosis of "Greenland's icy mountains and India's coral strand"
will have been put into the record. That book will then justify
what an overenthusiastic admirer has said of this one: "A revelation not only of what education among a primitive people
may be but of what real education essentially is."

Professor Westermann is co-director of the International Institute of African Languages and Cultures, and writes almost
pontifically on *The African To-Day*. The point of view is that
of modified imperialism, naturally,—the benevolent trustee-
ship conception, the advocacy of the new compromise of indirect rule and the encouragement of integral African traditions
with economic but not serious cultural penetration. Of course,
it remains to be proved that this reconstructed imperialism is
possible; and sound and just, even if possible. However, the
brief for it is carefully and humanely advanced by Dr. Westermann, with as much detailed anthropological information as
to what is really going on in Africa by reason of the contact
and conflict of cultures as is gathered between any two book
covers. The study is, therefore, a gift horse that cannot be
looked too harshly in the mouth by serious students of the African scene, even though the inspiration is too extra-racial to
be a final or a truly representative picture of the African today.

That picture must, of course, come eventually from the African himself. But in the process that we have been discussing all along, namely the recanting of Nordicism, this book and its dominant point of view represent one long delayed and welcome admission,—namely, that there are elements of permanent value in African cultures and their tradition, and that the complete displacement of these cultures would be an irreparable loss. The idea that they yet have their complementary contribution to make to the cultures of the white man is, of course, below the horizon as yet, but not so far below as not to give some hints of its impending rise.

33

DEEP RIVER, DEEPER SEA

Retrospective Review of the
Literature of the Negro for 1935

PART I

Deep river; deeper sea!—even a landlubber knows that! How much water, then, is under our literary keel? Out with the critical plummet! But there's the hitch; in 1934 we felt and announced the shock of the breakwater, we know we are further downstream,—the view has suddenly widened, the sense and tang of the sea are anticipating the actual sight of it, and yet,— the waters are shallower than they were upstream and the current has slackened. Where, then, are we?

If the reader has patience, let us try a simile. A generation back, Negro literature and art were shallow trickles and stagnant puddles in the foothills; in some instance, perhaps, choked sluggish creeks behind rural millponds. Meanwhile, the poets cried out: "Yonder's Parnassus," and the critics blubbered: "We want the sea, nothing will do but the sea." But art had no such magic; water cannot run uphill and doesn't forthright leap dams and ditches. So 'poetic justice,' 'universal values,' 'high life and vindication' were yearned for in vain. Consequently, racial expression had to run inevitably the traditional course; in turns; to trickle in babbling brooks of rhetoric, dally in sentimental shallows and romantic meadows, run headlong and raucously over the sticks and stones of controversy, slow down as it gathered soil and complexion from its native banks and clay bars, chafe im-the Negro. Both, incidentally, insist that each must be understood in basic common terms, and that the tragedy of the one is the tragedy of the other. Such developments, coming at this critical time of social reconstruction, have a meaning all too obvious. What is more amazing is the acceptance of these truths in substantial quarters in the South, due somewhat to the irrefutability of the facts, but also in large part to the happy circumstance that most of this writing is "indigenous criticism." Human nature is pretty much like that, every-where,—and here's a toast to,—and a prayer for, the most desired of all desirables,—indigenous criticism on the part of the creative and articulate Negro himself. Until this shall come, the Negro can really produce no truly universal or even fully repre-sentative art. Let the white artist study Negro life objectively and wholly in terms both of itself and its context, as he is show-ing rapid and wholesome signs of doing; let the Negro artist do so likewise! There is the sea, of which I have spoken.

Some of the younger Negro writers and artists see this situ-ation in terms of what is crystallizing in America and through-out the world as "proletarian literature." What is inevitable is, to that extent at least, right. There will be a quick broadening of the base of Negro art in terms of the literature of class pro-test and proletarian realism. My disagreement is merely in terms of a long-term view and ultimate values. To my think-ing, the approaching proletarian phase is not the hoped-for sea but the inescapable delta. I even grant its practical role as a suddenly looming middle passage, but still these difficult and trying shoals of propagandist realism are not, never can be, the oceanic depths of universal art; even granting that no art is ever groundless or timeless.

But to return briefly to our 1935 crop of Negro fiction. Readers keen on comparative values may wonder why I have not yet mentioned *Deep Dark River*, Robert Rylee's moving tragedy of Mississippi injustice and persecution. It is more of a novel structurally and more a specific study of Negro charac-ter than *Siesta*. But the last few years of fiction have just about illuminated us on the question "What is the South"; the for-ward turn now is to tackle that more courageous and hopeful analysis; "What makes it like that," in other words the *why* rather than just the *how* of the South. In these terms then, even Frederick Wight's half aesthetic travelogue *South* is more significant, though less powerful, for it tries to explain and is ever conscious of the great dilemmas in southern life by which it is set over against itself. It is important and brave for Mr. Rylee, himself a southerner, to admit, through the mouth of his white Portia, Mary Winston, in talking to Mose, in jail for murder: "You see, Mose, the story you have told me is not a story that can be told in a court room. You are a Negro and Mr. Birney is a white man. A Negro can't tell that a white man was living with his wife or that a white man sent a Negro to kill him. No jury would free you if you made that defense," but it is still more important and profound to say of the eastern Cotton Belt, as Berry Fleming does, "This is the heart of the South; you can't get any farther into the South than this. This is Anglo-Saxon and African, this is the original cotton country . . . and these three states have one-third of all the fertilizer factories in the United States. The fertilizer factory isn't on any of their state seals, but it ought to be . . . the unfertility of the soil makes a hard living. You have to put almost as much money into the ground as you get out." For when Mr. Fleming goes on to say that beauty doesn't grow out of soil like that, he might also have included justice. Diagnosis is better than description; although the day is yet young since frank description came on the horizon, this sort of analysis is still younger.

Mrs. Hallie Dickerman has written an interesting first novel, *Stephen Kent*, frank in theme, true enough to fact, but handled with timid sentimentality. Several years ago it would have been an advanced novel because of its frank treatment of miscegenation and the peculiar Southern dilemmas of the "blot on the escutcheon." However, it does not break with the old conventional formula of blood atavism and calmly accepts the rules of caste as framing irrevocable tragedy even for the thoughts of the characters themselves: Thus Stephen Kent's magnanimity in not claiming his white mother actualizes few of the deep potentialities of the plot, and despite a courageous theme, makes a milk and water contrast to the blood, iron and steel of the prevailing trend.

Negro writers of fiction come forward with but two offerings out of the rapidly increasing field. However, both are real contributions to local color and characterization, though unfortunately not in theme or social philosophy. George Wylie Henderson's first novel *Ollie Miss* is a mature and competent study of Negro farm life and its elementals so far as that can take us without any suggestion of its place in the general scheme of things. Just such detached but intimate recording is also done in Miss Hurston's folklore collection, *Mules and Men*, which has the effect of novel vignettes because of her great power of evoking atmosphere and character. It has been many years since [Negro fiction beat] patiently against barriers of prejudice, give over much of its substance to alien exploitation before gaining depth and strength enough to overleap the dam of provincialism, spurt forward, dangerously, in a waterfall of deceptive freedom, spin and eddy in self-confusion, labor toward a junction with the mainstream, press along jointly in an ever-deepening channel, though at the cost of the muddy murk of realism and the smelly muck of commercialism, at last, under the accumulated impetus of all this, to meet and challenge,—and lose, to the sea.

The reader has a right to query: "And are we really there?" Even by the simile,—not yet. Just on the threshold of the sea, nature gives us the paradox of the shallow delta with its unproductive mixture of sea sand and river soil and its unpalatable blend of salt and fresh water. And so, in this matter of the literary course of the deep, dark river of Negro literature, here we are at the end of 1935, I think, on the wide brackish waters of the delta, waiting not too comfortably or patiently in the uninviting vestibule of the ocean of great, universalized art. The scenery is monotonous, the air unsavory, the course weed-grown and tricky; half of the literature of the year isn't literature but a strange bitter bracken of commingled propaganda and art. Yet one optimistic factor stands out, in spite of all this, the horizons are wider,—wider than they have ever been: and thus the promise of the sea is assuredly there. Before too very long, the tang, taste, color and rhythm of our art will have changed irreparably from the purely racial to the universal, and those who have cried for the sea will doubtless cry for the loss of their river.

Meanwhile, our art is again turning prosaic, partisan, and propagandist, but this time not in behalf of striving, strident racialism, but rather in a protestant and belligerent universalism of social analysis and protest. In a word, our art is going proletarian; if the signs mean anything. Yesterday it was Beauty at all costs and local color with a vengeance; today, it is Truth by all means and social justice at any price. Except for the occasional detached example, those who hope for the eventual golden mean of truth with beauty must wait patiently,—and perhaps, long. Just now, all the slime and hidden secrets of the river are shouldered up on the hard, gritty sandbars and relentlessly exposed to view. Almost overnight, in the fiction and drama of Negro life, generation-old taboos have been completely broken down; in a dozen steely mirrors, miscegenation shows not its intriguing profile but its tragic full face and economic exploitation and social injustice their central tragedy of common guilt and imminent retribution, not just the stock sideshow of Negro melodrama. Hollywood still plays with a picture-book version of the old romantic South, but in serious contemporary letters, the work of Erskine Caldwell, though extreme, is typical. Here, the South is on the grill of a merciless realism, administered for the most part by disillusioned and disillusioning white southerners to whom the poor white and the Negro peasant are common victims of a decadent, top-heavy and inhuman system, for which they see no glory and no excuse. This increasing trend has caught the southern defensive completely off guard because it has made no concessions to its argumentative set; it has just confronted the orators and propagandists with overwhelming and almost photographic reporting. After all, none of us can get away from bare facts in the glare of sun or spotlight; no one can read through Caldwell's *Kneel to the Rising Sun* or Berry Fleming's *Siesta*, or out of the field of fiction, Clarence Cason's *90° in the Shade* and ever be quite the same. Especially important are they for the Negro reader, who suffers acutely from the blindness of familiarity as well as from the blinkered distortion of his own case and problem. As incurable a southern as Edward Larocque Tinker calls *Siesta* "a truthful picture of how the present generation in deep Dixie lives, loves and thinks,"—"an adult novel drawn from true American sources."

I suppose that in this matter of the new radical literature of the American South, there will always be two schools, both for the creators and the consumers, the artists and the critics. Caldwell, of course, represents the social protest approach and Miss Lumpkin's *Sign for Cain* is the most daring and logical expression of that point of view to date, barring, of course, Mr. Caldwell's own brilliant pioneering; Clarence Cason will, I think, more and more come to fame as the brave pioneer of the 'psychographic' analysts, for whom the mind-sets of the South are the keys to the situation rather than the class economics of the Marxian Caldwellites. In which case, it seems to me, Cason, though no novelist, has founded or grounded a school of southern fiction, of which Berry Fleming is, to date, the most brilliant and promising exponent. My own sympathies, temperamentally determined no doubt, are with the psychoanalysts; but I grant the power, integrity, and increasing vogue of the Marxians. What is of greater importance than this issue of approach and technique is the overwhelming agreement of both schools on the evidence of fact. They corroborate each other on the facts of the case startlingly; and together they raise up a new plateau both for the artistic and the social understanding of the South and younger Negro writers have had as firm a grip on their material as here indicated; which is so positive a gain that it is probably ungracious to complain of the lack of social perspective and philosophy. While not particularly incumbent on Miss Hurston by reason of the folklore objective of her work, there is yet something too Arcadian about hers and Mr. Henderson's work, considering the framework of contemporary American life and fiction. The depression has broken this peasant Arcady even in the few places where it still persisted, and while it is humanly interesting and refreshing enough, it is a critical duty to point out that it is so extinct that our only possible approach to it is the idyllic and retrospective. On the other hand, this same rare native material and local color in the flesh and bone of either the proletarian or the sociological strains of fiction would carry into them the one lacking dimension of great art.

On the dramatic front, however, folklore is in the ascendancy with the undoubted and deserved success of *Porgy and Bess*; since in the field of the problem play no real succession to last season's strong play *Stevedore* has come forward in spite of the obvious candidacy of Langston Hughes's current Broadway offering of *Mulatto*. Granting the difficulty of any unpleasant theme on the American stage, it is strange to account for the general lack of success of the serious Negro problem play. Playwrights, black and white, must meet this challenge, for the audience cannot be entirely blamed when one after the other, with the most sympathetic reading, plays in this category smolder rather than flame. I think it is a problem of craftsmanship primarily, recalling how long the southern realistic novel smoldered before it broke clear and bright. *Porgy* deserves its success, both as a play and as opera, it surges irresistibly with life and is totally convincing. The other themes can do the same, when master craftsmanship appears. Even without master craft a certain flare for the dramatically vital gave real life to *Stevedore*. But *Roll, Sweet Chariot*, though well studied, over-studied perhaps, is cryptic; Raphaelson's *White Man*, with an incandescent theme, sputters and goes feebly defeatist at the end—(though even at that, it is a considerable advance in the treatment of the psychology of intermarriage over *All God's Chillun Got Wings*),—and *Mulatto* merely noses through on the magnificent potentialities of its theme, which for the most part are amateurishly smothered in talk and naïve melodrama. Of course, Broadway merely takes a pot chance as yet on serious Negro plays; they are usually hastily rehearsed, poorly staged, and superficially seasoned. But the playwrights themselves must force the issue and above all else let their characters grow up to the full stature of the heroic. Well studied genre or pastiche characters carrying through great themes in only two dimensions will never put over the serious drama of Negro life.

The Negro actor has demonstrated his capacity under great handicaps of inadequate materials; it is tragic, especially in view of her enforced and we hope temporary retirement, to think of the puny roles Rose MacClendon has had for the expression of her truly great dramatic genius. Of course, any role in which she would not have been positively miscast ought to have been open to her. But she has had to battle not only a limited chance, but even there, half-baked characterization, type roles that ill befit great dramatic powers. Imagine, for example, to take the case of *Mulatto*, a Cora who really became the Colonel's mistress as the door closed and then shifted suddenly back to the mode of the domestic servant as it opened again to company; it is for such reasons that I place primary blame, not on the audience, the producers, and Broadway traditions, but upon the faulty dramaturgy of two-thirds of the plays of Negro life, irrespective of the authorship being professional or amateur, black or white. Negro drama needs full gamut and an open throttle; and not what it has so often had, either skill without courage, or courage without skill.

Turning to belles lettres, we witness an obvious revival of biography, and this with the rumors of a projected biographical series of Negro leaders and the promised revival of the plans for an Encyclopedia of the Negro, indicates a decided awakening of the historical impulse. All three of the books in this field extend to the general reading public little known historical material that should be theirs. In the context of a vindication of saintliness and mystical apprehension of the supernatural, Arnold Lunn gives us a vivid biography of St. Peter Claver; who labored thirty-eight years during the eighteenth century for the alleviation of the victims of the slave trade. Professor Brawley brings within reach of the general reader biographical and critical material on the least known of our literary fields—the Negro writers of the colonial and early anti-slavery periods, with well-culled selections from their works. Professor Wesley has written the first complete biography of *Richard Allen*, founder of African

Methodism and pioneer racialist. All this is more than welcome, even though none of the work is in the contemporary vein of biography. Paucity of material and the Puritan repressions of those who did make the contemporary records of these worthies has undoubtedly crippled their biographers for drawing psychological portraits of their subjects. They will possibly thus remain in the daguerreotype and woodcut outlines in which they are already familiar to researchers; the gain is that this material is now at the ready disposal of the general reader, competently presented and attractively readable.

Two veteran poets have come to the fore with their medals on, so to speak. In spite of the new material, there are no new notes and no new poetic highs. In general, these two volumes of Countee Cullen and James Weldon Johnson do not advance their poetic reputations. The choruses of Cullen's translated *Medea* are finely turned, with virtuosity in fact, and it is good to have available again the cream of Weldon Johnson's *Fifty Years and Other Poems*, now out of print. However, Negro poetry cannot expect in this day of changing styles and viewpoints to live successfully on its past. That is why I turned most feverishly to the pages of *The Brown Thrush: Anthology of Verse by Negro Students*. Perhaps my present impatience with the elder generation is that I found so many weak and tiring echoes of Dunbar, Johnson, Hughes, and Cullen there. Natural enough, no doubt, but if so, why not Whitman, Swinburne, Frost, Millay, or Jeffers? In fact, Negro poetry has no excuse today for being imitative at all, and little excuse for being tenuous and trite in substance. For the new notes and the strong virile accents in our poetry today, we must shift from Harlem to Chicago; for there are Willard Wright whose verse sees the light in the *New Masses* and other radical periodicals and Frank Marshall Davis, who really brings fresh talent and creative imagination to this waning field. Both of these younger poets owe more to the Langston Hughes inspiration than to the academicians, but each in his own individual way has gone deeper into the substance of the folk life, though neither of them so deeply as that other more mature poet, Sterling Brown, who regrettably publishes so little of what he writes. I insist that we shall not know the full flavor and potentialities either of tragic or comic irony as applied to Negro experience until this sturdy, incisive verse of Brown's is fully published. For years we have waited for the sealed vials of irony and satire to open and for their purging and illuminating fire to come down in poetic flashes and chastising thunderbolts. And for some reason, the gods withhold the boon. The puny thrust that passes for irony, the burlesque smirk that masquerades as satire try one's critical soul, until one remembers illuminatingly that outside antiquity, only the Irish and the French have the gift of it. But it might have been in the gift-box of the Negro, seeing he had such need of it.

ADDENDA:
LITERATURE OF THE NEGRO,—1935
PART II

Even in the cold ashes of sociology, some new fires are burning; like a refiner's furnace in books like Cason's *90° in the Shade*, like a flaming torch in a book like Dr. Du Bois's *Black Reconstruction*. The subject needs both heat and light; more light, but in the impending crisis, heat, too, is salutary. In the small but searching volume, *The Collapse of Cotton Tenancy*, even that arch-advocate of objective sociology, Professor Charles S. Johnson, in the company of Edward R. Embree and Will W. Alexander, points an accusing finger and calls for present-day social reconstruction. This is a healthy symptom of progress in the artificially isolated and conservative field of Negro history and sociology. I take it that there will not be many more books written in this field that will ignore the general social and economic crisis and the necessary and vital linkage of the Negro situation with the general issues. Although not fully repudiated, this handicap and blight of several generations standing is now definitely on the wane.

Of course, separate discussion of racial issues and interests is necessary and inevitable, but a separate and special ideology, especially one based on outmoded social concepts, never has been desirable, although until recently it has been all too frequent. Yet one can scarcely approve in full of Dr. Du Bois's passionate leap to close the gap and throw the discussion of the Negro problem to the forefront battle-line of Marxian economics, even though *Black Reconstruction* is one of the most challenging worthwhile books of the year. This merely because it is more difficult to apply the Marxian formula to the past decades of Negro history, and that inaccurately done, really detracts considerably from the main purpose and accomplishment of the work,—viz. a crashing counter-interpretation of the Reconstruction period and a justifiable impeachment of its American historians. Ultimately,—soon perhaps, we shall have the other problem realized in a scientifically economic interpretation of the Negro's status in American life and history; meanwhile we gratefully salute Dr. Du Bois's spirited and successful historical challenge.

A useful publication, purely factual and statistical, comes from the government press, compiling the figures of the 1930 U.S. Census as they relate to the Negroes in the United States. For the first time, this appears under the acknowledged editorial supervision of Charles E. Hall, veteran Negro statistician of the Census department. Under the editorial supervision of Dr. Ambrose Caliver, and the imprint of the U.S. Department of Education, comes a small but pithy publication,— *Fundamentals in the Education of Negroes*, collating the findings of last year's conference on Negro education. The pamphlet gives the best statement available of the state of Negro education in terms of the present crisis.

The Year Book issue of the *Journal of Negro Education* brings forward, similarly, a most opportune subject, in fact the crucial one of the separate Negro school. Although the pattern of previous volumes is followed, and thus the symposium issues are well balanced, *pro* and *con*, the trend of the argument is decidedly against the principle and practice of educational segregation, and forecasts a militant reaction against it. Most of the disputants advocate challenging its legality before the courts, such as has been recently done in the University of Maryland case, so successfully prosecuted under NAACP auspices by the young Washington attorney, Charles H. Houston. The symposium and its conclusions anticipated the case, it should be noted, in estimating its significance as a gauge of educational opinion among Negroes.

As has been hinted, *The Collapse of Cotton Tenancy*, although not completely militant, turns its back definitely upon palliative measures in the problems of the rural South. It pictures vividly the present plight of the cotton tenant farmer, and though interested in the Negro particularly, uses the more scientific concept of the sharecropper, be he black or white. The authors conclude that the present crisis in southern agriculture is the final stage of the generation-old breakdown of the plantation system, that this system must be radically changed, and that there is no solution short of converting the share-tenant into an owner tenant with whatever legal and governmental aids are necessary. So, whichever way we turn, from the economic, historical, or psychological angle, a more radical and challenging point of view confronts us. One warns, another challenges, still another, as with Cason, almost vivisects; but none condone, placate, or play hopeful Pollyanna. We ought, at least, know where we are and not be victims of time-old illusions.

As one might expect, the field of Africana is a baffling mixture of tinsel and gold: this year's yield has some of the profoundest and some of the most superficial interpretations yet made of primitive life and custom. Surely one of the worst is Loederer's *Voodoo Fire in Haiti*, where again the unhappy isle is distorted by the flippant sensation monger, looking for cheap, glamorous exotic primitivism. The verdict of competent scholarship is that the Haiti of Seabrook, Craige, and Loederer simply does not exist except in the hectic imagination of these journalist-adventurers. They see largely what they preconceive, superficially document it, and are off with their wares to the eager but misguided devotees of the cult of the jungle. Those who know the jungle life more expertly come out with sober and radically different interpretations.

An instance, and an encouraging contrast is Captain Rat-tray's novel of a primitive African cult, *The Leopard Priestess*. It is a novel, and should perhaps have been listed with our fiction, but for the fact that its folklore and background are too important. The author knows his Africa from years of study and intensive experience. Authentic mystery, accurate primitive magic, and ceremonial, appropriate tropic situations follow the fate of the guilty lovers; they are enmeshed in an even more typical African guilt than the lovers of *Batouala*, and the stark simplicity of their fate convinces us that a real African romance has been written. Had it the stylistic excellence of *Batouala*, it would be the undisputed classic that the latter still is.

Another competent and illuminating record of African custom and thought is the story of a native African chieftain's son, told by Akiki Nyabongo, himself an educated native of Uganda. Mr. Nyabongo has little need of a dubious veil of fiction to decorate his narrative, unless it be to save some embarrassment in this nearly autobiographical story of the conflict between native and European mores in the youth and adolescence of little Prince Ati. In some respects, this is the first book to bring out from the inside the dilemmas of the intelligent African involved in education at the hands of missionaries and tutelage from the self-appointed trustees of their civilization. Time and again the ignorant disdain of native custom is clearly and cleverly illustrated, and more than once, the native tradition comes off best. One cannot refrain from repeating the refreshing incident of the young prince reading to his father and his assembled wives, after the yearlong diatribes of the Reverend Mr. Hubert on polygamy, of the passages from the Holy Bible detailing the story of King Solomon with his seven hundred wives and three hundred concubines. A gale of laughter is sometimes more effective than a blast of polemics.

In a Province, a problem novel of South Africa, reports for the first time effectively the main outlines of the class struggle and the industrial dilemmas of that quarter of the globe. Laurens van der Post is a painstaking artist as well as a competent reporter,—and the book betokens a new breath of artistic liberalism from the stagnant conservatism of its traditional background.

Professor Fitzgerald's social and economic geography of Africa is a pathbreaking analysis that ought to be the base of whatever prescribed studies of Africa are given in our colleges. The arts and antiquities of Africa are important for the true understanding of African life, and nothing is less known and more misunderstood by the average American Negro but without a scientific, objective basis such as this study of the great continent affords, they are a deceptive veneer. That is why, with an interest of long standing in such subjects as Professor Sadler's book on the *Arts of West Africa*, Mr. James Sweeney's admirable essay and catalogue on African art prepared for the Museum of Modern Art's remarkable spring show, or even Monsieur Carré's fine preface on the Benin civilization and its art prepared for the recent Knoedler gallery show, I still insist that a fundamental knowledge of African geography and the economics of the colonial situation are indispensable in any sound and comprehending knowledge of the land of our forefathers.

Those who need the shortcut of an interpretation combining several of these factors into a single book will, therefore, welcome and praise Geoffrey Gorer's *Africa Dances*, to my thinking, the book of the year. Starting out as an aesthetic caravan, studying the African dance, the magic key of taking Feral Benga, the talented Senegalese dancer, as devoted and respected travel companion, opened for Mr. Gorer, though a novice in Africa, doors closed to missionaries, traders, government agents, and even canny anthropologists. And so, natives, chiefs, fetish priests, colonial society, high, low, and middle-rank, townsmen, coastmen, hinterlanders all flit graphically across Mr. Gorer's diary pages with a lifelike vividness and candid reality. Of course, all praise to Mr. Gorer's own temperamental equipment, sensitiveness, amazing candor, freedom from prejudice of civilization and color (many who have immunity from one of these are chronic victims of the other), and a contagious power of description; but with all these, he could have forgotten the magic open sesame of an African friend and sponsor. He magnanimously admits this, so there is little virtue in calling attention to it, except to praise the book, which I do in everything but its pessimistic conclusions,—and this only because Africa has survived so much that it seems likely that she will survive even the modern plagues of imperialistic exploitation.

34

JINGO, COUNTER-JINGO, AND US

*Retrospective Review of the
Literature of the Negro: 1937*

PART I

The literature of the year, both by Negro and white authors, still continues to be racially tinged, some of it pro, some of it anti, little or none of it objective enough to be called "neutral." And yet some of it, for all that, is healthy and sane and true enough to be called art rather than propaganda and science rather than polemic or partisan jingo. Jingo is a touchy word since the caustic but stimulating article of Mr. Benjamin Stolberg on "Minority Jingo" in the *Nation*, (October 23). Nevertheless let's consider, by way of an aperitif, jingo, counter-jingo and "us"; us meaning Negro.

Like Mr. Stolberg, I also say: "Good Lord, deliver us from jingo!"—But unlike him, yet like a philosopher, I must begin with the beginning. And 'minority jingo' isn't the beginning, and so, not the root of the evil, evil though it may be. Minority jingo is counter-jingo; the real jingo is majority jingo and there lies the original sin. Minority jingo is the defensive reaction, sadly inevitable as an antidote, and even science has had to learn to fight poison with poison. However, for cure or compensation, it must be the right poison and in the right amount. And just as sure as revolution is successful treason and treason

is unsuccessful revolution, minority jingo is good when it succeeds in offsetting either the effects or the habits of majority
jingo and bad when it reinfects the minority with the majority
disease. Similarly, while we are on fundamentals, good art is
sound and honest propaganda, while obvious and dishonest
propaganda are bad art. Thus, I think, we must not load all
the onus (and ridicule) upon the pathetic compensations, of
the harassed minority, though I grant it is a real disservice not
to chastise both unsound and ineffective counterargument.
The Negro has a right to state his side of the case (or even to
have it stated for him), as for example in Professor Lips's *The
Savage Hits Back* and Melville Herskovits's *Life in a Haitian Valley*, antidotal to reams of falsification like Seabrook's
Magic Island, or Erskine Caldwell's *You Have Seen Their
Faces* poking out its realistic tongue at *Gone with the Wind*
and *So Red the Rose*. But some of these counterarguments
have the racial angle and are interested in the group particularities, (notice I didn't say pecularities) while another has the
class angle and significantly includes the Negro material relevant to that. We must not praise or condemn either because of
its point of view but rather because of its accomplishment in
terms of its point of view. It happens that in each of these cases
there is sound science and good art on the side of the opposition, and much majority jingo is debunked accordingly. The
minority is entitled to its racial point of view provided it is
soundly and successfully carried through. However, we shall
have to take account of volumes a little later,—and some of
them by Negro authors, that deserve every inch of Mr. Stolberg's birch.

As I see it, then, there is the chaff and there is the wheat. A
Negro, or anyone, who writes African history inaccurately or
in distorted perspective should be scorned as a "black chau-
vinist," but he can also be scotched as a tyro. A minority apologist who overcompensates or turns to quackish demagoguery
should be exposed, but the front trench of controversy which
he allowed to become a dangerous salient must be remanned
with sturdier stuff and saner strategy. Or the racialist to whom
group egotism is more precious than truth or who parades in

the tawdry trappings of adolescent exhibitionism is, likewise, to be silenced and laughed off stage; but that does not invalidate all racialism. There are, in short, sound degrees and varieties of these things, which their extremisms discount and discredit but cannot completely invalidate. I am not defending fanaticism, Nordic or Negro or condoning chauvinism, black or white; nor even calling "stalemate" because the same rot can be discovered in both the majority and the minority baskets.

I merely want to point out that minority expression has its healthy as well as its unhealthy growths, and that the same garden of which jingo and counter-jingo are the vexatious and even dangerous weeds has its wholesome grains and vegetables, its precious fruits and flowers. Selective cultivation, then, rather than wholesale plowing-under or burning over should be the sane order of the day. Transposing back to our main theme, which is literary, this would mean corrective criticism rather than general excommunication, intelligent refereeing instead of ex-cathedra outlawing. For there can be proletarian jingo as well as bourgeois and capitalist jingo and class jingoism as well as the credal and racial varieties.

As for the Negro cause in literature there is a double concern,—we are threatened both by the plague of bad art and the blight of false jingo. And jingo is more deceptive with the gloss of art and more subtly effective with the assumed innocence and disinterest of art. By all means let us be on our guard against both. Mr. Stolberg was performing a much needed critical service, then, in giving a forceful warning against any double standard in criticism, against any soft tolerance of the fallacies and opiates of internal minority chauvinism at the very time when we were making a point of the exposure and discrediting of majority jingoism. It is a matter of keen regret that much of the cultural racialism of the "New Negro" movement was choked in shallow cultural soil by the cheap weeds of group flattery, vainglory, and escapist emotionalism. To that extent it was neither sound racialism nor effective and lasting counter-assertion. The first generation of these artists, (1917–1934), were primarily handicapped by having no internal racial support for their art, and as the movement became a fad the taint of exhibitionism and demagoguery inevitably crept in. They are not to be excused entirely for having prostituted their wares and their artistic integrity. But a sounder cultural racialism would have avoided these pitfalls, would have aimed at folk realism and the discovery of basic human and social denominators to be thrown under the numerators of racial particularities for a balanced and factorable view of our group life, and in my judgment a second generation of Negro writers and artists, along with their white collaborators, are well on the way toward such a development. Some of them are writers like Langston Hughes, Zora Hurston, Arna Bontemps, Sterling Brown, whose life bridges both generations, while others, like Richard Wright, Waters Turpin, Hughes Allison, Frank Davis belong entirely to the younger generation. Their more penetrating, evenhanded, and less-illusioned portrayal of Negro life is realizing more deeply the original aims of what was too poetically and glibly styled "The Negro Renaissance." Although in self-extenuation, may I say that as early as 1927 I said:—(*Ebony and Topaz*: "Our Little Renaissance")—"Remember, the Renaissance was followed by the Reformation." Another quotation,—if I may:—"The Negro Renaissance must be an integral phase of contemporary American art and literature; more and more we must divorce it in our minds from propaganda and politics . . . the self-expression of the New Negro, if conditions in the South were more conducive to the development of Negro culture without transplanting, would spring up as just one branch of the new literature of the South, and as one additional phase of its cultural reawakening."

This is just what has happened or is happening. Josephine Johnson's *Jordanstown* is in the strict sense not a novel of Negro life, but a novel of the tragedy of labor organization in the sharecropper South; but it is notable for its rare and penetrating perception of the basis of the race problem and the Negro's position in the small town rural areas and for its daring analysis of the integration of Negro and white lives. Similarly Theodore Strauss's *Night at Hogwallow*, which details not only the lynching of an innocent Negro by a labor gang of mixed southerners and northerners but gives a more detailed account of the crowd psychology of the mob than I recall having ever read. It is both good art and good sociology; all the more notable and promising because it is Mr. Strauss's first publication. Mrs. Johnson is a Pulitzer Prize veteran which gives weight and occasionally edge to her laurels. Her sociology, too, is indisputable; she goes as far as balanced realism can go, and gives a vital sense of tragedy over and above the documentation. Incidentally, it is to be noted that most socialistic novels refuse to consider themselves defeatist in the tragic death of their main characters, as in this case of the martyrdom of Adam, the militant labor leader. Why should they? Yet why should tragedy in other contexts invariably raise the hue and cry of "defeatism"?

Defeatism in art is where the issues are unfairly joined, and where the implications, social or psychological, are vicious or misrepresentative. Both bad art and poor sociology alike can lead to that. In sinister conjunction they lead to falsity in a novel like *Us Three Women*, for all its profession of detailed documentation of the lives of three Negro women and their southern friends. The book is a deceptive survival of the old Plantation Tradition, which still thrives perniciously and unabashed in Hollywood plots, children's stories, and popular romance fiction very generally. However, one is meeting it less and less on the level of serious realistic writing: *Us Three Women* being one of these exceptions.

Two novels, one by a white and the other by a Negro author, although unevenly matched in artistry, go a long way toward proving that the return to the plantation need not be trite or reactionary. Lyle Saxon's *Children of Strangers*, has some sentimental tourists looking on at the crucial scene in Famie's tragic life, taking snapshots in the assurance that she looks "so typical" and that they are the "happiest people—not a care in the world." This after a lifetime of struggle after her early seduction, her ostracism by her proud Creole relatives, her vain and pathetic sacrifices for her illegitimate son, and the final breach of the law of her land-owning clan that spells her final sacrifice. Even with the romantic touch and the charm of the old tradition, Saxon sacrifices neither truth nor social perspective; and this novel will only seem defeatist to local color tourists on the one hand and fanatical proletarians on the other. With far less artistic power, George Lee's *River George* is yet noteworthy. The flaw probably lies in the too concocted expansion of the legend of River George, so dramatically told in the author's *Beale Street*, who was just a John Henry "bad man" of the slums, into a race-defiant protagonist of the oppressed sharecroppers. So, as other critics have noted, the first half or more of the story runs convincingly and the second not at all. Arty dialogue and sophomoric interlardings contribute to this; but the attempt to over-modernize material out of its tradition is risky. But the Negro novelist, though he needs criticism, needs to be read. He is definitely on his way somewhere. And the average Negro should know what is being written about him; he needs that analytical dimension in his life. Otherwise, his life is the cultural equivalent of living in a house without a mirror.

Part of the Negro novelist's dilemma is his obviously divided public. Few have the courage to write straight across the stereotypes of the whites and the hypersensitive susceptibilities of the blacks. And yet in no other way can great writing or a great master emerge. As good an author as Arna Bontemps, for example, writing belligerent and heroic *Black Thunder* (Macmillan, 1936),—which by the way was inadvertently and regrettably omitted from our 1936 list, this year writes a children's story which barely escapes from the melon-patch stereotypes. Wistful here and there, in a revamped setting of three little black southern adventurers in Harlem, there is still an unfortunate reversion to type even after all allowances are made for the unrealistic tradition of the child story. Whereas *Black Thunder* was historical fiction of considerable power and decided promise. Even though a highly fictionalized version of a historic slave insurrection, it documented Negro character and motivation in unconventional and all but convention-breaking ways.

And now, Zora Hurston and her magical title: *Their Eyes Were Watching God*. Janie's story should not be retold; it must be read. But as always thus far with this talented writer, setting and surprising flashes of contemporary folklore are the main point. Her gift for poetic phrase, for rare dialect and folk humor keep her flashing on the surface of her community and her characters and from diving down deep, either to the inner psychology of characterization or to sharp analysis of the social background. It is folklore fiction at its best, which we gratefully accept as an overdue replacement for so much faulty local color fiction about Negroes. But when will the Negro novelist of maturity who knows how to tell a story convincingly, which is Miss Hurston's cradle-gift, come to grips with motive fiction and social document fiction? Progressive southern fiction has already banished the legend of these entertaining pseudo-primitives whom the reading public still loves to laugh with, weep over, and envy. Having gotten rid of condescension, let us now get over over-simplification!

Just this Waters Turpin attempts in *These Low Grounds*,— and for a first novel more than half succeeds in accomplishing. A saga sweep of four generations of a family is daring for a fledgling writer, but the attempt is significant, not merely in breadth of canvas but in the conception that the Negro social tragedy is accumulative and the fight with the environment, dramatic or melodramatic for the individual, is heroic and epical for the race. So from pre–Civil War Virginia to Baltimore, Philadelphia, New York, and the contemporary Eastern Shore Maryland of the Salisbury lynching (Shrewsbury is the fictional name of the town), Turpin doggedly carries his story and the succession of parents, children, and grandchildren. The modern scene, especially rural Maryland, is well painted, and the futility of the odds of prejudice dramatically shown. It is in the dating of the generations—a task for a scholarly writer of historical fiction, and the characterization of his central figures that one finds it necessary to speak of the high promise rather than the finished attainment of this book. As it should be, it is a moving tale of courageous matriarchy, closer to

Heyward's *Mamba's Daughters* than anything else in the fiction of Negro life unless still further back we recall, as we oftener should, Clement Wood's *Nigger.*

In *American Stuff*, under the editorship of Henry Alsberg, the Federal Writers' Project presents its cross-section miscellany, with a reasonably representative participation of Negro writers and poets. Of the prose, Richard Wright's thumbnail sketches of prejudice,—"The Ethics of Living Jim Crow," is by far the most powerful and thought-provoking. However, one is left wondering whether cold steel rather than hot steel would not have been better as an etching tool; but it is encouraging to see Negro writers turning to irony on their way to the maturer mastery of satire. Incidentally, gleams of the latter are in Sterling Brown's poetic contribution to this volume,—"All Are Gay." To me the growing significance of Richard Wright still pivots on his last year's performance of 1936 in *The New Caravan.*—"Big Boy Leaves Home," the second serious omission of my last year's chronicle. It must be mentioned even after this delay because it is the strongest note yet struck by one of our own writers in the staccato protest realism of the rising school of 'proletarian fiction.' There is a legend that the spring really begins in some surprising after-midnight March clash of lightning and thunder. To my ears and with reference to the new generation note, "Big Boy Leaves Home" sounds like an opener similarly significant to Jean Toomer's startling and prophetic *Cane.* Lusty crude realism though it is, it has its salty peasant tang and poetic glint, two things that one likes to think necessary for Negro folk portraiture rather than drab, reportorial realism, no matter how often tried.

Poetry proper still lags, as indeed for the last four years. A creditable anthology of Negro poets for popular use has come from the Newark, New Jersey, WPA project and a slender volume of original verse has been printed in New Orleans under the guidance of Marcus B. Christian, himself a rising poet of some distinction. His "Southern Sharecropper" in July *Opportunity* excels anything in this small volume, however. Frank Davis's *I Am the American Negro* becomes thus the outstanding verse effort of the year. Yet the book has too many

echoes of the author's first volume and overworks its mechanism of rhapsodic apostrophes flung out in flamboyant Whit-
manesque prose poetry. The mannerism dulls the edge of his
social protest and again suggests hot untempered steel. Alone
it would be notable, but it is not a crescendo in the light of the
achievement and promise of the author's initial volume. In occasional publication there is also another Chicagoan poet,
Robert Davis, with much the same ideology, but a more restrained style. Indeed until the recent publication of the *New
Challenge* under the sponsorship of a New York group, it
began to look as though the center of the literary scene was
shifting from Harlem out to the Midwest, and even with that
promising recovery, Harlem must still look to its literary
laurels.

In the Bronze Booklet series, Sterling Brown has outlined in
carefully documented sequence and penetrating interpretation
the course of the Negro theme in American poetry and drama
in *Negro Poetry and Drama* and of the Negro theme in American fiction in *The Negro in American Fiction*. It is not too
much to say that this is a greatly needed critical service, especially since the dimension of social interpretation has been
brilliantly stressed. On the contrary, in *The Negro Genius*,
Professor Brawley, enlarging and bringing up to date his *The
Negro in Literature and Art*, has stuck to his previous method
of mere chronicle narrative with trite praise and blame evaluations. Apart from the lack of social interpretation, this is not
analytical criticism of the kind it models itself after,—Arnold,
Lowell, and Gates. But more of that later. Concluding our
belles lettres, Rosamond Johnson has a creditable anthology
of Negro folk song, in which he has achieved considerable perspective and corrected in a simpler style of arrangement the
over-ornate style of arrangement that somewhat marred his
volumes on the Spirituals.

Proportionately, it seems, as poetry has withered away, biography has waxed strong, following a dominant trend in contemporary letters. Negro biography is a province of potential
importance; if ever the anomalies of the race problem are
caught between the cross fire of close-grained fiction and

well-defined biography, we shall at last know something about its intriguing dilemmas and paradoxes. But Negro biography has yet to grow up either to the grand manner or the expertness of contemporary biography and autobiography. The single figure in the grand manner is a figure of purely historical interest and only sentimentally connected,—Pushkin. The extent to which his mixed ancestry influenced either his career or his personality are highly debatable; he was Russian among the Russians, and stands clearly only as a striking example of cultural assimilation and the timeless and spaceless universality of first-water genius, over and above cultural and national traits. But while I would not loud pedal Pushkin's ancestry, I also see no point in ignoring it, and some point in giving it a sustained pedal for a bar or so for the color-deaf ears of the prejudiced.

Coming nearer to our time and locality, the other biographies stack up interestingly, but to no Alpine heights. Curiously in contrast, McKay's autobiography exploits a personality while Angelo Herndon's exploits a cause. Balanced biography can come from neither overemphasis. Yet an important chapter of the younger generation Negro life has been documented and oddly enough both trails lead to Moscow, one in terms of cosmopolitan vagabondage and the pursuit of experience for experience's sake, the other in the hard rut of labor struggle and the proletarian movement in the deep South. The clash of individualism and collectivism, of aestheticism versus reform, of the contemporary dilemmas of race and class could not be better illustrated if these books had been prearranged and their respective authors' lives accordingly. Because of its live issues and heroic attitude *Let Me Live* has no apologies to offer even in juxtaposition with the clever style and picaresque charm of *A Long Way From Home*.

It was Professor Brawley's *Negro Builders and Heroes* that precipitated the Stolberg article and that had to sustain the full force of that blast against compensatory racialism. Exhibit A sociology, as I have said before, has bred a vicious double standard; the American success story (a majority pathology, by the way) has added its shabby psychology of Pollyanna optimism and sentimentalism, and the combination, I agree, although still the meat and bread of many professional interracialists and well-intentioned interracial movements, is stale cake on the contemporary table. Not so indigestible, once you acquire a taste for it, its chronic use induces, if I may keep up the metaphor, two serious symptoms of acute indigestion, cultural vertigo and split or dislocated social vision. Inevitable a generation ago, tolerable a half generation back, it is today not only outmoded but for the younger generation, dangerously misleading. Irrespective of personalities, then, it is time to call a halt on it.

The Incredible Messiah, from the other side of the racial fence points to the same moral: its readers and its author forget the characteristic American phenomenon from Barnum to Billy Sunday, and regard the black "Father Divine" as peculiar and racially characteristic. That's what racialism at its worst does for us; and after that, it is a hardy soul that elects not to abandon the racialist point of view altogether. Yet we cannot even if we would, and should not, as I said in the beginning, just because many cannot be sane and fair and honest about it. After all, cultural racialism has better odds on long futures than nationalism, which incidentally has similarly fallen into the hands of the emotional extremists until some reaction of sanity comes to its rescue,—if it can.

Unless the sanity index of the literary discussion of race rises more rapidly, although I think it is slowly rising, we shall perhaps have to turn to other arts for out truest view of the social scene. Two books, in each of which the Negro is incidental but perhaps all the more significant, Caldwell and Margaret Bourke-White's *You Have Seen Their Faces* and Thomas Benton's *An Artist in America* tell more of life than chapters of biography and reams of fiction.

PART II

Drama, as far as propaganda is concerned, is the bronco of the arts; most playwrights who venture dramatic jingo finish in the dust while a riderless horse makes a hasty and disorderly exit. It takes genius to balance a problem in the dramatic saddle; yet if ever a problem gets itself effectively dramatized, nothing in the whole run of art can be as spectacular or compelling. But the many-phased Negro problem still awaits its Ibsen or even its Bernard Shaw. *Stevedore, Turpentine, Run, Little Chillun,* and *Mulatto* are still the best we have to show, and with each the dramatist finishes out of control and nearly unhorsed. As for the 1937 drama field, only in combination do they register any noteworthy placing; as single performances they scarcely rate as successes. Donald Heywood's *How Come, Lawd?*, on which the promising Negro Theatre Guild unwisely gambled away its future, was a flat failure. It attempted to raise the previously successful formulae of *Stevedore* and *Turpentine* to a melodramatic folk-play, but instead of generating the conviction of persecution or the premonition of class war, *How Come, Lawd?* hatched a Deadwood Dick welter of corpses. Leaning on an already successful play for support, Gus Smith of the Lafayette Federal Theatre project, more than half successfully dramatized *The Case of Philip Lawrence.* Here was the setup for a great Negro play,—the ghetto drag-down of a successful college athlete whose family and friends had no bootstraps to lift themselves by, and little helpful conception of the success he yearned for. But a gangster racket and infatuation bring him down with a melodramatically contrived "framing" for murder, from which he escapes at the end only by a hair's breadth capture of the racket boss. Had social fate rather than a jealous, revengeful gangster been Philip Lawrence's downfall, real tragedy might have ensued instead of a Hollywood finish. Dramatically the strongest of the crop, *The Trial of Dr. Beck* revealed a promising newcomer to the thin ranks of Negro playwrights, Hughes Allison. His play, a success of the Newark Federal Theatre project, enjoyed a brief but effective Broadway showing at the Maxine Elliott. But here again a vital racial theme was overlaid with the trappings of an Oppenheimer crime story and two acts of well-documented but melodramatic court scenes. Though there is much talk of color complexes and considerable arraignment of the paradoxes of prejudice,—all to the good as among the first effective dramatization of these issues, both Dr. Beck's lily-whitism and his sister's-in-law counter color hate are far from being what they should be, the real protagonists of the play. Instead, Pinkertonian detective tactics and an over-idealized lawyer are the short-circuiting artifices by which Mr. Allison gets justice done and his moral put over. Still the talent of Hughes Allison, more mature in dramatic technique and depth of characterization than any Negro playwright to date, warrants hopeful watching and encouragement. The Morgan College Players are responsible for presenting the one creditable work of the white dramatist in Negro drama for 1937. Various professional concoctions of Broadway producers, two of them by George Abbott, have fortunately been as short-lived as they were mercenary and misrepresentative. At least this negative gain seems to have come about, that except in the movies and on the vaudeville stage, the Broadway stage formula for a successful Negro play has obviously worn itself out. *Jute*, on the other hand, is the very antithesis of the Broadway play, but probably for that very reason a portent of what Broadway must come around to. Its strong bitter social realism, smacking of *Tobacco Road* on the one hand and *Stevedore* and *Waiting for Lefty* on the other, is the much needed antidote to too much *Black Boy, Sweet River* and *Brown Sugar*. In social content, Philistine Negro protests notwithstanding, *Jute* is significant and promising for the social content of vital Negro drama.

In the ever important field of social analysis and criticism, one general change is increasingly obvious; "race sociology" is growing up. It is less frequently nowadays a puny missionary foundling or the awkward patronized protégé of the interracial sentimentalists. Here and there it is sociology of full strength and maturity. And even where it is not, the pretension to scientific accuracy and objectivity is a significant omen. Certainly one of the best and most illuminating of this year's race studies is Cedric Dover's *Half-Caste*. With a panoramic swoop of world perspective on the race question, the book achieves a unique coordination of the phenomena of race.

With eagle-like penetration of vision, international imperialism and fascist nationalism are seen to have common denominators of repressive, self-righteous racialism. Relentlessly the biological and cultural stalking horses of race prejudice are unmasked and the politico-economic objectives of race policies exposed. This is deftly done because the problem is tackled in terms of its crucial dilemma, the half caste, who as Mr. Dover senses, is the Dalmatian sword over the heads of all racialists: For the factualities of the human hybrids contradict either the theories or the practices of racialism; which then stands biologically contradicted or morally condemned. No other survey to date has given so wide a perspective on human hybridization or such a realization of its common factors, the similarity of situations and policies, the uniformity of its social dilemmas, and perhaps most important of all, the preponderant numbers of the mixed bloods. In the chapter on the American Negro, "God's Own Chillun," the author achieves an illuminating analysis of the general situation, with pardonable lapses of proportion in the detailed statements of Negro achievement in which he has followed several uncritical and provincial sources. But the general soundness of his main thesis saves serious distortion, and it will be salutary for all who lack objective perspective on the American race question, Negro chauvinists included, to review the situation in this unusual and broad scientific frame of reference.

In *Our Racial and National Minorities*, under the editorship of Professors Brown and Roucek, the polyglot character of America is documented by some thirty spokesmen for national and racial subgroups of our population. James Weldon Johnson has a double inning on Negro American achievement history and "The Negro and Racial Conflicts." The approach of the whole study is too superficial for any sound interpretation of the interaction of minorities or the cultural problems involved in dual loyalties. Cultural pluralism and its educational objectives are, however, rather convincingly presented. The special degrees of isolation and differential treatment involved in the cases of the Negro, Indian, Mexican, and Oriental minorities are dangerously minimized in the interest of the general thesis that we are all cultural hyphenates and that cultural reciprocity is our soundest, most progressive type of Americanism. Professor Johnson in keying his chapters in with this platform has not glossed over the particular injustices and inconsistencies of the Negro's position, but he has not sufficiently stressed the unusual cultural assimilation of the American Negro as compared with other minorities or the special inconsistencies of majority behavior toward the Negro.

With *Caste and Class in a Southern Town* and *The Etiquette of Race Relations in the South*, we pass to sociological anatomy of the most scientific and painstaking sort. And yet what we get eventually in both cases is not any enlightenment as to social causes but only elaborations of the mechanisms of caste control and majority dominance. Can it be that this descriptive analytic point of view is hopelessly un-diagnostic and therefore just so much academic "busy work?" Both works agree that caste rather than class describes the racial cleavage, and that its outlines are only correctly traced by examining in detail custom patterns in the social mores. But neither gives any very clear understanding of what economic interests and political policies all these elaborate mechanisms serve. In short, the vital question, it seems to me, is not the *how* but the *why* of these social differences and differentials.

In *The Negro's Struggle for Survival*, subtitled "a study in human ecology," Professor Holmes of the University of California assembles the Negro's biological statistics elaborately and tries to trace trends and prospects. In most of these balancings, our author finds Negro survival outdistancing or offsetting its handicaps, whether directly biological like the birthrate or socioeconomic like the influence of poverty, migration, and hybridization. However, toward the conclusion the banished bugaboo of race ascendancy comes back to threaten serious issues should the Negro rate of population increase decidedly to disturb the present balance. The author then predicts "population control" as the probable outcome. Even with the pseudoscientific coating of "eugenics," this is the abandonment of the plane of science for that of politics and is a disappointing conclusion for an otherwise factual and objective book.

On the sound platform that "the essential human rights of Negroes do not appertain to them as Negroes, but simply as members of the human family" and that "modern Catholic sociologists see in the tendency to subordinate all considerations of the dignity of the human person to the unbridled quest of material gain the primary source of interracial, as well as of economic, industrial and international injustice," Father La-Farge works out a program of really radical equalitarianism differing only in its sanctions and reform machinery from the economic radicals. In spite of this wide difference of proposed remedy, it is interesting to note this startling agreement in diagnosis. "Cheap labor," says Reverend LaFarge, "brings cheap lives. And from cheap lives follow customs and maxims sanctioning the cheapening of lives."

In *The Negroes in a Soviet America*, J. W. Ford and J. S. Allen expound the now familiar Communist formula for revolutionary socialism and minority self-determination. It has become too much of a formula perhaps, but that does not remove its realistic thrust as a contending alternative to the yet unsuccessful reformism of moral appeal and legislative guarantees. *Reconstruction* by J. S. Allen gives a much less doctrinaire analysis of the relation of the Negro to the political and economic interests of the nation and the South. Particularly revealing are documentary evidences of Negro statesmanship in realistic political and labor programs from 1865 to 1879 that were frustrated by the tacit alliance of Northern industrialists and Southern Bourbons not to insist on thoroughgoing reconstruction or political power for the Negro in the South. This picture of American history after 1878 as a counterrevolution to the Civil War is an important and plausible interpretation; it culminated not merely in the setback to Negro advance but in the stultification of the labor movement for several decades and of the full functioning of democratic machinery even up to the present. A few close students of history have known this all along, but it is important that the layman should know it as well.

T. Arnold Hill's *The Negro and Economic Reconstruction* in the Bronze Booklet series also presents an indispensable layman's manual on the connection of the Negro question with past and present labor issues and programs. Volume No. 8 of the same series presents a readable and well-proportioned outline of *Negro History*, by the well-known bibliographer and source collector Arturo A. Schomburg. But also in social history, which has been so neglected in Negro historical effort, most promising beginnings have now been made in various guidebooks of the Federal Writers' Project. With Virginia, Louisiana, and New York documentary chronicles in preparation, the project leads off very auspiciously with a revealing account, edited by Sterling Brown, of "The Negro in Washington" in the Washington: American Guide Series.

In *Life in a Haitian Valley*, Professor Herskovits vindicates even more brilliantly than in his previous books his thesis of acculturation. Studying the Haitian peasant rituals, he discovers not only substantial traces of African religions, especially the Dahomean Vodun cults, but clearly demonstrates the prevailing Haitian popular religion to be an amalgam of this, Catholicism, and local superstition. This points to a completely general human pattern of acculturation, with none of the specious doctrines of innate racial primitivism or mysterious blood survivals, the favorite formulae of the culture-mongers who thrive on fashionable exoticism and bad anthropology. Cut free from such false implications, the search for African survivals is merely an excursion into social history. There is cold comfort for Nordicism or any other racial condescension in any such results, and for this service the Haitian cause in particular and the Negro cause in general have much to be grateful for in such studies as this and the previous volume of *Suriname Folk-Lore*, documenting even more extensively striking survivals and parallels in the folklore of the Negroes of Dutch Guiana. Nigerian and Dahomean patterns, both of behavior and thought, are found strikingly perpetuated.

But while we are shutting doors to Nordic jingoists, we should not be opening them to Negro jingoism. And such we must frankly label *Introduction to African Civilizations* by

Huggins and Jackson. On a brittle thread of sentimental interest in Negro blood admixture, prehistoric Cro-Magnons, semi-Semitic Mediterraneans, Egyptians, Ethiopians, ancient and modern, South and West African peoples of diverse stocks are all hodgepodged into an amateurish hash of the black man's vindication. Such facts and conjectures are warrantable offsets to rampant and hysterical Nordicism provided they escape the same fallacies they challenge. But when they commit the same errors of overgeneralization, assumption of fixed racial character and instinctive heredities, and worse than all, the ignoring of distinct culture groupings, the results must be repudiated as just as pseudoscientific as the conclusions and prejudices they try to counteract. A much more intelligent and effective statement of the counter-case comes from an African author, Akiki Nyabongo, whose *Africa Answers Back* continues the pointed critique he began with his *Story of an African Chief.*

With a most laudatory preface by Malinowski, and a thrilling and trenchant account of his own liberal stand against German Nazi oppression and censorship, Professor Lips launches out in his *The Savage Hits Back* into an extensive documentation of the manner in which primitive peoples have represented the white man,—ruler, trader, missionary, and colonial administrator. It is sufficient indictment of fascism that so indirect a criticism of colonial exploitation should seem dangerous enough to persecute and exile a scholar for daring to compile it. But this is neither the first nor the most impressive vindication of the primitive or even the African as artist. In fact most of the representations treated betray the native art in a bastard genre both with respect to style and subject matter, and necessarily we must discount its artistic and allow principally its sociological or cultural importance. Most of this work is therefore in the minor category of genre and even caricature; though of course it is interesting documentary proof that the native both sees and sees through the white overlords and takes due recourse to shrewd and half-concealed ridicule. Only rarely, however, do the European forms and accoutrements blend harmoniously with the native styles of expression, so that there is much more that must be labelled curiosa than can be called art proper. Nevertheless Professor Lips has documented very unmistakably the colored world's reaction to cultural jingoism and the loss of prestige which is taking place under the surface of professed respect. For exposing this significant symptom he merits our gratitude, even though we may not entirely grant his prophesy of a "future collision of the white and colored worlds" and his contention that "it is not class cohesion that will be the decisive factor in such a collision but the sense of race unity."

A joy to the scientific type of mind is the way in which both anthropology and the analysis of culture contacts are slowly disengaging themselves from the fog of prejudice and preconceived racialisms. Whether one grants the thesis of Frobenius that the similarities of prehistoric art indicate wide diffusion into Europe of African peoples or whether one holds with Leakey that parallel or roughly similar culture sequences worked themselves out both in Europe and different areas of the African continent, it is only too obvious in either case that the net conclusion is one of the basic similarity and parity of the human species. No sounder antidote for false racial pride or propagandist history could be found than in the cultural anthropology which is giving us increasing evidence along these new lines of the antiquity and the versatility of primitive man.

To the same collaborated authorship as *Prehistoric Rock Pictures* we owe the illuminating collection of African fables and creation myths in *African Genesis* (Stackpole Sons, N.Y—$3.00). Berber, Fulbe, Sudanese, Rhodesian,—these tales are of wide range and diverse cultural quality, but they are all indicative of a more seasoned folklore and a higher level of literary form than other collections reveal, even the celebrated Cendrars *Anthologie Nègre*. Interestingly enough, in some of them Frobenius believes he has discovered common symbols and rituals to early Egyptian mythology.

The really authoritative studies of African colonial contacts as they effect changes and breakdowns and fusions of cultures bear out the same liberal relativism of values. Notable among such are Monica Hunter's *Reaction to Conquest* and

MacCrone's *Race Attitudes in South Africa*, each of which in a very different way illustrates the principle that one civilization more often demoralizes a different culture than it civilizes or improves it. In brief, according to the more recent scientific accounts, the white man makes his own burden and then has to carry it, not to mention the disproportionate profit he makes on the other side of the imperialistic ledger.

Although unnecessarily fictional for so detailed and painstaking a narrative of native folkways, Carnochan and Adamson's *Out of Africa* is a remarkably sympathetic biography of Kalola, chief of the Nyamwezi serpent cult. Nowhere has a better analysis of such ritual fetishism been drawn, with the balance carefully kept between black and white magic, conjure and tribal medicine, superstition and sound institutional tradition. In such books as we have reviewed, the African counter-statement is just beginning to gather momentum, but it certainly will have its day of assertion. However, let us hope that it will be a scientific, sanely directed counter-statement, and not another deluge of bigotry, hysteria, and counter-prejudice. Not for moral reasons, but for effectiveness, let us be saner than our opponents. And let us welcome as champions only those who are scientifically convinced and convincing.

35

FREEDOM THROUGH ART

A Review of Negro Art, 1870–1938

Every oppressed group is under the necessity, both after and before its physical emancipation from the shackles of slavery,—be that slavery chattel or wage—of establishing a spiritual freedom of the mind and spirit. This cultural emancipation must needs be self-emancipation and is the proper and peculiar function of a minority literature and art. It gives unusual social significance to all forms of art expression among minorities, often shading them unduly with propaganda or semi-propaganda and for whole periods inflicting them also with an unusual degree of self-consciousness and self-vindication, even to the point of cultural exhibitionism and belligerency. But for these faults and dangers we have compensation in the more vital role and more representative character of artistic self-expression among "the disinherited;" they cannot afford the luxury, or shall we say the vice, of a literature and art of pure entertainment.

The literature and art of the Negro, and to an extent all serious literature and art about the Negro, have had almost universally this quality of moral seriousness and social significance. That has not been an unmixed blessing, since the arts of the Negro have had to struggle through to some degree of artistic freedom from these fetters of polemics and didacticism. The Negro artist has worn mental chains, and his achievements are all the more creditable. He has always faced two dilemmas;— how to speak for himself as an individual at the same time that he was being considered a racial spokesman; how to galvanize inert propaganda and racial doctrines with the electric and moving qualities of art. His present achievement of recognized contribution to universally significant and nationally representative art is thus a double achievement; in the first instance a mastery over the inherent difficulties of his art, in the second instance, a victory over the artificial odds of cultural stigma and persecution. In this double aspect we must review briefly the career of Negro art and literature from Emancipation till now.

It is hard to realize that at the beginning of the brief period of 75 years which this issue of *The Crisis* is retrospecting, the Negro artist was a cultural freak of circus proportions in the North and proscribed cultural contraband in the South. The characteristic Negro author was then a runaway slave with an Abolitionist amanuensis or a natural born orator who had only become literate as an adult. There were exceptions, but this was the rule. But the astonishing thing was the way in which these slave-born narrators, poets, and orators mastered the art of powerful and influential expression, conspicuously challenging their more advantaged freeborn contemporaries, white and black. There was the poetic power of Horton and Albery Whitman for example, quite excelling the early literate Ellen Harper and Madison Bell; there was the dominance of Douglass, Pennington, and William Wells Brown, slave-born, over the university-trained McCune Smith, Highland Garnet, Daniel Payne, and Samuel Ward. Indeed the fervor of the anti-slavery movement and the rare cultural comradeship of that cause seem to have raised Negro literary expression on all sides to a high level in the 1850s and '60s from which it actually receded in the dull early Reconstruction decades.

THE '70S AND '80S DULL

Anti-slavery controversy and the hope of freedom brought poetry and fire to the Negro tongue and pen: whereas the setbacks and strained ambitions of Reconstruction brought forth, in the main, leaden rhetoric and alloyed pedantry. Thus the

'70s and the '80s were the awkward age in our artistic development. They were the period of prosaic self-justification and painful apprenticeship to formal culture. Yet these years saw the creditable beginnings of Negro historical and sociological scholarship, even at the expense of an endless elaboration of problem discussion themes, and saw also an adolescent attack on the more formal arts of the novel, the drama, formal music, painting, and sculpture. Before this almost all of our artistic expression had flowed in the narrow channels of the sermon, the oration, the slave narrative, and didactic poetry.

But in spite of their talents and labors, authors like Highland Garnet, Alexander Crummell, George Williams, the historian, Martin Delany, and even Frederick Douglass in these later days had a restricted audience, much narrower than the wide national and international stage of anti-slavery times. There was, instead of the glamour of the crusade against the slave power, the dull grind of the unexpected fight against reaction. The larger audience and a more positive mood were not recaptured until the mid-nineties, when strangely enough a clustered group of significant events came together, any one of which would have been notable. In 1895, Booker Washington caught national attention with his Atlanta Exposition speech; in 1896 Paul Laurence Dunbar rode into fame and popular favor; in the same year the first Negro musical comedy took Broadway; in '98 and '99, Chesnutt, the novelist, came to the fore; in '95 Burleigh was helping Dvořák with the Negro folk themes of the *New World Symphony* and at the same time making his first entry to the New York concert world; in '98 Will Marion Cook launched serious syncopated music with *Clorindy*; '96 was the year of Tanner's first substantial Paris recognition; and in '98 Coleridge-Taylor came to maturity and fame in the first part of the *Hiawatha Trilogy*. The only other stellar artistic event of this period for which we have to wait is the appearance in 1903 of Dr. Du Bois's *Souls of Black Folk*.

Quite obviously there was a sudden change of trend as this blaze of talent ushered in a new era of racial expression. It was more than a mere accession of new talent; it was the discovery of a new racial attitude. The leading motive of Reconstruction thought was assimilation and political equality; following the cry for physical freedom there had been the fight for the larger freedom of status and the right to be the same and equal. But the leading motive of the new era (1895–1910) seems to have been racialism and its new dynamic of self-help and self-assertion. Even the motivations of Du Bois's equal lights crusade were militantly self-conscious and racial; in fact, race consciousness was now definitely in the saddle driving to redirect the stalled logic of the assimilation program and revive the balked hopes of the thwarted equal rights struggle. The formula of special gifts and particular paths had been discovered, and became the dominant rationalization of the period. The leading conception of freedom now was the right to be oneself and different. Thus the groundwork was laid for the cultural racialism of the "Negro Renaissance" movement which, however, was not to appear definitely till the mid-twenties and the next literary generation. In its first phase this racialism was naïve emotional, and almost provincial; later under the influence of the World War principles of self-determination and the rise of other cultural nationalisms, it was to become sophisticated and historically grounded in Africanism and the philosophy of cultural revivals.

REACTION FROM RACIALISM

Of course, no such formula held undisputed sway, either in the first or second decade of the new century. Nor were most writers or artists formal converts to it. But historically it is characteristic just the same, and helps us in retrospect to symbolize and understand the composite mind of this generation. Race pride, self-respect, race solidarity, the folk-spirit are to anyone who has lived through these decades slogans vibrating vitally with the thought of the time. The art of these decades keynoted them; they were its spiritual dynamic. And that is all the more apparent as this phase of our cultural life begins to pass with the new issues and ideology of the present crisis and its struggle for economic freedom and social reform. For new viewpoints and values, geared in with these social forces, are again changing the whole cast and direction of Negro expression in literature and art. Thus in the latest generation thought was veered away from racialism and sharply repudiated historical romanticism, and while still continuing some of the folk interests of cultural racialism, it is definitely realistic, socialistic, and proletarian. Its ideals and objectives, like those of the anti-slavery epoch, are radical and broadly humanitarian and its slogans of economic equality, freedom, and justice are not distinctly racial.

The reader may wonder what this has to do with a brief review of Negro artistic achievements. The answer is that except from the point of view of these shifts in Negro thought as cultural tactics veering to the changing drift of social forces, there is no sane and significant account of our art expression, especially in panoramic perspective. Every quickening of the pulse and change in the flow of our art has represented some intensification of social forces, the peak of some social movement. In 1914–17, when the sensitive minds of the group faced the growing dilemmas of democracy and the World War from the racial angle, they could not share its enthusiasms, and a whole school of challenge and ironic protest sprang up keyed to Fenton Johnson's "We are tired of building up somebody-else's civilization," James Weldon Johnson's challenging "To America," and the social protest verse of Claude McKay. Then with the urban migration and its accompaniments came the more positively toned movement of cultural racialism and solidarity, coupled with a fresh interest in the peasant folk life. One wing of this movement was caught up and diverted in the neurotic jazz age with its freakish aesthetics and its irresponsible individualism while another linked on to a realistic rediscovery of the folk; both over the common denominator of racialism. Finally with the depression and the second disillusionment of the elite came the reformist and socialistic reaction of the present day, which we have already described. Personalities and individual achievements may stand out, do stand out on close inspection, but this is the general path and, we think, the major significance.

In the main, each generation, with a shift of tactic almost each decade, has been seeking cultural freedom through art; at one time with a moralistic goal, at another through aestheticism; in one phase in terms of a social program, in another, highly individualistically; its motivation now racialistic, now socialistic; for a while dominated by disillusionment and protest, at another by optimistic forecast and crusading reform. The tempers of each phase are clearly discernible as, with few exceptions, the art follows the social trends. Of course, if aestheticism, realism, regionalism, or proletarianism are the general cultural vogue, Negro art reflects it, but always caught up in the texture of a racially determined phase, as might also be expected. There is no possibility of a separate account of the course of the Negro's art, but there is great point to a special secondary line following the fluctuations of racial situation and attitude.

36

THE NEGRO: "NEW" OR NEWER

A Retrospective Review of the Literature of the Negro for 1938

PART I

It is now fifteen years, nearly a half a generation, since the literary advent of the "New Negro." In such an interval a new generation of creative talent should have come to the fore and presumably those talents who in 1924–25 were young and new should today be approaching maturity or have arrived at it. Normally too, at the rate of contemporary cultural advance, a new ideology with a changed world outlook and social orientation should have evolved. And the question back of all this needs to be raised, has it so developed or hasn't it, and do we confront today on the cultural front another Negro, either a newer Negro or a maturer "New Negro"?

A critic's business is not solely with the single file reviewing-stand view of endless squads of books in momentary dress parade but with the route and leadership of cultural advance, in short, with the march of ideas. There is no doubt in the panoramic retrospect of the years 1924 to 1938 about certain positive achievements:—a wider range of Negro self-expression in more of the arts, an increasing maturity and objectivity of approach on the part of the Negro artist to his subject matter, a greater diversity of styles and artistic creeds, a healthier and firmer trend toward self-criticism, and perhaps most important of all, a deepening channel toward the mainstream of American literature and art as white and Negro artists share in ever-increasing collaboration the growing interest in Negro life and subject matter. These are encouraging and praiseworthy gains, all of which were confidently predicted under the convenient but dangerous caption of "The New Negro."

But a caption's convenience is part of its danger; so is its brevity. In addition, in the case in question, there was inevitable indefiniteness as to what was meant by the "New Negro." Just that question must be answered, however, before we can judge whether today's Negro represents a matured phase of the movement of the '20s or is, as many of the youngest Negroes think and contend, a counter-movement, for which incidentally they have a feeling but no name. These "bright young people" to the contrary, it is my conviction that the former is true and that the "New Negro" movement is just coming into its own after a frothy adolescence and a first-generation course which was more like a careen than a career. Using the nautical figure to drive home the metaphor, we may say that there was at first too little ballast in the boat for the heavy head of sail that was set. Moreover, the talents of that period (and some of them still) were far from skillful mariners; artistically and sociologically they sailed many a crooked course, mistaking their directions for the lack of steadying common sense and true group loyalty as a compass. But all that was inevitable in part; and was, as we shall later see, anticipated and predicted.

But the primary source of confusion perhaps was due to a deliberate decision not to define the "New Negro" dogmatically, but only to characterize his general traits and attitudes. And so, partly because of this indefiniteness, the phrase became a slogan for cheap race demagogues who wouldn't know a "cultural movement" if they could see one, a handy megaphone for petty exhibitionists who were only posing as "racialists" when in fact they were the rankest kind of egotists, and a gilded fetish for race idolaters who at heart were still sentimentalists seeking consolation for inferiority. But even as it was, certain greater evils were avoided—a growing race consciousness was not cramped down to a formula, and a movement with a popular groundswell and a folk significance was not tied to a partisan art creed or any one phase of culture politics.

The most deliberate aspect of the New Negro formulation—and it is to be hoped, its crowning wisdom—was just this repudiation of any and all one-formula solutions of the race question, (its own immediate emphases included), and the proposed substitution of a solidarity of group feeling for unity within a variety of artistic creeds and social programs. To quote: "The Negro today wishes to be known for what he is, even in his faults and shortcomings, and scorns a craven and precarious survival at the price of seeming to be what he is not. He thus resents being spoken of as a social ward or minor, even by his own, and to being regarded a chronic patient for the sociological clinic, the sick man of American Democracy. For the same reasons, *he himself is through with those social nostrums and panaceas, the so-called 'solutions' of his 'problem', with which he and the country have been so liberally dosed in the past. Religion, freedom, education, money—in turn he has ardently hoped for and peculiarly trusted these things: he still believes in them, but not in blind trust that they alone will solve his life-problem.*"

How then even the enfants terribles of today's youth movement could see "cultural expression" as a substitute formula proposed by the "New Negro" credo I cannot understand, except on the ground that they did not read carefully what had been carefully written. Nor would a careful reading have been auspicious for their own one-formula diagnosis of "economic exploitation" and solution by "class action." Not only was there no foolish illusion that "racial prejudice would soon disappear before the altars of truth, art, and intellectual achievement," as has been asserted, but a philosophy of cultural isolation from the folk ("masses") and of cultural separatism were expressly repudiated. It was the bright young talents of the '20s who themselves went cosmopolite when they were advised to go racial, who went exhibitionist instead of going documentarian, who got jazz-mad and cabaret-crazy instead of getting folk-wise and sociologically sober. Lest this, too, seem sheer rationalizing hindsight, let a few direct quotations from *The New Negro* testify to the contrary. Even more, the same excerpts will show that a social Reformation was called for as the sequel and proper goal of a cultural Renaissance, and that the present trends of second generation "New Negro" literature which we are now passing in review were predicted and reasonably anticipated. For reasons of space, quotations must be broken and for reasons of emphasis, some are italicized:

"A transformed and transforming psychology permeates the masses. . . . In a real sense it is the rank and file who are leading, and the leaders who are following. . . . It does not follow that if the Negro were better known, he would be better liked or better treated. (p. 10) . . . Not all the new art is in the field of pure art values. There is poetry of sturdy social protest and fiction of calm dispassionate social analysis. But reason and realism have cured us of sentimentality: instead of the wail and appeal, there is challenge and indictment. Satire is just beneath the surface of our latest prose and tonic irony has come into our poetic wells. These are good medicines for the common mind, for us they are the necessary antidotes against social poison. Their influence means that *at least for us* the worst symptoms of the social distemper are passing. And so the social promise of our recent art is as great as the artistic. (p. 52) . . . Each generation, however, will have its creed, and *that of the present* is the belief in the efficacy of collective effort, in race cooperation. This deep feeling of race is *at present* the mainspring of Negro life. . . . It is radical in tone, but not in purpose and only the most stupid forms of opposition, misunderstanding, or persecution could make it otherwise. Of course, the thinking Negro has shifted a little toward the left with the world trend, and there is an increasing group who affiliate with radical and liberal movements. But fundamentally *for the present* the Negro is radical on race matters, conservative on others, in other words a "forced radical," a social protestant rather than a genuine radical. Yet under further pressure and injustice iconoclastic thought and motives will inevitably increase. Harlem's quixotic radicalisms call for their ounce of democracy today lest tomorrow they be beyond cure. (p. 11).

It is important, finally, to sum up the social aspect of the New Negro front with clarity because today's literature and art, an art of searching social documentation and criticism, thus becomes a consistent development and matured expression of the trends that were seen and analyzed in 1925.

"The Negro mind reaches out as yet to nothing but American wants, American ideas. But this forced attempt to build his Americanism on race values *is a unique social experiment*, and its ultimate success *is impossible except through the fullest sharing of American culture and institutions. There should be no delusion about this.* American nerves in sections unstrung with race hysteria are often fed the opiate that the trend of Negro advance is wholly separatist, and that the effect of its operation will be to encyst the Negro as a benign foreign body in the body politic. This cannot be even if it were desirable. The racialism of the Negro is no limitation or reservation with respect to American life; it is only a constructive effort to build the obstructions in the stream of his progress into an efficient dam of social energy and power. Democracy itself is obstructed and stagnated to the extent that any of its channels are closed. Indeed they cannot be selectively closed. So the choice is not between one way for the Negro and another for the rest, but between American institutions frustrated on the one hand and American ideals progressively fulfilled and realized on the other." (p. 12).

The generation of the late '30s is nearer such a cultural course and closer to such social insight than the tangential generation of the late '20s. Artistic exploitation is just as possible from the inside as from the outside, and if our writers and artists are becoming sounder in their conception of the social role of themselves and their art, as indeed they are, it is all the more welcome after considerable delay and error. If, also, they no longer see cultural racialism as cultural separatism, which it never was or was meant to be, then, too, an illusory dilemma has lost its paralyzing spell. And so, we have only to march forward instead of to counter-march; only to broaden the phalanx and flatten out the opposition salients that threaten divided ranks. Today we pivot on a sociological front with our novelists, dramatists, and social analysts in deployed formation. But for vision and morale we have to thank the spiritual surge and aesthetic inspiration of the first-generation artists of the renaissance decade.

And now, to the literature of this year of reformation, stir, and strife.

In fiction, two novels by white authors remind us of the background use of Negro materials that used to be so universal. Many such have been ignored as not basically "Negro literature" at all. However these two, Clelie Benton Huggins's *Point Noir* and Arthur Smith's *The Dead Go Overside*, do exhibit significant if limited use of Negro historical and local color materials. The latter particularly, documenting intensively New England's part in the slave traffic, weaves a melodramatic love story and sea rescue over the somber details of a New Bedford fishing schooner's conversion into a slave raider and a sturdy personality deteriorating as it passes from codfishing to the more prosperous job of man-hunting. Also picaresque is Ed Bell's *Tommy Lee Feathers*, a local color novel of Marrow-town, a Tennessee Negro community. Reasonably well studied local color and characterization are seldom met with in the rustic humor school of Negro fiction, so *Tommy Lee Feathers* registers progress even in its broad stroke characterizations of the exploits of the town's "Black Angels," Tommy's football team, and the more conscious angels of Sister Feather's "Sanctified Church." One does not, of course, expect serious social commentary under this idiom. But too much "safe" entertainment of this sort has laid the groundwork for bad sociology.

However, it is noteworthy how much serious social commentary there really is in this year's crop of fiction, from both the white and the Negro authors. Already we are used to the semi-doctrinal criticism of the Erskine Caldwell school, which by the way he continues with usual unsparing and unrelieved realism in his latest volume of stories, *Southways*, but there are other and as I think more effective brands of realism. Certainly one of the most convincing and moving bits of documentary fiction on the racial situation is Don Tracy's reportorial but beautifully restrained *How Sleeps the Beast*. More even than the famous movie *Fury*, this novel gives the physiology of American lynching; not just its horror and bestialities, but its moods and its social mechanisms. Vince, who starts out by saying to his girl, "I ain't goin', I got no truck with lynchin's" eventually goes under her taunts; Al Purvis, whose life poor Jim had saved, starts out to rescue him but succumbs to social cowardice and mob hysteria; the Sheriff is jostled from official indifference to sectional hate at the sign of a "Yankee meddler," and a newspaper reporter hunted by the mob for fear of exposure barely escapes the same fate by sleeping the night through in the "malodorous room marked 'Ladies'," after having been ordered out the back door of the local Eastern Maryland Shore hotel while the mob pickets the entrance. In realism charged with terror, but tempered with pity and understanding, Don Tracy has written in the Steinbeckian vein the best version yet of this great American tragedy and of the social obsessions that make it happen.

More notable still, because about a more normal social subject, is Julian Meade's saga of Mary Lou Payton, the most fully characterized domestic Negro servant in all the tedious range of Negro servitors in American fiction. *The Back Door* is a book of truthful, artistically balanced human documentation. Mary Lou's always precarious hold on the good things in life, on both domestic job and self-respect, on her amiable tobacco-worker lover beset by the wiles of looser women on the one hand and unemployment and occupational disease on the other, on her cherished but socially unrewarded respectability that every other week or so confronts the dreaded advances of Frank Anderson, the philandering white rent-collector, on even the job itself, are all portrayed with pity and sympathetic irony.

The Back Door is as much a step above *Porgy* as *Porgy* was above its predecessors. Its deftly true touches—the wedding ring bought on installments and eventually confiscated, the lay-off that enables Jim to half conquer his consumptive cough, the juvenile blackmail of "Mr. Willie's" retort, "I know durn well *you* hook a plenty on the sly" as reply to Mary's frantic, "Mr. Willie, please don't bother them sandwiches," even the unwitting irony of the waiting ladies' missionary hymn,

> *Can we whose souls are lighted*
> *With wisdom from on high,*
> *Can we to men benighted*
> *The lamp of life deny?*

are all triumphs of the school of delicate realism well contrasted with the bludgeoning effects of the school of rough-shod realism. To the small sum of Southern classics must be added this tender saga of Stoke Alley and Chinch Row.

To the fine achievements just mentioned, two Negro writers make this year a sizeable contribution. In the first, Mercedes Gilbert's *Aunt Sara's Wooden God*, the theme of the story is more important than its literary execution. Despite a too lenient introduction by Langston Hughes, this first novel is no masterpiece, not even a companion for *Ollie Miss* or *Jonah's Gourd Vine* with which it is bracketed; but it is promising and in subject matter significant. William Gordon, the illegitimate son, is the favored but profligate brother, Aunt Sara's "Wooden God." From the beginning a martyr to his mother's blind partiality, Jim, the darker brother, takes from start to finish the brunt of the situation, the childhood taunts, the lesser chance, the lion's share of the farm work while William is in school or frittering away time in Macon, then the loss of his sweetheart, Ruth, through the machinations of William, and finally imprisonment for William's crime. Amateurish overloading, as well as the anecdotal style of developing the episodes of the story, robs the book of its full tragic possibilities. William's eventual return to a deathbed reconciliation and Aunt Sara's pious blessings is only relieved by his attempted confession and Jim's heroic resolve not to disillusion Aunt Sara. Our novelists must learn to master the medium before attacking the heavier themes; a smaller canvas dimensionally done is better than a thin epic or a melodramatic saga. Here is a great and typical theme only half developed, which someone—perhaps the author herself—must someday do with narrative power and character insight.

In contrast, Richard Wright in *Uncle Tom's Children* uses the novella with the sweep and power of epic tragedy. Last year the first of these four gripping tales, "Big Boy Leaves Home," was hailed as the most significant Negro prose since Toomer's *Cane*. Since then it has won the *Story Magazine* award for the national WPA's Writers' Project contest, and a second story, "Fire and Cloud," has won second prize in the O. Henry awards. This is a well-merited literary launching for what must be watched as a major literary career. Mr. Wright's full-length novel is eagerly awaited; perhaps in the longer form the nemesis of race injustice which stalks the fate of every chief character in the four stories will stalk with a more natural stride. One often feels in the shorter form that the nemesis makes forced marches. This is not a nerve-wrecked reader's cry for mercy; for we grant the author the terrible truth of his situations, but merely a plea for posterity that judges finally on the note of universality and artistry. By this criterion "Big Boy" and "Long Black Song" will last longer for their poignant beauty than "Down By the Riverside," certainly, and perhaps also, "Fire and Cloud." Yet as social indictments, the one of white oppression and ingratitude and the other of black cowardice and gullibility, these very two have the most documentary significance. The force of Wright's versions of Negro tragedy in the South lies in the correct reading of the trivialities that in that hate-charged atmosphere precipitate these frightful climaxes of death and persecution; an innocent boy's swimming prank in "Big Boy," a man's desperate need for a boat to rescue his pregnant wife during a Mississippi flood, a white salesman's casual infatuation while trying to sell a prosperous black farmer's wife a gramophone, a relatively tame-hearted demonstration for food relief in the other three stories. And so, by this simple but profound discovery, Richard Wright has found a key to mass interpretation through symbolic individual instances which many have been fumbling for this long while. With this, our Negro fiction of social interpretation comes of age.

Love at the Mission is Mr. R. Hernekin Baptist's sternly tense story of the frustrations of three daughters of Pastor Oguey, a South African missionary. Hedged about by the double barriers of race and puritanism, Hortense, the eldest, becomes involved in morbid jealousy of her younger sister's love affair, plots to poison her father, the symbol of this isolation, blames it after the fashion of the country on the African serving boy. But finally she has to stand for her intended crime and wither jealously in prison. Fani, the African nurse and housekeeper, is the counter-symbol of black paganism tolerant of this intruding puritanism but never quite corrupted by it. Indeed the novel is really a pictorialized analysis of the futility of missionarism, and is of considerable significance because of its frank and carefully studied approach to the clash of native and Nordic mores. In key so far as conclusions go, Sarah Gertrude Millin, with greater maturity, has analyzed the South African paradox from the point of view of an English civil servant with a tender conscience. Henry Ormandy, the hero of *What Hath a Man?*, is outwardly successful as an individual but is haunted to the end of his career by his realization of the futility of the white man's self-imposed mission of imperialism. Mrs. Millin has woven into the earlier part of the story, when Ormandy encounters Cecil Rhodes just after the raid of Matabeleland, remarkable documentary evidence that Rhodes himself had a troubled conscience and paused once in his ruthlessness. But the very brevity of such a gesture in a coldblooded game keynotes Mrs. Millin's indirect but quite effective indictment of imperialism as does also Henry's lonely, terrorful death. This too, although on the surface a novel of character study, is a novel of social protest; another David's pebble against our modern Goliath. The cause of social justice has been well served this year by the novelists.

A promising symptom is the rapid growth of serious and sympathetic juvenile books on the Negro theme. Mrs. Florence Means in *Shuttered Windows* has written a story of an educated girl from the North, Harriet Freeman, and her struggle for the enlightenment of the illiterate South Carolina Island folk. Eva Knox Evans adds to her already well-known Jerome Anthony series of Negro child stories a sympathetic and quizzical tale of *Araminta's Goat*. Two gifted Negro teachers have collaborated to bring out a laudable public school reader series, beginning with *Country Life Stories*, a book that deserves wide circulation. Mrs. Helen Adele Whiting, Miss Cannon's collaborator in the foregoing, has independently brought out through the Associated Publishers two attractively bound and illustrated child's books, *Negro Folk Tales* and *Negro Art, Music and Rhyme*; the first much more successful in diction than the latter, but both only laudable pathbreakers in the important direction of introducing African legends and simplified race history to children. Dutton has also brought out Pattie Price's rhymed versions of *Bantu Tales*, genuinely true to folk idiom, which is all to their credit, but not too successfully adapted to the average child mind. All this is symptomatic of an important trend, of as much significance for general social education as for mere child entertainment. The crowning achievement in this field, however, is *The Child's Story of the Negro*, written by Miss Jane Shackelford. Here in fascinating style the riches of race history are minted down in sound coin for juvenile consumption and inspiration. More attractive format would make this real contribution a child's classic, and it is to be hoped that a second edition will make this advantageous addition.

Returning to the adult plane, the situation of poetry must claim our attention briefly. Time was when poetry was one of the main considerations of the Negro renaissance. But obviously our verse output has shrunk, if not in quantity, certainly in quality, and for obvious reasons. Poetry of social analysis requires maturity and group contacts, while the poetry of personal lyricism finds it hard to thrive anywhere in our day.

Especially so with the Negro poet whose cultural isolation is marked; to me it seems that this strain of expression is dying a natural death of spiritual suffocation, Beatrice Murphy's anthology of fledgling poets, *Negro Voices*, to the contrary. Here and there in this volume one hears a promising note; almost invariably, however, it is a poem of social analysis and reaction rather than one of personal lyricism. To the one or two veterans, like Hughes, Frank Davis, Louis Alexander, a small bevy can be added as discoveries of this meritorious but not too successful volume: Katherine Beverly, Iola Brister, Conrad Chittick, Marcus Christian, Randolph Edmonds, Leona Lyons, and Helen Johnson. However it is clear that the imitation of successful poets will never give us anything but feeble echoes, whether these models be the classical masters or the outstanding poets of the Negro renaissance, Cullen, McKay, and Hughes. If our poets are to serve well this generation they must go deeper and more courageously into the heart of real Negro experience. The postponement of Sterling Brown's expected volume *No Hidin' Place* thus leaves a lean poetic year of which the best garnerings, uneven at that, are Frank Marshall Davis's *Through Sepia Eyes* and Langston Hughes's *A New Song*. Both of these writers are vehemently poets of social protest now; so much so indeed that they have twangy lyres, except for moments of clear vibrancy such as Hughes's "Ballad of Ozzie Powell" and "Song of Spain" and Davis's "Chicago Skyscrapers," the latter seemingly the master poem of the year in a not too golden or plentiful poetic harvest. On the foreign horizon the appearance of the young Martinican poet L. G. Damas, is significant; otherwise the foreign output, like the domestic, is plaintive and derivative.

Whereas poetry languishes, drama seems to flourish. The honors are about evenly divided between the experimental theaters and the Federal Theatre Project. The latter, with several successful revivals, *Run, Little Chillun* among them, had as new hits Theodore Ward's *Big White Fog* and William Du Bois's moving though melodramatic *Haiti* to its credit. On the other hand, the experimental theater has given two Negro playwrights a chance for experimentation both in form and substance that may eventually lead somewhere. Dodson's *Divine Comedy*, the Yale Theatre's contribution, is a somewhat over-ambitious expressionistic rendition of Negro cult religion that shows promise of a new writing talent, while the Harlem Suitcase Theatre's *Don't You Want to Be Free?* has vindicated the possibilities of a new dramatic approach. Both are to be watched hopefully, but especially the latter, because a people's theater with an intimate reaction of the audience to materials familiar to it is one of the sound new items of a cultural program that in some of the arts, drama particularly, has stalled unnecessarily. This theater and the Richmond Peoples' Theatre, under the auspices of the Southern Youth Congress and the direction of Thomas Richardson, supply even better laboratory facilities than the drama groups of the Negro colleges, laudable as their Intercollegiate Dramatic Association is. It is to be hoped that real folk portraiture in drama may soon issue from these experiments. In the dramatized "Blues Episodes" of *Don't You Want to Be Free?*, and in the promising satirical sketches that the same theater has recently begun, I see potentialities such as I have previously discussed at length. I am not only anxious to see them develop but anxious for some further confirmation of the predicted role of the drama in the Negro movement of self-expression in the arts. Not that an individual critic needs to be sustained, but since the course was plotted by close comparative study of other cultural movements, some national and some racial, rather that the history of this phase of our cultural development should demonstrate the wholesome principle that the Negro is no exception to the human rule. For after all, it is the lesson of history that a cultural revival has been both the symptom and initiating cause of most people's awakenings.

PART II

As we turn now to the biographic, historical, and sociological literature of the year, we find the treatment of the Negro, almost without exception, maturing significantly. There is, on the whole, less shoddy in the material, less warping in the weaving, and even what is propaganda has at least the virtue of frank, honest labeling. The historical cloth particularly is of more expert manufacture and only here and there exhibits the frowsy irregularities of amateur homespun. General social criticism reaches a record yardage; and so far as I can see, only the patient needlepoint of self-criticism has lagged in a year of unusual, perhaps forced production. Forced, because undoubtedly and obviously the pressure behind much of this prose of social interpretation is that of the serious contemporary economic and political crisis. But fortunately also, a considerable part of this literature is for that very reason, deliberately integrated with the general issues and the competing philosophies of that crisis.

Before inspecting the varied stock of the year, a brief retrospective word is needed. Committed to no one cult of aesthetics (and least of all to the creed of "art for art's sake," since it tried to focus the Negro creative writer upon the task of "folk interpretation"), "The New Negro" movement did have a rather definite set of objectives for its historical and sociological literature. These were a non-apologetic sort of biography; a boldly racial but not narrowly sectarian history; an objective, unsentimental sociology; an independent cultural anthropology that did not accept Nordic values as necessarily final; and a social critique that used the same yardstick for both external and internal criticism. A long order—which it is no marvel to see take shape gradually and by difficult stages. Again to satisfy the skeptical, let quotations from "The Negro Digs Up His Past" attest:

> The American Negro must remake his past in order to make his future. Though it is orthodox to think of America as the one country where it is unnecessary to have a past, what is a luxury for the nation as a whole becomes a prime social necessity for the Negro. For him, a group tradition must supply compensation for persecution and pride of race the antidote for prejudice. History must restore what slavery took away, for it is the social damage of slavery that the present generation must repair and offset.

But this call for a reconstructed group tradition was not necessarily pitched to the key of chauvinism, though there is some inevitable chauvinism in its train. Chauvinism is, however, the mark and brand of the tyro, the unskilled and unscientific amateur in this line, and we have had, still have, and maybe always will have our brash amateurs who rush on where scientists pause and hesitate. However, this was recognized, and warned against, and was spoken of as the mark of the old, not of the newer generation. It was said:

This sort of thing (chauvinistic biography and history) was on the whole pathetically over-corrective, ridiculously over-laudatory; it was apologetics turned into biography. But today, *even if for the ultimate purpose of group justification*, history has become less a matter of argument and more a matter of record. There is the definite desire and determination to have a history, well documented, widely known at least within race circles, and administered as a stimulating and inspiring tradition for the coming generations. But gradually as the study of the Negro's past has come out of the vagaries of rhetoric and propaganda and become systematic and scientific, three outstanding conclusions have been established:

First, that the Negro has been throughout the centuries of controversy an active collaborator, and often a pioneer, in the struggle for his own freedom and advancement. This is true to a degree which makes it the more surprising that it has not been recognized earlier.

Second, that by virtue of their being regarded as something "exceptional," even by friends and well-wishers, Negroes of attainment and genius have been unfairly disassociated from the group, and group credit lost accordingly.

Third, that the remote racial origins of the Negro, far from being what the race and the world have been given to understand, offer a record of creditable group achievement when scientifically viewed, and more important still, that they are of vital *general* interest because of their bearing upon the beginnings and early development of culture.

   With such crucial truths to document and establish, an ounce
of fact is worth a pound of controversy. So the Negro historian
today digs under the spot where his predecessor stood and argued.

The mere re-statement of this historical credo of *The New
Negro* (1925) shows clearly that not only has it not been super-
seded, but that it has yet to be fully realized. Indeed it was
maintained at that time that the proper use of such materials as
were available or could be unearthed by research was "not only
for the first true writing of Negro history, but for *the rewriting
of many important paragraphs of our common American history.*" One only needs an obvious ditto for sociology, anthropology, economics, and social criticism to get the lineaments of
a point of view as progressive, as valid, and as incontestable in
1939 as fifteen years ago.

   Indeed we may well and warrantably take this as a yardstick
for the literature which we now have to review. Professor Brawley has excellently edited the *Best Stories of Paul Laurence Dunbar*; a service as much to social as to literary criticism. For by
including with the short stories excerpts from his novels, Dunbar's pioneer attempts at the social documentation of Negro
life are brought clearly to attention. Less artistic than his verse,
Dunbar's prose becomes nevertheless more significant with the
years; here for the most part he redeems the superficial and too
stereotyped social portraiture of his poetry and shakes off the
minstrel's motley for truer even if less attractive garb. Robinson's volume of stories, *Out of Bondage*, is, on the other hand,
such thinly fictionalized history as to have little literary value
and only to be of antiquarian interest. It is hard, no doubt, to
galvanize history either in fiction or biography, but Arthur Huff
Fauset's crisp and vivid *Sojourner Truth* proves that it can be
done. This—beyond doubt the prize biography of the year and
one of the best Negro biographies ever done—takes the fragile
legend of Sojourner and reconstructs a historical portrait of illuminating value and charm. It lacks only a larger canvas giving the social background of the anti-slavery movement to be of
as much historical as biographic value; and even this is from

time to time hinted back of the vigorous etching of this black peasant crusader.

Just this galvanic touch is missed in the scholarly and painstaking biography, historical critique, and translation of the poems of *Juan Latino*, by Professor Valaurez Spratlin. Thus this detailed documentation of the ex-slave Humanist, the best Latinist of Spain in the reign of Philip V and incumbent of the chair of Poetry at the University of Granada, rises only momentarily above the level of purely historical and antiquarian interest. In the verses of Latino there was more poetics than poetry, but the *Austriad* faithfully reflected the florid Neoclassicism of Spain of the 1570s; the biography could and should have shed a portraitistic light, if not on the man, then at least on his times, for concerning them there is plenty of material.

The Life of George Washington Carver, under the slushy caption of *From Captivity to Fame*, is a good example of what race biography once was, and today should not be. Purely anecdotal, with an incongruous mixture of petty detail and sententious moralisms, it not only does not do the subject justice, but makes Dr. Carver a "race exhibit" rather than a real human interest life and character. One is indeed impressed with the antithesis between the sentimental, philanthropic, moralistic approach and the historico-social and psychological approaches of modern-day biography. They are perhaps irreconcilable. Mrs. Addie Hunton's biography of her well-known husband, William Alphaeus Hunton, pioneer leader of the YMCA work among Negroes, is an example and case in point. A point of view that spots a career only by its idealistic highlights, that is committed to making a life symbolic, whether of an ideal or a movement, that necessarily omits social criticism and psychological realism, scarcely can yield us what the modern age calls biography. It is more apt to be the apologia of a "cause." In spite of such limitations, the Hunton biography is a record worth reading just as the life behind it was thoroughly worth living, but neither a moralistic allegory nor a thrilling success story like Pastor Clayton Powell's creditable autobiography will give us the objective social or human portraiture which the present generation needs and for the most part, desires.

The Black Jacobins by the talented C. L. R. James is, on the other hand, individual and social analysis of high order and deep penetration. Had it been written in a tone in harmony with its careful historical research into the background of French Jacobinism, this story of the great Haitian rebel Toussaint Louverture and his compatriots Christophe and Dessalines, would be the definitive study in this field. However, the issues of today are pushed too passionately back to their historic parallels—which is not to discount by any means the economic interpretation of colonial slavery in the Caribbean, but only a caution to read the ideology of each age more accurately and to have historical heroes motivated by their own contemporary idiom of thought and ideas. There is more correctness in the historical materials, therefore, than in the psychological interpretation of these truly great and fascinating figures of Negro history.

Unless it be characterized as the breezy biography of a cult, Zora Neale Hurston's story of Voodoo life in Haiti and Jamaica is more folklore and belles lettres than true human or social documentation. Scientific folklore, it surely is not, being too shot through with personal reactions and the piquant thrills of a travelogue. Recently another study has given Voodooism a more scientifically functional interpretation and defense, and Voodooism certainly merits an analysis going deeper than a playful description of it as "a harmless pagan cult that sacrifices domestic animals at its worst." Too much of *Tell My Horse* is anthropological gossip in spite of many unforgettable word pictures; and by the way, the fine photographic illustrations are in themselves worth the price of the book. The social and political criticism, especially of the upper-class Haitians, is thought-provoking; and caustic as it is, seems no doubt deserved in part at least. One priceless epigram just must be quoted: "Gods always behave like the people who make them."

Contrasting in thoroughness and sobriety with these excursions into Caribbeana are the two works of the Uruguayan race scholar, Ildefonso Pereda Valdés. Through the studies of

Fernando Ortiz, the learned scholar of Afro-Cubana, and the work in Afro-Braziliana by Dr. Arthur Ramos, shortly to be published in abridged translation by the Association for the Study of Negro Life and History, the field of the Negro elements in Latin American culture is at last being opened up to the scientific world generally, and to the North American reader in particular. Not yet translated, Señor Valdés's studies are an important extension of this most important field. In *Linea de Color*, he largely interprets the contemporary culture of the American and Cuban Negro while in *El Negro Rioplatense*, he documents the Negro and African elements in the history, folklore, and culture of Brazil, the Argentine, and Uruguay, and traces Negro influences from Brazil right down into furthermost South America. Important studies of Negro idioms in the popular music of Brazil, of African festivals and superstitions in Uruguay and the valley of the Rio de la Plata open up a fresh vein of research in the history and influence of the Negro in the Americas. In *Linea de Color* are to be found pithy urbane essays on Nicolás Guillén, the Afro-Cuban poet, the mulatto Brazilian poet Cruz e Sousa, and on African dances in Brazil. In the other volume, more academic essays on the Negro as seen by the great Spanish writers of the Golden Age in Spain and several other cosmopolitan themes attest to the wide scholarship of Señor Valdés. It is refreshing and significant to discover in far South America an independently motivated analogue of the New Negro cultural movement. *Linea de Color* reciprocates gracefully by giving a rather detailed account of the North American Negro renaissance in terms of its chief contemporary exponents, cultural and political. It has been an unusual year for Negro biography and folklore, the latter capped academically by the exhaustive collation of African and Negro American proverbs in Champion's monumental *Racial Proverbs*.

As is to be expected, the documentation of Negro life in the Federal Writers' Project, the American Guide series, is varied, uneven, and ranges through history to folklore and from mere opinion to sociology. But on the whole the yield is sound and representative, due in considerable measure to the careful direction of these projects from the Federal editorial office. *New York Panorama,* however, in its sections on the Negro, misses its chances in spite of the collation of much new and striking material. Moderately successful in treating early New York, it fails to interpret contemporary Harlem soundly or deeply. Indeed it vacillates between superficial flippancy and hectic propagandist exposé, seldom touching the golden mean of sober interpretation. In *The New Orleans City Guide* the Negro items are progressively integrated into the several topics of art, music, architecture, folklore, and civic history in a positively refreshing way. This exceeds the usual play-up of the Creole tradition at the expense of the Negro, and for once in the Creole account the Negro element is given reasonable mention. The *Mississippi Guide* is casual, notable for its omissions in its treatment of the Negro; and savors as much of the reactionary tradition of the Old South as the New Orleans Guide does of the liberal New South that we all prefer to hold with and believe in. The Old South is an undeniable part of the historical past; but as a mirror for the present it is out of place and pernicious.

Thus liberal studies like *A Southerner Discovers the South* by Jonathan Daniels and Frank Shay's *Judge Lynch: His First Hundred Years* become the really important guides to social understanding and action. They, with most of the solid literature of the New South—which someone has said is the necessary complement of the New Negro—keep accumulatively verifying these basic truths: that the history of the South itself is the history of the slave regime, that the sociology of the South is its aftermath and retribution, and that the reconstruction of the entire South is its dilemma and only possible solution. Whatever common denominator solution can be found is the problem of the present generation. Thus for Mr. Shay, lynching is rightly not just the plight of the Negro but the disease of law and public opinion; while for Mr. Daniels the Negro is not so much a problem as a symptom. This realistic third dimension now being projected into the consideration of the race problem is the best hope of the whole situation, and should never be lost sight of by any observer, black or white, who wishes today to get credence or give enlightenment.

For this reason, Professor Stephenson's study of *Isaac Franklin: Slave Trader and Planter of the Old South* is as social history of the newer, realistic type, as much a document of Negro history as it is of the socioeconomic story of the plantation regime. Factual almost to a fault, it is a model of careful objective statement; no one can accuse this author of seeing history through colored spectacles of opinions. Only slightly less objective, and even more revealing is Professor Bell Wiley's study of *Southern Negroes: 1861–1865*. But a decade ago so frank and fair an account of the Negroes during the crisis of the Civil War would have been very unlikely from the pen of a Southern professor of history and certainly unthinkable as a prize award of the United Daughters of the Confederacy. Southern abolitionism, Negro unrest and military service to both sides, the dilemmas of Southern policy and strategy, are not at all glossed over in a work of most creditable historical honesty. Almost a companion volume, by chance has come Professor Wesley's penetrating study entitled *The Collapse of the Confederacy*. Here surely is a fascinating division of labor—an analysis of the policy of the Confederacy by a Negro historian and of the status and behavior of the Negro population during the same period by a white historian. Dr. Wesley carefully and incisively documents the economic breakdown of the Confederate economy, showing its military defeat as merely its sequel. He is also insistent on the too often forgotten facts of the Confederacy's last frantic dilemma about military emancipation and the proposed use of Negro soldiers to bolster its shattered manpower. Thus both the historical and the contemporary Southern scene have this year had significant, almost definitive interpretations.

The fascinating subject of *The Negro in Louisiana* has unfortunately not had anything approaching definitive treatment at the hands of Professor Rousseve; for his volume, a creditable groundbreaker, has too much sketchiness and far too little social interpretation to match worthily the rapidly rising level of Southern historical studies.

Turning from the regional to the national front, we find the discussion of the race problem gains by the wider angle of vision and attack. We find also one great virtue in the economic approach, apart from its specific hypotheses—an insistence on basic and common factors in the social equation. The economic interpretation of the race question is definitely gaining ground and favor among students of the situation. Both studies in the long anticipated Volume I of the *Howard University Studies in Social Science* have this emphasis, the one explicitly, the other by implication. Wilson E. Williams's dissertation on "Africa and the Rise of Capitalism" breaks pioneer ground on the importance of the slave trade in the development of European commerce and industry in the 16th, 17th, and 18th centuries and establishes the thesis that it was a "very important factor in the development of the capitalist economy in England"—one might warrantably add, of Western capitalism. The second essay, by Robert E. Martin, skillfully analyzes "Negro Disfranchisement in Virginia," not in the traditional historical way, but by documenting the shifts of political policy and the mechanisms of majority-minority interaction, thus bringing to the surface conflicts of interest and motives too often unnoticed or ignored. Apart from such clarifying information these studies, reflecting the trend of the graduate instruction of which they are products, seem to predict a new approach in this field with broad implications and deep potentialities.

In contrast to this critical economic attack, J. W. Ford's *The Negro and the Democratic Front* hews rather dogmatically to the official Marxist line, but with frank and zealous insistence. Its frankness is a virtue to be praised; as is also the value of having a clear, simply put statement of the Communist interpretation of major national and world issues from the angle of the Negro's position. Though largely a compendium of Mr. Ford's addresses, it does focus for the layman a unified picture

of radical thought and programs of action. Quite to the opposite, John G. Van Deusen in *The Black Man in White America*
has taken up the cudgels for gradualism, gratuitously and with
feeble effect. To a book seven-eighths full of patiently assembled and well-organized facts about every important phase
of Negro life, Professor Van Deusen adds the banalities of
philanthropic platitudes and dubious advice. He counsels "patience," expects "education and understanding" and in another paragraph "that universal solvent: Time" to solve the
Negro problem, yet admits that "the greatest part of the work
of conciliation remains to be accomplished." If there were
some automatic strainer to separate fact from advice and opinion, this book would be a boon to the average reader, for there
are regrettably few up-to-date compendiums of the facts about
Negro life.

In education, there are three books of note this year. The
Yearbook of the *Journal of Negro Education*, in keeping with
the high standard of all its five annual year-book issues, documents exhaustively and in many regards critically "The Relation of the Federal Government to Negro Education." Similarly
exhaustive, with elaborate deduction of trends but little or no
overt social criticism, Professor Charles Johnson's study of
The Negro College Graduate offers for the first time since Du
Bois's Atlanta Studies an objective and composite picture of
the college-bred Negro. Significant conclusions are the relatively low economic standard of the Negro in professional service and the serious displacement of trained Negro leadership
from the areas of greatest mass need. It may be pled that an
objective survey study should only diagnose and must not
judge or blame. But just such vital correlation with social policy and criticism of majority attitudes is boldly attempted in
President Buell Gallagher's book, *American Caste and the
Negro College*. Instead of just describing the Negro college,
Dr. Gallagher spends seven of his fourteen chapters analyzing
the social setting and frame of reference of the Negro college,
namely the American system of color caste with its taboos and
techniques of majority domination and minority repression.

Then he illuminatingly decides that in addition to its regular function as a college, a Negro college has imposed upon it the function of transforming and transcending caste, or to quote: "the segregated college has a special set of responsibilities connected first, with the problem of transforming the caste system" and second, "with the success of the individual member of the minority group in maintaining his own personal integrity in the face of defeat, or of partial achievement." If for no other reason, such keen analysis of the social function of Negro education would make this an outstanding contribution; but in addition, the diagnosis is sound, the prescriptions liberal and suggestive, and the style charming. Indeed a noteworthy contribution!

African life has a disproportionately voluminous literature, since any European who has been there over six weeks may write a book about it. It is safe to say that over half of this literature is false both as to fact and values, that more than half of what is true to fact is false in interpretation, and that more than half of that minimal residue is falsely generalized—for Africa is a continent of hundreds of different cultures. So, the best of all possible interpreters is the intelligent native who also knows, without having become de-racialized, the civilization of the West. Next best is the scientific interpreter who uses the native informer as the open sesame to African social values. The virtue of René Maran's *Livingstone* is that he himself knows by long acquaintance that same equatorial Africa which was Livingstone's country. José Saco speaking of slavery in Brazil, Dantès Bellegarde speaking for Haiti and, with some reservation for amateurishness, J. A. Jarvis speaking for the Virgin Islands make their respective books welcome and trustworthy as native opinion upon native materials. The same should have been true for Nnamdi Azikiwe's *Renascent Africa* but for the almost adolescent indignation distorting the outlines of a statement of native West African conditions, grievances, and programs. Even so, an expression of native opinion is valuable at any price. Just as radical, in fact more so in spite of its cool reasoning, is George Padmore's *Africa and World Peace*. In addition to being one of the sharpest critiques of imperialism in a decade of increasing anti-imperialist attack, this book vividly expounds the close connection between fascism and imperialism, on the one hand, and fascism and African interests and issues on the other.

Turning to the less controversial, we have from Professor Herskovits a monumental and definitive two-volume study of the Dahomean culture. A careful historical and functional approach yields a sympathetic view of a much misunderstood people, and both illustrates and fortifies a growing trend toward the independent interpretation of African life not in terms of Nordic mores and standards but of its own.

So conceded is this point of view becoming that even the best travel literature is now being keyed to it. *Black and Beautiful* is one such, not just by wishful thinking in its title but by virtue of twenty-five years of "going native" by the author, Marius Fortie. His natives are individuals, not types; several of them were his "wives" and sons, and he speaks passionately for and in behalf of his "adopted people," a far cry indeed from the supercilious traveler, missionary, or civil servant. Even Andre Mikhelson's *Kings and Knaves in the Cameroons*, mock-heroic and ironic, is a cynical fable castigating "so-called European civilization"; while Isak Dinesen's *Out of Africa* gives a delicately sensitive and respectful account of Kenya native life and the Kikuyu, the Somali, and the Masai. The approach is human rather than anthropological and we have that to thank for a general impression that these peoples have a future and not merely a tragic present and an irretrievable primitive past. An impassioned defense of pagan primitivism is the subtle theme uniting the impressionistic diary pictures of *African Mirage*, by Hoyningen-Huene, by considerable odds one of the most understandingly observed and beautifully written volumes in the whole range of this literature. Even with all of our scientific revaluation, all our "New Negro" compensations, all our anti-Nordic polemics, a certain disrespect for Africa still persists widely. There is only one sure remedy—an anointing of the eyes. *African Mirage* seems to me almost a miraculous cure for cultural color blindness. Such normality of social vision is surely one of the prerequisites also for effective history, sociology, and economics; no scientific lens is better except mechanically than the eye that looks through it. Let us above all else pray for clear-minded interpreters.

37

DRY FIELDS AND
GREEN PASTURES

PART I

There are two traditions in the portrayal of Negro life and character, the realistic and the romantic, and it seems that they are coming into sharper contrast and conflict. This is more than the usual aesthetic controversy between realism and romanticism, for that is an issue of the past which realism has won decidedly, at least as far as seriously creative literature is concerned. But as relating to Negro materials, either the battle has to be fought all over again, belatedly; or else there is something more to the issue in this field—and the latter, I think, is the case. A minority literature is likely to suffer the orphan's fate of being forced always to wear hand-me-down, ill-fitting clothes. And even minority artistic spokesmen are apt to revel in these tatters of the past, especially if they once have been "elegant." This accounts for some of the shoddy, secondhand romanticism that perennially pervades the Negro literature of this or any typical year. But, as has already been said, I think there is even more to it than that.

What can it be—this additional something? Well, it is surely obvious to all but Hollywood and the Southern obscurantists that there are several sorts of Negroes, in addition to those that never were except in the imagination and tradition of the school of official Southern romance. Even the progressive and creatively original Southern writers have abandoned these stereotypes, but for all that, they are still very much alive and unbelievably popular. We should stop to consider this, for not all of it is Southern obscurantism and regional propaganda. There is a legitimate appetite for the picturesque, the naïve the zestful, and the exuberantly imaginative, and even in their baneful social misrepresentativeness, these traditional Negro types do have a deep human appeal that in some measure accounts for their wide vogue. They were, for example, the charm of *Green Pastures*, and against them realistically drab and drear characters, even though sociologically sound, have little chance in competition for general favor and interest. Putting it in a phrase, folk life, as poetically picturesque, enjoys a more than ten-to-one advantage over folk life as prosaically pictorial. A small section of reformists, a disillusioned intelligentsia, will accept sociological realism, and an occasional wider hearing may come to it as in the recent vogue of *Grapes of Wrath*, but on the whole and in the long run, romantic versions of life, especially minority life, are bound to have greater currency and popularity.

Personally in spite of the charm and the diversion I vote for the realistic art of the "dry fields," even the parched meadows and the scorched earth of our contemporary social crises, as against the romantic art of the "green pastures." We need more informative and less escapist literature and art. But that is not to ignore the general human inclination to lie down, mentally and emotionally, in the cool green shade beside pleasantly running waters. So it remains a very practical question for us partisans of truth in art to figure out what can and must be done about it. Here I think the literature of the year gives us a clue, and to those of us who have special interests in Negro materials and subject matter, gives also a new hope.

One form of realism can shorten the long odds against it, and that is poetic realism; for that, without making concessions to the truth, still manages somehow to lift the drab sordidness of the prosaic varieties of realism and give instead the warm human touch, the throbbing rhythm, the vital balance of contrast so necessary to an art that would make us see and feel and move rather than merely sit and stare and listen.

Certainly here and there touches of a particularly successful poetic realism are to be detected in Negro literature—amid, I admit, a terrific amount of realistic slag and romantic dross, but worth all the hard prospecting that it takes to find it and all the patient refining and careful vouching that may be necessary to get it into accepted and profitable circulation.

Such art combines beauty with truth, and reconciles the dilemma of having to have one at the expense of the other. For some time now I have had the conviction that not only the Negro writer, but whatever artist worked long and hard and deeply with Negro materials would find, by virtue of some things deeply characteristic of Negro life, the rare formula of poetic realism. And where it does crop out, we have, I am sure, the best of this or any year's production.

Fiction, especially with this rare combination, should not be expected of the average writer, nor of a period like ours which is so inevitably commercial. Yet it is to be marveled at that unconventional fiction is so much the order of the day. New types and new backgrounds are fairly frequent these days. Arna Bontemps, after a fine apprenticeship in the unromantic historical novel, follows his *Black Thunder* of several years back with a novelette of the Haitian revolution, *Drums at Dusk*. He has a grand theme, the young aristocrat intrigued by the impending slave revolt and dabbling back and forth between the moribund world of the Breda estate and the rising black Haiti of the peasants. But for all the broad canvas and the carefully studied historical and local color, *Drums at Dusk* fails to be either thrilling romance or moving realism. It is, however, a competent second novel in a field that promises a great deal.

The Negro historical novel is still in the making, but we can begin to glimpse what it will be in its full stature, with the homely epic character and unusually dramatic incident, in this book. In pioneering quality, *Drums at Dusk* is most significant, but it falls between the old and the new traditions.

So does another ambitious historical novel by two white writers, Roland Barker and William Doerflinger, a semi-realistic romance of the slave trade entitled *The Middle Passage*. So divided are the two parts of the canvas, and so different their brushstrokes, that one can almost imagine that it was a divided assignment.

Some commendable research has dug up vivid and true details of the slave trade, particularly about the African slave raids, the trading compounds on the Guinea coast, and the ruthless intertribal wars that fed the slave markets. Against this admirably realistic background, however, a melodramatic romance acts itself through, in too swashbuckling a fashion to be either convincing or in key. Stephen Bishop's blighted romance, his desperate resort to slave trading, his gradual conformation to type, his bitter feuds with his ship companions and trade rivals, and his final disappointment when, on his return for his last cargo, he finds his Emilia married to the Spanish trader, Esperanza, all move on another stage, and not until the ironic escape from capture by the British brig tracking down the outlawed slavers does the main plot mesh in effectively with the subplot. Again, then, a good beginning in an important new vein of historical material; or better than a mere beginning if we recall last year's slave melodrama, *The Dead Go Overside*, for in *Middle Passage* the local color is genuine.

We now come to an interesting but painful contrast, with some of the worst and best of Southern fiction on our hands. In fact we have, interestingly enough, four literary traditions represented in four books. Two of them are traditional and stereotyped; two, modern and pioneering. There is, on the one side, the sentimental paternalism of the old Southern school, the carefully studied indifference of the Neo-Confederates, for whom Negroes are but so much necessary background and local color; and on the other, the modern humanist tradition, folklore-ing the Negro with careful but not too-well-integrated realism, and the school of sociological realism integrating him with increasing skill and success. *It Will Be Daybreak Soon* typifies the first; *Journey Proud*, the second; *Star Spangled Virgin*, the third; and *Some Like Them Short*, the last. Here one really has the full gamut of Negro characterization exemplified.

Archibald Rutledge is an old and honorable name; undoubtedly *It Will Be Daybreak Soon* is well-intentioned. But the
practical upshot of this moribund paternalism is mawkish
sentimentality, unconvincing moralism, condescension, and
worse than these from the literary point of view, bad characterization.

"Lifelong and affectionate association with the presentation
Negro, who is, I think, the Negro at his very best," has produced a classic of the old-school attitude; a palpable misreading of fact and character in spite of the author's statement: "I
frequently feel inferior to these humble and beloved people;
inferior in the most important thing in life, in matters pertain-
ing to the human spirit, both here and hereafter." One can understand, after reading this, why the Old South turned to
Romance; it dared not face reality.

Journey Proud, by Thomasine McGehee, is, on the other
hand, modernized ancient tradition. It passes for realism, and
is realism in part. The Old South of Virginia from 1845 to
1879 is carefully resurrected, and the lives of the Mackays and
the Wyatts are lovingly documented from antebellum ease
and prosperity, through the shattering storm of Harpers Ferry
and Wilderness, Cold Harbor and Petersburg, to postbellum
decadence and proud maintenance of tradition. But, if possible, more pride cometh after than went before the fall: this is a
tradition glossed over, steadily romanticized and only superficially representative.

Not only are the Negro characters stereotyped, but many
human sides of Southern life are as carefully omitted as in any
prudish Victorian novel. In fact, Victorianism still survives in
the Southern aristocratic tradition although elsewhere it is
outmoded. With no apparent conception of their own society,
these figures move on in pasteboard serenity. Ellen asks her
husband if the man who is to buy the estate "expected to take
the Negroes," and Thomas says: "Of course! My Lord, what
could he do without 'em!"

It must not be overlooked, however, that the Southern tradition has been undone by enlightened Southern writers, and
among them none has a more honorable record than DuBose

Heyward, the author of *Star Spangled Virgin*. This time he has gone to the Virgin Islands for his background, and pens as usual a well-studied story. But this ironic idyll of the New Deal regime in the Islands, for all its careful technique, is not a moving portrait and it will not make a trilogy with *Porgy* and *Mamba's Daughters*. Perhaps it is not intended so seriously, but Rhoda, star-spangled virgin with five children, and her primitivisms may pass with many readers for serious social portraiture. Mr. Heyward seems to be falling too much into the exotic formula of a childlike Negro, which is the pitfall of the South Carolina school.

In contrast, it is important to see what William March does with a more enlightened and penetrating realism. There are twenty stories in *Some Like Them Short*, and only two are about Negroes. But some years back I said, apropos of Mr. March's *Come In at the Door*, here is the beginning of a new tradition in Southern fiction. The great stars of that day were William Faulkner, Erskine Caldwell, and Thomas Wolfe. I felt then that the first was too doctrinaire and insistent; the second too morbid and introspective; and the third too inchoate and kaleidoscopic. Truly great art has clarity, perspective, balance, sanity, and the human touch. March's two stories of Negro character, "Runagate Niggers" and "The Funeral," are the most significant bits of Southern fiction in this regard that I have ever read. Here is poetic realism at its best: and oddly enough, for all the brevity and naturalness, there is more effective social indictment and protest, more anatomizing of the Southern regime, than in reams of Faulkner and Caldwell.

Lafe Rockett's share tenants complain and sink deeper into debt; they try to run away to Chicago, are intercepted by the sheriff, and are on their way back to Lafe's farm when a Northern newspaper woman hears the story from the modern slave catchers, reports the case to Washington, and Lafe is indicted for peonage by Federal agents. Six staccato pages end with the ironic complaint of one of Lafe's friends: "For two cents I'd move out of this country and go to some place where people still enjoy liberty. That's how disgusted I am with this here country, and I don't much keer who knows it, either!"

"The Funeral" is even more tragic, but with greater poetic depth. Reba, the cook's little mistreated child, is whipped for spying on the little white girl's funeral. Her mother, in the thwarted role of the domestic, sees the child's behavior only in the light of the white folk's command and pleasure, which to her are the laws of life itself. When she turns to the backyard after the busy spells of kitchen duty on the funeral supper, it is to find Reba hanging from the backyard tree, for she too wanted kind words, a great to-do over her, a magnificent funeral. Here, too, the force of the social indictment flows naturally and justly from the mere description of scene and character; this is art, not a tract, tragedy rather than diatribes or dialectic. And when a reader finishes with the feeling, "*this is the truth, the whole truth*," realism has really triumphed.

In ineffectual contrast is a novel like *Boss Man* true enough in detail, but packed so overfull with harrowing incidents that it fails both of conviction and social understanding. Such raw-document literature has its place, and has served a social purpose, but it has one great failing: it isn't literature. When this is fully realized we shall prefer tracts that are not fictionalized and fiction that is not tractarian.

Four Negro writers conclude the year's fiction, with increasing collective power and penetration, but not in every case with completely successful literary grasp and style. Zora Neale Hurston's *Moses, Man of the Mountain* might have escaped the category of fiction had her characterization and dialogue been less sustained. And it would have been better so, for after all this is cleverly adapted *Green Pastures* in conception, point of view, and execution. Genuine folk portraiture it is not; and, lacking the vital dramatization that superb acting gave to *Green Pastures*, it sinks back to the level of the original Roark Bradford. What if the stereotyping is benign instead of sinister, warmly intimate instead of cynical or condescending? It is still caricature instead of portraiture. Gay anecdotes there are aplenty, but somehow black Moses is neither reverent nor epic, two things I should think that any Moses, Hebrew, Negroid, or Nordic, ought to be.

Waters E. Turpin's second novel has a great epical theme,

the saga of a family living in Chicago after a successful trans-plantation from the deep South. The Benson family intro-duces, from intimate Negro portrayal, a new milieu into our current fiction, and essays for the first time on any grand scale the migration theme. But somehow there is lacking the in-creased maturity one should expect of a second novel after so good a first as *These Low Grounds*. *O, Canaan!* is needle-point realism, too detailed and close focused for epic sweep or deep social perspective. More than one reviewer has therefore had to regard the book as a groundbreaker of merit rather than a definitive treatment of a novel and important theme. *O, Canaan!*, too, could have gained by treating its theme less pro-saically and with something of the fire of poetry and swift dramatic movement.

Just that lilt which is missing in so much realism comes into the style of William Attaway's first novel, *Let Me Breathe Thunder*. The title says so, and the narrative bears it out. Much ado has been made over the fact that this is not a novel of Negro character and situation. I thought that old Ghetto question was long since buried, but if it isn't, let this novel heap the last spadeful. What is significant, beyond some excel-lent local color and picaresque narration, is the strong natural-ness of characterization and the subtly conceived human trio of Step, Ed, and Hi Boy. The little Mexican waif is almost a symbol, yet very much alive. I call this the second triumph of the poetic kind of realism, and it marks Attaway's career as promiseful. And should he never write of Negro life—which is just as inconceivable as that he or any other free artist should write only of Negroes—there will still be something Negro in the equation. By that I do not refer to race or complexion, but to a brand of homely, folky imagination which I regard as characteristically Negro. *Let Me Breathe Thunder* has that rare quality in the overtones of its prose-poetic style.

Richard Wright, who has that quality too, was to have pub-lished his first novel this year, but it has been delayed. "Bright Morning Star," regarded by many as his best short story, reap-pears, after its first publication in the *New Masses*, in the Val-halla of O'Brien's *Best American Short Stories*. It deserves this

place, although personally I think it misses superlative great-
ness by an over-insistence on its theme and a redundancy that
still betrays a young artist, albeit perhaps a young genius. The
Caldwell influence has done much harm to many young writers, who pack it on too thick for credence and crisp flowing
outline. An over-documented or over-insistent realism is too
prosy even for good prose. One can readily see the temptation
to overdo and overstress, for Stribling, Caldwell, and Faulkner
had to tilt a risky tournament against the plumed Knights of
the Confederacy—Dixon, Page, Cohen, Roark Bradford, and
Stark Young. But the best Southern fiction will come neither
from the glamour boys nor from the calamity boys, but from
the nonpartisans to whom truth is dearer than either Marx or
Caesar.

Juvenile fiction continues to improve, as it should but as for
a long time it didn't. Publishers and authors are beginning to
awaken to the possibilities of this neglected market. *Tobe,* by
Stella Sharpe, is a beautifully pictorialized story for small children, and comes near to being the long-awaited antidote for
the "pickaninny" tradition. It has been tried before, but *Tobe*
achieves it, more than half by virtue of its beautiful photo-
graphs.

Junior, A Colored Boy of Charleston, by Eleanor F. Latti-
more, a book for older children, has much of the same charm
and inspirational lift. It has even touches, here and there, of
social implications, as for instance in the appeal of the children
for their unemployed seniors. William C. White's *Mouseknees*
reverts to the comic tradition, but sympathetically so. It is a
good West Indian picnic story, artistically carried through.
Lion Boy, by Alden G. Stevens, goes to East Africa and presents well-documented tribal folklore. It, too, follows in the pioneer footsteps of the better fiction and like Erick Berry's
work, offers American children for the first time a sane and
fair idea of Africa. The importance of that, to the Negro child
particularly, cannot be overestimated.

Turning next to poetry, the yield is still meager. One can
scarcely believe that verse-making has so suddenly ceased, and
I have much reason, from manuscript experience, to know that

it has not. The financial depression has clipped Melpomene's wings: poetry seldom paid, nowadays it bankrupts. A. S. Cripps, an English missionary, has succeeded in having the Oxford Press bring out a volume of serious but over-sophisticated verse, a great deal of it of African locale or inspiration. Here and there are important notes of insight and revaluation, as in "The Dirge for Dead Porters"; and in "A Mashona Husbandman:"

> You find him listless, of but little worth
> To drudge for you, and dull to understand?
> Come watch him hoe his own rain-mellowed land:
> See how the man outbulks his body's girth!

Gwendolyn Bennett has resumed writing in periodicals, and exhibits a maturing of a talent that always was promising. Her "Threnody for Spain," in extended ode form, bears the quotation of two sample stanzas of considerable beauty and competence:

> The lovely names of Spain are hushed today—
> Their music, whispering with a muted tone,
> Caresses softly mounds of restless clay
> Where urgent seeds of liberty were sown. . . .
>
> And from your soil and from the bones beneath,
> For those who guest anew a Golden Fleece,
> A sword will rise, undaunted from its sheath,
> To cleave a path for universal peace!

In the significant anthology *This Generation*, edited by George Anderson and Eda Lou Walton, Sterling Brown is represented by seven poems of his later "social criticism" vein, "Transfer," "Old Lem," "Conjured," "Colloquy of a Black and White Worker," "Bitter Fruit of the Tree," "Slim in Hell," "Break of Day," and "Glory, Glory." Here, too, is successful poetic realism, all the more so when the turn of thought is ironic and farcical than when it is socially indignant. The satire of "Slim in Hell" is effective social indictment and protest, perhaps more so than verse like "Old Lem" and "Colloquy." However, we need more of both from one of the strongest of our younger poets. For there is Negro grief and tragedy that needs forceful telling; the grief, for example, of Mame, waiting for her murdered Big Jess, waylaid fireman on the Alabama Central:

> *Sweet Mame sits rocking, waiting for the whistle*
> *Long past due, babe, long past due.*
> *The grits are cold, and the coffee's boiled over,*
> *But Jess done gone, baby; he done gone.*

and there is Negro desperation also, on many minds though fewer tongues, as in this from "Transfer:"

> *But this is the wrong line we been ridin',*
> *This route doan git us where we got to go.*
> *Got to git transferred to a new direction.*
> *We can stand so much, then doan stand no mo.'*

For the most effective social discussion and the most potent realism we must in the end, I think, turn to the drama. Yet here it seems to come so slowly; on the issue of the effective portrayal of Negro life, drama is still in the hands of the enemy; and of late in the hands of that difficult variety, the friendly enemy. The commercial theater has increased the Negro vogue but has not capitulated yet either to complete truth or sincere art. *Mamba's Daughters*, for instance, although it offered Ethel Waters a chance for a spectacular role, took a great deal of the balanced social documentation out of the original novel, and concentrated on a pitiful and almost moronic primitivism in Hagar—good theater but not necessarily good drama. Then along comes the new *John Henry*, with the potentialities of a moving folk epic, but throttled down to melodramatic pageantry and musical-comedy triteness in many of its big scenes. It is still doubtful whether Paul Robeson's talent and fine singing presence can make a success of this pastiche of the John Henry saga, that as a libretto has cast too green an eye toward

Show Boat, Porgy, and *Green Pastures* and as a musical score
has set gems of genuine folk song in too stylized a matrix. The
success curse of the stereotype was also on *Swingin' the Dream,*
where only the truly genuine Negro things like the dancers and
the inset jazz, were moving. The rest was farce, and of the
vaudeville variety at that, but with *The Hot Mikado* still in circulation, it would appear that we are in for plenty of it. The
Negro *Macbeth,* a fine thing in itself, has had a fearful
progeny—all of them black sheep, in my opinion, except *The
Swing Mikado.*

   In more serious drama, the little-theater groups are experi-
menting feverishly, but not as yet with great success. The
Karamu theater produced Langston Hughes's three-act drama
of labor, *The Front Porch.* It proved to be not as strong as either
Mulatto or *Don't You Want to Be Free.* The Rose MacClendon
Players of New York presented several novelties, most promising among them George Norford's *Foy Exceeding Glory.* The
Yale University Theatre presented Owen Dodson's *The Garden
of Time.* This second play of the talented author of *Divine
Comedy* is the most competent piece of playwriting that any of
our young authors has yet turned out. Very skillfully it drama-
tizes, in beautiful prose poetry, the story of Jason and Medea,
first in its ancient Greek setting and then, breaking over to a
Southern analogue, the clandestine interracial romance of John
and Miranda. With the good acting and superb setting which it
received at New Haven, this was a powerful and challenging
play despite its occasional expressionistic mannerisms. In its
big scenes—Medea's seduction, Medea's appeal to Jason, and
Blue Boy's comforting of Miranda—*The Garden of Time*
achieved exceptional but restrained dramatic effect. Dodson's
is a career to be watched. We badly need a dramatist who
knows his theater and who is not too lazy to polish his lines.
Serious Negro drama must shake off the blight of the amateur
just as the regular drama must shake off the curse of the "sure-
fire success" and the box office.

   Negro music has done extraordinarily well this year. The
University of North Carolina Press is bringing out Harold
Courlander's carefully annotated anthology of Haitian

folklore, melodies, drum-rhythms, and dances; and the Clar-ence Williams Music Publishing Company has issued the ex-cellent *Voice of Haiti*, another annotated collection of Haitian folk songs by Laura Bowman and LeRoy Antoine. The year has also brought an array of careful and technically competent analyses of jazz, all three studies notable for the absence of that flippant and fashionable faddism so associated with this all-too-popular subject.

Wilder Hobson's study, *American Jazz Music*, traces the or-igins of the various jazz styles with important new sidelights on the "musical underground" that has been going on for twenty-five years between the white and the Negro exponents of popular American music. This documents all the more the Negro's claim to the origination of this musical material, with-out in any way detracting from the genuine talent and artistic democracy of the white musicians. On the whole, they have behaved well; it has been public opinion largely that has been responsible for the clandestine character of the close associa-tion: Negro music was bootlegged in the "bootleg era."

Winthrop Sargeant's *Jazz: Hot and Hybrid* is the best and most scholarly analysis of jazz and Negro secular folk music to date, and *Jazzmen*, by Frederic Ramsey and Charles E. Smith—a careful and zestful pilgrimage to the home sources of jazz, recounting firsthand reminiscences of the 'old masters' which were about to die out—has performed an inestimable service to present and future students of this important musi-cal tradition. It has also done belated justice to many a humble unknown who deserves the credit and should have had his share of Tin Pan Alley's millions. In the December issue of *Es-quire*, Elmer Simms Campbell has a well-documented article on "The Blues: The Negro's Lament," with very fortunate au-thoritative material given by Charles C. Cooke and Clarence Williams.

Interestingly enough, the streams of realism and romance, the traditions of dry fields and green pastures, meet and min-gle gloriously in Negro folk music and above all, in Negro jazz.

PART II

There is a *Green Pastures* tradition in the sociological and economic interpretation of Negro life and history as well as in the fictional. Once it dominated its field about as definitely as the lush and sentimentally romantic tradition dominated the literary and artistic treatment of the race life. However it, too, is now on the defensive, and at points it is in disorganized retreat. The "dry fields" view of objective and factualist versions of the racial situation has the backing of the new scholarship, both of the white and Negro scholars who concern themselves with the American minority scene. Once the sociologists wrote with one eye on the scene and another on some forecast solution of the "race problem," and there was many a fine talent and intention led astray by the ideological mirage. For the real opponents of Negro interests this was a boon, for under cover of race formulas, they were deadly realistic in sinister ways of repression, exploitation, and unrelenting persecution. The panaceas and the millennial hopes of the Negroes and their advocates covered up their antagonists' animosity and social rascality, and the glowing treatises and prolonged oratorical sessions and interracial meetings served, often unwittingly enough, as smoke screens and alibis for the white opposition. That situation seems to have changed materially and, let us hope, permanently, and the sociological literature of 1939 definitely shows it. Most encouraging of all is the growth of younger Negro social scholars, demonstrating an ability to handle social analysis of situations in which they are themselves deeply involved, with competence and objectivity, and an ability, also, to interpret and indict in an impartial fashion as well as to describe scientifically. There are this year a half dozen books on the American racial situation that are outstanding, three of them by Negro scholars, with notable race participation in one of the others. That is a record, though I am not enough in favor of "race statistics" to mention it except for its objective significance, which is qualitative. It is the quality of these studies that counts.

Nominally in another field, in fact entitled *Negro Education in Alabama*, Horace Mann Bond's book is actually a thorough and incisive socioeconomic analysis of the Southern scene. He connects up, almost for the first time, the trends of education with the economic policy and issues of a significant region. Alabama is significant in this sense, not only in being representative of the lower South, but of having in it two economies—the lowland cotton economy, and the mining industrial economy around Birmingham. Bond traces the fight between them, and then the alliance with Northern industrialism in this region, and probably gives us our best account, to date, of why it was (and is) that the Southern policy toward the Negro has had such tacit support from Northern industrial forces, in spite of the traditional Northern espousal of the Negro's cause. Bond definitely suggests that the improvement of Negro education in the South is contingent on the social reconstruction of the South as such. The information on educational history and trends is also thoroughly competent and clearly interpreted.

Dr. Hortense Powdermaker has provided another top flight analysis in her semi-anthropological survey of a Delta town, alias "Cottonville," to save the inhabitants embarrassment. This is the same community investigated a short while back by Dr. Dollard of Yale, as the basis of his book, *Caste and Class in a Southern Town*. In *After Freedom*, which she subtitles *A Cultural Study in the Deep South*, Miss Powdermaker investigated the background, attitudes, and class structure of this typical Southern biracial community. Her notable results are her tracing of the roots of the Southern code not to tradition alone but to a continuance of a system of economic exploitation; her documentation of the class structure of the Negro group, with its differential values and attitudes; and her report of the increasing acculturation of the Negro, even in an unprogressive community. She also reports the growing spirit of resentment and incipient revolt which that entails, and gives a rather vivid picture of the inner workings of the Southern biracial code, with all its inconsistencies anatomized. Such a study could not have been made without other pioneer work such as

Dollard, Guy Johnson, Odum, Raper, and Gallagher did in previous years. Books like *The Tragedy of Lynching, Black Yeomanry, The Collapse of Cotton Tenancy,* and *American Caste and the Negro College* have directly led up to it by laying down a basis of frank, realistic social analysis for the Southern social scene. That movement has now matured, and is bringing powerful scientific criticism of the Southern regime; the sort upon which social reconstruction can be based whenever there is sufficient courage and practical incentive.

After Freedom is particularly good in revealing the interaction of majority and minority life, and in locating a large part of the trouble in the general economic predicament of the South, black and white. A penetrating analysis of the Negro church as an agency of palliative and escapist influence is another of its important contributions.

What the Powdermaker volume does for one community and for one rather static segment of the racial scene, the Negro sections of the North Carolina, Tennessee, and Georgia Federal Writers' Project publication, *These Are Our Lives,* does for a wider and more changing field and over both rural, small-town, and industrial centers. It is not too much to say that this self-portraiture of the lower and lower-middle classes in terms of typical life histories is a new and promising procedure in sociological analysis. It vindicates both the project and its editorship, and gives us a vital and humanized understanding of social conditions instead of merely objective scientific reporting. The Negro sharecropper, cash-renter, independent farm owner, unskilled worker, freight handler, odd-job worker, bootblack, housemaid, and dentist—all have their respective say, and tell a revealing story in their substantial parallels with white lives on the same levels. What is striking, in spite of the differentials of race prejudice and proscription, is the basic similarity of the social situations and reactions; telling the progressive-minded reader what is basically wrong with Southern society, irrespective of racial discrimination. Here is a great supplementary human document on the "Number one economic problem."

Professor Burgess calls E. Franklin Frazier's study of *The Negro Family in the United States* the most valuable contribution to the literature of the family since the publication, twenty years ago, of Znaniecki's *The Polish Peasant in Europe and America*, and with considerable warrant. For Professor Frazier's exhaustive study, with a historical background unusual for the average sociological study, gives both a cross-section and an evolutional view of Negro life and the social forces that have played upon it, by using the Negro family as a frame of reference. As a study of progressive acculturation, under great odds, it is important beyond the narrow field of Negro social data and history. It traces the original adaptations during slavery, the development of the Negro class structure, the readaptations after slavery in the Reconstruction, and most important of all, the more recent changes of urbanization, which in the author's opinion are gradually but surely integrating the Negro minority with the working classes and the contemporary economic order. No superficial optimism, but a careful analysis of current social forces and their trends yields these conclusions, illustrating what was said at the beginning about the growing value of an interpretive rather than a purely descriptive brand of sociology.

Of almost equal importance is Horace Cayton and George Mitchell's study of the relation of Negro and white labor in their *Black Workers and the New Unions*. The very process which Professor Frazier found most significant—urbanization with gradual industrial integration—is here traced and analyzed both with respect to its factors of progress and factors of retardation. A differential between the CIO and the AF of L policies of unionization permits an illuminating picture of both, although it is obvious from the data reported that the more liberal CIO program has put indirect pressure on the American Federation of Labor and is beginning to affect its attitude toward the wider unionization of Negro labor. Not only the more liberal policy, but also the fact that the bulk of Negro workers are in the relatively more unorganized sections of labor, puts the CIO in a vital relationship to Negro industrial interests.

The volume traces the story of the Negro in the iron and steel industries, the meat-packing firms, railroad car shops, and the mines and factories of the Birmingham district. These latter are most important, for successful biracial unionization is taking place in this Southern center and its importance is being recognized increasingly by the white workers. This means, if a relatively successful nationwide extension can follow, conscious industrial cooperation between large sections of the white and the Negro masses; something having potentialities for the removal or modification of race prejudice on a realistic basis and in terms of self-interest such as could not have been imagined ten years ago. "A movement for the single purpose of integrating Negroes into the trade union movement" is seen by the authors as one of the needs of the hour, and one of the greatest prospects on the contemporary social horizon.

Under the editorship of Edgar T. Thompson, Duke University Press has published a notable study with a traditional title but an untraditional approach, *Race Relations and the Race Problem.* The novelty of the book—another milestone in advancing Southern sociological scholarship—is the more generalized approach to the race question as neither local nor national solely, but as an instance of a minority situation and its adjustment. With an introduction by Professor Robert E. Park validating this point of view, ten other scholars, two of them colored, discuss various aspects of changing race relations. Edward B. Reuter discusses what he calls the racial division of labor; Guy B. Johnson, patterns of race conflict; Lloyd Warner and Allison Davis, a comparative study of the class and caste cleavages in the South, or the way racial caste modifies the class structure; and Edgar Thompson, the plantation tradition as a basic pattern for Southern life. Particularly notable, it seems to me, are Copeland's article on the "Negro as a Contrast Conception," showing the origin and basis in the socioeconomic order of the false stereotypes of the whites about the Negro and their role in facilitating and rationalizing prejudice and social discrimination; Stonequist's study of the mulatto, which, in addition to a historical review of the status of the mulatto in the United States, makes an excellent comparison of the mulatto status under the Latin and South American pattern of society; and Charles S. Johnson's admirable study on "Race Relations and Social Change," in which he goes over unequivocally, for perhaps the first time, to large-scale interpretive conclusions. There were suggestions of this trend in Professor Johnson's cotton tenancy study, but here he definitely declares for the economic factors as basically determining race conflict issues, as the factors in terms of which he thinks the dominant trends of minority-majority relations can be forecast, and as revealing the common denominators between the race problem and other issues of social conflict and reconstruction. Quite evidently, then, this is an important book with a progressive and objective outlook on the racial situation.

Professor Ira Reid's doctoral study on *The Negro Immigrant* opens up the important new field of the investigation of the West Indian Negro in the United States. This is a contingent of about a hundred thousand persons, not by any means all concentrated in New York, who have had a disproportionate influence on Negro life generally, so much so that it is rather to be regretted that the study does not run back to the migrations before 1899, the opening date of the book. The study shows that even in this later period of mass migration, the West Indian Negro has taken important leadership in the fight against racial discrimination. In the period prior, this was also importantly true. This seems due to the galvanizing experience of migration and reaction to new social conditions.

Dr. Reid also shows the initial hostile reactions of the native-born Negroes, both in their aspect of economic competition and in their less pardonable aspect of nativist prejudice, but shows how the common situation of proscription has gradually forged a solidarity of interest and cooperation, beginning at about the period of the Garvey movement, but continuing with appreciable momentum since. A few typical life histories are given, as are statistical tables of much interest and value for the further study of the transplanted Negro West Indian.

The 1939 Year Book of the *Journal of Negro Education*, on *The Position of the Negro in the American Social Order*, is, among its many outstanding previous issues, easily the most comprehensive and provocative. Every aspect of the minority group life is analyzed critically by an expert, generally with reference to current trends. A critical forecast section is added to insure more than mere analysis as the outcome of this elaborately collaborated study.

The recent volume by Dr. Du Bois, *Black Folk, Then and Now*, immediately challenges attention in the historical field because of its tremendous scope: it is a vivid sketch of the world history of the Negro. Partly for that very reason, but also due, no doubt, to the strong dramatic strain in Dr. Du Bois's outlook and style, there is considerable of what I have called *Green Pastures* romanticizing in this book, particularly in the earlier sections on the prehistory of the Negro, where, after all, there is unfortunately more opinion than fact available. Readers familiar with the author's *The Negro*, of which the present book is something of a modernized version, will remember with gratitude that brilliant, effective defense and apologia of the darker peoples. In its day it rendered great service in widening the historical perspective on the Negro and in challenging Nordic versions of world history. However, scientific scholarship now needs no such challenge and merits no such indictment on the whole. The general public still needs the facts, perhaps, written as Dr. Du Bois can write them, but from the scientific point of view no extended historic polemic is now necessary. Consequently, the reviewer finds other parts of the present book more worthwhile, especially the section on "Black Europe"—a vivid picture of the colonial scene and the alignments of the black-white world under imperialism. Here the book will serve to break through the provincialism of the average American reader, black or white, and open out to him color as a world situation and problem. Dr. Du Bois's interpretation here is, briefly, that of the incompatibility of real democracy and economic empire, and the common interests, hardly yet realized, of the economic emancipation of the white European masses, and of the black and yellow masses in the colonies and protectorates, exploited by the same machinery of ruthlessly expansive and competitive capitalism. This is undoubtedly the stronger section of the book, for which its too-racially-conceived earlier history can be forgiven.

The difficulty with historical apologetics is the fact that the other side always has its inning, and from that point of view, one is doomed to a relay of heated statements in partisan succession. Such a book, from the other side, is Arthur Lloyd's *The Slavery Controversy*, which really blames the war on the provocative tactics of the extreme Garrisonian Abolitionists. The thesis is that the North was precipitated into challenging the South by propagandized over-statements indicting the slave system, which, as the controversy progressed, entered into the political issues of the time. This construction of the "sectional struggle" is far from new, Dr. Lloyd's evidence is factually interesting, and some readers may be convinced by its interpretation. The old formula of states' rights and the confederation concept of the Union is really the pivot of the author's argument, and according as one takes sides on this, he will agree or disagree with the conclusions.

Admitting, too, the important influence of the abolitionist controversy, W. Sherman Savage documents rather competently the controversy from 1816 to 1860 in terms of the quarrel over the distribution of the movement's literature. Here, undoubtedly, was one of the earliest and greatest propaganda movements in our national history, and even as Lloyd claims, the public opinion it crystallized did finally flow into political channels. But the point Lloyd overlooks is the formidable counter-movement of Southern pro-slavery controversy and propaganda that also had its day and chance, and lost. So that to blame the issue on the provocative tactics of one side merely, and to represent the South's economy as a misunderstood sectional system or a martyred minority cause has little or no historical warrant. Indirectly, by showing the frantic tactics of Southern statesmen, particularly Calhoun and Jackson, the Savage book restores historical impartiality to the record.

———

A powerful book, particularly well-documented, is Joseph Carroll's sketch of *Slave Insurrections in the United States*. The theme has become popular of late, and is an important restoration of a glossed-over chapter in the Negro's social history. This is one of the most extensive of the studies from the point of view of documentation, although the pioneer work of Aptheker, barely mentioned by this author, must not be forgotten. The study lacks much mention of the social conditions behind these insurrections, although the Wilberforce historian lists some 78 slave conspiracies.

Professor Ralph V. Harlow of Syracuse adds to the growing historical literature of the abolition movement a competent biography of Gerrit Smith, a narrative that might have gained in social importance had it discussed at greater length the abolitionist conception of the Negro's possibilities and future as it figured so largely in Smith's controversies with his contemporaries. Professor Harlow has almost the Lloyd thesis about the provocative effect of the uncompromising wing of the Abolitionists, and rather blames them for precipitating a Civil War that could have been avoided by compromise. Closer to Negro life and interests therefore, is Alphonse Miller's thoroughly vital biography of *Thaddeus Stevens*, whom he styles the "Sinister Patriot," referring to his complex for stubborn, tactless, but brave opposition to both convention and tyranny. Fortunately for the veracity of the portrait, none of Stevens's life is glossed over, including his close associations with Negroes; so here is the definitive biography of this most belligerent of the Negro's advocates.

A slight but interesting contribution to the biographic field is *Five North Carolina Negro Educators*, edited by N. C. Newbold and written by persons acquainted with the lives of Simon Atkins, J. B. Dudley, Annie Holland, Peter W. Moore, and Ezekiel E. Smith, all pioneers of public school education in North Carolina. The significance of their cooperative contribution toward developing the first progressive policy of state education in the South is not without its social significance.

An autobiography of Colonel D. P. Calixte, former commandant of the Haitian army, detailing his disagreement with the Vincent regime and consequent exile, is an interesting contemporary document, far too much a personal apologia to be good biography, but perhaps of considerable historical value on the none-too-liberal administration of the first nominally Haitian government after the withdrawal of the American occupation. Mainly of personal interest is the volume supplementing his autobiography of last year, Rev. A. Clayton Powell's travel sketches from the Holy Land, and decidedly more ephemeral, even, is J. Irving Scott's homiletic guidance and pedagogic manual, *Living with Others*, based on his personal teaching experience.

A book that might easily have been just as ephemeral, *The Negro in Sports*, has been saved from that fate by careful documentation and a sound educational perspective on a popular subject, the Negro's athletic achievements. Not enough of the social history and influence of the sports is given, however, for here we could have had a discussion of the interaction of racial discrimination upon the players and upon the standards of American collegiate competition. In this sense the book could have been a side treatise on the paradoxes of American public opinion on the race issue, and not just a primer of athletic prowess and success.

Heading the list in belles lettres is an opinionated critique of the Negro author in relation to his public, or rather what the author considers his "two opposed publics." J. Saunders Redding's *To Make a Poet Black* is groundbreaking, in a very important field, the psychological conditioning of the Negro author throughout the various periods of Negro literary expression; but Mr. Redding is too insistent on his pet thesis, mentioned above, to do justice to many of the writers and movements he surveys. It is questionable that the dilemma of trying to please two audiences is the root of the Negro author's trouble. An academic but competent study of the development of the *Negro Character in the Southern Novel* has been published in the Louisiana State University abstracts.

Compiled under the supervision of Mrs. Dorothy Porter, the catalogue of the Howard University Moorland Collection of books by and on the Negro has appeared, and is an invaluable addition to Negro bibliography.

In another province of belles lettres in spite of its appearance in 1938, attention must be called to a brilliant anthology of Afro-Cuban poetry, *Orbita de la Poesía Afro-Cubana, 1928–1937*, edited by Ramón Guirao, for it introduces an important new province of Negro creative talent. The work of these Cuban poets of mixed blood is of superior talent, both technically and in social interpretation. It almost appears that the declining stream of fresh creative effort in poetry has shifted South.

Along the same line, Richard Pattee's welcome but unfortunately abridged translation of Arthur Ramos's *The Negro in Brazil*, has appeared under the Associated Publishers' imprint. This is a cultural history primarily, giving particular attention to Negro influences on the music, folklore, and the arts in Brazil.

More sociological, but discussing the cultural issues of the world problem of color, comes an important French publication, under Catholic auspices, *L'Homme de Couleur*. It ranges from Indochina, Japan, and Polynesia to the contacts of white civilization and cultural policies as they affect the Negro in East, West, and South Africa, in the United States, the West Indies, and the Philippines. The frame of reference is the new and highly significant campaign for racial and social justice being emphasized in Roman Catholic circles today, which, launched by certain liberal circles in the church, has lately achieved, under the new Pontificate, special emphasis and the status of an official policy.

In criticism from a more realistic angle, Cedric Dover's book, *Know This of Race*, covers the same ground of the world problems of racialism, with the author's usual trenchant and broadly informed criticism of contemporary prejudice— Nazi, British, American, and colonial. James W. Ford's *Anti-Semitism, The Struggle for Democracy, and the Negro People* covers the same ground from the angle of Marxist social criticism and solutions of class structure reform. All in all, the consideration of race on the world and cultural fronts is steadily increasing, and the American race problem is gaining in perspective thereby.

Even in the African literature there seems this year, to be more science than romance. The only significant sentimental document is F. Clement Egerton's spicy narrative of a personal journey to the Cameroons, *African Majesty*. It is one of the more penetrating travelogues, with sympathetic and valuable data on the Bangante people and their social customs. Quite factual in approach, on the other hand, and almost too noncommittal, is the simply written but authoritative account of *The Southern Bantu* by L. Marquard and T. G. Standing. This becomes now the best available handbook on the race situation of the Union of South Africa: it is only mildly liberal in viewpoint, but is unimpeachable as to its factual information on a segment of the race question which should be better known, especially to Negro Americans.

Stupendously comprehensive and official is the publication of the African Research Survey of the Royal Institute for International Affairs, Lord Hailey's *An African Survey*. It is a digest of the whole area of colonial black Africa south of the Sahara, and especially from the side of political administration and policy, it states exhaustively the latest details on imperialism in Africa. Indispensable to the student, it cannot be expected to give the general reader any clear picture, despite its wealth of detail. From such official, documentary literature, it is a relief, then, to turn to penetrating insight into native life and social problems in the African scene. This one gets from the simple but revealing narratives of the veteran scholar-missionary, Albert Schweitzer, in his *African Notebook*. Schweitzer knows his Africans not as problems but as human beings, and etches indelibly aspects of their lives and character. It might almost be characterized by paraphrasing the North Carolina project title, *These Are Their Lives*. In such a tradition and spirit, the lives and the folklore of the African peoples must someday be presented: it will eventually take the educated native, and not the detribalized half-educated native, to do it authoritatively and adequately. Signs are not wanting of such native authorship, although this year no titles of native writings, beyond some linguistic primers, have come this way.

38

OF NATIVE SONS

Real and Otherwise

PART I

Minorities have their artistic troubles as well as their social and economic ones, and one of them is to secure proper imaginative representation, particularly in fiction and drama. For here the warped social perspective induces a twisted artistic one. In these arts characterization must be abstract enough to be typical, individual enough to be convincingly human. The delicate balance between the type and the concrete individual can be struck more easily where social groups, on the one hand, have not been made supersensitive and morbid by caste and persecution, or on the other, where majority prejudice does not encourage hasty and fallacious generalization. An artist is then free to create with a single eye to his own artistic vision. Under such circumstances, Macbeth's deed does not make all Scotchmen treacherous hosts, nor Emma Bovary's infidelity blot the escutcheon of all French bourgeois spouses. Nana and Magda represent their type, and not their respective nations, and *An American Tragedy* scarcely becomes a national libel. But it is often a different matter with Shylock, and oftener still with Uncle Tom or Porgy, and for that matter, too, with the denizens of *Tobacco Road*, or even Southern colonels, if too realistically portrayed. All of which is apropos of the Negro literary phenomenon of 1940, Bigger Thomas. What about Bigger? Is he typical, or as some hotly contest, misrepresentative? And whose "native son" is he, anyway?

These questions, as I see them, cannot be answered by reference to Negro life and art alone. That indeed is the fallacy of much of the popular and critical argument about this masterwork. Only in the context of contemporary American literature, its viewpoints and trends, is it possible to get a sound and objective appraisal of *Native Son*. For all its great daring and originality, it is significant because it is in step with the advance guard of contemporary American fiction, and has dared to go a half step farther. Year by year, we have been noticing the rising tide of realism, with its accompanying boon of social honesty and artistic integrity. Gradually it has transformed both the fiction of the American South and of the Negro. The movement by which Stribling, Caldwell, and Faulkner have released us from the banal stereotypes—where all Southern ladies were irreproachable and all Southern colonels paragons of honor and chivalry—has simply meant, eventually, as a natural corollary, another sort of Negro hero and heroine. It is to Richard Wright's everlasting credit to have hung the portrait of Bigger Thomas alongside in this gallery of stark contemporary realism. There was artistic courage and integrity of the first order in his decision to ignore both the squeamishness of the Negro minority and the deprecating bias of the prejudiced majority, full knowing that one side would like to ignore the fact that there are any Negroes like Bigger and the other like to think that Bigger is the prototype of all. Eventually, of course, this must involve the clarifying recognition that there is no one type of Negro, and that Bigger's type has the right to its day in the literary calendar, not only for what it might add in his own right to Negro portraiture, but for what it could say about America. In fact Wright's portrait of Bigger Thomas says more about America than it does about the Negro, for he is the native son of the black city ghetto, with its tensions, frustrations, and resentments. The brunt of the action and the tragedy involves social forces rather than persons; it is in the first instance a Zolaesque *j'accuse* pointing to the danger symptoms of a self-frustrating democracy. Warping prejudice, shortsighted exploitation, impotent philanthropy, aggravating sympathy, inconsistent human relations, doctrinaire reform, equally impotent punishment stand behind the figures of Bigger, the Daltons, Mary, Jan, and Max, as the real protagonists of the conflict. This is timely and incisive analysis of the core dilemmas of the situation of race and American democracy. Indeed in the present crisis, the social import of *Native Son*, with its bold warnings and its clear lessons, temporarily overshadows its artistic significance. Its vivid and vital revelations should be a considerable factor in awakening a social sense and conscience willing at last, after much evasion and self-deception, to face the basic issues realistically and constructively. No sociological treatise or economic analysis has proved half so well just where the crucial problems lie or what common interests are at stake: America cannot any more afford to ignore the issues presented in this book than she could in 1853, when *Uncle Tom's Cabin* anticipated Lincoln's insight in saying: "This land cannot long continue to exist half-slave and half-free." And as before, it is not just a plea for the Negro, but a challenge to the nation and its own enlightened self-interest.

Just to make this clear, let me quote briefly from Wright's brilliant critical postscript, "How Bigger Was Born." Says he:

I felt that Bigger, an American product, a native son of this land, carried within him the potentialities of either Communism or Fascism. I don't mean to say that the Negro boy I depicted in *Native Son* is either a Communist or a Fascist. He is not either. But he is a product of a dislocated society; he is a dispossessed and disinherited man; he is all of this, and he lives amid the greatest possible plenty on earth and he is looking and feeling for a way out. Whether he'll follow some gaudy, hysterical leader who'll promise rashly to fill the void in him, or whether he'll come to an understanding with the millions of his kindred fellow workers under trade-union or revolutionary guidance depends upon the future drift of events in America. But, granting the emotional state, the tensity, the fear, the hate, the impatience, the sense of exclusion, the ache for violent action, the emotional and cultural hunger, Bigger Thomas, conditioned as his organism is, will not become an ardent, or even a lukewarm, supporter of the status quo.

This is why I call *Native Son* Zolaesque, and insist that it is an important book for these times, and that it has done a great national service in making this acute diagnosis and putting American democracy, if it will act intelligently, on the defensive.

Native Son has brilliant and imposing collaboration from other novelists of the American scene. It seems as though our writers had all resolved to tear chapters out of Zola and probe society's wounds and ulcers. They have little need for the old-fashioned romantic imagination that was once the novelist's chief stock-in-trade. They do, however, need the realist's imagination to set both the social and the psychological perspectives so that we have another and more enlightening experience than from reading the notations in a psychiatrist's or a social case worker's notebook.

Edward Heth, for example, anatomizes Ruby Street, a marginal city community of white pleasure-seekers and semi-impoverished Negroes, demoralized into parasitic living as merchants of gaiety and joy. This borderline situation, the sex analogue of Wright's laboring class ghetto—and an equally sinister and explosive by-product of the half-insulated lives of the two races—is drawn with bold, ironic skill by Heth, and with evident understanding of its basic factors of thwarted opportunity and easy victimization. It is Aggie's chief ambition that her daughter Julee escape the physical and moral barriers of Ruby Street, but environment tragically conquers and Julee chooses to remain and follow the precarious path that, unfortunately, is one way in our pattern of life, liberty, and the pursuit of happiness.

The Southern scene takes its turn, too, before the same unrelenting literary analysis. Erskine Caldwell, veteran of this fiction of actualities, has come back with an analysis of the Southern small town and its modern lower-middle class hatreds and racial problems. A hysterical woman vents her spleen against Negroes in a false rumor, and Sonny Clark pays the penalty as a Saturday crowd of townsmen and sharecroppers track him down for a race riot and lynching bee in *Trouble in July*. Unpleasant reading, it is nevertheless part of the bitter medicine we must take to find a true diagnosis and cure for a sick democracy. Less macabre, but just as diagnostic, are his many Negro situation vignettes in the newly issued volume of collected stories, *Jackpot*, where we meet again such challenging sketches as "Blue Boy," "Daughter," "Runaway," and "Yellow Girl." All these incidents have the stamp of unimpeachable truth, and what is significant now is not so much that they could have happened, as that nowadays they can be told, and by a native son of the white South. With something of his own individual brand of irony, Caldwell says in the epilogue to one of these stories:

"Does it make any difference, after all, whether an event actually happened or whether it might have happened?" Well, except as the South can see itself in the literary mirror that the new realism is burnishing, there is no hope; for, as has happened before in history, it is easier to stand the fact than its portrayal.

Gwen Bristow completes her trilogy of the Southern plantation with *This Side of Glory*, showing the double clash of the poor white and the lapsing aristocratic traditions and the economy of the old plantation and tenant sharecropping. The title is itself a text, for she finds the glory gone and a new order the only hope of survival from mortgages, boll weevil, and restive workers. Samuel Elam's *Weevil in the Cotton* is even more revealing, because he pictures the corrupt political machinery which is in the Southern saddle, and rides the tottering system through its last decades. Somewhat too melodramatic and not the artistic equal of these other novels, it still has something important to add to the new realistic tale of the South.

Follow the Drinking Gourd reverts a little to the romantic tradition, with a story of an Alabama plantation. However even here, there is a Banquo at the romantic feast—absentee ownership—and the estate finally winds up in bankruptcy and a foreclosed mortgage. In *The Keepers of the House*, Harrison

Kroll actually comes to grips with the plantation cycle and almost writes its obituary in terms of Bart Dowell's losing struggle with fertile soil but a declining market and a disintegrating social order. *God Rides a Gale* also has Mississippi for a locale, and includes more of a class study of the interactions of tradesmen, landlords, sharecroppers, black and white, than his first novel, *Stark Summer*. It is not strictly a novel of the Negro's situation, but has significance as a relatively new use of the Negro as background material.

Finally, Willa Cather breaks a long silence and many precedents in her story of *Sapphira and the Slave Girl*, pivoting this novel of her native Virginia on the jealousy of Sapphira for the mulatto slave girl whom she suspects of being her husband's mistress. Here is the frank admission and analysis by one of the master novelists of our generation of the canker at the heart of the plantation rose, even in its heyday of bloom and prosperity—a significant note in the contemporary reconstruction of Southern fiction.

In *The Caballero*, Harold Courlander evidently fictionalizes on his observations in Haiti to paint the drama of the clash of the mulatto and the black, the patois and the peasant culture in the Caribbean. Romantically seasoned by the story of the rise of a native dictator, the story, for all its mythical location in the island of Puerta Negra, is sufficiently realistic as to have some thinly veiled analogies with the American occupation of Haiti and the rise of Trujillo in Santo Domingo. Here too, in the guise of fiction, we get an important analysis of present-day social forces in the West Indies.

Our year's fiction is so factual that one turns to the biography with a positive thirst for adventure. Langston Hughes provides it—perhaps too much of it—in his biographic memoir, *The Big Sea*. Too much by way of contrast certainly, for the broad areas of his life's wide wanderings—Europe, Africa, and America from east to west coast—are not plumbed to any depth of analysis or understanding, with the possible exception of Washington society. If, as in this case, righteous anger is the mainspring of an interest in social analysis with Langston Hughes, one wishes that more of life had irked him. For time and again important things are glossed over in anecdotal fashion, entertainingly but superficially, without giving us any clear idea as to what a really important participant in the events of the last two decades thinks about the issues and trends of his generation and the Negro's relationship to them. Occasional hints of attitudes on such matters argue for an awareness of their existence, and seem to call for a more penetrating analysis even if it should sober down the irresponsible charm of the present narrative.

Of such things Dr. Du Bois does speak at considerable length in his *Dusk of Dawn* autobiography, projected, as one might expect, through an experienced and observant personality. This might easily have been one of the important biographic memoirs of the generation had there been greater psychological perspective on the issues and events. But an egocentric predicament involves the author all too frequently, so that his judgments of men and issues, warrantably personal in a biography, are not stated as that, but are promulgated dogmatically as though by a historian who had objectively examined all sides of the evidence. Valuable then only as the chronicle of an important career, *Dusk of Dawn* scarcely justifies the promise of its subtitle to give us reliably the outlines of race programs and race thinking over the five active decades of the author's eventful and useful life.

Two entirely anecdotal publications document interestingly the careers of live pioneer Negro educators in North Carolina, and John Paynter's fifty years of government service in Washington. It is of considerable importance to have more of such memoir materials appear in print, for the sake of a fuller documentation of Negro experience and accomplishment. These are however, but the raw material of adequate social history, which in most cases comes a generation or so after the event and the firsthand publication of the factual evidence.

In a more ambitious mold, Mrs. Mary Church Terrell has published her memoirs, under the title of *A Colored Woman in a White World*, prefaced by what to this reviewer seems an unnecessarily patronizing introduction by H. G. Wells, for all his well-intentioned moralizing on the analogies of racial and class prejudice. Essentially Mrs. Terrell's story is that of the generation when the so-called "talented tenth" were struggling for recognition, and were confronting, with considerable embarrassment, the paradoxes of the educated mulatto. It is to Mrs. Terrell's great credit that she overcame most of these, and rendered public service with some considerable recognition of what race leadership involves as to responsibilities. Too many of her generation thought of it merely in terms of special personal honors and privileges. This is a valuable factual chronicle of that particular overlapping generation of Reconstruction, one that will be even more helpful as it recedes into history. However, it must pale to relative insignificance in comparison with the reissue by the Douglass Literary and Cultural League of the *Life and Times of Frederick Douglass*; a much needed new access to this classic among Negro biographies.

One of the outstanding items of belles lettres has already been quoted from: it is Richard Wright's "How Bigger Was Born"—the critical account of the literary genesis of his novel. From it we learn that Bigger Thomas was really a synthetic character of five individuals observed in different years and places, and we get an insight seldom given by an author into the crucible of his art and experience. This is a great critical document, noteworthy for that very objectivity of self-analysis which we have complained of as lacking in the two outstanding biographies of the year. Perhaps it is saner to rejoice over its attainment here than its absence there, for a sensitive and intelligent Negro has to compensate mightily if he is ever to achieve poise and detachment on situations in which he is personally and socially involved. Wright is clearly conscious of the basic issues involved both in the Negro artist's relation to himself and to contemporary society.

Another important analysis of the social position of the Negro artist and writer is to be found in *Fighting Words*, in the symposium on the subject by Langston Hughes, Melville Herskovits, and Alain Locke, reprinted from the proceedings of the League of American Writers. Langston Hughes is also represented in a critical study of his work and social philosophy by René Piquion, in which his social slant is too definitely platformed, for though it is emotionally radical, it is not as Piquion claims, overtly Marxist.

The music field is richer this year by a one-volume reissue of the still-popular James Weldon and Rosamond Johnson *American Negro Spirituals*, and the addition to Laurence Gellert's valuable collecting of contemporary Negro work songs of new numbers, *Ale and My Captain*. In the art field, Alain Locke has edited, as illustrative sequel to his *Negro Art: Past and Present*, the first comprehensive illustrated portfolio of the *Negro in Art*; embracing both the work of Negro artists and the treatment and development by artists generally of the Negro subject as an art theme.

In poetry the yield is slender, and but for Countee Cullen's cleverly conceived and executed poetic fable would be negligible. *The Lost Zoo*, with its fascinating color illustrations by the gifted young artist Charles Sebree, is bound to be one of the notable specimens of its genre; at least it belongs on the same shelf with *Alice in Wonderland*. The posthumous volume of David Camon's poems, *Black Labor Chant*, can only be condoned as a sentimental tribute to a very amateur talent. Cullen, however, shows in a new vein of epigrammatic comedy a rare quaint imagination and all the old knack of clever versifying.

In *The Negro and the Drama*, Frederick Bond had the chance to bring the analysis of this field up to date and with some critical finality. But he is historically not as inclusive nor critically as sound as either the prefaces to *Plays of Negro Life* or the three short but pithy chapters of Sterling Brown's *Negro Poetry and Drama* (1937).

Indeed, drama is still but a half-conquered province for us as yet, both critically and creatively. The year's drama offerings were considerably disappointing. In the first place there was Paul Robeson's regrettable decision to create the flimsy role of *John Henry*, which is even more obviously threadbare in published print than in the acted presentation. Only one Broadway production to date on the Negro theme registers favorably, and that excites as much through marvelous acting on the part of Ethel Waters as through its whimsical but not overly profound script. However, the play, *Cabin in the Sky*, does convey an authentic and characteristic Negro feeling, which for Broadway is quite a commendable accomplishment. Its comedy is inoffensive, particularly as so deftly portrayed by Dooley Wilson, and its tempo and emotional tone are set true to real folk values, thanks again especially to the great talent of Miss Waters.

In the non-commercial theater, where we had great promise and hopes for the year, there have been considerable disappointments. The blame must be divided between the actors and their public. In the first place, Harlem can support both financially and artistically one good repertory company and theater, and only in pooling all possible resources there can success be optimistically anticipated. Then, too, the serious vehicles lack, through over-seriousness, sufficient theater to be compelling, a fault to be found in all three of the major new efforts by Negro playwrights that this season has brought forth. *Big White Fog*, by Theodore Ward, as reset for the Negro Playwrights Group, was competently staged and acted. It holds a situation with first-class dramatic possibilities. But instead of holding to its excellently posed character conflicts, over money and race loyalty, Americanism and Garveyism, it swerves to a solution by way of radical social action for its denouement. Harlem is to be blamed at that, for not taking sufficient interest in one of the few meaty, serious plays it has had a chance to support, but the Playwrights Group should have had a more balanced repertory to offer before it ventured so boldly with a regularly leased theater. The MacClendon Players have continued their policy of plays by Negro authorship, but have as yet this season only found one play of even moderate merit, William Ashby's *Booker T. Washington*—and that a revived play from their previous repertoire. We still await the much needed drama revival.

PART II, AND A POSTSCRIPT ON POETRY

Nineteen hundred and forty ends one decade and begins another. In some minds, with the world crisis in view, it portentously looms through the mist like the threshold of an epoch. One is tempted, therefore, to take this sense of crisis and critical change as the touchstone of an author's real significance and vitality. More than ever we want either the truth and nothing but the truth, or what we feel is the writer's humanly best effort to get at it. Yesterday's charm and irresponsibility we now think reprehensible, and do not lightly forgive whoever writes with his tongue in his check or prissily à la mode or with conscious reservations. In the light of the times, we have the right to ask this honest integrity of the novelist, the playwright, even of the poet—and some we have seen live up to this expectation.

All the more necessary and obligatory, then, is this criterion for the historian, the economist, and the sociologist. For, born of the crisis, we have the wish to know what in the crisis of illness we tritely call "the worst," but what we really mean as the truth without reservation.

Now factual literature, historical, sociological, and economic, has been for generations notorious for its conventions and its formulae, and these, from the very nature of the case, have been traditional deceptions and conventional lies. They haven't all been sinister; most indeed have been placatory and polite. Discussions of race and class have been almost as discreet and polite—and therefore as superficial—as discussions of religion and morals. Basic realism in social science has been relatively rare and in many cases, from the point of view of the tradition-breakers, costly. And so with that in mind as a fair and now imperative criterion, we glance at the social literature of the year as it relates to our subject of special interest, the Negro.

Although threadbare in treatment from the conventional point of view, slavery and anti-slavery analysis has an important bearing on our social attitudes in contemporary race relations. In fact, we get our cues for the present from the past, and when we do change in contemporary alignments, we are apt to reorganize our history. The changed views, or rather perspectives, on slavery are thus indicative of today's changing attitudes and mores. Though of late 1939 vintage, here is a significant book, Dumond's *Antislavery Origins of the Civil War*. It is neither pro nor anti-slavery, and is probably the most objective analysis of slavery ever offered in so small a compass. Thus it should be prescribed reading, particularly for Negroes, who, on the whole, do not understand the historical issues involved, and to that extent have only a sentimental grasp on the basic factors of race and class status in America. Dumond has done a great service in trying to focus historical evidence on the explanation of a situation rather than to vindicate either personalities, regional sections, or even schools of historical opinion. Particularly does he bring out the importance of the Midwest and the Southwest and their economic interests and political opinions in complicating and finally balancing the traditional rivalry between the North and the South.

Coleman's *Slavery Times in Kentucky* is similarly a far cry from the usual documentary local history: for it presents factual evidence primarily, and leaves evaluations to the reader. One of the main lines of this evidence shows what is now conceded by modern historians of the institution, the complete interdependence of the master and slave and their common deterioration in both human and economic fortunes as the economy matures. In Kentucky, as the narrative shows, black and white were, at first, mutually helpful frontier pioneers and retained much of that independence and vigor in sections of the state which did not embrace the cotton economy. Mangum's exhaustive treatise on *The Legal Status of the Negro*, on the other hand, merely perpetuates a lapsing tradition of scholarship. Even in bringing its subject up to date, it performs one very useful historical service, for in its ultra-legalistic approach, the important connection between law and public opinion is relatively overlooked. Hence the fluctuations of degrees of civic privilege and disability are merely chronicled, carefully it is true, but unexplained.

The Negro in Congress, however, is a serious and fairly successful attempt at interpretation. Stemming from the liberal traditions of Chapel Hill, this is as successful as a groundbreaking treatise could hope to be, and strikes a rather happy mid-ground between the violent detractions of the Negro reconstruction politicians and equally partisan vindications. The wide diversity of these Negro legislators is wisely emphasized, and some of them are shown to have been men of considerable acumen and statesmanship. The study is really, it seems to me, a challenge to Negro historians to supplement the picture from documentary evidence likely to be more accessible in the correspondence of some of these men, or if not available, then from the closest scrutiny of their legislative records. Our historical scholarship is, as yet, strangely weak on the biographical side.

Mabry's analysis of *The Negro in North Carolina Politics Since Reconstruction* adds little beyond mere detail to the repeated studies of the sad aftermath of slavery: in all the Southern states practically the same forces were in operation, and North Carolina history only makes a little more clear the role of the poor white faction in the drama of reaction. Obstruction was the real character of the Reconstruction period, postponing to our day the real reconstruction problems. In this basic interpretation Herbert Aptheker is right in regarding both the Civil War as a postponed act of the original American struggle for human rights, and today's reconstruction efforts as the further development of an abortive emancipation of the Negro. However sound this reading of American history is, Aptheker pushes his thesis too hard and dogmatically either for general conviction or for an unforced interpretation of the historical facts. Insinuated into the history of *The Negro in the American Revolution*, the conclusions fall out suspiciously. More overtly Marxist, Elizabeth Lawson's intelligently consistent study outline of *Negro History* commands attention and respect, even where one does not agree with its emphases. It has the virtues of a frank economic and labor interpretation of the issues, and of less dogmatic statement than most readings of this school of historical thought.

It is to be regretted that Mr. Newcomb's study of Henri Christophe is cast in so romantic a vein; for its length and apparent intent promise what should have been a definitive life of this important historical character. Haitian history, except in French treatises, has generally run to the popularized and superficial type, with the exception of James's still unsurpassed *Black Jacobins*. Consonant with the growing interest in the Caribbean, we do have two competent diplomatic histories of Haiti, which oddly enough almost parallel each other. Mr. Montague's work looks very comprehensive and final until one compares it closely with the Logan book, which has much more extensive bibliographic sources. With contemporary hemispheric politics tending toward the same objectives, the celebrated affair of the coaling base at Môle Saint-Nicolas takes on a revived interest, and throws a dimension of statesmanship into what many have regarded a mere political incident. Frederick Douglass's connection with this affair and his dilemma between racial and national patriotism are definitively treated in Professor Logan's book, and that along with closer regard for Haitian sources and interests stamps this as the more objective and permanently valuable contribution to the subject.

Mr. Van Voorhis has assembled a much too partisan and unobjective narrative of *Negro Masonry*; the earlier history of Prince Saunders, though out of print, still remains by all odds the more acceptable historical source. Dr. Cobb has documented an interesting chapter in Negro professional history in his study of *The First Negro Medical Society* of the District of Columbia; it has more than memoir significance since it recounts also the early history of the first fight of Negro professional men for recognized professional standing and association—a fight not yet won as far as the National Medical Association membership is concerned.

Dr. Murphy, in his *Analysis of the Attitudes of American Catholics Toward the Immigrant and the Negro*, traces very objectively the gradual liberalization of Catholic thought on matters of race, linking reactionary Americanism somewhat too superficially with the attitudes toward the immigrant, since, after all, race prejudice is many degrees more violent and often of more traditional derivation.

M. S. Stuart's book on *Negro Life Insurance* has ironically chosen its own obituary in its title: at best a flimsy Who's Who of Negro insurance, it itself makes a wide economic detour around the basic problems and trends of Negro business enterprise. So the studies of Professor Harris remain almost our sole reliable guide in this crucially vital field; much needed, however, is bringing such objective and competent analyses up to date through the later years of the depression crisis.

Turning to sociology proper, we have a number of creditable documentations both of Negro history and present-day conditions in the various state guides, among others the Pennsylvania and the Nebraska guides. Two state WPA projects have extensive special studies—the Georgia project in *Drums and Shadows* and the Virginia project in *The Negro in Virginia*. The former focuses on the coastal communities and undoubtedly has gathered the crude materials of several further anthropological studies. In their present shape they suggest a little too strongly the thesis of straight African survivals, and need to be gone over carefully from the acculturation angle as composite folkways and folklore, which in the main they seem to represent.

The Negro in Virginia, on the other hand, is much more than a compendium of raw materials; it is a well-balanced and illuminating historical and social analysis, one of the best overall accomplishments of the Writers' Project in toto.

Able editing has integrated into it a panoramic review of the Negro experience, which since Virginia is the oldest site, save Florida, of Negro settlement, makes it a readable and enlightening epitome of the Negro's history. Especially the slave narratives have rescued important material that in another decade would have lapsed completely, and much new light is thrown both on the domestic pattern of slavery and on the slave insurrections.

Two contrasted community studies also challenge comparison, this time to the disparagement of the more elaborate volume. For Crum Mason's simple, straightforward description of the *Gullah* has merit of a factual sort, while Claude McKay's more pretentious analysis of *Harlem* is disappointingly shallow and misleading. Coming from the inside and from a well-known participant in a good deal of the movements considered, this is particularly inexcusable.

Quite clearly there have been two abortive motivations behind McKay's work—the desire on the one hand to be journalistically spectacular, and on the other to be personally vindicating. There is accordingly a double distortion, of facts out of true proportion and of movements and personalities seen askew. McKay outdoes *The Big Sea* for superficiality and lack of serious evaluation, and the Du Bois biography, which is professedly historical also, in personalisms of under- and over-emphasis—according, of course, to personal whim. In all frankness this is what I meant in my prefatory remarks. If ever warrantable, this flippancy and egocentrism is not to be condoned in a time like this. Which doesn't mean that we insist at all times on documentary treatises and case studies, but rather upon a more sober regard for factuality and fair play. Sufi and Garvey in parallel panels, the Harlem literary movement and the numbers racket bracketed, are examples in point: they hardly spell good journalism, certainly not representative social analysis.

Great strides in such analysis have nevertheless been made, some from the point of view of enlarged scope in the papers published under the caption of *The Negro in the Americas*, where the subject benefits considerably from the contrast consideration of the Caribbean and the South American Negro; but still greater strides in the group of American Youth Commission studies which are the climax of the social literature of the year. Perhaps even they would be challenged in modernity and thoroughness by the yet unpublished and extensive monograph studies of the staff of the Carnegie Myrdal collaborative research, tentatively styled, *The Negro in America*. But the published and announced Youth Commission analyses of contemporary Negro life—five in all—represent high-water marks of the younger generation scholarship.

Ira Reid's volume is a readable and graphic epitome of the Negro's situation in America, useful for beginners and for a panoramic review of the situation. Professor Frazier's volume covers youth in the borderline states, Professor Charles Johnson's is to cover youth in the rural South, while the Davis-Dollard study covers the Southern cities.

Each in its way is committed to combining psychological with sociological findings, to going beyond statistics to trends and if possible beyond trends to attitudes and other causal factors of explanation. Each also tries to resolve the over-generalizations so conventional previously, and to take account of class position and economic background as variants in the social experience.

Frazier's conclusions show the variation of class status to be quite as important as sectional differences, and also reveal considerable difference in reaction according to the personality patterns of the individual. However, they also show in the main how appallingly oppressive the minority predicament is, and suggest it as one of the grave unsolved problems both of education and of social reform.

A comparison with other minority groups undoubtedly would throw up such common denominators, in varying degree of course, as to suggest entirely new approaches both to the study and the remedial treatment of the so-called racial problem. This indeed seems to be the final upshot of what is perhaps the most provocative study of them all, the progressive Davis-Dollard book with the unprogressive title, *Children of Bondage*. Here, by a promising attack on the situations of class and race psychoanalytically, a general contribution to social analysis seems on the verge of realization. It is to the effect that social conditions operate through their action upon the psyche of the individual, which gives education a diagnostic and possibly corrective approach to these problems both of class and race. The study also shows the roots of the considerable variation within the same community of the individual reactions and the individual aspects of the problem, and fortunately, too, shows them to have common denominators with the general human situations of frustration and limited opportunity. This, it seems to me, even at the price of a too doctrinaire theory of caste and class, is a contribution of general significance in addition to being an advance step in the concrete and realistic study of racial situations.

The war clouds have almost grounded the scholarly flights

of African studies, despite the increasingly crucial relation of African situations to world politics. A revised reissue of Seligman's *Races of Africa* is more than welcome, as one of the few anthropological analyses both readable and reliable at the same time. C. K. Meek's *Europe and West Africa*, probably written before recent developments of the African campaigns, clearly admits and documents the vital stakes of the imperialistic system in the colonial markets and sources of raw products.

Yet few scholars have the courage to press the obvious corollaries as to the imperative need for colonial fair play and reform. Professor Hoernlé alone seems willing to go to the moral roots of the imperialistic dilemmas between democracy's creed and its practices. Says he:

> There have been many champions of liberty. . . . But they have all been content to re-state the ideal of liberty on traditional lines against attacks upon it, and denials of it, by "totalitarian" thinkers, whether belonging to the Communist or the Fascist "ideologies." What none has done is to re-examine, in the light of a multi-racial society, like South Africa, what liberty means and how, if at all, it can be realized in that sort of society. Yet, if "liberty" as the Balfour Declaration has it, "is the life-blood of the British Commonwealth," then, so long as the Commonwealth includes multi-racial societies, the realization of liberty for all races is the most urgent and important problem, both in theory and practice, which the members of the Commonwealth have to solve.

Where "natives" are outcasts, as in colonial South Africa, or native sons are sub-citizens and "children of bondage" as in the United States, society is manifestly in the throes of paradox and crisis: the literature that calls these facts and dilemmas to our attention may not be so pleasant or entertaining, but certainly it is sound and potentially constructive. More of it, let us hope, in 1941!

I must append a poetry postscript, for two volumes of verse have come to hand since Part I was written: Nick Aaron Ford's *Songs from the Dark* and Robert Hayden's *Heart-Shape in the*

Dust. Mr. Ford is a competent versifier of the academic sort, and his emphasis is racial rhetoric in the main; a variant, in short, on the formula of the last decade. Though some of Mr. Hayden's poems are also in this vein, his obvious bent and stronger talent is the direction of social poetry, of contemporary mood, and he can occasionally speak with an accent of real power and promise, as in the lines on "Coleman, Negro Veteran Murdered by the Black Legion:"

> In the tolerated weeds of murder,
> Coleman lies. . . .
> Blood is the color of this season's flower,
> Fires, blood-colored, consume our days. . . .
>
> They leave him bleeding there,
> Believing that his death
> Can prove their superior aliveness,
> Loosen the vises of defeat.
>
> (Coleman, all had been saved,
> Had we forestalled your lonely martyrdom)
>
> O cancelled face that stares
> Into the desolate windows of our long night,
> Tell us it is not yet too late;
>
> Tell us the blood seeps down
> To give rich suck unto the roots
> Of yet another season.

39

FROM *NATIVE SON* TO *INVISIBLE MAN*

A Review of the Literature of the Negro for 1952

In the thirty years' span of my active reviewing experience, there have been in my judgment three points of peak development in Negro fiction by Negro writers. In 1923 from a relatively low plateau of previous problem fiction, Jean Toomer's *Cane* rose to unprecedented artistic heights. Not only in style but in conception it raised a new summit, as it soared above the plane of propaganda and apologetics to a self-sufficient presentation of Negro life in its own idiom and gave it proud and self-revealing evaluation. More than that, the emotional essences of the Southland were hauntingly evoked in an impressionistic poetic sort of realism; it captured as well some of the more distinctive tone and color of Negro living. Its only shortcomings were that it was a series of character sketches rather than a full length canvas: a succession of vignettes rather than an entire landscape—and that its author chose not to continue. In 1940, Richard Wright's skillful sociological realism turned a hard but brilliant searchlight on Negro urban life in Chicago and outlined the somber tragedy of Bigger Thomas in a well-studied setting of Northside wealth and Southside poverty. Artistically not the equal of the more masterful series of short stories, *Uncle Tom's Children*, that preceded it, *Native Son's* narrative was masterful and its character delineation as skillful as any work of Dreiser's or Farrell's. The book was marred only by Wright's overreliance on the communist ideology with which he encumbered his powerful indictment of society for Bigger, the double pariah of the slum and the color-line. Wright was essentially sound in his alignment of the social forces involved but erred artistically in the doctrinally propagandist tone which crept into his novel chapter by chapter until the angry, ineffective end. The greater pity it was—and is—that later he disavowed this ideological commitment that cheated him of an all-time classic of American fiction. Despite this, *Native Son* has remained all these intervening years the Negro novelist's strongest bid for fiction of the first magnitude.

But 1952 is the significant year of Ellison's *Invisible Man*, a great novel although also not without its artistic flaws, sad to say. Ralph Ellison is a protégé of Wright, who predicted for him a bright literary future. Written in a style of great force and originality, although its talent is literally smothered with verbosity and hyperbole, *Invisible Man* is both in style and conception a new height of literary achievement. The life story of its hero, obviously semi-autobiographic, ranges from the typical South of a few years back to the metropolitan North of New York and vicinity. Conceptually it runs also almost the whole gamut of class in American society and is interracial at all stages even in the deep South from the benefactor patron of the college visiting for Founders Day to the sinister "crackers" of the rural backwoods. It is in fact one of the best integrated accounts of interaction between whites and Negroes in American society that has yet been presented, with all characters portrayed in the same balance and perspective. Ellison's philosophy of characterization, incisive, realistic, unsparing of physical and psychological detail—all his major characters are stripped bare to the skin and bone, so to speak—is close to the best European realism in that it is so three-dimensional. We see a grand caravan of types, all registered first person on the sensitive but rather cynical retina of the young Negro protagonist. In the South, the patronizing but well-intentioned school trustee, the piously hypocritical Negro school principal, the gauche, naïve, but not too honest students, the disillusioned, institutionalized war veterans, the townsfolk, the peasants of the countryside, white and black, and most particularly the unforgettable earthy peasant character of Jim Trueblood. In the North, the pageant resumes with all sorts and manner of men and women: the financiers of Wall Street and their decadent jazz-loving sons, factory workers, pro and anti-union varieties, the urban peasants and their homely oddities, parlor-pinks and hard inner-core communists, race leaders, educated and illiterate, each after his kind—and the Harlem community generally displayed finally at frenetic tension in its one big authentic riot. Stylistically all this unrolls in a volcanic flow of vivid, sometimes livid imagery, a tour de force of psychological realism. A double symbolic meaning piled on top of this realism gives the book its distinctive and most original tone and flavor: *Invisible Man* is actually a surrealistic novel because of this, and but for its lack of restraint would rank among the very best of the genre. But the unrestrained bravado of treatment, riding loose rein at full gallop most of the time, and the over-precious bravura of phrase and diction weight it down where otherwise it would soar in well-controlled virtuosity. Many readers will be shocked at Ellison's daring franknesses and dazed by his emotional intensity but these are an integral part of the book's great merit. For once, too, here is a Negro writer capable of real and sustained irony. *Invisible Man*, evidently years in the making, must not be Ralph Ellison's last novel.

Lonnie Coleman's *Clara* is uniquely different, but it deserves placement in the same high bracket of fiction of the first magnitude. Within a four- or five-year period it is the top product of the fiction of Negro life by white southern novelists. Coleman, Georgia-born and Alabama-bred, needs no authentication as truly of the South; his easygoing intimate knowledge of southern ways, Negro included, testifies sufficiently to that. No southern novel has gone further, also, in that ultimate candor of insight and outspoken courage toward which the younger generation of southern writers seems to be moving. In handling the interracial triangle of his plot from the woman's side and by putting the narrative first person in the words of Lillian Sayre, the white wife, Coleman approaches his subject the steep, bold way, but he succeeds. Lillian, marrying largely for convenience, finds herself not quite mistress of the Sayre household, already routined by her husband's recently deceased mother under the competent management of Clara, the Negro housekeeper, who, with her mulatto son, Petie, lives in a small cabin behind the house. Rivalry begins instantly between the two women and mounts as it is goaded on by Clara's more seasoned knowledge of the husband's ways. Particularly is this so as with the passing years Sayre relapses into chronic alcoholism, partly in frustration from Lillian's frigidity. Clara stands out more and more in her bossy dignity as the pillar of the household, while Lillian appeases her unhappiness in doting on her godchild, Randall, her sister's son, who becomes the inseparable playmate of Clara's Pete. Soon Lillian's suspicions are aroused, and by bold accusation she learns from Clara that Petie is Sayre's child. Clara is forced to leave and that night her cabin burns to the ground. In Pluma, Alabama, Lillian is automatically above suspicion, so she has her moment of triumph.

But the household caves in after Clara's departure, and shortly Clara must come back to manage and to hold the roof up over an increasingly drunken Carl; Lillian's steadily declining maiden Aunt Aster; the growing exigencies of Randall and Pete, still bosom friends; and Lillian's own frustrated dependence. Tragic events, mutually endured, gradually alter the tensions—Carl's death, Randall killed in war, Pete successfully installed on Aunt Aster's farm, married to Lutie and happy father of a son, "Randy," after Randall. But Pete, disliked both for his success and his progressive farming, marked as "an uppity nigger," is in that community already doomed. The trigger incident finally happens—Toll Cannon, white reactionary with whom he has been feuding, is murdered; in Pluma's eyes "no one but Pete could have done it," and with similarly anonymous bullets, Pete himself is lynched. Lillian, resolutely matured by now, gathers up the remnants, and the triangle that began with prejudice, jealousy, and hate resolves into a strange household trio for that community; Lutie, Clara, and Lillian, protectively focused in Lillian's house as mother, grandmother, foster-mother around Randy, Petie's child. In the bare telling the story of *Clara* seems melodramatic, but in full length reading it is a moving and convincing drama of character transformation. It has balanced, consistent characterization, three dimensional, not type treatment for all, and makes Clara, who plays the title role, the most wholesome and dignified member of the cast.

Earl Conrad's *Rock Bottom* is the South documented well but too laboriously to register vitally. It, too, is told in the first person, by Leeha, the heroine who is supposed to move us as she moves from one vicissitude to another, from one sordid environment to the next. But all the way from Mississippi to Harlem, even in the bogs of Florida's muck swamps, she is a pasteboard pillar for propagandist indictments of society. Not that this is untrue, but all the more pity if it does not move to pity and terror. Why, we ask ourselves, knowing the earnest intentions of these tractarian authors? The answer is an old one; excess is never good art. *Rock Bottom* accordingly misses its target by shooting it, so to speak, to shreds. Thirty years of unrelieved sordidness and oppression are quite possible in life, unfortunately, but only a Gorky could have brought this sort of story out of its overdone effect.

With *Strangers and Afraid* and *Trespass*, we come to another overdone subject, the Harlem interracial, which threatens to become the Waterloo of so many serious but overambitious junior authors. There is a field here, but no one has quite mastered it. Of course, one of the first difficulties is to realize that life and character and circumstances are pretty much the same everywhere. There is no magic in the Harlem setting that will rectify a poor plot or vivify shallow characterization or evoke a philosophy of life when an author has none. But such things have to be there in any work of art, and color, skin color or local color, cannot compensate for the lack of them. Though obviously most seriously intentioned, Eugene Brown's story is merely an excursion into Harlem, and really should end with the discovery that Harlem and Flatbush are very much alike after all. And why not? Far too many think it should not be so, and go stubbornly on to proclaim the difference. Particularly on this moot subject of mixed marriage, all novelists should be instructed that it is an old human phenomenon; sometimes successful, in other cases not, but always for specific, never general reasons. The prejudices which with one couple would wreck a marriage would be cementing pressures in another instance: in telling a story, to be successful one must tell a specific story. A stock situation documented to death will never bring a real situation to literary life. The notebooks, yes, but when it comes to the crucial point of writing, young authors must have the courage to throw away the notebooks.

There is much more of moment and substance in *Strangers and Afraid* and yet it, too, is not successful. Here the two protagonists are too much of a polarity: Lyle Bishop, the reformer, and Maccabee David, the perfect foil. The die is cast from the beginning, and once again the plausibility is gone. This novel is wrecked on the shoals of formula character, a little more interestingly than the average Harlem adventure, but wrecked just the same without the sense of a profitable struggle. I think sometimes that there persists, especially with the racially "enlightened," one damaging vestige of the corporate prejudice from which they think they have detached themselves completely, and that is the notion that the Negro character is foredoomed to a defeatist end. The very essence of tragedy is the chance of evading defeat, which in good tragedy is indeterminate until near the end, or even when destined is fought out to the very end. This is not a novel of moving tragedy in spite of all its tragic happenings, and it well may stem from some such attitude, conscious or more likely subconscious.

Truman Nelson has novelized the Boston anti-slavery story of a celebrated fugitive case, that of Anthony Burns, espoused by Theodore Parker, Wendell Phillips, and the Ward Howes. He has done a colossal amount of research on this celebrated case, and used much, perhaps most of it in his novel, *The Sin of the Prophet*. It can never be asserted against it that it is not authentic; but even in the historical novel authenticity is but the beginning. And for all the dialogue, and the direct quotation of sermon, court pleas, and conversations, this is hardly a genuine novel, but a case history. It is true, an important case history for the times and for the anti-slavery cause, as well as for the revelation of the inner niceties of difference of opinion among both abolitionists and their proslavery opponents, most of all for a portrait of a Boston divided deeply enough on the issue to cause violence and intrigue normally alien to its cold-blooded ways; but I will be much surprised if the novelization adds much to either the circulation or the comprehension of the facts. *The Case of Anthony Burns* could well have been the title, and the nonhistorically minded would have been forewarned.

Laughing to Keep from Crying is typical Langston Hughes. That means many things, among them uneven writing, flashes of genius, epigrammatic insight, tantalizing lack of follow-through, dishwater—and then suddenly crystal springs. Fortunately, this is a motley of anecdotal scenes and stories, scattered from his own cosmopolitan experience—Africa, Hong Kong, Frisco, Paris, and the like, but all pointing up to Harlem and its theme of color. The title story, a very good one, has the dominant key and clue: "Who's Passing for Who?" It pokes ironic fun at the color line, as for example also does "Something in Common"—the encounter of a white Kentuckian and a color-weary Negro in a Hong Kong bar, where after falling out violently over the color question and being ejected by the bartender, they stagger back together to fight for their rights, presumably including the right to fight over the color question. This is a fair sample; as thumbnail sketches both are well observed and in that sense anecdotally good; one, however, is well told, the other, just an anecdote. And so it goes, not alternately as in this case, but spotty to the end. "Saratoga Rain," a two-page cameo of incisive etching, suggests that this type of thing is Hughes's forte, and that sustained development is not, whether it be plot or character. Why complain? Simply because from the point of evoking it, Langston Hughes knows Harlem so much more surely than all the rest that his vignettes are, with all their faults, worth dozens of so-called "Harlem novels," and with just a little more art. Hughes could be Harlem's Daumier, or to change to the right figure, its Maupassant. How true what W. C. Handy says of another book of his, "Read it for yourself and have a laugh on Harlem, not at it." There's the difference—and the right approach for all writing about this province of Negro life: to see, feel, and show not its difference but its different way of being human.

The review of the year's fiction should include mention of Frank Yerby's most recent best-seller achievement, *Saracen Blade*, one of his best and most elaborate historical romances. In this, Mr. Yerby vindicates once more the right of the Negro as artist to any theme and province he chooses as a freeman of the world of letters. This particular work shows cumulative maturity in his chosen field, and its success with the general public will be an incentive to younger Negro writers that may spread our creative production over wider subject-matter fields than usual.

POETRY AND BELLES-LETTRES

Langston Hughes as poet has received this year the recognition of a translation of a volume of selected poems in Spanish, doubly appropriate because of a long standing constructive interest of his in Cuban, Haitian, and other Latin American poets and writers. The quite neglected field of literary criticism comes in for welcome mention at last: serious sustained work in straight criticism, Dr. Nathan A. Scott's *Rehearsals of Discomposure* and Helen Chesnutt's biography of her father, which has a valuable dimension of literary criticism because of the light it sheds on his literary philosophy and on his relations with his publishers and literary contemporaries.

Dr. Scott's scholarly and thought-provoking contribution is a series of essays in philosophical criticism dealing with four great literary figures of contemporary culture, Franz Kafka, D. H. Lawrence, Ignazio Silone, and T. S. Eliot. What he is interested in is the twentieth century concept of man, what he calls "the human predicament" as it presents itself to these representative modern thinkers. After chastising formal academic

philosophy for its evasion of this urgent problem, Dr. Scott
goes on with an acute, enlightening analysis of what he considers the common denominator problem of these more sensitive artist-thinkers, who do attempt to resolve the confusions
of our contemporary culture. Dissatisfied with what he regards a superficial diagnosis of their reaction as "disillusionment," Dr. Scott suggests viewing it as "spiritual withdrawal"
or "cosmic isolation and exile," connecting it with existential-
ism as a parallel phenomenon. With a conviction that the common question is more significant as "the modern intellectual's
dilemma" than any individual answer, he then compares the
several specific solutions, and concludes that the grand overall
objective of creative thinking in our time is the quest for the
rediscovery of inner, life-sustaining values. Whether we agree
or not with Dr. Scott's suggestion that a rethinking of Christianity along more mystic but more humane lines is the goal of
the search, all serious readers can agree on the indisputable
value of his incisive comparative analysis of some of the most
significant trends in contemporary thought.

The Chesnutt item is drawn from the family treasury of
Charles Waddell Chesnutt's private correspondence as well as
from the memories of an objectively intelligent daughter. It
gives us definitive light on the personality background of a
man who, with time, looms more and more as the important
literary Negro of his generation. His stature should be considerably helped by this revelation of high seriousness on the race
question, for his group loyalty was really deeper than that of
many of his more vociferous contemporaries. Or at least, it
was based on more intelligent courage, the resolution to tell
the full objective truth about Negro-white relations as he saw
them in his day. This was disinterested truth telling, since it is
evident from the account of his family life and of his interracial circle of admiring friends in Cleveland, that as a personal
problem, race discrimination was already satisfactorily solved
for him. This justifies quite meaningfully Miss Chesnutt's subtitle, calling him a "pioneer of the color line."

Both the history and the analysis of Negro music enjoy unusual contributions this year. Rex Harris's small but scholarly

booklet, *Jazz*, is illuminating both for the layman and the expert, and treats jazz as a world phenomenon, with adequate documentation of its European developments; while Barry Ulanov's work is restricted by title to the history of jazz in America. It, too, brings the common sense and the expert approaches together fruitfully. Particularly sane is Mr. Ulanov's rejection of "the legend of African origins," confirming, as he says, "the average man's impression of the Negro as a jungle-formed primitive whose basic expression is inevitably savage." Jazz, for him, is correctly an American social development, and his close analysis of its various schools and idioms is a valuable contribution to the subject. In addition to an enlightening discussion of the various locales and what they have contributed to jazz idiomatically, Ulanov gives us an almost complete genealogy of the outstanding jazz musicians, Negro and white. These biographical details are in themselves a priceless contribution; and his discussion of these player-composers by instrument groups adds greatly to our understanding of jazz style development. Harris, on the other hand, is a special devotee of the New Orleans school, and though he therefore exhibits definite partiality to New Orleans and St. Louis, in return he has given us one of the best documentations of the early roots of jazz in these two seedbed centers. With the voluminous literature of the last decade or so, there is little more now to be said on the subject.

HISTORICAL AND SOCIOLOGICAL

In the third volume of *Life and Writings of Frederick Douglass*, Dr. Foner brings his monumental edition and biography of Douglass through the critical period of the Civil War. Admirably edited and documented, and for the most part objectively interpreted, this is indispensable reading for whomever would really understand the intricate issues of slavery, emancipation, the inner politics of the abolition movement, and the fateful vicissitudes of the Civil War. How near this or that historic decision came to disaster, including the Emancipation

Proclamation, is a lesson all need to learn, as also how to admire and evaluate the resourceful strategy which combined with Douglass's fixed convictions to make him so powerful an advocate of freedom's cause. He emerges from the record of these five years, 1860–65, in the full stature of a statesman, and this account, documented point by point, establishes it as has no previous study.

Similar recognition and gratitude are due Herbert Aptheker for another arduous editorial task, the compiling from tons of old records, most of them nearly inaccessible to any but the research historian, of *A Documentary History of the Negro People*. With a pardonable stress on the rebel traits and reactions—and it is indeed noteworthy to see how continuous this strain is in Negro leadership, especially in the earlier years, 1790–1860, there has been gathered together from all sides an amazing mass of evidence showing how much a collaborator the Negro was in the fight for his own freedom. The full gamut of Negro cultural activity is also well represented from church and politics to labor, social welfare, and artistic and literary expression, again a rather unusual coverage. Along with the full time span of the Negro's whole articulate life in this country, this, then, is a unique offering. It is good to remember, though, that it was Carter Woodson who laid down the model for all this sort of work, especially in his little known *The Mind of the Negro as Reflected in Letters Written During the Crisis, 1800–1860* (1926). *The Negro Freedman*, a contribution of Dr. Henderson H. Donald, is a welcome but somewhat superficial sketch of the conditions of the Negro in the early emancipation period. Of course, the evidence itself is patchy for this period, and biased pro or con; but still there ought to be enough indirect documentary evidence to check by—sufficient, for example, to avoid accepting obvious bias and hearsay for fact as well as to safeguard against over-inclusive generalization. These occur more than occasionally, particularly in the sections on religious and social customs and "on social classes and traits." *The Romance of African Methodism* by George A. Singleton has somewhat similar flaws, in this case more faults of perspective and over-heroic interpretation than of incompleteness of historical facts.

We come finally, in this group, to a brief discussion of a significant and probably very influential book, Carl Rowan's *South of Freedom*. *South of Freedom* represents effective and skillful journalism, detailing the positive as well as the negative challenges of a changing South. Its great virtue and special service, it seems to me, is his presentation of the situation as still a challenging touch-and-go between the forces of reaction and the forces of progress. One comes away with the feeling that the American South is an open battleground in a current war for political, economic, and cultural democracy—this time involving Negro reactionaries, the vested interests of segregation as well as the white die-hards on the one side and the liberal white South, the "New South" of the younger generation for the most part, and the progressive Negroes on the other. As Mr. Rowan vividly documents it here and there over a wide area of the South, deep, middle, and southwest, a reader gets a dramatic account of a struggle, the scope and import of which few actually realize—even those who are engaged and involved in it. But in Rowan's sharp, graphic account it reads like a war correspondent's journal of a tour crisscross the South along six thousand miles of American democracy's internal battlefront.

EXOTICA AND AFRICANA

Liberia by R. Earle Anderson, which he correctly subtitles *America's African Friend*, recognizing her past and future usefulness as a keystone base of our transcontinental military air routes, is a realistic but appreciative analysis of a country in transition. It forecasts for Liberia both a great economic and cultural development, which is all the more certain now because of the new development plans for the adjacent Gold Coast and Nigeria. The author is unusually fair in his appraisal of the Liberian government and of native life and customs, giving more justice to both than probably any previous study. The reading public, for example, needs to know that tribal bride-buying is a family contract of amends for the loss of a family worker, subject even to repayment if the wife is "divorced," and that the ancient custom of women trekking behind, carrying heavy burdens on their heads, stems from the time when the man was traditionally kept unburdened to be ready to fight or protect from any hazards of the journey. Liberia, or any other country, seen through such understanding lenses, is well served by its foreign observers. In this case, the situation seems full of promise, especially as the tragic rift between Americo-Liberians and the natives seems, at last, on the constructive mend.

Of the increasing number of books on South Africa, the most incisive seems to be Dvorin's *Racial Separation in South Africa*. By any account, it is an appalling story, this fantastic outbreak of hysterical racism. But it must be faced, as in this study with realistic intelligence. Obviously liberal, Dvorin makes sure not to be partisan in his factual statements, and although warrantably apprehensive, does see some possibility, with a divided white opinion, of some eventual solution.

Strange Altars by Marcus Bach adds still another item to the unending bibliography of Haitian voodoo "research," research in quotation marks. Without condemning either the motive or the genuine interest of many of these books, this one included, one must at last realize that no amount of dramatic description adds up to what is now needed on this subject of Haitian voodoo: detailed study of the rites and symbolic interpretation of the rituals, a job for professional anthropologists only. Neither Mr. Bach, nor his worthy sponsor, the ex-marine Doc Reser, for all their special entree and kindly interest, is capable of that.

The literature of Negro African art, hitherto scant, has grown to an all-time high. After last year's competent treatise by Professor Wingert, *The Sculpture of Negro Africa*, now come two studies of equal competence but superior deluxe format. The Ladislas Segy and Paul Radin volumes are among the most beautiful art books produced in America in the last quarter century; the former, *African Sculpture Speaks*, is exclusively devoted to African sculpture and a stylistic study of its tribal varieties while the latter, *African Folktales*, written with the collaboration of Elinore Marvel and James Johnson Sweeney, is a superb collection of African folk tales paralleled by equally superb reproductions (165 folio plates) of African sculpture tribally arranged. The higher levels of African culture, as known already to the present-day cultural anthropologist, are now graphically available to the lay reader, who cannot—if he has a grain of artistic and literary sensibility—ignore or misinterpret them. These tales, many of them cosmological myths of deep symbolic significance, and these plastic creations are indisputable evidence of qualities and culture traits comparable to the better known culture traditions of the whole human race. One yearns for the time when such knowledge and its transforming evaluations will percolate down to the level of generally educated men and women. That they are not yet so disseminated, even among educated American Negroes, is just to be put down to contemporary medievalism or cultural lag. Consider the evidence objectively, especially since the Greeks and the Teutons were "pagan" and the Jews non- or at least pre-Christian: some African creation myths are all "good" or meaningful as any, Genesis included, and some African fables are, even in their moral values, equal to the parables of the New Testament. Considering the billions of dollars' worth of psychological damage missionary and racist misconceptions of Africa and the African have wrought, on both countless Negro and Caucasian minds, books such as these, though relatively expensive, are cheap and welcome antidotes—good medicine for the mind diseased.

40

SELF-CRITICISM

The Third Dimension in Culture

The symposium section in this issue of *Phylon*, which I have had the opportunity of reading in manuscript, seems to signal the emergence of a long-awaited stage in Negro cultural development. For these eight essays analyzing our literary output and its implications mark a considerable step forward toward objective self-criticism. This is a necessary and welcome sign of cultural maturity. It was predicated twenty-five years ago as one of the objectives of the so-called Negro Renaissance, along with the companion aim of objective self-expression, but unfortunately such criticism was not forthcoming in any large volume. Its lack was unquestionably indicative of a certain lingering immaturity, the reasons for which it will be interesting to assess a little later on. For the moment it may be noted that the conditions which delayed it may also have been considerably responsible for the admitted shortcomings of our literary and artistic output in the Nineteen-twenties, thirties, and forties. Indeed this seems to be the present consensus of the new criticism which is so significantly emerging.

It is now obvious in retrospect, as many of these articles point out, that for many generations Negro creative expression was inevitably imitative and marked with a double provincialism of cultural immaturity and a racial sense of subordination. It ran a one-dimensional gamut from self-pity through sentimental appeal to hortatory moralizing and rhetorical threat—a child's gamut of tears, sobs, sulks, and passionate protest. All of us probably expected too much of the Negro Renaissance, but its new vitality of independence, pride, and self-respect, its scoff and defiance of prejudice and limitations were so welcome and heartening.

Like the adolescence it was, the New Negro era was gawky and pimply, indiscreet and overconfident, vainglorious and irresponsible; but its testy dynamic gave the Negro new spiritual stature and an added dimension of self-reliance. As several of the critics point out, adolescence was mistaken for manhood, so there was in the creative expression of the Twenties and Thirties pride without poise, vision without true perspective, self-esteem without the necessary tempering of full self-understanding.

Beginning with the broader social identifications of *Native Son*, and the social discoveries of common-denominator human universals between Negro situations and others, these critics rightly claim, artistic expression with Negroes has become increasingly sounder, more objective, and less racialistic—in the limiting sense of chauvinism—but withal even more racial in the better sense of being more deeply felt and projected. This third dimension of objective universality, they feel, is the ultimate desideratum for a literature that seeks universal appeal and acceptance. I agree. In fact, have always agreed, though this is neither the time nor place for self-justifying quotations.

Suffice it to say that even in 1925, some original proponents of the "Negro Renaissance" forecast the position which seems to be the new consensus of the "new criticism." That is, that when the racial themes are imposed upon the Negro author either from within or without, they become an intolerable and limiting artistic ghetto, but that accepted by choice, either on the ground of best known material or preferred opportunity, they stake off a cultural bonanza. Mr. Gloster, for example, does well to inveigh against the triple snares of "race defense, protest and glorification," but it still remains that Negro life and experience contain one of the unworked mines of American dramatic and fictional material, overworked and shabby as their superficial exploitation has been. For both the white and the Negro author in this area, the era of pan-mining is about over or should be; the promising techniques are now deep-mining and better artistic smelting of the crude ore. In provincial and chauvinistic rendering, of which we have been offered far too much, especially from Negro authors, as Messrs. Redding and Reddick bravely point out, Negro materials pan out shallow, brittle, and unrefined. But in objective, thoroughly humanized treatment they still promise artistic gold fit for universal currency. The necessary alchemy is, of course, universalized rendering, for in universalized particularity there has always resided the world's greatest and most enduring art.

Though rare, this quality has appeared sporadically in Negro writing. Mr. Chandler is right in giving us the proper historical perspective, however, by reminding us how long it took American literature itself to achieve this dimension of universalized power and insight. Perhaps it would be invidious to be too specific for the current generation, though I think all would agree that the first two chapters of *Native Son* had such quality, not to mention how and why the book as a whole lost these virtues as it became more and more involved in propagandist formulae. I am personally surprised that no one referred to the phenomenal early appearance of such "universal particularity" in Jean Toomer's *Cane* in 1923. Here was something admirably removed from what Mr. Chandler calls very aptly "promotional literature," but it is Negro through and through as well as deeply and movingly human. It was also exempt from any limitation of provincialism although it gave local color convincingly. To wish for more of this is to ask for the transmuting quality of expert craftsmanship combined with broad perspective or intuitive insight, one or the other. For we must remember the two ways in which Russian literature achieved its great era; through the cosmopolitan way of Turgenev, Tolstoy, and Chekhov and the nativist way of Dostoyevsky, Gogol, and Gorky, each of which produced great writing and universal understanding for Russian experience.

Our problem now seems to be how to translate this new insight into creative action. So far as a body of sound criticism can point the way, we have in this group of critical essays the beginnings of a new objective criticism, and henceforth can have little excuse if a considerable part of our creative expression does not follow its lead and guidance. At least we have within our artistic grasp the final resolution of the old dilemma of the proper attitude of the Negro writer toward race materials. Agreeing that this should be, to quote Mr. Gloster, "to consider all life as his proper milieu, yet treat race (when he chooses) from the universal point of view, shunning the cultural isolation that results from racial preoccupation and Jim-Crow aesthetics," we have as a net result, however, the mandate: Give us Negro life and experience in all the arts but with a third dimension of universalized common-denominator humanity.

A final word or so of constructive criticism may be in order. Let us start with the shameful fact that out of the whole range of Negro experience, the very areas on which the Negro author has almost monopolistic control, there has been little else than strange silence. On this matter, Mr. Reddick hints provocatively. I will venture to speak even more plainly on my own responsibility. Three taboos that seal doors that must be broken through to release greatly original and moving revelations about Negro life and experience remain unbroken, partly through convention-ridden cowardice, partly through misconceived protective strategy. If William March and Erskine Caldwell, Lillian Smith and William Faulkner, can boldly break with the tribal taboos of the White South to release the full potentials of Southern drama and fiction, so in turn must the Negro author boldly break the seals of analogous Negro conventionality. Of course, easier said than done! The Negro intellectual is still largely in psychological bondage not only, as Reddick puts it, "to the laws and customs of the local (Southern) culture," but to the fear of breaking the taboos of puritanism, Philistinism, and falsely conceived conventions of "race respectability." Consciously and subconsciously, these repressions work great artistic harm, especially the fear of being accused of group disloyalty and "misrepresentation" in portraying the full gamut of Negro type, character, and thinking. We are still in the throes of counter-stereotypes.

The releasing formula is to realize that in all human things we are basically and inevitably human, and that even the special racial complexities and overtones are only interesting variants. Why, then, this protective silence about the ambivalences of the Negro upper classes, about the dilemmas of intra-group prejudice and rivalry, about the dramatic inner paradoxes of mixed heritage, both biological and cultural, or the tragic breach between the Negro elite and the Negro masses, or the conflict between integration and vested-interest separatism in the present-day life of the Negro? These, among others, are the great themes, but they molder in closed closets like family skeletons rather than shine brightly as the Aladdin's lamps that they really are.

To break such taboos is the crucial artistic question of the moment, the wrath of the Negro Rotarians, preachers, college presidents, and journalists notwithstanding. It is this inner tyranny that must next be conquered, now that the outer tyrannies of prejudice and intellectual ostracism are being so suddenly relaxed. I am far from suggesting that even a considerable part of this revelation will be morally risqué or socially explosive; some of it will be, of course. But I do sense a strange and widely diffused feeling that many of these situations are Masonic secrets—things to be talked about, but not written or officially disclosed. Maybe, now that a few Negro authors have demonstrated the possibility of financial independence and success as writers, some of our younger talents can shake free of the white-collar servitudes of job dependency on the one hand and conventional "race loyalty" on the other. If so, we may confidently anticipate an era of fuller and more objective presentation by Negro authors of their versions of contemporary living in general and Negro life and experience in particular.